Revolutionizing Cybersecurity With Deep Learning and Large Language Models

Hewa Majeed Zangana
Duhok Polytechnic University, Iraq

Jamal Al-Karaki
Zayed University, UAE

Marwan Omar
Illinois Institute of Technology, USA

IGI Global
Scientific Publishing
Publishing Tomorrow's Research Today

Vice President of Editorial — Melissa Wagner
Managing Editor of Acquisitions — Mikaela Felty
Managing Editor of Book Development — Jocelynn Hessler
Production Manager — Mike Brehm
Cover Design — Phillip Shickler

Published in the United States of America by
IGI Global Scientific Publishing
701 East Chocolate Avenue
Hershey, PA, 17033, USA
Tel: 717-533-8845
Fax: 717-533-8661
Website: https://www.igi-global.com E-mail: cust@igi-global.com

Library of Congress Cataloging-in-Publication Data

LCCN: 2025011854 (CIP Data Pending)
ISBN13: 979-8-3373-3296-3
Isbn13Softcover: 979-8-3373-3297-0
EISBN13: 979-8-3373-3298-7

British Cataloguing in Publication Data
A Cataloguing in Publication record for this book is available from the British Library.

Table of Contents

Detailed Table of Contents

The integration of deep learning (DL) and large language models (LLMs) has significantly advanced the field of cybersecurity, offering innovative approaches to threat detection, anomaly identification, and secure communication. Deep learning techniques, such as neural networks and reinforcement learning, have demonstrated robust capabilities in detecting previously unknown threats by learning patterns from vast amounts of cybersecurity data. Similarly, LLMs, particularly transformers, have revolutionized natural language processing tasks, enabling effective vulnerability analysis, malware classification, and phishing detection. This chapter explores the foundational concepts of deep learning and LLMs, highlighting their applications and challenges within the cybersecurity landscape. Additionally, it discusses the synergy between these technologies, focusing on how they complement traditional cybersecurity measures and drive the evolution of intelligent defense mechanisms.

The rapid advancement of artificial intelligence (AI) has transformed contract security, offering innovative solutions for managing contract expiry, ensuring compliance, and mitigating risks. Traditional contract management systems often struggle with scalability, accuracy, and adaptability, leading to inefficiencies and potential legal vulnerabilities. This chapter explores how deep learning and large language models (LLMs) enhance contract security by automating contract review, expiration tracking, and regulatory compliance assessment. By leveraging natural language processing (NLP) and predictive analytics, AI-driven solutions can proactively identify risks, flag anomalies, and ensure adherence to contractual obligations. Furthermore, this chapter discusses key challenges such as bias in AI models, data privacy concerns, and the need for robust regulatory frameworks. Through case studies and experimental results, we demonstrate how AI-powered contract security improves efficiency, reduces human errors, and enhances organizational risk management.

Cyber threats are increasingly complex, requiring advanced detection and mitigation strategies. Deep learning (DL) offers powerful solutions for threat detection and anomaly identification, thanks to its ability to process large data volumes and uncover subtle indicators of cyber threats. This chapter discusses the integration of various DL techniques—CNNs, RNNs, autoencoders, and GANs—for detecting malicious activities and anomalies across diverse cybersecurity contexts. By examining both supervised and unsupervised approaches, it highlights strengths and limitations in tackling threats such as zero-day attacks, insider threats, and APTs. Real-world applications, case studies, and the role of explainable AI (XAI) in enhancing transparency and trust are also explored. Finally, challenges like adversarial attacks, data quality, and computational constraints are addressed, along with future directions for improving the robustness and efficiency of DL-driven threat detection systems.

Large Language Models (LLMs) are revolutionizing cybersecurity in healthcare, government, and industrial sectors by enabling real-time threat detection, anomaly identification, and compliance automation. This chapter explores the transformative role of LLMs in mitigating cyber risks while addressing challenges such as adversarial attacks, data privacy, and bias. It examines real-world applications, highlighting their effectiveness in securing critical infrastructures. Additionally, ethical, legal, and regulatory considerations are discussed to ensure responsible AI deployment. The chapter provides strategic recommendations for integrating LLM-powered security solutions while mitigating risks, enhancing resilience, and improving automated incident response. By leveraging LLMs effectively, organizations can strengthen cybersecurity frameworks and safeguard sensitive data against evolving threats in an increasingly digital landscape.

Preface

INTRODUCTION

The rapid advancement of artificial intelligence (AI) has significantly reshaped the landscape of cybersecurity, introducing both groundbreaking opportunities and formidable challenges. Among AI-driven innovations, deep learning and large language models (LLMs) have emerged as transformative tools in the detection, prevention, and mitigation of cyber threats. These technologies are redefining cybersecurity paradigms, enabling intelligent, proactive, and adaptive security mechanisms that surpass traditional approaches.

Deep learning, with its capacity to analyze vast datasets and identify intricate patterns, has become indispensable in intrusion detection systems (IDS), behavioral analysis, fraud detection, and other critical security applications. Simultaneously, LLMs—exemplified by models such as OpenAI's GPT and Google's Gemini—are revolutionizing cybersecurity by enhancing natural language processing (NLP)-based threat detection, automating vulnerability assessments, and supporting security analysts in real-time decision-making. The convergence of these two AI domains is driving an era of unprecedented cybersecurity innovation.

Despite the immense potential, the integration of deep learning and LLMs into cybersecurity frameworks is not without challenges. Issues such as adversarial attacks, data privacy concerns, bias in AI-driven decision-making, and the ethical implications of automated threat responses necessitate careful consideration. Addressing these complexities requires a concerted effort from researchers, practitioners, and industry leaders to develop robust, explainable, and resilient AI-based security solutions.

This edited volume, *Revolutionizing Cybersecurity With Deep Learning and Large Language Models*, aims to explore the latest advancements, methodologies, applications, and challenges associated with leveraging deep learning and LLMs for cybersecurity. By compiling contributions from leading experts in AI and security, this book serves as a valuable resource for researchers, cybersecurity professionals, and policymakers striving to harness the full potential of these transformative technologies.

The primary objective of this book is to bridge the gap between theoretical research and practical implementations by examining how AI-driven technologies can enhance security strategies, automate threat detection, and optimize response mechanisms. Through expert contributions, this book seeks to:

- Advance Research in AI-Driven Cybersecurity: Provide an in-depth analysis of how deep learning architectures and LLMs are transforming traditional cybersecurity methodologies, offering novel insights into AI-driven anomaly detection, behavioral analysis, and threat intelligence.
- Enhance Practical Applications: Showcase real-world use cases, case studies, and implementations of AI models in cybersecurity to demonstrate their effectiveness in mitigating cyber threats across various industries.
- Address Emerging Challenges: Identify and critically assess challenges such as adversarial AI attacks, ethical concerns, bias in AI decision-making, and the computational costs associated with deploying deep learning and LLM-based security systems.
- Foster Innovation and Collaboration: Serve as a platform for researchers, security professionals, and policymakers to exchange knowledge, propose new frameworks, and discuss the future trajectory of AI-powered cybersecurity solutions.
- Support Decision-Making and Policy Development: Equip cybersecurity professionals, industry leaders, and governmental organizations with the knowledge needed to implement AI-based security measures effectively while considering ethical, regulatory, and technical implications.

This book is designed to cater to a diverse audience engaged in cybersecurity, artificial intelligence, and related disciplines, including:

- Academics and Researchers: Scholars in AI, cybersecurity, and data science seeking to explore the latest advancements in deep learning and LLMs for security applications.
- Cybersecurity Professionals: Security analysts, incident response teams, and IT security practitioners looking to enhance their defensive and offensive cybersecurity strategies with AI-driven techniques.
- Data Scientists and AI Engineers: Professionals developing deep learning models and LLMs who wish to understand their cybersecurity implications and applications.

- Industry Leaders and Decision-Makers: Executives, CISOs (Chief Information Security Officers), and policymakers responsible for implementing AI-powered security frameworks across various sectors.
- Students and Educators: Graduate and advanced undergraduate students in cybersecurity, computer science, and AI-related fields seeking to deepen their understanding of AI-driven security solutions.
- Government and Law Enforcement Agencies: Organizations involved in national cybersecurity initiatives, cybercrime investigations, and the development of AI-driven regulatory policies.

By addressing both theoretical and practical dimensions, this book aims to bridge the gap between research and real-world applications, offering insights that can drive innovation and strengthen cybersecurity defenses in an increasingly AI-driven digital world. We hope that this volume serves as an essential reference for those navigating the evolving intersection of artificial intelligence and cybersecurity.

ORGANIZATION OF THE BOOK

Chapter 1: Foundations of Deep Learning and Large Language Models in Cybersecurity

Deep learning (DL) and large language models (LLMs) have emerged as pivotal tools in modern cybersecurity, transforming the way threats are detected and mitigated. This chapter lays the groundwork by exploring the fundamental principles of DL and LLMs, detailing their applications in threat analysis, anomaly detection, and secure communication. By leveraging neural networks, reinforcement learning, and transformer-based models, cybersecurity systems can proactively identify and respond to threats in real-time. Additionally, the chapter examines the integration of these advanced AI-driven technologies with traditional security frameworks, shedding light on both their potential and the challenges they present in an evolving digital landscape.

Chapter 2: AI-Powered Contract Security: Managing Expiry, Compliance, and Risk Mitigation through Deep Learning and LLMs

The integration of artificial intelligence (AI) in contract security has transformed how organizations manage contractual obligations, compliance, and risk. This chapter delves into the role of deep learning and LLMs in automating contract review, expiration tracking, and regulatory adherence. AI-powered solutions offer enhanced accuracy and efficiency in identifying risks, mitigating legal vulnerabilities, and ensuring compliance. By utilizing natural language processing (NLP) and predictive analytics, organizations can streamline contract management and proactively address potential pitfalls. The chapter also explores key challenges, including AI bias, data privacy concerns, and the evolving regulatory landscape, while presenting case studies that highlight the tangible benefits of AI-driven contract security.

Chapter 3: Threat Detection and Anomaly Identification Using Deep Learning

With cyber threats becoming increasingly sophisticated, traditional security measures often fall short in detecting and responding to emerging dangers. This chapter investigates how deep learning techniques, including convolutional neural networks (CNNs), recurrent neural networks (RNNs), and generative adversarial networks (GANs), are redefining threat detection and anomaly identification. By examining real-world applications and case studies, the chapter underscores the strengths of DL-based cybersecurity systems in identifying zero-day threats, insider attacks, and advanced persistent threats (APTs). Additionally, it explores challenges such as adversarial attacks and computational limitations, emphasizing the role of explainable AI (XAI) in ensuring transparency and trust in DL-driven security measures.

Chapter 4: LLM-Powered Security Solutions in Healthcare, Government, and Industrial Cybersecurity

Large Language Models (LLMs) have become instrumental in fortifying cybersecurity across critical sectors, including healthcare, government, and industrial systems. This chapter explores the transformative impact of LLMs in enhancing real-time threat detection, automating compliance checks, and mitigating cyber risks. Addressing concerns related to adversarial attacks, data privacy, and bias, the chapter presents best practices for the ethical deployment of LLM-driven security solutions. By incorporating case studies and strategic recommendations, the discussion underscores how these models can strengthen cybersecurity frameworks, improve incident response, and ensure resilience against evolving digital threats.

Chapter 5: Phishing and Social Engineering Attack Prevention with LLMs

Phishing and social engineering attacks have become increasingly complex, exploiting human psychology to manipulate individuals and organizations. This chapter examines how LLMs enhance cybersecurity by enabling automated phishing detection, email classification, and user education through NLP-based chatbots and behavioral analysis tools. By integrating deep learning with traditional cybersecurity measures, organizations can develop adaptive defense mechanisms against these evolving threats. The chapter also addresses challenges such as adversarial manipulation of LLMs, ethical considerations, and the importance of continuous model refinement to prevent exploitation by cybercriminals.

Chapter 6: Malware Analysis and Classification Using Deep Learning

The increasing sophistication of malware demands advanced analytical techniques for effective detection and classification. This chapter explores how deep learning models, particularly CNNs and RNNs, are revolutionizing malware analysis by automating feature extraction and pattern recognition. The discussion highlights how AI-driven malware classification enhances detection accuracy while addressing challenges such as data imbalance, model interpretability, and overfitting. Additionally, the integration of large-scale datasets and LLMs is examined, providing insights into their potential to further refine malware classification techniques and bolster cybersecurity defenses.

Chapter 7: AI Automated Incident Response and Threat Mitigation Using AI

Artificial Intelligence (AI) has redefined cybersecurity by enabling automated incident response and threat mitigation. This chapter explores how deep learning and LLMs empower organizations to detect, analyze, and mitigate threats in real-time, improving overall security postures. Key technologies, such as AI-driven security orchestration, automation, and response (SOAR) systems, are examined alongside their applications in modern cybersecurity frameworks. The chapter also discusses challenges related to AI deployment, including data security, adversarial attacks, and the need for robust governance models, while highlighting future trends in AI-driven cybersecurity operations.

Chapter 8: Empowering Cybersecurity with LLMs: Overcoming Automation Challenges in Threat Intelligence and Detection Systems

As cybercriminals employ increasingly sophisticated techniques, traditional threat detection methods struggle to keep pace. This chapter explores how LLMs are revolutionizing threat intelligence and detection by automating complex cybersecurity processes. By leveraging models such as OpenAI's GPT and Google's BERT, cybersecurity systems can process vast amounts of unstructured data, identify attack patterns, and enhance real-time decision-making. The discussion also addresses the challenges of automating threat detection, including model interpretability, adversarial manipulation, and scalability, while presenting innovative methodologies, such as hybrid AI approaches and transfer learning, to overcome these obstacles.

Chapter 9: Secure Authentication and Identity Management with AI

Authentication and identity management are essential components of cybersecurity, yet traditional methods often fall short in preventing unauthorized access and credential theft. This chapter examines how AI-driven solutions, including biometric recognition, behavioral analysis, and anomaly detection, are transforming identity verification processes. By leveraging deep learning and federated learning techniques, modern authentication systems enhance security while preserving user privacy. The discussion also explores the challenges of implementing AI-driven authentication, including ethical concerns, data protection, and the evolving landscape of decentralized identity frameworks.

Chapter 10: Enhancing Agricultural Cybersecurity: Leveraging Deep Learning and Large Language Models for Smart Farming Protection

The digital transformation of agriculture has introduced new cybersecurity vulnerabilities, particularly with the adoption of precision farming, IoT-enabled sensors, and automated decision-making systems. This chapter explores how deep learning and LLMs enhance agricultural cybersecurity by providing real-time threat detection, adaptive defense mechanisms, and automated incident response. Case studies illustrate the application of AI-driven security solutions in agricultural environments, highlighting strategies to mitigate cyber risks associated with data breaches, ransomware attacks, and supply chain vulnerabilities. The chapter concludes with recommendations for strengthening cybersecurity frameworks in the rapidly evolving domain of smart farming.

CONCLUSION

As cyber threats continue to evolve in complexity and sophistication, the integration of advanced artificial intelligence techniques—particularly deep learning and large language models—has become a crucial component in modern cybersecurity strategies. This book has explored the foundational principles, applications, and challenges associated with these cutting-edge technologies, offering valuable insights into their role in fortifying digital infrastructures across various sectors. From automated threat detection and malware classification to AI-driven incident response and secure authentication, each chapter has demonstrated the transformative potential of AI-powered cybersecurity solutions.

However, with great technological advancements come critical challenges, including ethical considerations, adversarial vulnerabilities, data privacy concerns, and regulatory compliance. As researchers, practitioners, and policymakers strive to harness the power of AI for cybersecurity, a balanced approach is necessary—one that ensures security enhancements without compromising transparency, fairness, or user trust. Addressing these challenges will require interdisciplinary collaboration, continuous innovation, and a commitment to responsible AI deployment.

By bringing together expert contributions from leading researchers and practitioners, this book serves as both a reference and a call to action for the future of AI in cybersecurity. It is our hope that the insights provided herein will not only deepen the understanding of AI-driven security solutions but also inspire further advancements in the field. As AI technologies continue to evolve, so too must our approaches to cybersecurity—adapting, innovating, and strengthening our digital defenses to safeguard the increasingly interconnected world.

Hewa Majeed Zangana
Duhok Polytechnic University, Iraq

Jamal Al-Karaki
Zayed University, UAE

Marwan Omar
Illinois Institute of Technology, USA

Chapter 1
Foundations of Deep Learning and Large Language Models in Cybersecurity

Hewa Majeed Zangana
https://orcid.org/0000-0001-7909-254X
Duhok Polytechnic University, Iraq

Marwan Omar
Illinois Institute of Technology, USA

Jamal N. Al-Karaki
https://orcid.org/0009-0000-7833-3970
Zayed University, UAE

ABSTRACT

The integration of deep learning (DL) and large language models (LLMs) has significantly advanced the field of cybersecurity, offering innovative approaches to threat detection, anomaly identification, and secure communication. Deep learning techniques, such as neural networks and reinforcement learning, have demonstrated robust capabilities in detecting previously unknown threats by learning patterns from vast amounts of cybersecurity data. Similarly, LLMs, particularly transformers, have revolutionized natural language processing tasks, enabling effective vulnerability analysis, malware classification, and phishing detection. This chapter explores the foundational concepts of deep learning and LLMs, highlighting their applications and challenges within the cybersecurity landscape. Additionally, it discusses the synergy between these technologies, focusing on how they complement traditional

DOI: 10.4018/979-8-3373-3296-3.ch001

cybersecurity measures and drive the evolution of intelligent defense mechanisms.

1. INTRODUCTION

The landscape of cybersecurity is undergoing a profound transformation, fueled by advancements in artificial intelligence (AI), machine learning (ML), and, notably, large language models (LLMs). As cyber threats evolve in complexity and scale, traditional defense mechanisms are increasingly becoming inadequate, necessitating the integration of more advanced technologies. Deep learning and LLMs have emerged as powerful tools in addressing the ever-growing security challenges. These technologies not only enhance threat detection but also enable predictive capabilities, automated responses, and more robust defenses, revolutionizing the field of cybersecurity.

The cybersecurity landscape is evolving rapidly, with threats becoming more complex and sophisticated. The following diagram categorizes cyber threats into different types, illustrating their interconnections.

Figure 1. Categories of cyber threats

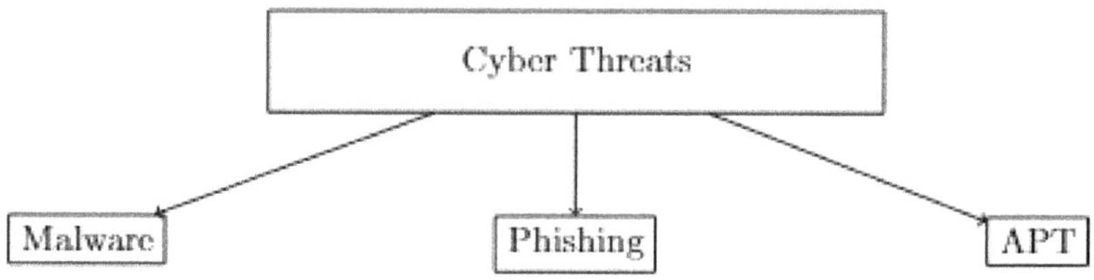

The rapid advancement of LLMs such as GPT (Generative Pretrained Transformer) and BERT (Bidirectional Encoder Representations from Transformers) has significantly reshaped how security systems analyze and process data. Initially developed for natural language processing (NLP), these models are now being adapted to cybersecurity tasks, ranging from detecting vulnerabilities to predicting potential cyber-attacks (Ferrag et al., 2024; Xu et al., 2024). LLMs excel in understanding context, identifying patterns in massive datasets, and offering more accurate threat intelligence compared to traditional approaches.

The application of LLMs in cybersecurity spans multiple domains, including intrusion detection, malware analysis, phishing detection, and even cyber attack prediction (Santos, Salam, & Dahir, 2024; Kasri et al., 2025). These models have shown remarkable promise in automating complex security tasks that would otherwise require human expertise and extensive resources. Moreover, as cyber attackers become more sophisticated, the ability of LLMs to continuously learn from new data and adapt to emerging threats is crucial to staying ahead in the cyber battle.

One of the key advantages of LLMs in cybersecurity is their ability to process large volumes of unstructured data, such as logs, network traffic, and threat intelligence reports. This capability allows for quicker identification of security breaches and reduces the time it takes to respond to threats (Motlagh et al., 2024; Ferrag et al., 2023). Additionally, LLMs are increasingly being used to enhance the privacy and security of IoT (Internet of Things) and IIoT (Industrial Internet of Things) devices, which are often targeted by cybercriminals due to their inherent vulnerabilities (Ferrag et al., 2024).

However, while LLMs offer a wealth of opportunities, their application in cybersecurity is not without challenges. Issues such as model interpretability, ethical concerns, and the risk of adversarial attacks on the models themselves require careful consideration (Zangana et al., 2024). Despite these challenges, the integration of LLMs into cybersecurity practices is poised to usher in a new era of defense systems that are more intelligent, proactive, and resilient.

This chapter aims to provide an in-depth exploration of the foundations of deep learning and large language models within the realm of cybersecurity. It will delve into their theoretical underpinnings, practical applications, and the emerging trends shaping their role in revolutionizing cyber defenses. By examining the most recent research and developments, this chapter will highlight how LLMs are reshaping the cybersecurity landscape and driving the evolution of next-generation defense strategies.

Through a detailed review of current advancements (Hassanin & Moustafa, 2024; Ferrag et al., 2024), the chapter will also explore the synergies between deep learning techniques and LLMs, addressing how their combined capabilities enhance security protocols across various sectors, from enterprise systems to critical infrastructure. Furthermore, it will discuss the potential future directions for integrating these technologies to address the most pressing cybersecurity challenges, such as securing emerging technologies and addressing the growing number of cyber threats targeting global networks (Sarker, 2024; Ghazal et al., 2024).

In summary, deep learning and LLMs represent a paradigm shift in cybersecurity, offering powerful new tools for mitigating risks and enhancing overall system resilience. As these technologies continue to evolve, their integration into cybersecurity strategies will be essential for combating increasingly sophisticated cyber threats. This chapter sets the stage for understanding how these innovations are transforming the field, providing both theoretical insights and practical guidance for leveraging LLMs in cybersecurity practices.

2. EVOLUTION OF DEEP LEARNING AND LARGE LANGUAGE MODELS (LLMS)

The evolution of deep learning and large language models (LLMs) has revolutionized the field of artificial intelligence (AI), particularly in the domain of cybersecurity. Over the past two decades, deep learning techniques have gradually transformed from experimental concepts into powerful tools that drive many of today's AI applications. Deep learning is a subset of machine learning that uses neural networks with many layers (hence "deep") to model complex patterns in data. This capability, combined with the increase in computational power and the availability of large datasets, has enabled deep learning to achieve breakthroughs in tasks such as image recognition, natural language processing (NLP), and time-series forecasting.

In the early stages, deep learning models faced challenges related to limited data availability, high computational costs, and a lack of effective algorithms. However, key innovations, such as convolutional neural networks (CNNs) and recurrent neural networks (RNNs), have significantly improved the performance of models in tasks like speech recognition and computer vision. These advancements paved the way for the development of more sophisticated models, such as transformers, which have since become the backbone of modern LLMs (Vaswani et al., 2017).

2.1 Rise of Large Language Models (LLMs)

Large language models (LLMs) are designed to understand, generate, and manipulate human language with remarkable accuracy. The primary innovation that propelled the rise of LLMs was the introduction of the transformer architecture. Unlike previous models, transformers do not rely on sequential data processing, which makes them more efficient in handling large amounts of data and capturing long-range dependencies in text. This ability to process vast amounts of text data quickly has made LLMs highly effective in various applications, from text generation and translation to question answering and sentiment analysis.

The first significant milestone in the development of LLMs was the introduction of models like OpenAI's GPT (Generative Pretrained Transformer) and Google's BERT (Bidirectional Encoder Representations from Transformers). These models were pre-trained on massive corpora of text data, allowing them to learn intricate patterns in language. GPT models are autoregressive, meaning they predict the next word in a sequence based on the previous words, while BERT models use a bidirectional approach, capturing context from both directions of a sentence. These innovations enabled LLMs to achieve state-of-the-art performance on numerous NLP benchmarks (Vaswani et al., 2017).

LLMs such as GPT-2, GPT-3, and GPT-4 have become increasingly capable, not just for generating human-like text but for understanding context, answering complex questions, and performing tasks that were previously thought to be exclusively in the domain of human intelligence. These models are trained on billions (or even trillions) of parameters, making them highly versatile and adaptable to a range of applications, including those in cybersecurity (Sarker, 2024).

2.2 LLMs in Cybersecurity

As cybersecurity threats become increasingly sophisticated, the need for advanced AI models to detect, predict, and respond to attacks has never been more critical. The intersection of LLMs and cybersecurity is an area of intense research, as LLMs' ability to understand and generate human language makes them particularly useful in tasks like cyber threat detection, phishing detection, and incident response (Motlagh et al., 2024). The capabilities of LLMs have enabled more efficient threat identification through the analysis of unstructured data such as logs, network traffic, and email content.

For instance, Ferrag et al. (2024) introduced a privacy-preserving BERT-based lightweight model specifically designed for IoT/IIoT devices, revolutionizing cyber threat detection by enabling the detection of anomalies while preserving user privacy. In a similar vein, researchers like Thandi (2024) and Kasri et al. (2025) explore the potential of LLMs in enhancing cybersecurity defenses through automated anomaly detection, prediction of attack vectors, and real-time threat mitigation strategies. These efforts are crucial in the context of IoT networks, where devices are often vulnerable to a variety of cyber threats, including zero-day attacks and sophisticated malware.

The strength of LLMs lies in their ability to adapt to dynamic and ever-evolving threat landscapes. According to Zangana, Mustafa, and Li (2025), the use of LLMs allows cybersecurity systems to predict and mitigate cyberattacks proactively, rather than relying solely on reactive measures. This shift toward predictive and intelligent cybersecurity models is made possible by LLMs' ability to process vast amounts of security data and identify emerging threats before they can cause significant harm.

2.3 Challenges and Future Directions

Despite the impressive capabilities of LLMs in cybersecurity, their application is not without challenges. One major concern is the efficiency of these models, as their size and computational demands can be prohibitive in resource-constrained environments. Researchers are actively exploring methods to optimize these models without sacrificing their performance. Kasri et al. (2025) and Ferrag et al. (2024)

have worked on reducing the computational complexity of LLMs, which can make them more accessible and deployable in real-world cybersecurity applications.

Another challenge is ensuring that these models do not inadvertently introduce new vulnerabilities. As LLMs are trained on vast amounts of data, there is a risk that they may inadvertently learn biases or security flaws from the data they are exposed to. Ensuring the robustness and fairness of LLMs is a critical area of ongoing research, as highlighted by Xu et al. (2024) and Hasanov et al. (2024).

Looking forward, the integration of LLMs with other emerging technologies, such as blockchain, quantum computing, and edge computing, is expected to further enhance their capabilities in cybersecurity. The combination of LLMs with these technologies holds the promise of creating even more secure and resilient systems (Santos et al., 2024). As the field continues to evolve, the development of specialized LLMs tailored to specific cybersecurity domains—such as IoT, industrial control systems, and cloud security—will be a key area of research and innovation (Sarker, 2024).

In conclusion, the evolution of deep learning and large language models has had a transformative impact on cybersecurity. From enhancing threat detection to automating response mechanisms, LLMs are proving to be indispensable tools in the ongoing battle against cyber threats. As research and innovation continue, the potential of LLMs in cybersecurity will only grow, leading to more intelligent, proactive, and resilient defense mechanisms.

3. KEY CONCEPTS: NEURAL NETWORKS, TRANSFORMERS, AND PRETRAINED MODELS

3.1 Neural Networks

Neural networks (NNs) are a fundamental component of artificial intelligence (AI) systems, designed to mimic the way the human brain processes information. At their core, neural networks consist of layers of interconnected nodes or "neurons," which communicate by passing data through weighted connections. This structure enables the network to learn complex patterns from large datasets, making it particularly effective in tasks such as classification, regression, and pattern recognition.

NNs can be categorized into various architectures, including feedforward neural networks, convolutional neural networks (CNNs), and recurrent neural networks (RNNs). Each of these architectures has its own strengths, depending on the nature of the problem. For example, CNNs are particularly useful for image and video processing due to their ability to capture spatial hierarchies, while RNNs excel in sequence-based tasks like speech recognition or time-series prediction.

Recent developments in deep learning, especially in the area of large-scale neural networks, have contributed significantly to advances in cybersecurity. Neural networks, particularly deep learning models, are capable of detecting complex patterns in cyber threats, such as identifying anomalies in network traffic or predicting potential vulnerabilities (Sarker, 2024; Zangana, 2025). These networks offer automated threat detection with improved accuracy and adaptability over traditional methods.

Neural networks form the backbone of many AI-driven cybersecurity systems. The diagram below illustrates a simple feedforward neural network used in threat detection.

Figure 2. Neural network structure for threat detection

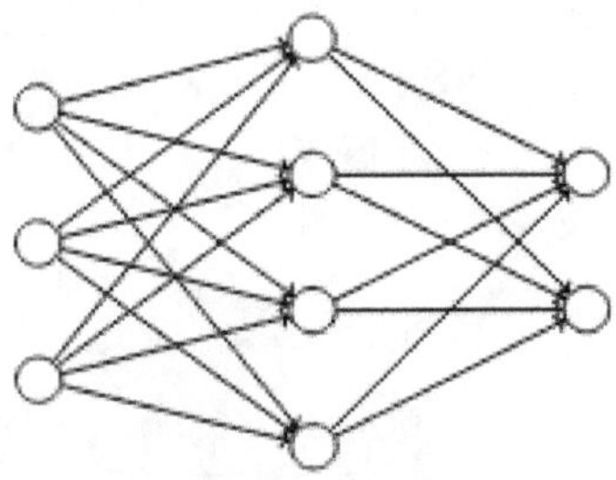

3.2 Transformers

Transformers are a class of neural network architectures that have revolutionized natural language processing (NLP) and are now expanding into other domains like cybersecurity. Introduced by Vaswani et al. (2017), transformers address limitations of previous models by using self-attention mechanisms that allow them to capture dependencies across long sequences of data, without the need for recurrent structures. This ability to process input data in parallel rather than sequentially makes transformers more efficient, particularly when dealing with large datasets.

Transformers have revolutionized natural language processing and are now extensively used in cybersecurity. The following diagram illustrates the basic transformer architecture.

Figure 3. Transformer architecture for cybersecurity applications

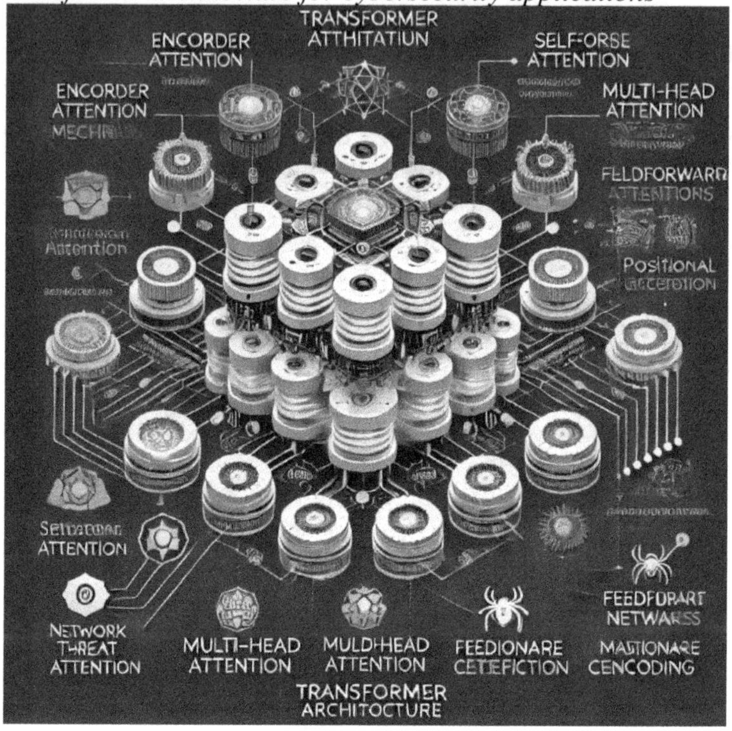

The core innovation of transformers lies in their self-attention mechanism, which enables the model to weigh the importance of different words or tokens in a sentence (or elements in a dataset) relative to one another. This results in more accurate contextual representations, which is why transformers have become the architecture of choice for state-of-the-art models in tasks like language translation, text generation, and even cybersecurity.

Transformers are particularly suited for cybersecurity applications due to their scalability and flexibility. They can handle the massive amounts of data involved in threat detection, analyze vast logs of network activity, and detect patterns that may indicate cyberattacks (Kasri et al., 2025). The application of transformers in cybersecurity tasks has led to significant advancements in threat detection and response systems (Ferrag et al., 2024; Motlagh et al., 2024).

3.3 Pretrained Models

Pretrained models are machine learning models that have been trained on large, general-purpose datasets and can then be fine-tuned for specific tasks. The rise of pretrained models in AI, particularly large language models (LLMs) such as BERT,

GPT, and their derivatives, has significantly impacted many fields, including cybersecurity. These models are pretrained on vast corpora of text, enabling them to learn language patterns, relationships, and structures before being adapted to specific tasks.

In the context of cybersecurity, pretrained models are used to enhance threat detection, vulnerability assessment, and automated response. These models provide a powerful way to leverage existing knowledge for tasks like detecting malicious activity, analyzing security logs, and identifying vulnerabilities without needing to retrain from scratch. Pretraining allows cybersecurity systems to benefit from models that have already learned fundamental language and pattern recognition capabilities, which can then be fine-tuned to the specific needs of security applications (Ghazal et al., 2024; Liu, 2024).

The use of pretrained models like BERT and GPT has enabled breakthroughs in the cybersecurity domain. For example, Ferrag et al. (2023) explore how BERT-based models can be employed for lightweight, privacy-preserving detection of cyber threats in IoT/IIoT devices. These pretrained models are capable of learning the intricacies of threat behavior and improving response time, thus enhancing cybersecurity resilience. Furthermore, pretrained models such as GPT can automate the generation of threat mitigation strategies, offering a dynamic approach to cybersecurity (Zangana, 2024). These models continue to evolve, paving the way for more intelligent, scalable, and effective cybersecurity solutions (Hadi et al., 2023; Thandi, 2024).

In addition to their direct applications in cybersecurity, pretrained models also contribute to the overall evolution of AI in security contexts. By leveraging the transfer learning paradigm, pretrained models help to reduce the need for large, labeled datasets, a challenge in cybersecurity due to the constantly evolving nature of cyber threats (Xu et al., 2024). This capability is essential in addressing the ever-changing landscape of cybersecurity, where new threats emerge regularly, and previous data may quickly become outdated.

3.4 Summary

The integration of neural networks, transformers, and pretrained models represents a significant advancement in the field of cybersecurity. These technologies provide the foundation for intelligent, scalable, and efficient threat detection and mitigation systems. As AI and machine learning continue to evolve, the ability to harness large language models and other pretrained architectures will become increasingly crucial in the ongoing battle to secure digital infrastructures (Kasri et al., 2025; Ferrag et al., 2024).

These advancements will not only enhance threat detection capabilities but also ensure that cybersecurity systems remain adaptive and capable of addressing the most sophisticated and emerging cyber threats (Santos et al., 2024; Hassanin & Moustafa, 2024). As the field continues to develop, we can expect even more innovative applications of these models, further revolutionizing the landscape of cybersecurity.

4. DEEP LEARNING VS. TRADITIONAL CYBERSECURITY APPROACHES

In the field of cybersecurity, traditional defense mechanisms have long been the cornerstone of protecting networks, data, and systems from malicious threats. These approaches typically rely on signature-based detection systems, rule-based engines, and heuristics to identify known threats and anomalies. However, as cyberattacks grow in sophistication and complexity, these traditional methods are proving inadequate, leading to the adoption of more advanced techniques, notably deep learning (DL).

4.1 Traditional Cybersecurity Approaches

Traditional cybersecurity solutions focus heavily on predefined signatures or patterns of known attacks to detect and mitigate threats. These systems rely on a database of attack signatures, which are created based on previously discovered threats. Signature-based methods can be highly effective for detecting known vulnerabilities but are limited when it comes to addressing zero-day attacks or novel forms of cyber threats. Additionally, rule-based systems, while capable of addressing specific vulnerabilities, often lack the flexibility to adapt to new or evolving attack methods.

Despite their long-standing use, these traditional systems suffer from various limitations, such as high false-positive rates, slow response times, and the inability to detect sophisticated and unknown attacks. For example, firewalls and intrusion detection systems (IDS) traditionally function by recognizing known attack signatures or suspicious behavior patterns, but these systems fall short when confronted with new or polymorphic threats (Sarker, 2024; Ferrag et al., 2024a). Moreover, their effectiveness often declines in highly dynamic environments like the Internet of Things (IoT) or Industrial Internet of Things (IIoT), where attack surfaces and threat vectors are continuously evolving.

4.2 The Emergence of Deep Learning in Cybersecurity

Deep learning, a subset of machine learning (ML), has emerged as a transformative technology in the field of cybersecurity. Unlike traditional methods that rely on manually defined rules or patterns, deep learning algorithms can automatically detect complex, unseen patterns within vast amounts of data, making them highly effective for identifying unknown and novel threats. By using large datasets to train models, deep learning techniques can adapt and improve over time, making them far more resilient to new attack strategies compared to traditional methods.

The adoption of deep learning in cybersecurity has grown significantly. The following bar chart illustrates the increasing trend of deep learning models used for cybersecurity applications over the past decade.

Figure 4. Growth of deep learning in cybersecurity

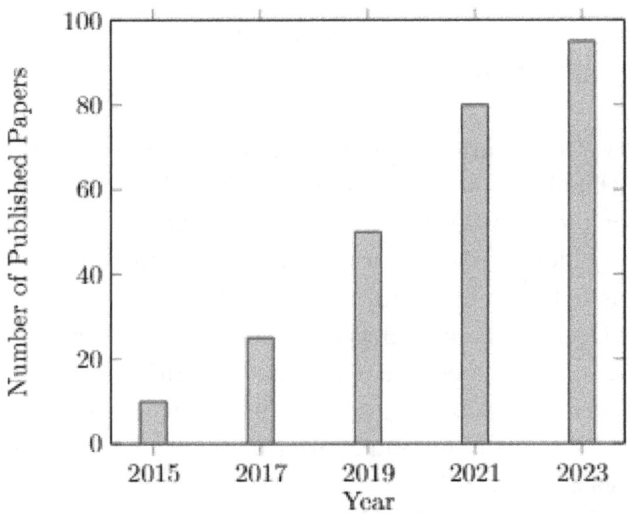

Deep learning approaches in cybersecurity, such as deep neural networks (DNN), convolutional neural networks (CNN), and recurrent neural networks (RNN), excel at identifying hidden patterns in network traffic, user behavior, and system logs. These models are particularly useful for anomaly detection, malware classification, and intrusion detection, offering more robust performance in dynamic environments (Liu, 2024; Ferrag et al., 2023). Furthermore, deep learning models are highly scalable and can be integrated into real-time security systems, providing immediate responses to potential threats.

A key advantage of deep learning is its ability to improve its performance as more data becomes available. Models such as those built on large language models (LLMs) like BERT (Bidirectional Encoder Representations from Transformers) are revolutionizing cybersecurity by enabling more accurate and real-time detection of attacks (Ferrag et al., 2024b). LLMs are particularly powerful because they can process unstructured data from a variety of sources, such as network traffic, logs, and even textual data from security reports, to detect malicious activity with higher accuracy than traditional methods.

Moreover, the integration of explainable AI (XAI) in deep learning models further enhances the transparency of threat detection. With the increasing adoption of large language models in cybersecurity, explainability becomes crucial for understanding how and why specific threats are detected. This transparency helps organizations fine-tune their security systems, making them more adaptive and accurate (Hasanov et al., 2024; Ghazal et al., 2024).

4.3 Key Advantages of Deep Learning Over Traditional Approaches

1. **Adaptability**: Deep learning systems are capable of learning from new data, making them highly adaptable to emerging threats. Unlike traditional approaches, which rely on predefined signatures, deep learning can detect novel and zero-day attacks by identifying patterns and anomalies that may not be present in existing datasets (Kasri et al., 2025; Sarker, 2024).
2. **Scalability**: Deep learning models can scale to handle large volumes of data, which is essential for modern networks and IoT/IIoT environments where the amount of data is continuously growing. These models can process and analyze millions of data points in real-time, offering rapid detection and mitigation of threats (Zangana et al., 2025).
3. **Accuracy and Precision**: With their ability to learn from large and complex datasets, deep learning models tend to be more accurate in identifying subtle attack patterns, reducing the likelihood of false positives. This capability significantly improves the efficiency of threat detection systems and reduces the workload for cybersecurity professionals (Motlagh et al., 2024).
4. **Detection of Advanced Persistent Threats (APTs)**: Deep learning's ability to analyze long-term patterns of network behavior allows it to detect advanced persistent threats (APTs), which traditional systems may miss. APTs are often stealthy and can evolve over time, making them difficult to identify using traditional methods (Chen et al., 2024; Ferrag et al., 2023).

5. **Automated Threat Detection**: By leveraging the power of LLMs and deep learning, cybersecurity systems can operate with minimal human intervention. This level of automation not only improves response times but also frees up resources for other critical tasks, such as investigating threats or strengthening preventive measures (Asoronye et al., 2024; Motlagh et al., 2024).

Traditional cybersecurity approaches rely on rule-based systems, whereas AI-driven methods leverage deep learning for anomaly detection. The table below highlights key differences.

Table 1. Comparison of traditional and AI-driven cybersecurity

Feature	Traditional Approach	AI-Driven Approach
Detection Speed	Slow	Fast
Adaptability	Low	High
False Positives	High	Lower
Automation	Limited	Extensive

4.4 Challenges in Implementing Deep Learning in Cybersecurity

While deep learning offers significant advantages, its implementation in cybersecurity also comes with challenges. One major hurdle is the need for large, high-quality datasets for training models. Deep learning models require vast amounts of labeled data to achieve optimal performance, which can be difficult to obtain in the context of cybersecurity (Hadi et al., 2023). Additionally, training deep learning models requires significant computational resources, which may not be feasible for all organizations.

Another challenge is the potential for adversarial attacks on deep learning systems. Cybercriminals may attempt to manipulate the input data to deceive deep learning models, rendering them ineffective (Xu et al., 2024). This highlights the importance of incorporating robust security measures into deep learning systems to ensure their reliability and resilience.

4.5 Summary

The shift from traditional cybersecurity approaches to deep learning represents a significant evolution in the way organizations defend against cyber threats. While traditional methods remain important, the growing complexity and volume of cyber-attacks demand more advanced solutions that can adapt to new and evolving threats. Deep learning, particularly through the use of large language models, has emerged as a powerful tool for enhancing cybersecurity, offering improved detection capabilities, better scalability, and greater accuracy in identifying threats (Kasri et al., 2025; Ferrag et al., 2024a). However, successful implementation requires overcoming challenges related to data quality, computational power, and adversarial threats. With continued advancements in AI and deep learning technologies, the future of cybersecurity is poised to be significantly more proactive, adaptive, and resilient.

5. BENEFITS OF AI IN CYBERSECURITY

Artificial Intelligence (AI) is transforming the cybersecurity landscape, offering significant advancements in threat detection, prevention, and response. By utilizing advanced algorithms and machine learning models, AI improves the ability to detect vulnerabilities, predict potential threats, and respond faster and more effectively to cyberattacks. Below are the key benefits of AI in cybersecurity:

5.1. Enhanced Threat Detection and Prevention

AI-powered systems excel at identifying potential threats by analyzing large volumes of data in real time. Unlike traditional cybersecurity methods, AI systems can learn from vast datasets, enabling them to recognize new, previously unseen threats. Large language models (LLMs), for example, are increasingly utilized to detect anomalies and patterns indicative of cyberattacks (Ferrag et al., 2023; Liu, 2024). AI's capacity to analyze patterns in real-time ensures more rapid identification of cyber threats, which reduces the time attackers have to exploit vulnerabilities (Kasri et al., 2025).

Ferrag et al. (2024) demonstrated the application of AI in IoT/IIoT (Industrial Internet of Things) devices, where AI-driven threat detection systems, powered by BERT-based models, can protect devices against attacks while preserving privacy. This real-time detection, coupled with automated responses, is critical in environments where human intervention may not be swift enough.

5.2. Predictive Capabilities

AI models not only detect known threats but also predict potential future attacks based on historical data and behavioral patterns. Predictive cybersecurity utilizes machine learning to forecast threat trajectories, enabling organizations to adopt a proactive approach to defense rather than simply reacting to incidents as they arise. AI's ability to identify emerging threats and vulnerabilities that may not yet have been exploited gives organizations a valuable edge in cybersecurity (Santos et al., 2024; Motlagh et al., 2024).

For example, recent studies suggest that LLMs can significantly enhance the ability to predict and mitigate threats in IoT networks (Diaf et al., 2024), offering a proactive strategy against evolving attack methods, including zero-day exploits (Jones & Omar, 2024).

Different AI models offer varying levels of accuracy and speed. The following line graph compares the performance of several models.

Figure 5. Performance comparison of AI models

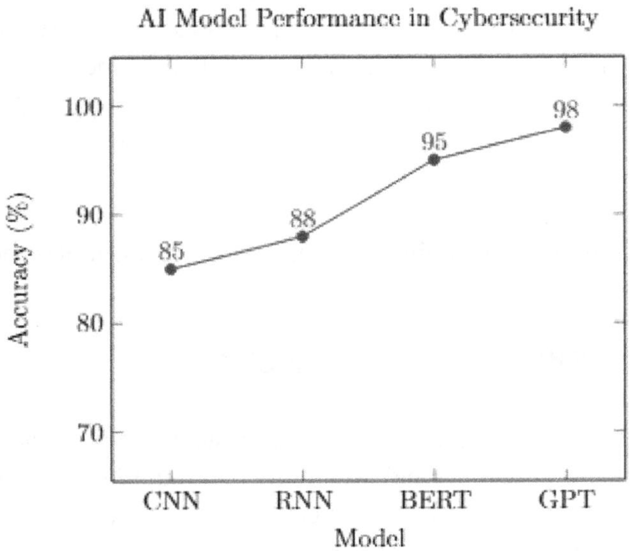

5.3. Automated Incident Response

One of the greatest advantages of AI in cybersecurity is its ability to automate responses to detected threats. This reduces the reliance on human intervention and ensures a faster response, which is crucial when mitigating the damage caused by cyberattacks. AI systems can trigger predefined actions, such as isolating affected systems or blocking suspicious IP addresses, without waiting for a human analyst to intervene.

Studies have highlighted the importance of automated threat responses in minimizing downtime and preventing the escalation of attacks (Sarker, 2024; Asoronye et al., 2024). Such systems are especially valuable in critical industries where the cost of a security breach can be catastrophic, such as healthcare and financial services.

5.4. Behavioral Analysis for Threat Identification

AI-driven behavioral analysis focuses on understanding the patterns of users and systems to detect abnormal activity indicative of a cyberattack. By learning what constitutes "normal" behavior within an organization's network, AI can spot deviations that might signal malicious activity, such as insider threats or advanced persistent threats (APT). This method has been shown to be highly effective in identifying attacks that traditional signature-based methods might miss (Hasanov et al., 2024; Ghazal et al., 2024).

This form of continuous monitoring ensures that security systems can adapt to the evolving tactics of cybercriminals, making AI a valuable tool in the fight against sophisticated threats.

5.5. Improved Efficiency and Scalability

AI systems can process large volumes of data faster than traditional cybersecurity methods, improving efficiency and scalability. Machine learning algorithms can quickly identify vulnerabilities across an entire network, flagging potential threats in real-time. This speed is critical, especially in large organizations or environments with complex infrastructure, where manual analysis would be slow and error-prone (Hassanin & Moustafa, 2024; Pleshakova et al., 2024).

By leveraging the power of AI, organizations can scale their cybersecurity measures without a linear increase in human resources. This allows for more comprehensive coverage without sacrificing performance.

5.6. AI-Powered Vulnerability Management

AI can automate the process of vulnerability scanning and risk assessment, identifying weaknesses before they can be exploited by attackers. The ability of AI to assess large and complex networks helps prioritize remediation efforts by focusing on the most critical vulnerabilities. As AI systems continue to improve, they will not only detect vulnerabilities more efficiently but will also recommend and implement patches or workarounds to mitigate identified risks (Gholami & Omar, 2023; Gupta et al., 2024).

The application of LLMs in vulnerability detection has also shown promise, with studies revealing their ability to significantly reduce false positives while increasing the accuracy of vulnerability identification (Gholami & Omar, 2024).

5.7. Data Privacy and Protection

AI enhances data privacy through more intelligent management of sensitive information. Advanced machine learning models can detect when sensitive data is at risk and take measures to protect it, such as encrypting data or blocking unauthorized access. In sectors like healthcare, where data privacy is paramount, AI can help mitigate risks related to data breaches and leaks (Motlagh et al., 2024; Zangana et al., 2025).

Generative AI models are particularly useful in maintaining privacy while ensuring robust cybersecurity. Ferrag et al. (2024) introduced a privacy-preserving BERT-based lightweight model for IoT/IIoT devices, which can effectively prevent cyber threats without compromising user privacy.

5.8. Enhanced Threat Intelligence Sharing

AI-powered systems enable organizations to share threat intelligence seamlessly and securely. By leveraging AI's capabilities to analyze and aggregate data from multiple sources, organizations can share insights on emerging threats with minimal risk of data leaks. This collaboration is essential for building a collective defense against global cyber threats (Chen et al., 2024; Sarker, 2024).

Moreover, AI allows for the automated translation of complex threat data into actionable intelligence, which can be shared in real-time with various stakeholders. This improves the overall cyber defense posture of the global cybersecurity community.

5.9 Summary

The benefits of AI in cybersecurity are vast and transformative. From enhanced threat detection to predictive capabilities and automated responses, AI equips organizations with powerful tools to combat cyber threats. The integration of LLMs into cybersecurity has particularly revolutionized threat detection and prevention, offering faster, more accurate, and scalable solutions. As AI continues to evolve, its role in cybersecurity will undoubtedly grow, offering even more advanced capabilities to protect against the increasingly complex and dynamic landscape of cyber threats (Kasri et al., 2025; Xu et al., 2024).

6. LIMITATIONS AND CHALLENGES OF AI-DRIVEN CYBERSECURITY

AI-driven cybersecurity has revolutionized the way security measures are applied in the digital realm, offering potential solutions to complex challenges. However, despite its rapid advancements, several limitations and challenges hinder the widespread adoption of these technologies. These challenges can be categorized into several key areas, including algorithmic limitations, data-related issues, privacy concerns, ethical considerations, and adversarial attacks.

6.1. Algorithmic Limitations

One of the most significant challenges in AI-driven cybersecurity is the intrinsic limitations of the algorithms themselves. While machine learning (ML) models, including large language models (LLMs), have shown promising results in threat detection and prevention, they are not infallible. For instance, models such as BERT and other deep learning-based architectures may suffer from overfitting, which leads to poor generalization on unseen data. As noted by Ferrag et al. (2024), a lack of robustness to new or emerging threats can undermine the model's ability to detect previously unknown attack patterns, leading to a false sense of security (Ferrag et al., 2024; Ferrag et al., 2023).

Furthermore, these models often require extensive computational resources to function optimally. This can result in inefficiencies, especially when deployed in resource-constrained environments such as Internet of Things (IoT) or Industrial IoT (IIoT) devices (Sarker, 2024). For instance, the computational overhead of real-time threat detection can significantly slow down system performance, making it less suitable for certain use cases.

6.2. Data-Related Issues

Data is central to the functioning of AI models. The quality and quantity of data used to train AI models can greatly impact their effectiveness. AI models, particularly in cybersecurity, are highly dependent on large, high-quality datasets to learn and adapt to the ever-evolving nature of cyber threats. However, obtaining such data can be problematic. In many cases, cybersecurity data can be scarce, particularly in areas related to zero-day attacks or new exploits (Hassanin & Moustafa, 2024).

Moreover, the need for labeled data for supervised learning can be a significant barrier, as labeling datasets can be time-consuming and costly.

Additionally, synthetic data, which is sometimes used to augment training sets, may not perfectly mimic real-world attack scenarios. As Gholami and Omar (2023) point out, the use of synthetic data might lead to less effective AI models that are unable to generalize well to real-world threats (Gholami & Omar, 2023). This highlights the ongoing need for more accurate and comprehensive datasets to train AI systems effectively.

6.3. Privacy Concerns

Another major challenge that arises with AI-driven cybersecurity solutions is the privacy implications associated with data collection and processing. As AI systems require vast amounts of data to perform their tasks, the risk of exposing sensitive information increases. Ferrag et al. (2024) highlight the importance of maintaining privacy, especially when deploying AI models in IoT and IIoT devices, where data often involves personally identifiable information (PII) or proprietary corporate data (Ferrag et al., 2024).

Privacy-preserving models, such as the privacy-preserving BERT-based lightweight model developed for IoT/IIoT devices, are gaining attention as potential solutions (Lestable & Thandi, 2024). However, these privacy-preserving techniques often introduce new challenges, such as the trade-off between performance and privacy, which can be a significant concern in high-stakes cybersecurity applications (Ferrag et al., 2023; Zangana, 2024). This balance remains an ongoing challenge as cybersecurity professionals aim to protect sensitive data without compromising the effectiveness of AI models.

6.4. Ethical Considerations

Ethical challenges also present significant hurdles in the development and deployment of AI in cybersecurity. These include concerns regarding bias in AI algorithms, transparency in decision-making, and the potential misuse of AI technologies for malicious purposes (Motlagh et al., 2024). Bias in AI models can lead to discrimination or inequity, especially when training data is not representative of diverse cybersecurity threats (Santos et al., 2024). Furthermore, the "black-box" nature of many AI models, including LLMs, makes it difficult to understand how decisions are made, potentially leading to accountability issues (Kasri et al., 2025).

Another pressing ethical concern is the risk of adversarial AI, where cyber attackers intentionally manipulate AI systems to bypass security measures (Hasanov et al., 2024). AI models that are not designed with robustness against adversarial attacks may be exploited by malicious actors, rendering them ineffective in protecting critical infrastructure (Sarker, 2024; Xu et al., 2024).

The ethical challenges in AI-driven cybersecurity include bias, privacy risks, and adversarial attacks. The pie chart below represents the distribution of these concerns.

Figure 6. Ethical concerns in AI cybersecurity

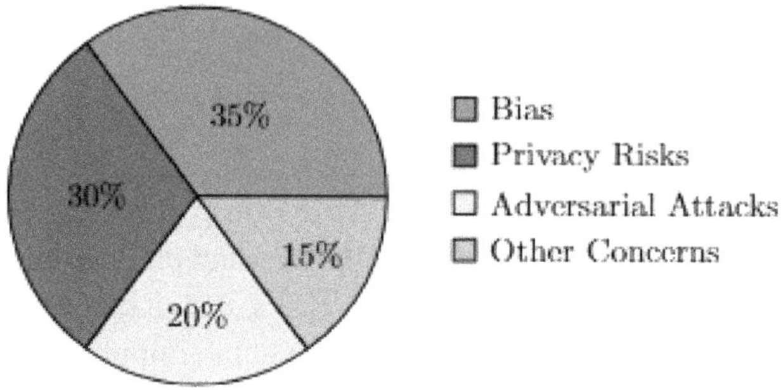

6.5. Adversarial Attacks

Adversarial attacks are a critical challenge to AI-driven cybersecurity. These attacks involve the deliberate manipulation of input data to mislead AI models, causing them to make incorrect decisions or fail to detect threats. The vulnerability of LLMs and other AI models to adversarial attacks is well-documented (Zangana, 2025). For example, slight modifications to input data can cause large language models to misclassify malicious content as benign, thereby allowing cyber threats to evade detection (Xu et al., 2024).

Researchers have been working on solutions to mitigate adversarial attacks, such as adversarial training, where models are trained with deliberately perturbed data to improve their robustness. However, the effectiveness of these countermeasures remains limited, and adversarial attacks continue to be a major concern in AI-based cybersecurity systems (Ghazal et al., 2024; Liu, 2024).

6.6. Regulatory and Compliance Issues

The deployment of AI-driven cybersecurity tools must also navigate the complex landscape of regulatory and compliance frameworks. As cybersecurity becomes increasingly reliant on AI, organizations must ensure that their AI systems comply with privacy laws, industry regulations, and ethical standards. The evolving nature of these regulations makes it challenging for organizations to stay compliant while leveraging cutting-edge AI technologies (Santos et al., 2024; Aghaei et al., 2022). This regulatory uncertainty can create barriers to adoption and hinder the integration of AI into existing cybersecurity frameworks.

6.7 Summary

Despite the promising potential of AI in cybersecurity, technology faces numerous limitations and challenges. Addressing these challenges requires a multifaceted approach, including improving the robustness of AI models, ensuring privacy and ethical standards are upheld, and developing more comprehensive data sets for training. Moreover, enhancing the resilience of AI-driven cybersecurity systems against adversarial attacks and navigating the complex regulatory landscape will be crucial for the continued success and adoption of these technologies. As Ferrag et al. (2024) and other researchers highlight, while AI offers significant advancements, its application in cybersecurity is still in its infancy, and much work remains to be done to fully harness its potential (Ferrag et al., 2024; Motlagh et al., 2024).

7. ETHICAL CONSIDERATIONS AND BIAS IN AI

The rapid development and deployment of artificial intelligence (AI), particularly large language models (LLMs), have introduced a range of ethical considerations and challenges, particularly in sensitive fields like cybersecurity. As AI systems become increasingly integrated into cybersecurity practices, it is vital to address ethical concerns regarding fairness, transparency, accountability, and potential bias in these technologies.

7.1 Privacy and Data Protection

One of the primary ethical concerns surrounding the use of AI in cybersecurity is privacy. LLMs often require vast amounts of data to train, which can include sensitive information. In many cases, these datasets may involve personal or confidential data that, if mishandled, could lead to violations of privacy rights. The ethical dilemma arises when AI systems are used to process or store data without sufficient safeguards to prevent unauthorized access or misuse. Researchers like Ferrag et al. (2024) have highlighted the importance of developing privacy-preserving models, such as their lightweight BERT-based approach for IoT/IIoT devices, to ensure data security while maintaining high detection accuracy.

Furthermore, the challenge of compliance with privacy regulations, such as GDPR, is paramount. The integration of AI into cybersecurity systems necessitates ensuring that personal data is handled responsibly. As noted by Hasanov et al. (2024), the rapid growth of AI technology often outpaces legal frameworks, creating a gap in regulations that must be addressed to prevent misuse.

7.2 Bias and Fairness

AI systems, including LLMs, are susceptible to biases inherent in the data they are trained on. Bias can manifest in various forms, such as gender, racial, or socioeconomic biases, and it can perpetuate existing inequalities in decision-making processes. This is a significant concern in cybersecurity applications, where biased models could lead to unfair treatment of certain groups or individuals, undermining the effectiveness and fairness of threat detection mechanisms.

Studies like those by Sarker (2024) and Ferrag et al. (2023) stress the importance of addressing bias in AI models to ensure that cybersecurity solutions are equitable and do not favor or disadvantage specific groups. Bias in AI can result from historical prejudices embedded in training data, and without proper oversight, these biases could affect the performance of cybersecurity systems, leading to misidentification of threats or overlooking certain vulnerabilities.

Incorporating fairness into AI models is not only an ethical imperative but also a practical necessity for ensuring the accuracy and reliability of cybersecurity tools. As Zangana et al. (2025) suggest, fair AI practices require constant monitoring and adjustments to minimize bias and ensure equitable treatment of all data inputs.

7.3 Transparency and Explainability

AI models, especially deep learning-based ones like LLMs, are often described as "black boxes," meaning their decision-making processes are opaque and difficult for humans to interpret. This lack of transparency raises ethical concerns, particularly in high-stakes domains like cybersecurity, where decisions made by AI systems can have significant consequences, such as blocking legitimate traffic or failing to detect novel threats.

The need for explainability in AI systems is critical to gaining trust and ensuring accountability. As noted by Liu (2024), transparency in AI models allows security professionals to understand why certain decisions were made, which is essential for troubleshooting, improving model performance, and mitigating any unintended negative impacts. For example, explainable AI (XAI) techniques, as explored by

Ferrag et al. (2024), can provide insights into the reasoning behind threat detection and help users interpret AI decisions more effectively, thereby enhancing trust in automated systems.

7.4 Accountability and Liability

As AI systems become more autonomous, determining accountability in the event of a cybersecurity breach or failure becomes increasingly complex. If an AI system wrongly identifies a cyberattack or fails to detect a legitimate threat, it raises questions about who is responsible for the resulting damages. Researchers like Thandi (2024) emphasize that establishing clear accountability structures is crucial for ensuring that AI technologies are used ethically in cybersecurity.

The use of LLMs in cybersecurity applications, especially in critical areas like threat detection and response, requires strict regulatory oversight to prevent misuse or errors. Ensuring that AI systems are designed with built-in accountability mechanisms will help mitigate the risks associated with relying too heavily on automated decision-making processes.

7.5 Impact on Employment and Human Roles

The increasing automation of cybersecurity tasks through AI technologies has the potential to displace human workers, raising ethical concerns about job security and the social implications of AI adoption. While LLMs can enhance efficiency and effectiveness in threat detection, they could reduce the need for certain cybersecurity professionals, such as those focused on manual monitoring and analysis. However, experts like Motlagh et al. (2024) argue that AI should be seen as a complement to human expertise, with AI systems supporting professionals in their decision-making rather than replacing them entirely. Ensuring that AI adoption is accompanied by workforce retraining and upskilling opportunities is crucial to minimizing negative social impacts.

7.6 Ethical Use in Threat Mitigation

AI's role in cybersecurity is ultimately to enhance defense mechanisms, but the ethics of deploying these systems in real-world scenarios should not be overlooked. The use of AI for predictive threat detection, as described by Diaf et al. (2024), raises the issue of how far AI should go in preemptively identifying and mitigating threats. The ethical question here is whether AI-driven responses, such as blocking certain

IP addresses or isolating devices based on predictive models, could inadvertently harm legitimate users or businesses.

As AI becomes more integrated into cybersecurity, it is essential to establish ethical guidelines for its use in threat mitigation. This includes ensuring that AI systems do not unjustly disrupt legitimate activities and that their deployment does not disproportionately target specific individuals or organizations without proper evidence.

7.7 Summary

Ethical considerations and bias in AI systems are critical concerns in the development and deployment of AI-driven cybersecurity solutions. As LLMs continue to evolve, it is essential to address these issues through transparent, fair, and accountable practices. Researchers and practitioners must work together to ensure that AI technologies are used ethically and do not harm individuals or communities. By prioritizing privacy, fairness, transparency, and accountability, the cybersecurity community can harness the power of AI while mitigating the associated ethical risks.

8. FUTURE TRENDS IN AI-DRIVEN CYBERSECURITY

As cybersecurity continues to evolve, artificial intelligence (AI), particularly large language models (LLMs), is shaping the next generation of defense mechanisms against increasingly sophisticated cyber threats. With their unparalleled ability to process vast amounts of data and identify patterns, LLMs are revolutionizing threat detection, response strategies, and overall security management in ways that were previously unimaginable. The future of AI-driven cybersecurity lies in the ability to harness these models for proactive threat intelligence, automated defense systems, and enhanced risk mitigation strategies.

The evolution of AI in cybersecurity has progressed through multiple stages, from basic automation to intelligent, self-learning systems.

Figure 7. Evolution of AI in cybersecurity

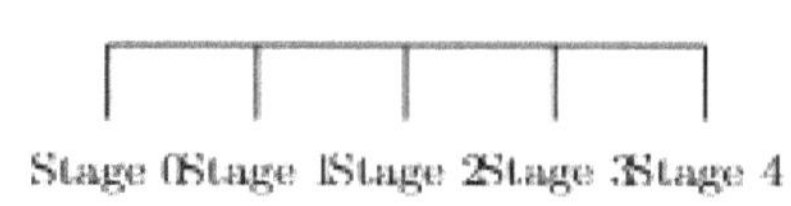

8.1 The Role of LLMs in Cyber Threat Detection

One of the most promising applications of AI in cybersecurity is its ability to detect and respond to threats in real-time. Large language models are particularly effective in processing natural language data, making them ideal for analyzing vast amounts of unstructured data such as network logs, security reports, and social media feeds. The ability of LLMs to learn from both structured and unstructured data enhances their ability to identify emerging threats faster and more accurately than traditional security tools (Kasri et al., 2025).

Recent studies have demonstrated the potential of LLMs like BERT and GPT-based models to detect cyber threats more efficiently. For example, Ferrag et al. (2024) propose a privacy-preserving BERT-based model specifically designed for IoT/IIoT devices, offering lightweight yet effective protection in resource-constrained environments. This marks a critical step in the integration of LLMs into cybersecurity tools, as lightweight models can be deployed across a range of devices without compromising performance or security (Thandi, 2024).

8.2 Threat Prediction and Mitigation Using LLMs

Beyond detection, AI models are increasingly used for predicting potential attacks and mitigating their impact. For instance, Diaf et al. (2024) explore the use of LLMs to predict cyberattacks in IoT networks, which are often susceptible to rapid escalation due to their vast and interconnected nature. Leveraging pre-trained language models in threat prediction allows security teams to anticipate attack vectors and develop strategies to counter them before they escalate.

The integration of generative AI techniques further enhances these prediction models. Sarker (2024) discusses how generative AI can simulate various attack scenarios, allowing organizations to test their cybersecurity protocols against hypothetical threats. This proactive approach is essential for developing resilient security systems that can quickly adapt to new types of attacks.

8.3 Enhancing Cyber Defense with Explainability

While LLMs are powerful tools for cybersecurity, one challenge that remains is the explainability of AI decisions. In the context of cybersecurity, understanding why a model flagged a particular event as suspicious or benign is critical for trust and verification. The rise of explainable AI (XAI) is crucial in addressing this issue, ensuring that cybersecurity professionals can interpret the reasoning behind model decisions and improve their decision-making processes (Ghazal et al., 2024). XAI will enable security teams to better understand model behavior, facilitating faster and more informed responses to potential threats.

LLMs like SecureBERT (Aghaei et al., 2022) are leading the way in integrating explainability with threat detection. These models not only offer robust security solutions but also provide transparency into how they classify and detect cyber threats, making them indispensable in high-stakes security environments.

8.4 Automating Cybersecurity Operations

AI's potential in automating cybersecurity operations cannot be overstated. Automation using LLMs can significantly reduce the response time to cyber incidents, allowing for faster containment and remediation of threats. Automated threat detection and mitigation workflows powered by LLMs will reduce the manual effort required in monitoring security systems, enabling organizations to focus on more complex security challenges.

Kasri et al. (2025) highlight the role of LLMs in automating key cybersecurity processes such as incident reporting, vulnerability management, and patch deployment. By leveraging generative models for dynamic responses, LLMs can not only identify and contain threats but also generate new defense strategies based on real-time attack data.

AI-driven threat detection follows a structured pipeline, from data collection to response automation. The diagram below illustrates this pipeline.

Figure 8. AI-powered cybersecurity pipeline

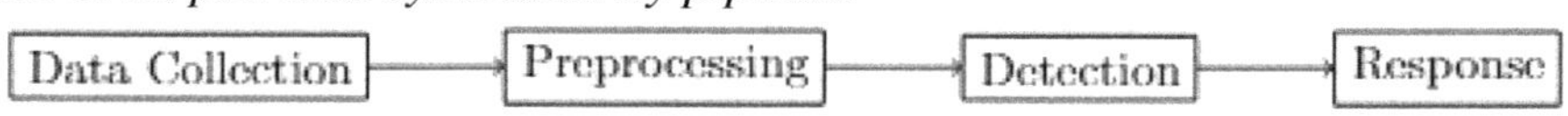

8.5 Privacy and Security Challenges in LLM Deployment

As LLMs become integral to cybersecurity systems, concerns surrounding data privacy and security must be addressed. While LLMs excel at processing vast amounts of data, they also pose risks if sensitive data is exposed during training or inference. Ferrag et al. (2023) highlight the importance of privacy-preserving techniques, such as differential privacy and federated learning, to ensure that user data remains protected when used to train models for cybersecurity applications.

These technologies enable the use of LLMs for cyber threat detection without compromising the privacy of the data being processed.

Moreover, the security of LLMs themselves is a growing concern. As these models become more complex and widely used, they may become targets for adversarial attacks. Liu (2024) discusses the potential vulnerabilities of LLMs and the need for robust security mechanisms to protect these models from exploitation.

8.6 The Future Landscape of AI-Driven Cybersecurity

Looking forward, the evolution of AI-driven cybersecurity will likely involve deeper integration with emerging technologies like quantum computing and blockchain. Zangana (2024) explores the use of LLMs in conjunction with quantum computing to enhance the encryption and decryption processes, ensuring that cybersecurity measures remain ahead of attackers who may also leverage quantum capabilities.

The integration of LLMs with blockchain technologies will also offer new opportunities for secure, decentralized cybersecurity solutions. As more organizations adopt blockchain for securing sensitive data, LLMs will be able to analyze blockchain transactions for signs of fraudulent or malicious activities, improving the overall security of decentralized networks (Santos et al., 2024).

8.7 Summary

In conclusion, the future of AI-driven cybersecurity is promising, with LLMs playing a central role in transforming how threats are detected, predicted, and mitigated. The ability of LLMs to handle vast amounts of unstructured data, predict potential attacks, and automate key cybersecurity tasks is already reshaping the landscape. However, challenges related to privacy, explainability, and model security must be addressed to fully realize the potential of LLMs in cybersecurity. As advancements continue, AI-driven solutions will become even more integral to building resilient, adaptive, and intelligent cybersecurity systems.

9. CONCLUSION

The evolution of artificial intelligence (AI), particularly through large language models (LLMs), is significantly transforming the cybersecurity landscape. From enhancing threat detection systems to automating incident responses, AI-driven cybersecurity solutions are becoming indispensable in addressing the complexities and volume of modern cyber threats. As organizations increasingly rely on AI technologies to secure their networks and data, LLMs are at the forefront of this revolution, offering innovative approaches to improving accuracy, efficiency, and scalability in cybersecurity operations.

This chapter has explored the multiple facets of AI-driven cybersecurity, emphasizing the transformative potential of LLMs in automating various security tasks such as malware detection, vulnerability management, and real-time threat intelligence. With advancements in machine learning algorithms and the advent of generative AI, LLMs are now able to process vast amounts of security data, identify emerging threats, and provide recommendations for proactive measures. These capabilities are crucial in the age of Industry 4.0, where threats are becoming more sophisticated and prevalent.

The integration of privacy-preserving mechanisms in AI models, especially when applied to Internet of Things (IoT) and Industrial IoT (IIoT) environments, is a notable trend in AI-driven cybersecurity. Research shows that the use of lightweight and privacy-aware models, such as those based on BERT, is increasingly gaining traction in providing secure and efficient threat detection without compromising user privacy. Furthermore, the ability of LLMs to continuously learn and adapt to new patterns of attack enhances the resilience of cybersecurity systems, making them more effective in countering novel and zero-day vulnerabilities.

Looking ahead, the role of AI in cybersecurity is expected to grow even more critical. As highlighted in the research, generative AI and LLMs will continue to evolve, enabling more advanced and robust defenses against cyberattacks. However, challenges remain, including ethical concerns, biases in model training, and the need for explainability in AI-driven decisions. Nevertheless, the continued refinement of LLM architecture and their applications in cybersecurity will play a pivotal role in shaping the future of cyber defense strategies.

In conclusion, the convergence of AI and cybersecurity holds immense promise for safeguarding digital ecosystems across industries. By leveraging the power of large language models, organizations can enhance their ability to predict, detect, and respond to cyber threats in real-time. As these technologies mature and further integrate with other emerging technologies such as quantum computing and blockchain, they will undoubtedly redefine the landscape of cybersecurity, creating a more secure and resilient digital world.

REFERENCES

Aghaei, E., Niu, X., Shadid, W., & Al-Shaer, E. (2022, October). Securebert: A domain-specific language model for cybersecurity. In *International Conference on Security and Privacy in Communication Systems* (pp. 39-56). Cham: Springer Nature Switzerland.

AlQenaei, Z. M. (2024, March). Evolution and Optimization of Language Model Architectures: From Foundations to Future Directions. In *International Conference on Computing and Machine Learning* (pp. 233-249). Singapore: Springer Nature Singapore.

Alturkistani, H., & Chuprat, S. (2024). Artificial Intelligence and Large Language Models in Advancing Cyber Threat Intelligence: A Systematic Literature Review.

Asoronye, G. O., Anthony, O. C., Ogbuikwu, R. I., Ogili, C. O., & Ali, H. U. (2024). SecLM: A Specialized Security Language Model for Advanced Cybersecurity Applications and Threat Mitigation. *EKETE-International Journal Of Advanced Research*, *2*(6), 33–42.

Bryce, C., Kalousis, A., Leroux, I., Madinier, H., Mermoud, A., Mulder, V., ... & Ruch, P. Trends in Large Language Models: Actors, Applications, and Impact on Cybersecurity.

Chen, Y., Cui, M., Wang, D., Cao, Y., Yang, P., Jiang, B., Lu, Z., & Liu, B. (2024). A survey of large language models for cyber threat detection. *Computers & Security*, *145*, 104016. DOI: 10.1016/j.cose.2024.104016

Diaf, A., Korba, A. A., Karabadji, N. E., & Ghamri-Doudane, Y. (2024, April). Beyond detection: Leveraging large language models for cyber attack prediction in iot networks. In *2024 20th International Conference on Distributed Computing in Smart Systems and the Internet of Things (DCOSS-IoT)* (pp. 117-123). IEEE.

Ferrag, M. A., Alwahedi, F., Battah, A., Cherif, B., Mechri, A., & Tihanyi, N. (2024). Generative ai and large language models for cyber security: All insights you need. *Available atSSRN* 4853709. DOI: 10.2139/ssrn.4853709

Ferrag, M. A., Ndhlovu, M., Tihanyi, N., Cordeiro, L. C., Debbah, M., & Lestable, T. (2023). Revolutionizing cyber threat detection with large language models. *arXiv preprint arXiv:2306.14263*, 195-202.

Ferrag, M. A., Ndhlovu, M., Tihanyi, N., Cordeiro, L. C., Debbah, M., Lestable, T., & Thandi, N. S. (2024). Revolutionizing cyber threat detection with large language models: A privacy-preserving bert-based lightweight model for iot/iiot devices. *IEEE Access : Practical Innovations, Open Solutions*, *12*, 23733–23750.
Ferrag, M. A., Ndhlovu, M., Tihanyi, N., Cordeiro, L. C., Debbah, M., Lestable, T., & Thandi, N. S. (2024). Revolutionizing cyber threat detection with large language models: A privacy-preserving bert-based lightweight model for iot/iiot devices. *IEEE Access : Practical Innovations, Open Solutions*, *12*, 23733–23750.
Ghazal, T. M., Janjua, J. I., Abushiba, W., Ahmad, M., Ihsan, A., & Al-Dmour, N. A. (2024, December). Cybersecurity Revolution via Large Language Models and Explainable AI. In *2024 17th International Conference on Security of Information and Networks (SIN)* (pp. 1-6). IEEE. DOI: 10.1109/SIN63213.2024.10871324

Gholami, S., & Omar, M. (2023). Does Synthetic Data Make Large Language Models More Efficient? *arXiv preprint arXiv:2310.07830.*

Gholami, S., & Omar, M. (2024). Can a student large language model perform as well as its teacher? In *Innovations, Securities, and Case Studies Across Healthcare, Business, and Technology* (pp. 122-139). IGI Global. DOI: 10.4018/979-8-3693-1906-2.ch007

Gupta, B. B., Gaurav, A., & Arya, V. (2024). Navigating the security landscape of large language models in enterprise information systems. *Enterprise Information Systems*, *18*(4), 2310846. DOI: 10.1080/17517575.2024.2310846

Hadi, M. A., Abdulredha, M. N., & Hasan, E. (2023). Introduction to ChatGPT: A new revolution of artificial intelligence with machine learning algorithms and cybersecurity. *Sci. Arch*, *4*(04), 276. DOI: 10.47587/SA.2023.4406

Hamza, Y. A., & Omar, M. D. (2013). Cloud computing security: Abuse and nefarious use of cloud computing. *International Journal of Computer Engineering Research*, *3*(6), 22–27.

Hasanov, I., Virtanen, S., Hakkala, A., & Isoaho, J. (2024). Application of Large Language Models in Cybersecurity: A Systematic Literature Review. *IEEE Access : Practical Innovations, Open Solutions*, *12*, 176751–176778. DOI: 10.1109/ACCESS.2024.3505983

Hassanin, M., & Moustafa, N. (2024). A comprehensive overview of large language models (llms) for cyber defences: Opportunities and directions. *arXiv preprint arXiv:2405.14487.*

Huff, A. J., Burrell, D. N., Nobles, C., Richardson, K., Wright, J. B., Burton, S. L., Jones, A. J., Springs, D., Omar, M., & Brown-Jackson, K. L. (2023). Management Practices for Mitigating Cybersecurity Threats to Biotechnology Companies, Laboratories, and Healthcare Research Organizations. In *Applied Research Approaches to Technology, Healthcare, and Business* (pp. 1-12). IGI Global.

Idelhaj, A., Abou El Houda, Z., & Khoukhi, L. (2024). Foundations models in cybersecurity. *Artificial Intelligence for Blockchain and Cybersecurity Powered IoT Applications*, 1.

Idelhaj, A., Abou El Houda, Z., & Khoukhi, L. Foundations models in cybersecurity: A comprehensive review and future direction. *Artificial Intelligence for Blockchain and Cybersecurity Powered IoT Applications*, 1-18.

Jones, R., & Omar, M. (2024). Revolutionizing Cybersecurity: The GPT-2 Enhanced Attack Detection and Defense (GEADD) Method for Zero-Day Threats. *International Journal of Informatics* [INJIISCOM]. *Information System and Computer Engineering*, *5*(2), 178–191.

Jones, R., Omar, M., Mohammed, D., Nobles, C., & Dawson, M. (2023). Harnessing the Speed and Accuracy of Machine Learning to Advance Cybersecurity. In *2023 Congress in Computer Science, Computer Engineering, & Applied Computing (CSCE)* (pp. 418-421). IEEE. DOI: 10.1109/CSCE60160.2023.00074

Kasri, W., Himeur, Y., Alkhazaleh, H. A., Tarapiah, S., Atalla, S., Mansoor, W., & Al-Ahmad, H. (2025). From Vulnerability to Defense: The Role of Large Language Models in Enhancing Cybersecurity. *Computation (Basel, Switzerland)*, *13*(2), 30.

Liu, Z. (2024, April). A review of advancements and applications of pre-trained language models in cybersecurity. In *2024 12th International Symposium on Digital Forensics and Security (ISDFS)* (pp. 1-10). IEEE.

Manoharan, A., & Sarker, M. (2023). Revolutionizing Cybersecurity: Unleashing the Power of Artificial Intelligence and Machine Learning for Next-Generation Threat Detection. *DOI:*https://www. doi. org/10.56726/IRJMETS32644, *1*.

Mohammed, D., Omar, M., & Nguyen, V. (2018). Wireless sensor network security: Approaches to detecting and avoiding wormhole attacks. *Journal of Research in Business. Economics and Management*, *10*(2), 1860–1864.

Motlagh, F. N., Hajizadeh, M., Majd, M., Najafi, P., Cheng, F., & Meinel, C. (2024). Large language models in cybersecurity: State-of-the-art. *arXiv preprint arXiv:2402.00891*.

Nguyen, V., Mohammed, D., Omar, M., & Banisakher, M. (2018). The Effects of the FCC Net Neutrality Repeal on Security and Privacy. [IJHIoT]. *International Journal of Hyperconnectivity and the Internet of Things*, *2*(2), 21–29. DOI: 10.4018/IJHIoT.2018070102

Omar, M. (2021). New insights into database security: An effective and integrated approach for applying access control mechanisms and cryptographic concepts in Microsoft Access environments.

Omar, M. (2022). *Machine Learning for Cybersecurity: Innovative Deep Learning Solutions*. Springer Brief. https://link.springer.com/book/978303115

Omar, M. (2024). From Attack to Defense: Strengthening DNN Text Classification Against Adversarial Examples. In *Innovations, Securities, and Case Studies Across Healthcare, Business, and Technology* (pp. 174-195). IGI Global.

Omar, M. (2024). Revolutionizing Malware Detection: A Paradigm Shift Through Optimized Convolutional Neural Networks. In *Innovations, Securities, and Case Studies Across Healthcare, Business, and Technology* (pp. 196-220). IGI Global. DOI: 10.4018/979-8-3693-1906-2.ch011

Omar, M., & Zangana, H. (Eds.). (2025). *Digital Forensics in the Age of AI*. IGI Global., DOI: 10.4018/979-8-3373-0857-9

Omar, M., & Zangana, H. M. (Eds.). (2024). *Redefining Security With Cyber AI*. IGI Global., DOI: 10.4018/979-8-3693-6517-5

Omar, M., & Zangana, H. M. (Eds.). (2025). *Application of Large Language Models (LLMs) for Software Vulnerability Detection*. IGI Global., DOI: 10.4018/979-8-3693-9311-6

Omar, M., Zangana, H. M., Al-Karaki, J. N., & Mohammed, D. (2024). Harnessing LLMs for IoT malware detection: A comparative analysis of BERT and GPT-2. In *2024 8th International Symposium on Multidisciplinary Studies and Innovative Technologies (ISMSIT)* (pp. 1-6). Ankara, Turkiye. https://doi.org/DOI: 10.1109/ISMSIT63511.2024.10757249

Omar, M., Zangana, H. M., & Mohammed, D. (Eds.). (2025). *Integrating Artificial Intelligence in Cybersecurity and Forensic Practices*. IGI Global., DOI: 10.4018/979-8-3373-0588-2

Ozkan-Okay, M., Akin, E., Aslan, Ö., Kosunalp, S., Iliev, T., Stoyanov, I., & Beloev, I. (2024). A comprehensive survey: Evaluating the efficiency of artificial intelligence and machine learning techniques on cyber security solutions. *IEEE Access : Practical Innovations, Open Solutions*, *12*, 12229–12256. DOI: 10.1109/ACCESS.2024.3355547

Pleshakova, E., Osipov, A., Gataullin, S., Gataullin, T., & Vasilakos, A. (2024). Next gen cybersecurity paradigm towards artificial general intelligence: Russian market challenges and future global technological trends. *Journal of Computer Virology and Hacking Techniques*, *20*(3), 429–440. DOI: 10.1007/s11416-024-00529-x

Santos, O., Salam, S., & Dahir, H. (2024). The AI revolution in networking, cybersecurity, and emerging technologies.

Sarker, I. H. (2024). Generative AI and large language modeling in cybersecurity. In *AI-Driven Cybersecurity and Threat Intelligence: Cyber Automation, Intelligent Decision-Making and Explainability* (pp. 79–99). Springer Nature Switzerland. DOI: 10.1007/978-3-031-54497-2_5

Taghavi, S. M., & Feyzi, F. (2024). Using large language models to better detect and handle software vulnerabilities and cyber security threats.

Wright, J., Dawson, M. E.Jr, & Omar, M. (2012). Cyber security and mobile threats: The need for antivirus applications for smartphones. *Journal of Information Systems Technology and Planning*, *5*(14), 40–60.

Xu, H., Wang, S., Li, N., Wang, K., Zhao, Y., Chen, K., . . . Wang, H. (2024). Large language models for cyber security: A systematic literature review. *arXiv preprint arXiv:2405.04760.*

Yu, J., Shvetsov, A. V., & Alsamhi, S. H. (2024). Leveraging machine learning for cybersecurity resilience in industry 4.0: Challenges and future directions. *IEEE Access : Practical Innovations, Open Solutions*, *12*, 159579–159596. DOI: 10.1109/ACCESS.2024.3482987

Zangana, H., & Omar, M. (Eds.). (2025). *Leveraging Large Language Models for Quantum-Aware Cybersecurity*. IGI Global., DOI: 10.4018/979-8-3373-1102-9

Zangana, H. M. (2024). Harnessing the Power of Large Language Models. *Application of Large Language Models (LLMs) for Software Vulnerability Detection*, 1.

Zangana, H. M. (2024). Exploring Blockchain-Based Timestamping Tools: A Comprehensive Review. *Redefining Security With Cyber AI*, 92-110.

Zangana, H. M. (2024). Exploring the Landscape of Website Vulnerability Scanners: A Comprehensive Review and Comparative Analysis. *Redefining Security With Cyber AI*, 111-129.

Zangana, H. M., & Li, S. (2025). Future Trends in AI and Digital Forensics. In Omar, M., & Zangana, H. (Eds.), *Digital Forensics in the Age of AI* (pp. 347–380). IGI Global Scientific Publishing., DOI: 10.4018/979-8-3373-0857-9.ch013

Zangana, H. M., Mohammed, A. K., Sallow, A. B., & Sallow, Z. B. (2024). Cybernetic Deception: Unraveling the Layers of Email Phishing Threats. [INJURATECH]. *International Journal of Research and Applied Technology*, *4*(1), 35–47.

Zangana, H. M., & Mohammed, D. (2025). Foundations of Large Language Models in Software Vulnerability Detection. In Omar, M., & Zangana, H. (Eds.), *Application of Large Language Models (LLMs) for Software Vulnerability Detection* (pp. 41–74). IGI Global., DOI: 10.4018/979-8-3693-9311-6.ch002

Zangana, H. M., & Mustafa, F. M. (2024). Hybrid Image Denoising Using Wavelet Transform and Deep Learning. *EAI Endorsed Transactions on AI and Robotics, 3*. Advance online publication. DOI: 10.4108/airo.7486

Zangana, H. M., & Mustafa, F. M. (2025). Image Denoising Techniques for Cybersecurity and Forensic Applications: AI-Driven Approaches. In Omar, M., Zangana, H., & Mohammed, D. (Eds.), *Integrating Artificial Intelligence in Cybersecurity and Forensic Practices* (pp. 117–142). IGI Global Scientific Publishing., DOI: 10.4018/979-8-3373-0588-2.ch005

Zangana, H. M., Mustafa, F. M., & Li, S. (2025). Large Language Models in Cybersecurity: From Automation to Intelligence. In *Leveraging Large Language Models for Quantum-Aware Cybersecurity* (pp. 277-300). IGI Global Scientific Publishing.

Zangana, H. M., Mustafa, F. M., & Li, S. (2025). Large Language Models in Cybersecurity: From Automation to Intelligence. In Zangana, H., & Omar, M. (Eds.), *Leveraging Large Language Models for Quantum-Aware Cybersecurity* (pp. 277–300). IGI Global Scientific Publishing., DOI: 10.4018/979-8-3373-1102-9.ch009

Zangana, H. M., Mustafa, F. M., Li, S., & Al-Karaki, J. N. (2025). Natural Language Processing for Cyber Threat Intelligence in a Quantum World. In Zangana, H., & Omar, M. (Eds.), *Leveraging Large Language Models for Quantum-Aware Cybersecurity* (pp. 345–388). IGI Global Scientific Publishing., DOI: 10.4018/979-8-3373-1102-9.ch011

Zangana, H. M., Mustafa, F. M., & Omar, M. (2024). A Hybrid Approach for Robust Object Detection: Integrating Template Matching and Faster R-CNN. *EAI Endorsed Transactions on AI and Robotics*, *3*. Advance online publication. DOI: 10.4108/airo.6858

Zangana, H. M., & Omar, M. (2020). Threats, Attacks, and Mitigations of Smartphone Security. *Academic Journal of Nawroz University*, *9*(4), 324–332. DOI: 10.25007/ajnu.v9n4a989

Zangana, H. M., & Omar, M. (2025). Harnessing the Power of Large Language Models for Cybersecurity: Applications, Challenges, and Future Directions. In Omar, M., & Zangana, H. (Eds.), *Application of Large Language Models (LLMs) for Software Vulnerability Detection* (pp. 1–40). IGI Global., DOI: 10.4018/979-8-3693-9311-6.ch001

Zangana, H. M., & Omar, M. (2025). Introduction to Quantum-Aware Cybersecurity: The Need for LLMs. In Zangana, H., & Omar, M. (Eds.), *Leveraging Large Language Models for Quantum-Aware Cybersecurity* (pp. 1–28). IGI Global Scientific Publishing., DOI: 10.4018/979-8-3373-1102-9.ch001

Zangana, H. M., & Omar, M. (2025). Introduction to Digital Forensics and Artificial Intelligence. In Omar, M., & Zangana, H. (Eds.), *Digital Forensics in the Age of AI* (pp. 1–30). IGI Global Scientific Publishing., DOI: 10.4018/979-8-3373-0857-9.ch001

Zangana, H. M., & Omar, M. (2025). The Role of Leadership in Advancing Inclusive Health Technologies. In Burrell, D., & Nguyen, C. (Eds.), *New Horizons in Leadership: Inclusive Explorations in Health, Technology, and Education* (pp. 203–220). IGI Global Scientific Publishing., DOI: 10.4018/979-8-3693-6437-6.ch009

Zangana, H. M., Omar, M., Al-Karaki, J. N., & Mohammed, D. (2024). Comprehensive Review and Analysis of Network Firewall Rule Analyzers: Enhancing Security Posture and Efficiency. *Redefining Security With Cyber AI*, 15-36.

Zangana, H. M., Sallow, Z. B., & Omar, M. (2025). The Human Factor in Cybersecurity: Addressing the Risks of Insider Threats. *Jurnal Ilmiah Computer Science*, *3*(2), 76–85. DOI: 10.58602/jics.v3i2.37

Chapter 2
AI-Powered Contract Security:
Managing Expiry, Compliance, and Risk Mitigation Through Deep Learning and LLMs

Dilshad Ahmad Mhia-Alddin
https://orcid.org/0009-0005-4046-1607
University of Mosul, Iraq

Akram Mahmoud Hussein
University of Mosul, Iraq

ABSTRACT

The rapid advancement of artificial intelligence (AI) has transformed contract security, offering innovative solutions for managing contract expiry, ensuring compliance, and mitigating risks. Traditional contract management systems often struggle with scalability, accuracy, and adaptability, leading to inefficiencies and potential legal vulnerabilities. This chapter explores how deep learning and large language models (LLMs) enhance contract security by automating contract review, expiration tracking, and regulatory compliance assessment. By leveraging natural language processing (NLP) and predictive analytics, AI-driven solutions can proactively identify risks, flag anomalies, and ensure adherence to contractual obligations. Furthermore, this chapter discusses key challenges such as bias in AI models, data privacy concerns, and the need for robust regulatory frameworks. Through case studies and experimental results, we demonstrate how AI-powered contract security improves efficiency, reduces human errors, and enhances organizational risk management.

DOI: 10.4018/979-8-3373-3296-3.ch002

1. INTRODUCTION

Contract security has long been a critical aspect of risk management in business and legal domains. Ensuring compliance, managing expiry, and mitigating risks are fundamental to maintaining robust contractual obligations. Traditionally, contract management relied heavily on manual oversight, legal expertise, and structured rule-based systems, which often resulted in inefficiencies, human errors, and compliance gaps (Ajmal et al., 2025; Albalate, Bel, & Reeves, 2021). However, recent advancements in artificial intelligence (AI), particularly deep learning and large language models (LLMs), have transformed contract security by automating and enhancing the monitoring, analysis, and execution of contractual obligations (Koshevaya, 2024).

AI-driven contract management systems integrate natural language processing (NLP), predictive analytics, and deep learning models to automate key aspects such as contract expiration tracking, risk detection, and regulatory compliance verification (de la Roche et al., 2024; Okegbola & Akiotu, 2024). These systems improve efficiency, reduce costs, and ensure a proactive approach to risk mitigation by analyzing large volumes of contractual data in real time (Sabharwal, Chhabra, & Aiden, 2024). Additionally, AI-powered contract analysis tools can identify hidden risks, detect inconsistencies, and provide recommendations for contract optimization, ultimately improving decision-making processes (Arya, 2024).

The application of AI in contract security is particularly relevant in highly regulated industries such as finance, healthcare, and government contracting, where compliance with evolving legal frameworks is essential (Huang et al., 2023). AI-powered tools enhance decision-making in contract lifecycle management by detecting potential fraud, monitoring contract execution, and automating renewal processes (Shan, 2025; Pingili, 2025). Furthermore, the integration of blockchain and AI enhances contract enforcement by providing immutable records and automated smart contract execution, ensuring transparency and security (Rouzel, Venkatesha, & Dreveton, 2024).

Despite these advancements, the deployment of AI in contract security raises several challenges. Issues such as bias in AI models, data privacy concerns, and the need for regulatory alignment must be addressed to ensure ethical and legal compliance (Rahaman et al., 2024; Santos & Radanliev, 2024). Moreover, the effectiveness of AI-driven contract security depends on high-quality data, robust training models, and continuous updates to adapt to changing legal requirements (Bloomfield & Rushby, 2024). Research highlights the importance of trustworthiness and interpretability in AI systems, emphasizing the need for human oversight in AI-powered contract management (Ferdaus et al., 2024).

This chapter explores the transformative impact of deep learning and LLMs on contract security, highlighting their role in managing contract expiry, ensuring compliance, and mitigating risks. The discussion covers AI-driven contract analysis, automation in compliance monitoring, risk prediction, and ethical considerations in deploying AI for legal and business applications. By analyzing real-world case studies and experimental results, this chapter provides insights into how organizations can leverage AI to enhance contract security and minimize risks in an increasingly digitalized world.

2. CYBERSECURITY RISKS IN CONTRACT EXPIRY

The expiration of contracts presents significant cybersecurity risks, particularly in digital environments where sensitive data, intellectual property, and compliance obligations are involved. Organizations must address these risks to prevent data breaches, unauthorized access, and regulatory non-compliance. As contract management increasingly integrates artificial intelligence (AI) and blockchain solutions, new challenges and vulnerabilities emerge, requiring proactive mitigation strategies (Albalate, Bel, & Reeves, 2021; Omar & Zangana, 2025).

2.1 Unauthorized Access and Data Breaches

One of the primary cybersecurity risks associated with contract expiry is unauthorized access to sensitive information. Expired contracts often leave behind residual data, including personally identifiable information (PII) and financial records, which can be exploited by malicious actors. If contract lifecycle management (CLM) systems lack robust access controls, attackers can gain unauthorized access to archived contracts, leading to data leaks (Koshevaya, 2024; Charfeddine, Kammoun, Hamdaoui, & Guizani, 2024). Cybercriminals may exploit vulnerabilities in outdated systems, particularly when security patches and compliance measures are not updated after contract termination (Heim, Starckjohann, & Torgersen, 2023).

2.2 Insider Threats and Contract Expiry Mismanagement

Insider threats pose a considerable risk when contracts expire without appropriate security measures. Employees, contractors, or third-party vendors with lingering access to expired agreements can misuse confidential data for personal or competitive advantage (Sabharwal, Chhabra, & Aiden, 2024). Without automated revocation of access privileges, sensitive documents remain vulnerable to exploitation, especially when firms rely on manual security audits (Kanabar, 2023).

2.3 Compliance Violations and Regulatory Risks

Failure to properly handle contract expiration can result in non-compliance with data protection regulations such as the General Data Protection Regulation (GDPR) and the California Consumer Privacy Act (CCPA). Expired contracts may contain obligations related to data retention and deletion that, if neglected, can lead to legal penalties and reputational damage (Ajmal et al., 2025; Okegbola & Akiotu, 2024). Regulatory frameworks increasingly emphasize data minimization, making automated contract expiry management essential for ensuring compliance (Rahaman, Pappachan, Orozco, Bansal, & Arya, 2024).

2.4 Phishing and Social Engineering Attacks

Expired contracts may be exploited in social engineering attacks, where cybercriminals use contract-related documents to impersonate legitimate business entities and manipulate stakeholders into divulging sensitive information. AI-generated phishing schemes leveraging contract metadata can deceive employees and vendors into granting unauthorized access to critical systems (Bergman Larsson & Talåsen, 2024; Santos & Radanliev, 2024). Large language models (LLMs) have also been weaponized to craft sophisticated phishing emails that mimic authentic contract renewal requests (Ferdaus et al., 2024).

2.5 Smart Contracts and Blockchain Vulnerabilities

While blockchain-based smart contracts offer automated contract execution and expiry, they are not immune to cybersecurity risks. Smart contract vulnerabilities, such as reentrancy attacks and flawed coding logic, can be exploited to manipulate contract terms post-expiry (de la Roche et al., 2024; Rouzel, Venkatesha, & Dreveton, 2024). Additionally, once a smart contract is deployed on a blockchain, it becomes immutable, making it difficult to correct errors or revoke expired agreements without implementing costly security patches (Poole, Devenney, & Shaw-Mellors, 2021).

2.6 Mitigation Strategies for Cybersecurity Risks in Contract Expiry

To address these cybersecurity risks, organizations should adopt proactive measures, including:

1. **Automated Contract Expiry Management:** Deploying AI-driven CLM solutions can ensure that expired contracts are securely archived or deleted in compliance with regulatory requirements (Koshevaya, 2024; Smits, 2021).
2. **Access Control and Privilege Revocation:** Implementing role-based access controls (RBAC) and automatic de-provisioning of credentials upon contract expiry can mitigate unauthorized access risks (Hermalin, Katz, & Craswell, 2007).
3. **Continuous Security Audits:** Regular audits and penetration testing can help identify vulnerabilities in contract storage and access mechanisms (Heim, Starckjohann, & Torgersen, 2023; Omar & Zangana, 2024).
4. **Blockchain Security Enhancements:** Ensuring that smart contracts undergo rigorous security audits before deployment can mitigate blockchain-related cybersecurity risks (de la Roche et al., 2024; Luhaibi & Al Ali, 2024).
5. **Employee Cybersecurity Training:** Educating employees about phishing threats and secure contract management practices can reduce the likelihood of social engineering attacks (Arya, 2024; Sadiq, 2023).

By implementing these strategies, organizations can enhance contract security, mitigate cybersecurity risks associated with contract expiry, and ensure regulatory compliance in an increasingly digital landscape.

The bar chart below shows the relative severity of different cybersecurity risks associated with contract expiry.

Figure 1. Cybersecurity risks associated with contract expiry

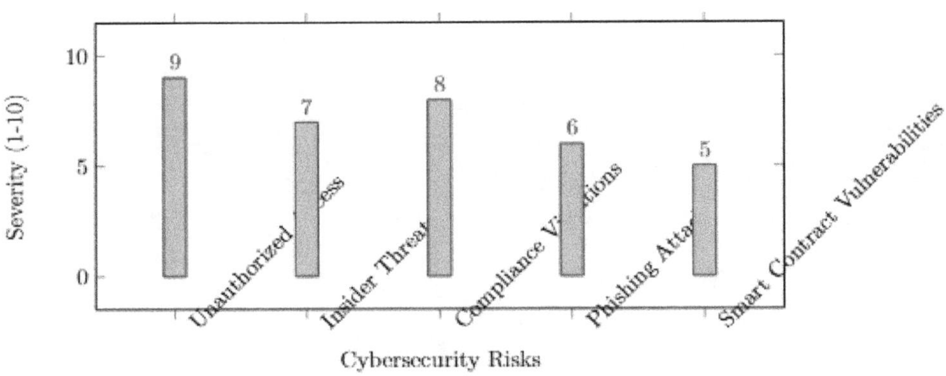

3. AI AND LLMS IN CONTRACT EXPIRY MANAGEMENT

Contract expiry management is a critical component of contract lifecycle management (CLM), requiring organizations to monitor, assess, and act upon expiring agreements to ensure continuity, compliance, and risk mitigation. With the rapid advancement of artificial intelligence (AI) and large language models (LLMs), contract expiry management has evolved significantly, enhancing efficiency, accuracy, and decision-making capabilities (Koshevaya, 2024). This section explores the role of AI and LLMs in contract expiry management, focusing on automation, predictive analytics, compliance adherence, and risk assessment.

3.1 Automation in Contract Expiry Management

AI-driven automation plays a pivotal role in streamlining contract expiry management by reducing manual interventions and human errors (Chotaliya, 2024). Traditional contract management systems often rely on human oversight, leading to inefficiencies and missed deadlines. However, AI-powered solutions can automatically track contract terms, send renewal notifications, and categorize contracts based on their significance and expiration timelines (Ajmal et al., 2025). These automated workflows improve operational efficiency and ensure that organizations do not overlook crucial agreements.

The flowchart below illustrates the automated workflow of AI-driven contract expiry management, showing how AI systems track contract expiration, assess risks, and automate compliance checks.

Figure 2. AI-driven contract expiry management workflow

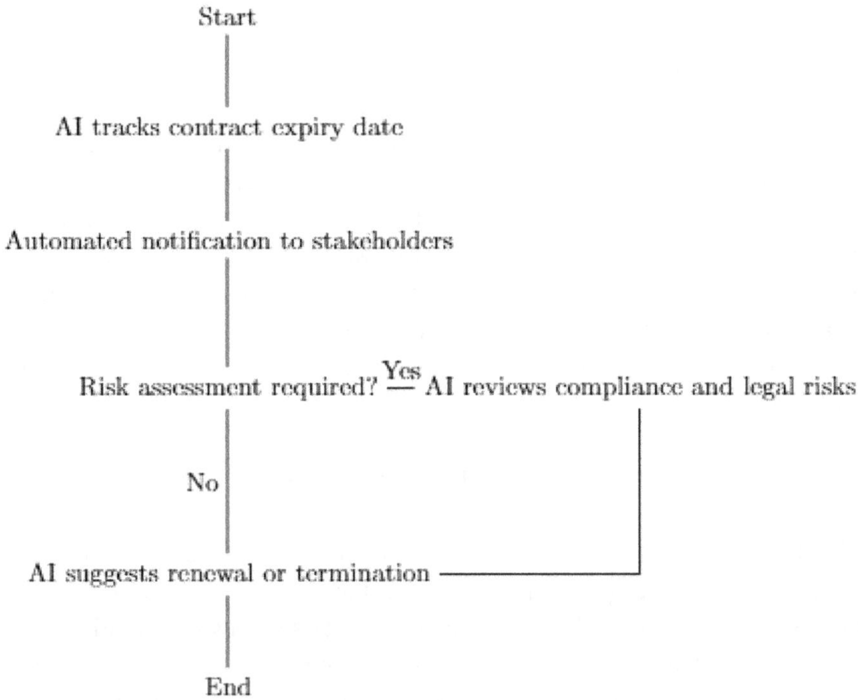

3.2 Predictive Analytics for Expiry Risk Mitigation

One of the most significant advantages of AI and LLMs in contract expiry management is their ability to leverage predictive analytics. Machine learning algorithms analyze historical contract data to identify patterns, assess risk factors, and predict potential disputes or financial implications associated with contract expiration (Al-Ebrahim, Bunian, & Nour, 2023). For instance, AI models can forecast vendor reliability, recommend optimal renewal strategies, and alert organizations about high-risk contracts (Kanabar, 2023).

Moreover, predictive analytics helps organizations in financial forecasting by analyzing contract performance trends and providing insights into potential revenue impacts due to contract expirations (Pingili, 2025). This ensures proactive decision-making, preventing financial disruptions or operational setbacks.

3.3 Compliance Adherence and Regulatory Considerations

Regulatory compliance is a critical concern in contract expiry management, especially in industries with stringent legal frameworks. AI-driven solutions enhance compliance by cross-referencing contract clauses with updated regulations and flagging non-compliant terms (Omar & Zangana, 2025). Large language models can process and interpret complex legal documents, ensuring that contract renewals align with evolving regulatory requirements (Okegbola & Akiotu, 2024).

For example, AI-powered CLM platforms can automatically adapt to changes in international trade agreements, data protection laws, or industry-specific regulations, reducing legal risks associated with non-compliance (Rai, 2022). Furthermore, AI-driven compliance checks improve transparency and minimize the risk of contractual disputes (Albalate, Bel, & Reeves, 2021).

3.4 Risk Assessment and Fraud Detection

AI and LLMs are instrumental in identifying potential fraud and mitigating risks associated with contract expirations. Natural language processing (NLP) models analyze contract language to detect anomalies, inconsistencies, or potential fraudulent clauses (Ferdaus et al., 2024). These models help legal teams conduct due diligence more efficiently, ensuring that contract terms align with organizational policies and legal standards (Bloomfield & Rushby, 2024).

Furthermore, AI enhances security measures by detecting unauthorized contract modifications or suspicious activities related to contract expirations (Heim, Starckjohann, & Torgersen, 2023). Blockchain-integrated AI solutions further bolster security by maintaining immutable records of contract amendments, ensuring authenticity and reducing the risk of contractual fraud (de la Roche et al., 2024).

The flowchart below illustrates how AI identifies and mitigates risks in contract security, ensuring compliance and fraud detection.

Figure 3. AI-driven risk mitigation in contract security

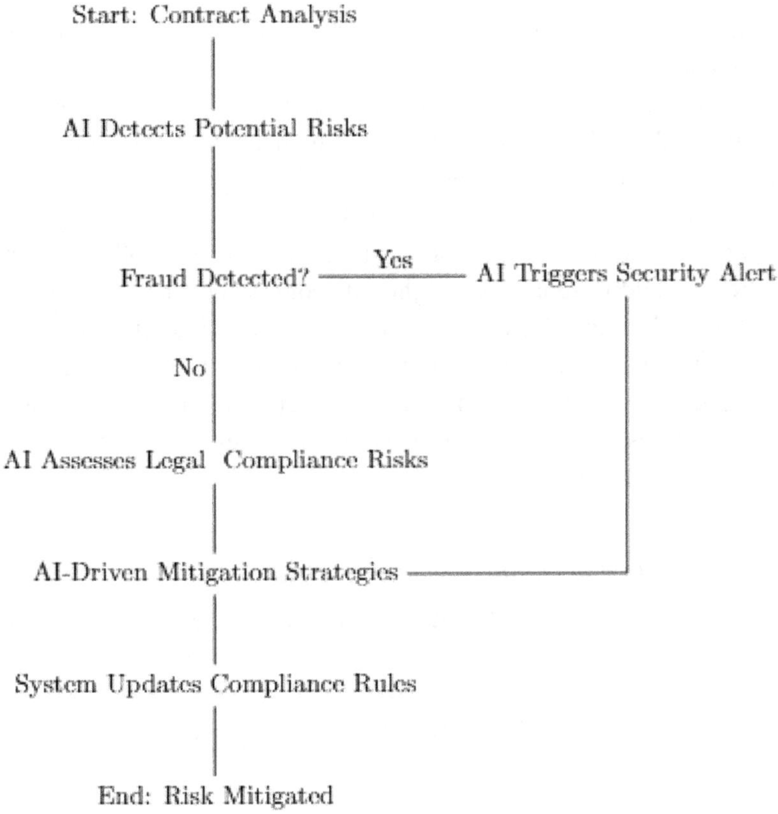

3.5 LLM-Powered Contract Review and Negotiation

Large language models have revolutionized contract review and negotiation processes by providing instant clause recommendations, summarizing contract terms, and offering legal insights (Bergman Larsson & Talåsen, 2024). LLMs can analyze vast repositories of legal documents, extracting critical information and providing contract managers with actionable insights (Schurer, 2024).

For example, AI-driven contract assistants help legal professionals draft renewal agreements with optimized terms, reducing the time spent on manual reviews and negotiations (Srivastawa, 2023). Additionally, AI-powered chatbots facilitate contract discussions by answering queries related to contract clauses, expiration terms, and potential risks (Sabharwal, Chhabra, & Aiden, 2024).

3.6 Integration of AI in Contract Lifecycle Management Systems

The integration of AI and LLMs into contract lifecycle management (CLM) platforms enhances contract expiry management by providing intelligent dashboards, automated alerts, and data-driven recommendations (Santos & Radanliev, 2024). AI-powered CLM systems improve document retrieval, version tracking, and contract auditing, ensuring that organizations maintain complete control over their contractual obligations (Rahaman et al., 2024).

Moreover, AI-driven CLM platforms facilitate seamless collaboration among stakeholders by providing real-time insights into contract performance and expiration timelines (Rouzel, Venkatesha, & Dreveton, 2024). Organizations leveraging AI for contract expiry management gain a competitive advantage by minimizing legal risks, reducing administrative burdens, and optimizing contract renewals (Sadiq, 2023).

The flowchart below outlines how AI is integrated into different phases of contract lifecycle management.

Figure 4. AI integration in contract lifecycle management

3.7 Summary

AI and LLMs have transformed contract expiry management by automating processes, enhancing compliance, and improving risk assessment. By leveraging predictive analytics, AI-driven automation, and advanced NLP models, organizations can proactively manage contract expirations, reduce legal uncertainties, and optimize contractual outcomes (Miller et al., 2025). As AI technologies continue to evolve, their integration into contract management will become increasingly sophisticated, driving efficiency and innovation across industries (Tabatabaei & Asadi, 2016).

The adoption of AI-driven contract expiry management solutions ensures that businesses remain compliant, secure, and well-prepared for contract renewals and terminations (Shan, 2025). Future research should explore the potential of AI in enhancing contract negotiations and dispute resolution, paving the way for a more intelligent and transparent legal ecosystem (Luhaibi & Al Ali, 2024).

4. SMART CONTRACTS AND BLOCKCHAIN SECURITY

Blockchain technology has revolutionized digital transactions by offering decentralized and immutable ledgers. Smart contracts, self-executing agreements with the terms directly written into code, are a crucial innovation in blockchain systems. They automate transactions, reduce the need for intermediaries, and enhance efficiency. However, security remains a significant challenge, as vulnerabilities in smart contracts can lead to financial losses and system breaches (Sabharwal et al., 2024).

4.1 Mechanisms of Smart Contracts

Smart contracts operate on blockchain networks such as Ethereum, Hyperledger, and Binance Smart Chain. These contracts execute predefined rules automatically when conditions are met. By leveraging cryptographic techniques and decentralized consensus, smart contracts eliminate the risks associated with traditional contractual agreements (Rouzel et al., 2024). The increasing adoption of AI-driven contract lifecycle management further enhances efficiency and compliance (Koshevaya, 2024).

The diagram below visually represents how blockchain-based smart contracts execute transactions securely and transparently.

Figure 5. Blockchain-based smart contract execution process

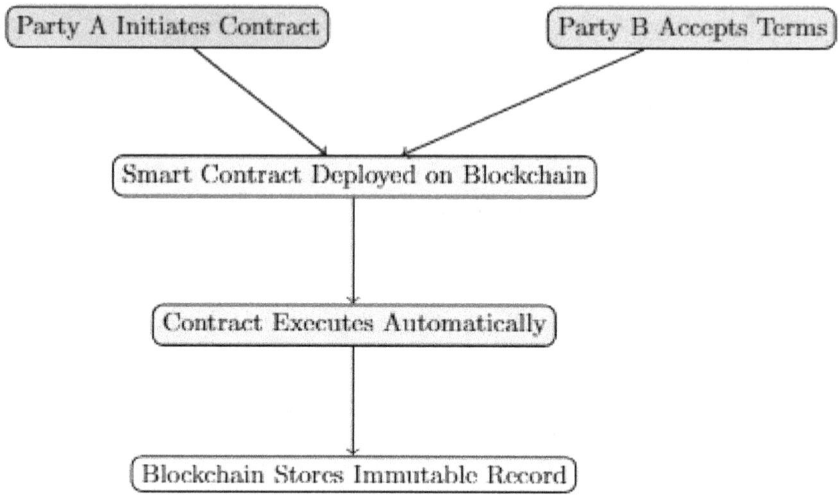

4.2 Security Vulnerabilities in Smart Contracts

Despite their benefits, smart contracts are prone to various security risks. Common vulnerabilities include reentrancy attacks, integer overflows/underflows, and unauthorized access. The DAO hack in 2016 demonstrated how a single vulnerability could lead to significant financial losses (Rahaman et al., 2024).

AI-driven approaches are now being integrated into smart contract security to mitigate these vulnerabilities. Machine learning algorithms help detect anomalies in contract execution, improving fraud detection (Shan, 2025). Additionally, AI-powered tools are being developed to automate security audits and ensure code integrity (Pingili, 2025).

The pie chart below represents the distribution of different security vulnerabilities in smart contracts.

Figure 6. Distribution of smart contract security vulnerabilities

compat−1.18

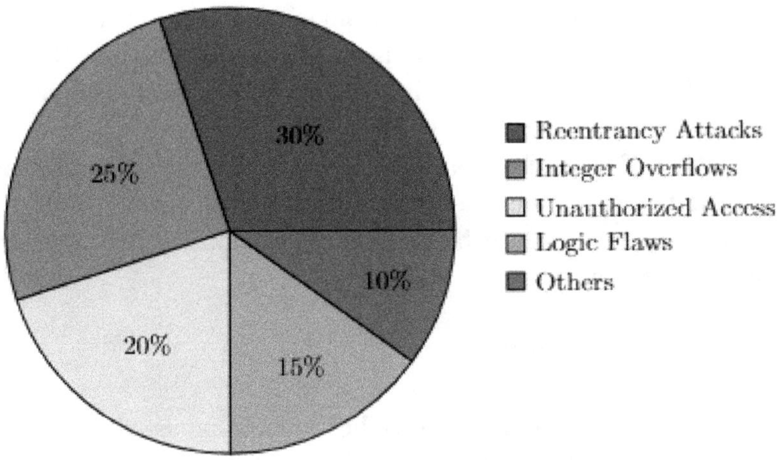

4.3 Regulatory and Legal Challenges

The legal landscape surrounding smart contracts is evolving. Unlike traditional contracts governed by legal frameworks, smart contracts exist in a decentralized ecosystem with ambiguous regulatory oversight. Issues such as contract expiration, liability, and enforceability remain critical concerns (Albalate, Bel, & Reeves, 2021; Sears, 2022). Studies highlight the need for robust legal frameworks to address disputes arising from smart contracts (Smits, 2021).

Efforts to standardize smart contract regulations are underway. For instance, AI-driven legal compliance tools are emerging to ensure adherence to international regulatory standards (Ajmal et al., 2025). Furthermore, blockchain's convergence with AI is helping refine automated contract negotiation and risk assessment (Schurer, 2024).

4.4 Enhancing Smart Contract Security

To address security concerns, various strategies have been proposed:

- **Formal Verification**: Mathematical techniques are used to validate smart contract logic before deployment, ensuring correctness and security (Bloomfield & Rushby, 2024).

- **Auditing and Testing**: Blockchain security firms conduct extensive audits to identify potential vulnerabilities. Automated penetration testing with AI is also becoming common (Heim, Starckjohann, & Torgersen, 2023).
- **AI-Driven Security Measures**: AI models enhance security by predicting threats and autonomously responding to suspicious activities (Ferdaus et al., 2024). AI's role in contract law is evolving, facilitating proactive threat mitigation (Hermalin, Katz, & Craswell, 2007).
- **Integration of Blockchain and AI**: The convergence of blockchain and AI is leading to smarter, more adaptive security mechanisms. AI-enabled fraud detection systems analyze blockchain transactions in real-time, improving anomaly detection (Santos & Radanliev, 2024).

4.5 Future Perspectives

The future of smart contract security lies in continuous advancements in AI, blockchain analytics, and regulatory compliance. AI-powered security frameworks will likely become a standard component of blockchain ecosystems (Luhaibi & Al Ali, 2024). Moreover, the use of large language models (LLMs) in legal compliance will enhance smart contract enforceability and adaptation to jurisdictional requirements (Omar & Zangana, 2025).

Emerging research focuses on AI's role in predictive security for blockchain networks, ensuring proactive threat mitigation. This includes the application of AI in supply chain management, healthcare, and financial contracts (Bergman Larsson & Talåsen, 2024; de la Roche et al., 2024).

4.6 Summary

Smart contracts represent a paradigm shift in digital transactions, offering automation, security, and efficiency. However, security vulnerabilities remain a critical challenge. AI-driven solutions and evolving legal frameworks are crucial for enhancing smart contract resilience. As blockchain and AI continue to converge, the future holds promising advancements in secure, autonomous, and legally compliant smart contracts.

5. REGULATORY AND ETHICAL CONSIDERATIONS

The increasing integration of artificial intelligence (AI) and blockchain technologies into various domains presents significant regulatory and ethical challenges. As these technologies become more sophisticated and pervasive, policymakers and organizations must navigate a complex landscape of compliance, governance, and ethical responsibilities (Okegbola & Akiotu, 2024; Rai, 2022). This section explores key regulatory frameworks, ethical implications, and emerging legal considerations surrounding AI-driven cybersecurity, blockchain applications, and large language models (LLMs).

5.1 Regulatory Frameworks and Compliance Challenges

Regulatory compliance remains a fundamental challenge in AI and blockchain adoption. Governments and international organizations have developed diverse regulations to ensure data protection, privacy, and cybersecurity (Ajmal et al., 2025). For instance, the General Data Protection Regulation (GDPR) and the California Consumer Privacy Act (CCPA) impose stringent guidelines on data processing and storage. In contrast, regulations such as the European Union's Artificial Intelligence Act aim to categorize AI systems based on risk levels, mandating transparency and accountability in their deployment (Sabharwal, Chhabra, & Aiden, 2024).

Blockchain technology introduces unique regulatory hurdles, particularly regarding smart contracts and decentralized finance (de la Roche et al., 2024). The self-executing nature of smart contracts complicates legal enforcement, requiring adaptations to existing contract laws (Hermalin, Katz, & Craswell, 2007; Poole, Devenney, & Shaw-Mellors, 2021). Moreover, financial regulators face challenges in overseeing cryptocurrency transactions, necessitating innovations in legal oversight (Shan, 2025).

5.2 Ethical Implications of AI and Blockchain

AI ethics remains a critical concern, particularly in the deployment of LLMs and automated decision-making systems. Issues such as bias, accountability, and transparency necessitate ethical AI governance frameworks (Ferdaus et al., 2024). The reliance on AI for legal contracts, healthcare, and financial decisions demands rigorous ethical considerations to prevent discriminatory outcomes (Rahaman et al., 2024).

Additionally, blockchain's promise of decentralization raises ethical questions regarding anonymity and responsibility (Rouzel, Venkatesha, & Dreveton, 2024). While blockchain ensures tamper-resistant record-keeping, it also facilitates illicit activities, necessitating a balanced approach between privacy rights and regulatory oversight (Albalate, Bel, & Reeves, 2021).

The Venn diagram below highlights the overlap between AI ethics, contract security, and regulatory compliance.

Figure 7. Ethical considerations in AI-powered contract security

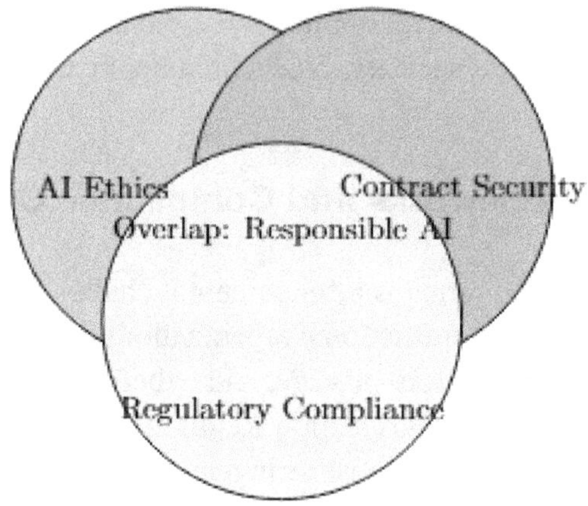

5.3 Legal Considerations in AI-Powered Contract Management

The legal landscape surrounding AI-driven contract management continues to evolve. AI systems are increasingly used in contract analysis, negotiation, and enforcement, raising concerns about liability and enforceability (Koshevaya, 2024; Srivastawa, 2023). The interpretation of implied contracts and liability issues when AI-driven systems execute agreements requires legal refinement (Sears, 2022; Smits, 2021).

Contract expiration and termination also present legal complexities, particularly in financial leasing and employment contracts (Helalat, n.d.; Luhaibi & Al Ali, 2024; Macijauskiene, 2006). Recent studies emphasize the importance of updating contract laws to reflect AI and automation-driven contract management trends (Arakcheev, n.d.; Schurer, 2024).

5.4 AI Governance and Policy Recommendations

Ensuring responsible AI deployment requires robust governance structures. Governments and organizations must collaborate to develop policies addressing algorithmic accountability, security risks, and ethical AI development (Arya, 2024; Santos & Radanliev, 2024). Recent research highlights the role of interdisciplinary regulatory bodies in harmonizing AI ethics with technological advancements (Miller et al., 2025).

Furthermore, AI and blockchain convergence necessitate adaptive legal frameworks to accommodate emerging use cases in finance, cybersecurity, and supply chain management (Charfeddine et al., 2024; Huang et al., 2023). By integrating AI ethics into regulatory frameworks, policymakers can mitigate risks associated with automated decision-making while fostering innovation (Kanabar, 2023).

5.5 Summary

Regulatory and ethical considerations play a pivotal role in the responsible deployment of AI and blockchain technologies. Addressing compliance challenges, ensuring ethical AI governance, and refining legal frameworks are essential steps toward sustainable innovation. As these technologies continue to evolve, interdisciplinary collaboration among policymakers, legal experts, and technologists will be crucial in shaping a secure and ethical digital future (Omar & Zangana, 2025a; Omar, Zangana, & Mohammed, 2025).

6. CASE STUDIES AND REAL-WORLD APPLICATIONS

The integration of artificial intelligence (AI) and large language models (LLMs) in real-world applications has significantly impacted various domains, from cybersecurity and finance to contract management and regulatory compliance. This section presents several case studies that illustrate the effectiveness, challenges, and future directions of AI-driven solutions across different industries.

6.1. AI in Cybersecurity and Digital Forensics

The role of AI in cybersecurity and forensic practices has grown exponentially, with LLMs being leveraged for threat detection, vulnerability analysis, and automated incident response. Omar and Zangana (2025) highlight how AI-powered digital forensics tools enhance investigative capabilities, allowing real-time anomaly detection and threat mitigation. Similarly, Heim, Starckjohann, and Torgersen (2023) explore how ChatGPT has been integrated into penetration testing, showcasing its potential in identifying security vulnerabilities and ethical challenges.

Additionally, Rahaman et al. (2024) emphasize the importance of AI safety in cybersecurity applications, discussing how organizations must address bias and robustness to avoid adversarial attacks. These insights underscore the need for continuous advancements in AI-driven security systems.

6.2. AI and Blockchain for Regulatory Compliance

The convergence of AI and blockchain technologies has introduced new paradigms in regulatory compliance and secure data management. De la Roche et al. (2024) provide an in-depth analysis of how AI-powered blockchain solutions enhance transparency, trust, and efficiency in regulatory reporting. Similarly, Sabharwal, Chhabra, and Aiden (2024) discuss the role of AI in secure data analytics, particularly within the realm of cybersecurity, demonstrating how blockchain and LLMs can work in tandem to mitigate risks.

Okegbola and Akiotu (2024) explore AI-driven regulatory compliance solutions, showing how AI can streamline complex legal and contractual obligations while maintaining adherence to global regulations. These applications demonstrate the potential of AI in automating compliance processes, reducing human error, and enhancing operational efficiency.

The network diagram below showcases how AI and blockchain technologies integrate to enhance contract security, compliance, and risk mitigation.

Figure 8. AI and blockchain convergence in contract security

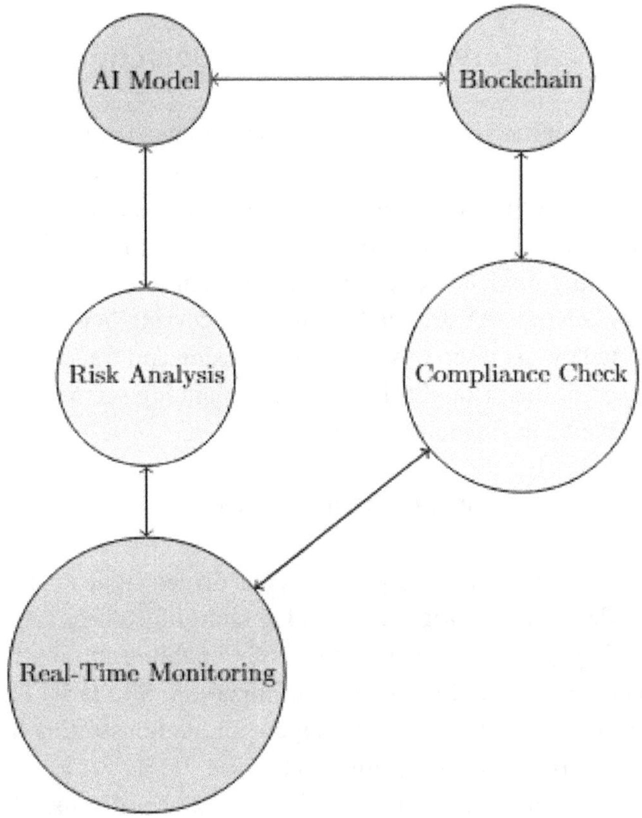

6.3. AI in Contract Lifecycle Management and Legal Applications

The automation of contract management through AI and LLMs has transformed traditional legal workflows. Koshevaya (2024) discusses the integration of AI models into contract lifecycle management, enabling organizations to streamline contract analysis, negotiation, and renewal processes. Similarly, Arakcheev (2024) examines the use of AI-powered legal tools in contract drafting and dispute resolution, demonstrating how AI can reduce manual workload and enhance decision-making.

From a broader legal perspective, Poole, Devenney, and Shaw-Mellors (2021) provide insights into how contract law has evolved with AI adoption. The automation of contract review processes using AI reduces delays and enhances accuracy, making legal operations more efficient. Furthermore, Rai (2022) explores the legal liability issues associated with AI-driven contract management, emphasizing the need for robust governance frameworks.

6.4. AI in Financial Services and Fraud Detection

The financial sector has seen significant advancements with the integration of AI in banking and fraud detection. Huang et al. (2023) discuss how ChatGPT is transforming financial operations, from customer service automation to risk assessment. Similarly, Shan (2025) highlights AI-powered fraud detection systems, showcasing how machine learning models identify fraudulent transactions in real-time.

Pingili (2025) explores AI-driven document processing in healthcare and insurance, emphasizing how AI improves claims processing and fraud prevention. These applications illustrate the critical role of AI in enhancing security, efficiency, and regulatory compliance in financial institutions.

6.5. AI in Business Process Automation

The adoption of AI in business operations has driven significant improvements in efficiency and decision-making. Bergman Larsson and Talåsen (2024) investigate how LLMs are being applied to business processes, enabling automation in customer interactions, data analysis, and workflow optimization. Similarly, Kanabar (2023) highlights the impact of AI in project management, demonstrating how generative AI enhances productivity and risk mitigation.

Furthermore, Al-Ebrahim, Bunian, and Nour (2023) discuss the role of AI-driven solutions in e-commerce, particularly in personalized recommendations and demand forecasting. These case studies underscore the transformative potential of AI in optimizing business operations across various sectors.

6.6. Ethical and Legal Considerations in AI Applications

While AI adoption presents numerous benefits, it also raises ethical and legal challenges. Bloomfield and Rushby (2024) provide an assurance framework for AI systems, ensuring their dependability and trustworthiness. Ferdaus et al. (2024) further explore the ethical implications of AI-driven decision-making, emphasizing the importance of fairness and transparency.

Additionally, Santos and Radanliev (2024) discuss the intersection of AI, security, privacy, and ethics, highlighting the need for regulatory frameworks to govern AI applications. As AI systems become increasingly integrated into critical infrastructure, addressing these ethical concerns is paramount.

6.7 Summary

The case studies presented in this section highlight the diverse applications of AI across multiple industries, from cybersecurity and finance to legal contract management and business process automation. While AI offers substantial benefits in terms of efficiency, security, and compliance, addressing its ethical, legal, and regulatory challenges remains a key priority. The continued evolution of AI-driven technologies, particularly with LLMs, will shape the future of automation and intelligent decision-making in the years to come.

7. FUTURE TRENDS AND CHALLENGES

The integration of Large Language Models (LLMs) and AI-driven automation into regulatory frameworks, cybersecurity, and contract management is expected to reshape industries. However, significant challenges remain in ensuring their safe, ethical, and effective use. This section explores emerging trends and key challenges, citing recent studies and expert insights.

7.1. AI-Driven Compliance and Regulatory Adaptation

AI is rapidly transforming compliance processes, enhancing efficiency in decision-making and regulatory affairs (Ajmal et al., 2025; Okegbola & Akiotu, 2024). The convergence of AI and blockchain is also being explored to improve transparency in compliance management (de la Roche et al., 2024). However, legal and ethical questions arise regarding accountability in AI-driven decisions, as regulatory frameworks struggle to keep pace with innovation (Rai, 2022).

7.2. AI in Contract Lifecycle Management

AI-based contract management tools are expected to automate contract drafting, risk assessment, and negotiations (Koshevaya, 2024). LLMs can analyze historical data to predict contract outcomes and enhance legal decision-making (Schurer, 2024). However, the risks of bias, misinterpretation, and security vulnerabilities in AI-generated contracts remain major concerns (Hermalin et al., 2007; Poole et al., 2021).

7.3. Cybersecurity Risks and AI in Defense Strategies

As AI adoption in cybersecurity increases, adversarial AI techniques and AI-powered cyber threats are also evolving (Omar & Zangana, 2024). Researchers highlight ChatGPT's dual role in cybersecurity—both as a penetration testing tool and as a potential threat vector (Charfeddine et al., 2024; Heim et al., 2023). Future developments will need to address these security gaps through robust AI governance and adversarial training methods (Bloomfield & Rushby, 2024).

7.4. AI and Decision-Making in Financial and Business Processes

LLMs are increasingly used in finance and banking, aiding in fraud detection and market analysis (Huang et al., 2023; Shan, 2025). AI-powered automation is also transforming business operations and project management (Bergman Larsson & Talåsen, 2024; Kanabar, 2023). However, ensuring the fairness and interpretability of AI-driven financial models remains an ongoing challenge (Sabharwal et al., 2024).

7.5. Ethical and Legal Considerations in AI Deployment

AI ethics and safety concerns are central to future research, particularly regarding AI biases, data privacy, and user safety (Ferdaus et al., 2024; Arya, 2024). Emerging trends focus on trustworthy AI frameworks that emphasize transparency, explainability, and human oversight (Miller et al., 2025; Santos & Radanliev, 2024). The legal implications of contract expiration, digital ownership, and liability are also evolving with AI integration (Helalat, 2024; Albalate et al., 2021).

7.6 Summary

While AI and LLMs continue to revolutionize multiple industries, their adoption presents new regulatory, security, and ethical challenges. Future research should focus on standardizing AI regulations, enhancing cybersecurity frameworks, and ensuring AI-driven systems remain ethical and unbiased. The interplay of law, AI governance, and technological advancements will shape the next era of AI-driven innovation (Omar & Zangana, 2025).

8. CONCLUSION

The rapid advancement of artificial intelligence, particularly in large language models and automated decision-making, is reshaping industries ranging from cybersecurity to regulatory compliance. AI-driven innovations are enhancing efficiency, automating complex processes, and transforming contract management, finance, and business operations. However, these advancements also bring significant challenges related to security risks, ethical concerns, and regulatory uncertainties. Striking a balance between innovation and risk mitigation is crucial for the sustainable integration of AI into critical domains.

As AI continues to evolve, its role in governance, compliance, and security will become increasingly complex. Organizations and policymakers must work collaboratively to establish robust frameworks that ensure transparency, accountability, and fairness in AI applications. Future research should focus on developing more explainable AI systems, strengthening cybersecurity defenses, and refining legal frameworks to address the evolving landscape of AI-driven decision-making.

Ultimately, the responsible deployment of AI requires a multidimensional approach that combines technological advancements with ethical considerations and regulatory oversight. The interplay between AI, law, and security will shape the future of intelligent systems, determining their impact on industries and society. By addressing the emerging challenges proactively, stakeholders can harness the full potential of AI while minimizing risks and ensuring equitable and secure implementations.

REFERENCES

Ajmal, C. S., Yerram, S., Abishek, V., Nizam, V. M., Aglave, G., Patnam, J. D., Raghuvanshi, R. S., & Srivastava, S. (2025). Innovative Approaches in Regulatory Affairs: Leveraging Artificial Intelligence and Machine Learning for Efficient Compliance and Decision-Making. *The AAPS Journal*, *27*(1), 22. DOI: 10.1208/s12248-024-01006-5 PMID: 39776314

Al-Ebrahim, M. A., Bunian, S., & Nour, A. A. (2023). Recent Machine-Learning-Driven Developments in E-Commerce: Current Challenges and Future Perspectives. [Arakcheev, A. Contract Smarter: Advancing Law with Technologies.]. *Engineering and Science*, *28*, 1044. DOI: 10.30919/es1044

Albalate, D., Bel, G., & Reeves, E. (2021). Government choice between contract termination and contract expiration in re-municipalization: A case of historical recurrence? *International Review of Administrative Sciences*, *87*(3), 461–479. DOI: 10.1177/00208523211002608

Arya, V. (2024). Al Safety and Security. *Challenges in Large Language Model Development and AI Ethics*, 354.

Bergman Larsson, N., & Talåsen, J. (2024). Applying Large Language Models in Business Processes: A contribution to Management Innovation.

Bloomfield, R., & Rushby, J. (2024). Assurance of AI systems from a dependability perspective. *arXiv preprint arXiv:2407.13948.*

Charfeddine, M., Kammoun, H. M., Hamdaoui, B., & Guizani, M. (2024). Chatgpt's security risks and benefits: Offensive and defensive use-cases, mitigation measures, and future implications. *IEEE Access : Practical Innovations, Open Solutions*, *12*, 30263–30310. DOI: 10.1109/ACCESS.2024.3367792

Chotaliya, H. M. (2024). *Artificial intelligence and its use cases in procurement* (Doctoral dissertation, Technische Hochschule Ingolstadt).

de la Roche, M., Voloder, E., Banerjee, A., Guerra, C., Cataldo Dell'Accio, D., Budris, F., & Sedej, T. (2024). Report on Artificial Intelligence and Blockchain Convergences. *Available atSSRN* 5023415.

Ferdaus, M. M., Abdelguerfi, M., Ioup, E., Niles, K. N., Pathak, K., & Sloan, S. (2024). Towards trustworthy ai: A review of ethical and robust large language models. *arXiv preprint arXiv:2407.13934.*

Heim, M. P., Starckjohann, N., & Torgersen, M. (2023). *The Convergence of AI and Cybersecurity: An Examination of ChatGPT's Role in Penetration Testing and its Ethical and Legal Implications* (Bachelor's thesis, NTNU). Helalat, M. A. The Expiry of the Financial Leasing Contract: A Comparative Study between the Jordanian Legislation and the Egyptian Legislation.

Hermalin, B. E., Katz, A. W., & Craswell, R. (2007). Contract law. *Handbook of law and economics, 1*, 3-138.

Huang, K., Chen, X., Yang, Y., Ponnapalli, J., & Huang, G. (2023). ChatGPT in finance and banking. In Beyond, A. I. (Ed.), *ChatGPT, Web3, and the Business Landscape of Tomorrow* (pp. 187–218). Springer Nature Switzerland. DOI: 10.1007/978-3-031-45282-6_7

Kanabar, V. (2023). *The AI Revolution in Project Management: Elevating Productivity with Generative AI*. Sams Publishing.

Koshevaya, V. (2024). Integration of Large Language Models in Contract Lifecycle Management.

Luhaibi, S. A., & Al Ali, I. A. (2024). Expiry of Family Ownership in the Public Property Law of the Emirate of Dubai No. 9 of 2020. *Library of Progress-Library Science, Information Technology & Computer, 44*(3).

Macijauskiene, R. (2006). The Expiry and Termination of an Employment Contract. *Jurisprudencija, 88*(10).

Miller, T., Durlik, I., Kostecka, E., Łobodzińska, A., Łazuga, K., & Kozlovska, P. (2025). Leveraging Large Language Models for Enhancing Safety in Maritime Operations. *Applied Sciences (Basel, Switzerland), 15*(3), 1666. DOI: 10.3390/app15031666

Okegbola, O., & Akiotu, C. A. (2024). Regulatory Compliance. *Perspectives on Digital Transformation in Contemporary Business*, 269.

Omar, M., & Zangana, H. (Eds.). (2025). *Digital Forensics in the Age of AI*. IGI Global., DOI: 10.4018/979-8-3373-0857-9

Omar, M., & Zangana, H. M. (Eds.). (2024). *Redefining Security With Cyber AI*. IGI Global., DOI: 10.4018/979-8-3693-6517-5

Omar, M., & Zangana, H. M. (Eds.). (2025). *Application of Large Language Models (LLMs) for Software Vulnerability Detection*. IGI Global., DOI: 10.4018/979-8-3693-9311-6

Omar, M., Zangana, H. M., & Mohammed, D. (Eds.). (2025). *Integrating Artificial Intelligence in Cybersecurity and Forensic Practices*. IGI Global., DOI: 10.4018/979-8-3373-0588-2

Pingili, R. (2025). AI-driven intelligent document processing for healthcare and insurance.

Poole, J., Devenney, J., & Shaw-Mellors, A. (2021). *Contract law concentrate: law revision and study guide*. Oxford University Press. DOI: 10.1093/he/9780192897336.001.0001

Rahaman, M., Pappachan, P., Orozco, S. M., Bansal, S., & Arya, V. (2024). AI Safety and Security. In *Challenges in Large Language Model Development and AI Ethics* (pp. 354–383). IGI Global. DOI: 10.4018/979-8-3693-3860-5.ch011

Rai, S. (2022). Legal Liability Issues and Regulation of Artificial Intelligence.

Rouzel, E., Venkatesha, G., & Dreveton, J. B. (2024). White Paper–B3X: The Ultimate AI-Powered Protocol for Decentralized Derivatives and Options Trading.

Sabharwal, S. M., Chhabra, S., & Aiden, M. K. (2024). AI and Blockchain for Secure Data Analytics. In *Next-Generation Cybersecurity: AI, ML, and Blockchain* (pp. 39–81). Springer Nature Singapore. DOI: 10.1007/978-981-97-1249-6_3

Sadiq, S. (2023). Generative AI: Language models and multimodal foundation models.

Santos, O., & Radanliev, P. (2024). *Beyond the Algorithm: AI, Security, Privacy, and Ethics*. Addison-Wesley Professional.

Schurer, J. A. (2024). *AI in negotiations: the perspective of procurement managers* (Doctoral dissertation).

Sears, B. (2022). Implied contract? When conduct continues after a contract expires.

Shan, W. (2025). *AI-powered fraud detection in banking: innovations, challenges and preventive strategies* (Doctoral dissertation).

Smits, J. M. (2021). *Contract law: a comparative introduction*. Edward Elgar Publishing.

Srivastawa, A. K. (2023). Exploring contract management in the digital age: The impact of artificial intelligence. *Jus Corpus LJ*, *4*, 737.

Tabatabaei, S. M. S., & Asadi, S. H. (2016). Reinvestigating the effect of act of God on condition of farming after expiry of farmletting contract. *Religious Researches*, *12*(4), 663–692.

Tang, A. (2025). *Safeguarding the Future: Security and Privacy by Design for AI, Metaverse, Blockchain, and Beyond*. CRC Press. DOI: 10.1201/9781003390695

Zangana, H., & Omar, M. (Eds.). (2025). *Leveraging Large Language Models for Quantum-Aware Cybersecurity*. IGI Global., DOI: 10.4018/979-8-3373-1102-9

Zangana, H. M., & Omar, M. (2025). The Role of Leadership in Advancing Inclusive Health Technologies. In Burrell, D., & Nguyen, C. (Eds.), *New Horizons in Leadership: Inclusive Explorations in Health, Technology, and Education* (pp. 203–220). IGI Global Scientific Publishing., DOI: 10.4018/979-8-3693-6437-6.ch009

Chapter 3
Threat Detection and Anomaly Identification Using Deep Learning

Hermano Jorge Da Silva De Queiroz
https://orcid.org/0000-0001-6738-6321
Lindsey Wilson College, USA

Helen MacLennan
https://orcid.org/0000-0002-0795-5008
Lindsey Wilson College, USA

ABSTRACT

Cyber threats are increasingly complex, requiring advanced detection and mitigation strategies. Deep learning (DL) offers powerful solutions for threat detection and anomaly identification, thanks to its ability to process large data volumes and uncover subtle indicators of cyber threats. This chapter discusses the integration of various DL techniques—CNNs, RNNs, autoencoders, and GANs—for detecting malicious activities and anomalies across diverse cybersecurity contexts. By examining both supervised and unsupervised approaches, it highlights strengths and limitations in tackling threats such as zero-day attacks, insider threats, and APTs. Real-world applications, case studies, and the role of explainable AI (XAI) in enhancing transparency and trust are also explored. Finally, challenges like adversarial attacks, data quality, and computational constraints are addressed, along with future directions for improving the robustness and efficiency of DL-driven threat detection systems.

DOI: 10.4018/979-8-3373-3296-3.ch003

1. INTRODUCTION

The rise of cybersecurity threats in the digital age has spurred significant advancements in defense mechanisms. As cyberattacks continue to evolve in sophistication and scale, traditional methods of detection and mitigation struggle to keep pace with the growing complexity of cyber threats. In response to these challenges, the integration of advanced technologies such as Deep Learning (DL) and Large Language Models (LLMs) has revolutionized the cybersecurity landscape. These technologies hold the potential to enhance the accuracy and efficiency of threat detection and anomaly identification, enabling organizations to respond proactively to cyber risks.

Deep Learning, a subset of artificial intelligence (AI), has demonstrated remarkable success in various domains, including image recognition, natural language processing, and cybersecurity. DL models, particularly neural networks, excel in identifying intricate patterns and relationships within vast amounts of data, making them highly effective for detecting anomalies and potential cyber threats (Ferrag et al., 2024). With the increasing use of Internet of Things (IoT) and Industrial Internet of Things (IIoT) devices, which are often vulnerable to cyber-attacks, DL has become an indispensable tool for improving the security of these connected environments (Sarker, 2024). Moreover, the convergence of DL with LLMs, such as the Bidirectional Encoder Representations from Transformers (BERT), has introduced a new dimension to cybersecurity defense by facilitating the detection of malicious activity and vulnerabilities in a privacy-preserving manner (Ferrag et al., 2024).

Large Language Models have proven to be exceptionally capable in processing and analyzing vast text data, making them highly valuable for cybersecurity tasks such as threat intelligence, vulnerability detection, and malware classification (Kasri et al., 2025). LLMs can automate the analysis of logs and network traffic, identifying suspicious patterns that might otherwise go undetected. Moreover, these models offer explainability features that allow for transparency in decision-making, a critical factor in the cybersecurity domain where accountability and clarity are paramount (Hasanov et al., 2024). As they are fine-tuned to domain-specific tasks, LLMs can further enhance threat detection by learning from historical attack data, detecting zero-day vulnerabilities, and anticipating new attack vectors (Motlagh et al., 2024).

The combination of Deep Learning and LLMs not only strengthens traditional cybersecurity measures but also introduces more adaptive, dynamic defense strategies that evolve in real-time as they learn from new attack patterns and methods. As a result, these integrated approaches are poised to play a pivotal role in shaping the future of cybersecurity, offering advanced solutions to combat emerging threats (Xu et al., 2024). In particular, their application in IoT and IIoT devices, which are critical to modern industrial infrastructure, exemplifies their importance in maintaining a robust defense against attacks targeting these vulnerable systems (Ghazal et al., 2024).

This chapter aims to explore the intersection of Deep Learning and Large Language Models in cybersecurity, highlighting their potential for improving threat detection and anomaly identification. We will examine how these technologies are being applied in real-world scenarios, discuss their challenges, and identify opportunities for further research. The chapter also aims to provide an overview of the latest developments in this area, emphasizing the role of these technologies in revolutionizing cybersecurity defense mechanisms across various sectors.

2. TRADITIONAL VS. AI-BASED THREAT DETECTION

Cybersecurity has evolved significantly in recent years, particularly with the integration of artificial intelligence (AI) and machine learning (ML) into threat detection systems. Traditional threat detection methods often rely on rule-based approaches, signature detection, and anomaly-based systems to identify and mitigate potential risks. These conventional techniques have been effective but also come with inherent limitations, especially in dealing with increasingly sophisticated cyber threats. In contrast, AI-based threat detection leverages advanced algorithms, particularly large language models (LLMs), to enhance cybersecurity capabilities and improve overall system resilience. In this section, we explore the differences between traditional and AI-based threat detection methods and highlight how AI is transforming the cybersecurity landscape.

2.1 Traditional Threat Detection Methods

Traditional threat detection systems, such as signature-based detection, anomaly detection, and rule-based detection, have been the backbone of cybersecurity for decades. Signature-based detection works by comparing incoming data against a predefined database of known threats or signatures. This method is effective at identifying previously encountered cyberattacks but struggles with detecting novel or evolving threats (Santos, Salam, & Dahir, 2024). Rule-based detection systems use predefined rules or heuristics to detect suspicious activity. While these systems are fast and can catch known threats, they can be inflexible and often require manual updates to stay current (Manoharan & Sarker, 2023).

Anomaly detection, another traditional method, relies on detecting deviations from the established baseline of system behavior. While this approach can identify new and unknown attacks by recognizing unusual patterns, it can produce high rates of false positives, particularly in dynamic and large-scale systems (Nguyen et al.,

2018). Traditional methods, despite their advantages, have significant drawbacks, especially when dealing with complex and polymorphic threats that evolve rapidly.

2.2 AI-Based Threat Detection

AI-based threat detection, on the other hand, uses advanced algorithms that can learn from large datasets and adapt to new patterns without relying solely on predefined rules or signatures. Machine learning and deep learning, subsets of AI, are the driving forces behind these systems, allowing them to continuously improve as they process more data (Ferrag, Ndhlovu, Tihanyi, Cordeiro, Debbah, Lestable, & Thandi, 2024). LLMs, specifically, are playing a pivotal role in advancing AI-based cybersecurity systems by offering enhanced capabilities for processing natural language and understanding the context of cyber threats (Ferrag, Ndhlovu, Tihanyi, Cordeiro, Debbah, & Lestable, 2023).

One of the key advantages of AI-based threat detection is its ability to identify previously unknown threats, including zero-day attacks. Unlike traditional systems, AI models do not rely on pre-existing signatures; instead, they can detect abnormal patterns of behavior or detect subtle deviations that might indicate an emerging threat (Motlagh et al., 2024). LLMs, such as SecureBERT and similar models, offer a highly effective means for enhancing cybersecurity defenses by understanding textual data, such as system logs, threat reports, and network communication patterns, to uncover complex attack strategies (Aghaei, Niu, Shadid, & Al-Shaer, 2022).

Furthermore, AI-based models are capable of providing real-time threat detection and responses, reducing the time between the identification of a threat and the initiation of a defensive action. The integration of explainable AI (XAI) into these systems enhances trust and accountability, enabling cybersecurity professionals to understand how the model arrived at its conclusions and to verify the system's decisions (Sarker, 2024; Liu, 2024). As AI models continue to evolve, they increasingly offer predictive capabilities, forecasting potential threats based on historical data, behavior patterns, and emerging vulnerabilities (Hasanov et al., 2024).

2.3 Key Differences Between Traditional and AI-Based Detection

The primary distinction between traditional and AI-based threat detection lies in their adaptability and efficiency in responding to novel and complex threats. Traditional systems, such as signature-based and anomaly detection, rely on static rules or known threat patterns, making them less effective at handling new attack techniques or zero-day vulnerabilities (Xu et al., 2024). In contrast, AI-based systems can adapt and evolve, learning from new data and detecting subtle patterns that may go unnoticed by traditional methods (Chen et al., 2024). These capabilities make AI models particularly effective in mitigating advanced persistent threats (APTs) and other sophisticated cyberattacks (Ghazal et al., 2024).

Another significant difference is the scalability of AI-based systems. Traditional threat detection methods often struggle with handling large volumes of data, particularly in modern enterprise environments with millions of devices and network traffic. AI models, however, can process and analyze vast amounts of data quickly, identifying threats across large and complex networks (Hadi, Abdulredha, & Hasan, 2023). The use of cloud-based AI systems further amplifies the scalability, enabling real-time monitoring and detection at a global scale (Ozkan-Okay et al., 2024).

To illustrate the differences between traditional and AI-based threat detection, Figure 1 compares key aspects of both approaches. Traditional methods rely heavily on predefined rules and known signatures, which limits their ability to detect novel threats. In contrast, AI-based methods, particularly those leveraging deep learning and large language models (LLMs), dynamically learn patterns from data, improving their ability to detect unknown and evolving cyber threats.

Figure 1. Comparison of traditional vs. AI-based threat detection

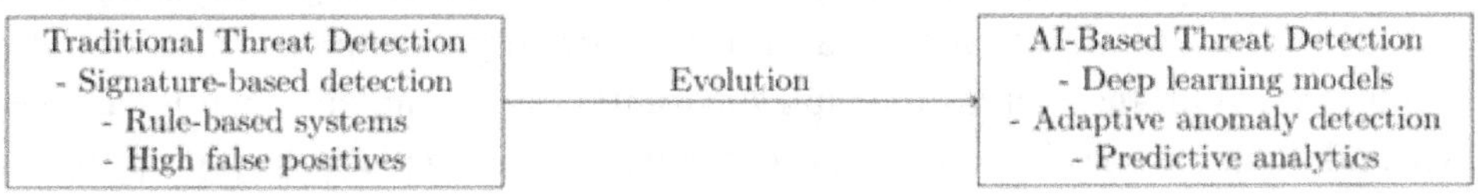

Moreover, AI-based threat detection systems can enhance the accuracy of threat identification, significantly reducing false positives and ensuring that security teams focus on the most critical issues (Zangana, 2024). By continually learning from new threats and adapting to changing attack patterns, AI systems can maintain high detection accuracy even in the face of evolving cyber threats.

2.4 Challenges and Future Directions

While AI-based threat detection offers significant improvements over traditional methods, it is not without its challenges. One key challenge is the need for large and high-quality datasets to train AI models. In cybersecurity, obtaining such datasets can be difficult due to privacy concerns, the need for diverse attack scenarios, and the dynamic nature of cyber threats (Motlagh et al., 2024). Additionally, AI-based systems require significant computational resources, which can be a barrier for smaller organizations.

Despite these challenges, the future of cybersecurity is undoubtedly AI-driven. As AI models become more efficient and accurate, they are expected to play an even more significant role in threat prevention, detection, and response. The integration of AI and LLMs will continue to revolutionize cybersecurity, with promising developments in areas such as autonomous threat hunting, advanced malware detection, and predictive analytics (Gholami & Omar, 2024; Hassanin & Moustafa, 2024).

In conclusion, while traditional threat detection methods have served their purpose in the past, AI-based systems, particularly those leveraging LLMs, are set to take the lead in modern cybersecurity strategies. Their ability to adapt, learn from new data, and detect complex threats will make them indispensable in the ongoing battle against cybercrime and other malicious activities.

3. DEEP LEARNING ARCHITECTURES FOR THREAT DETECTION

In the evolving field of cybersecurity, the use of deep learning architectures for threat detection has significantly transformed how organizations defend against cyberattacks. With the increasing sophistication of cyber threats, traditional rule-based and signature-based detection systems have become inadequate, prompting the need for more advanced methods. Deep learning models, particularly those utilizing large language models (LLMs), have emerged as pivotal tools for enhancing threat detection, response, and mitigation. This section explores various deep learning architectures, their applications, and their role in transforming cybersecurity practices.

3.1. Deep Learning Models in Cyber Threat Detection

Deep learning models, including Convolutional Neural Networks (CNNs), Recurrent Neural Networks (RNNs), Long Short-Term Memory networks (LSTMs), and Generative Adversarial Networks (GANs), have proven highly effective in detecting cybersecurity threats. These architectures are designed to automatically learn patterns from vast datasets, allowing them to detect anomalies, predict attacks, and identify new, previously unseen types of threats.

For example, CNNs are widely used in image recognition tasks but have also been successfully applied to analyze and detect anomalies in network traffic patterns. By treating network activity as an image-like structure, CNNs can learn spatial hierarchies that represent suspicious behavior. RNNs and LSTMs, on the other hand, excel in analyzing sequential data such as logs and network traffic, making them ideal for detecting patterns in time-series data that could indicate a cyberattack (Sarker, 2024; Motlagh et al., 2024).

Figure 2 provides an overview of deep learning architectures utilized in cybersecurity. Different models, including CNNs, RNNs, LSTMs, and GANs, are applied for tasks such as anomaly detection, network traffic analysis, and malware classification. Each model specializes in distinct aspects of cybersecurity, from recognizing sequential patterns to generating synthetic attack scenarios.

Figure 2. Deep learning architectures for cybersecurity

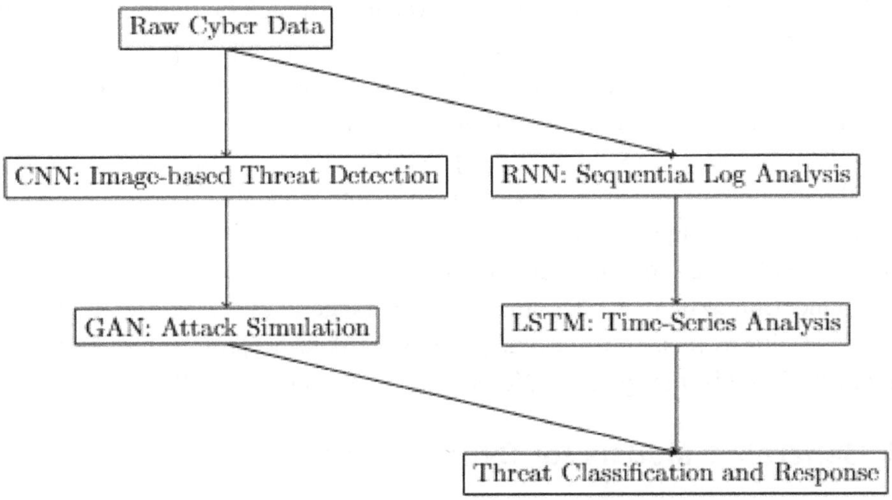

3.2. Large Language Models (LLMs) in Cyber Threat Detection

LLMs, such as BERT and GPT-based models, are transforming the landscape of cyber threat detection. These models have the capacity to process vast amounts of unstructured textual data and detect patterns indicative of malicious activities. LLMs can analyze the content of network packets, emails, or logs to detect phishing attempts, malware, and other social engineering attacks.

Ferrag et al. (2024) introduced a BERT-based lightweight model tailored for IoT/IIoT environments, which is able to detect threats with minimal computational overhead. The ability of LLMs to understand context, semantics, and intentions behind text enables them to perform more accurate detection, especially in environments with large amounts of unstructured data, such as social media or corporate communications (Ferrag et al., 2023; Kasri et al., 2025).

Furthermore, LLMs have been successfully integrated with other cybersecurity tools to automate the identification of zero-day vulnerabilities, detect suspicious behaviors in real time, and predict potential future threats. The architecture of these models allows them to process and understand intricate relationships between network events and security breaches, enabling proactive threat detection (Zangana et al., 2024; Ghazal et al., 2024).

3.3. Hybrid Models for Enhanced Threat Detection

To further enhance detection capabilities, hybrid models that combine traditional deep learning architectures with LLMs are gaining popularity. For instance, integrating CNNs with LLMs can allow for better handling of both structured and unstructured data. While CNNs excel in recognizing patterns in structured data, LLMs are adept at understanding the contextual and semantic nuances in unstructured textual data. Together, these models can provide a more comprehensive approach to cyber threat detection, reducing false positives and enhancing accuracy (Gholami & Omar, 2024; Ferrag et al., 2024).

Additionally, attention mechanisms such as the Transformer architecture, which is the foundation of many LLMs, are being leveraged in cybersecurity applications for their ability to focus on relevant portions of data, improving threat detection capabilities in real-time systems (Xu et al., 2024; Chen et al., 2024).

3.4. Generative Models for Cybersecurity

Generative models, particularly GANs, have also found applications in cybersecurity. GANs can generate synthetic data, such as network traffic or attack simulations, which is invaluable in training other machine learning models. These models are capable of learning from existing data and generating realistic examples of cyberattacks, which can be used to train detection systems without compromising privacy or relying on real attack data. GANs can simulate a variety of attack scenarios, making them crucial for testing and improving the resilience of security systems (Santos et al., 2024; Ferrag et al., 2024).

Furthermore, generative AI has been explored for developing defense mechanisms that automatically create countermeasures to known attacks, enhancing the adaptability and resilience of cybersecurity defenses (Hassanin & Moustafa, 2024; Zangana, 2024).

3.5. Challenges and Limitations

Despite their impressive capabilities, the use of deep learning and LLMs in cybersecurity also presents several challenges. One major concern is the need for large, high-quality datasets to train these models. In many cases, cybersecurity datasets are imbalanced or incomplete, which can affect the model's performance. Additionally, the computational resources required to train and deploy these models can be significant, particularly for real-time threat detection.

Another challenge is the interpretability of these models. While LLMs can achieve high accuracy in detecting threats, understanding the reasoning behind their decisions can be difficult, which is critical for trust and transparency in security-critical applications (Gholami & Omar, 2023; Liu, 2024). Explainable AI (XAI) approaches are being developed to address these issues, helping users understand how decisions are made by deep learning models (Ghazal et al., 2024; AlQenaei, 2024).

3.6. The Future of Deep Learning in Cybersecurity

The future of deep learning in cybersecurity looks promising, with continued advancements in both model architectures and techniques. As deep learning models become more efficient and adaptable, they are expected to play a central role in the development of autonomous cybersecurity systems capable of detecting and mitigating threats in real time. The integration of LLMs with other AI technologies, such as reinforcement learning and edge computing, will further enhance their capabilities, making them essential tools for protecting against the evolving landscape of cyber threats (Ferrag et al., 2024; Hassanin & Moustafa, 2024).

Moreover, as organizations adopt cloud computing and IoT technologies, the need for scalable and efficient threat detection models will grow. LLMs, particularly lightweight models like those proposed by Ferrag et al. (2024), will be critical in addressing the unique challenges posed by these environments.

In conclusion, deep learning architectures, particularly those leveraging LLMs, are reshaping the field of cybersecurity by providing advanced, adaptive, and automated methods for threat detection. Their integration into existing security infrastructures offers a promising solution to the growing complexity and scale of cyber threats.

4. DATASET PREPARATION AND FEATURE ENGINEERING

Effective dataset preparation and feature engineering are essential steps in the successful application of machine learning models, particularly in the context of cybersecurity, where accurate threat detection and response are paramount. In this section, we explore the key aspects of these processes, particularly when integrating large language models (LLMs) and advanced machine learning techniques to enhance cybersecurity systems.

4.1. Dataset Collection

The first step in preparing datasets for cybersecurity applications is the collection of relevant data. For effective threat detection, data must come from a variety of sources, including network traffic logs, system events, and historical attack data. Datasets typically include both labeled (with known attack types) and unlabeled data (where attack types are unknown), which allows for supervised and unsupervised learning techniques (Ferrag et al., 2023). Real-world cybersecurity datasets such as the CICIDS dataset or KDD99 are commonly used for training and evaluating machine learning models.

Moreover, the rapid development of IoT and Industrial IoT (IIoT) devices has led to the creation of specific datasets that focus on network security in these domains (Ferrag et al., 2024). These datasets contain information about device interactions, communication protocols, and potential vulnerabilities, all of which are critical for building effective threat detection systems.

4.2. Data Preprocessing

Data preprocessing is essential to ensure that the raw data can be used effectively by machine learning models. In the cybersecurity domain, preprocessing typically involves several steps:

- **Data Cleaning:** This step removes noise, errors, or irrelevant information from the dataset. In the case of cybersecurity, this could include removing duplicate logs, correcting misformatted data, or eliminating outliers that may distort the analysis.
- **Data Normalization:** Raw data often needs to be normalized to a common scale. For example, features such as packet size or frequency of access attempts are scaled to avoid biases toward variables with larger ranges.
- **Feature Selection and Extraction:** Identifying relevant features is critical for improving the model's performance and reducing overfitting. This involves selecting the most informative variables that contribute to distinguishing between normal and malicious activities. Feature selection techniques, such as Recursive Feature Elimination (RFE) or Principal Component Analysis (PCA), are commonly employed (Sarker, 2024).

4.3. Feature Engineering for Cybersecurity

Feature engineering plays a vital role in converting raw data into meaningful inputs for machine learning models. In the context of cybersecurity, several feature engineering techniques can be applied to improve the efficacy of large language models and machine learning classifiers:

- **Tokenization and Embeddings:** Given that LLMs operate on textual data, tokenizing network logs and security events into tokens or words is essential. Pre-trained embeddings such as BERT (Bidirectional Encoder Representations from Transformers) are used to convert textual data into fixed-length vectors that can capture the semantic meaning of the data (Ferrag et al., 2024; Kasri et al., 2025). These embeddings enable the model to process complex, high-dimensional security data more efficiently.
- **Time-based Features:** In cybersecurity, temporal patterns are often indicative of malicious activity. For example, analyzing the frequency and time intervals of login attempts, packet arrivals, or system access can help identify anomalies and potential threats. Feature extraction techniques such as Fourier Transform or Wavelet Transform can be used to detect periodic patterns that are indicative of normal or abnormal behaviors (Motlagh et al., 2024).
- **Categorical Encoding:** Features like device type, attack type, and protocol used can be encoded using methods such as one-hot encoding or label encoding to ensure compatibility with machine learning models.
- **Anomaly Detection Features:** Certain features related to anomaly detection, such as entropy (measuring randomness), average packet size, and connection attempts per second, can be used to detect network anomalies, which often indicate malicious activities (Ferrag et al., 2023).

4.4. Augmenting Datasets

Synthetic data generation techniques are also increasingly being used in cybersecurity to augment datasets, particularly when dealing with rare or unseen attacks. By generating synthetic data using models like Generative Adversarial Networks (GANs) or Variational Autoencoders (VAEs), researchers can create additional labeled examples of attack scenarios, which helps overcome class imbalance in attack datasets (Gholami & Omar, 2023). This can significantly improve the training and performance of cybersecurity models, as it allows them to better generalize to real-world scenarios.

Moreover, leveraging LLMs for data augmentation has been explored to generate realistic attack scenarios, which can be used to enhance model robustness (Gholami & Omar, 2024).

4.5. Privacy and Security Considerations

Data used in cybersecurity applications often contain sensitive information. Therefore, it is important to ensure that data preprocessing and feature engineering steps do not compromise user privacy. Techniques like differential privacy and federated learning allow the models to learn from decentralized data sources without accessing raw data, which helps in maintaining privacy while improving the accuracy of threat detection (Santos et al., 2024; Lestable & Thandi, 2024). The integration of LLMs in such privacy-preserving models has the potential to revolutionize the way cybersecurity data is utilized without compromising individual rights.

4.6. Model Training and Evaluation

Once the dataset has been preprocessed and the features engineered, the next step is training the machine learning model. In cybersecurity, different models like decision trees, support vector machines (SVM), or deep learning-based models such as convolutional neural networks (CNNs) are often used to classify data into benign or malicious categories. However, the growing importance of LLMs in this space has made it clear that transformers, such as BERT and GPT-based models, can offer significant advantages in detecting advanced threats (Ferrag et al., 2024).

The evaluation of these models requires robust metrics, including accuracy, precision, recall, F1-score, and ROC-AUC, to measure their ability to detect attacks and reduce false positives. Cross-validation techniques are often employed to ensure the model's generalizability across unseen data.

4.7 Summary

In conclusion, dataset preparation and feature engineering are crucial components in developing effective machine learning models for cybersecurity. By carefully selecting, processing, and enhancing features, cybersecurity systems can be trained to identify and mitigate a wide range of cyber threats. The integration of LLMs offers the potential to further enhance these systems, especially in areas such as anomaly detection, attack prediction, and privacy-preserving threat intelligence (Kasri et al., 2025; Zangana, 2024). Through thoughtful data preparation and feature engineering, the cybersecurity landscape can be significantly strengthened against emerging threats.

5. SUPERVISED VS. UNSUPERVISED LEARNING FOR ANOMALY DETECTION

Anomaly detection, a critical task in cybersecurity, aims to identify abnormal behavior or outliers in data that may signify potential threats or malicious activity. Machine learning techniques, particularly supervised and unsupervised learning, play a central role in this process. Both approaches have their strengths and weaknesses, and their suitability depends on the specific cybersecurity application at hand.

5.1 Supervised Learning for Anomaly Detection

Supervised learning involves training a model on labeled data, where the normal and anomalous patterns are already known. This approach is effective when sufficient labeled datasets are available for training. The model learns from these labels, identifying features that distinguish normal behavior from anomalous activities. Common algorithms used in supervised anomaly detection include decision trees, random forests, support vector machines (SVM), and neural networks.

In cybersecurity, supervised learning is particularly useful for detecting known attacks or patterns. For example, Jones et al. (2023) highlight the effectiveness of supervised learning models in threat detection, where specific attack signatures are learned from labeled data. Additionally, supervised learning models tend to perform well when the number of anomalies is relatively small and the training data is sufficiently diverse.

However, the main drawback of supervised learning in anomaly detection is the requirement for a large amount of labeled data, which may not always be available, especially for novel attacks. This is where unsupervised learning approaches become valuable, particularly when dealing with novel, previously unseen attack patterns.

5.2 Unsupervised Learning for Anomaly Detection

Unsupervised learning, on the other hand, does not rely on labeled data. Instead, it detects anomalies by identifying data points that deviate significantly from the normal data distribution. Common unsupervised learning techniques include clustering algorithms (such as K-means), isolation forests, and autoencoders. These methods are particularly useful when labeled data is scarce or nonexistent.

Unsupervised learning is gaining traction in cybersecurity, especially in the context of detecting zero-day attacks or emerging threats. Ferrag et al. (2024) underscore the potential of unsupervised methods, especially in Internet of Things (IoT) and Industrial Internet of Things (IIoT) environments, where new attack vectors are constantly emerging. Since unsupervised models do not require labeled data, they are more adaptable to evolving attack strategies and can help detect new, unknown threats in real time.

While unsupervised learning can detect novel anomalies, it may generate a higher number of false positives due to its inability to distinguish between truly anomalous behavior and natural data variability. Moreover, the performance of unsupervised models heavily relies on the quality of feature selection and the algorithm's ability to capture subtle patterns in the data, which can be challenging in complex cybersecurity scenarios.

5.3 Comparison of Supervised and Unsupervised Learning in Cybersecurity

When comparing supervised and unsupervised learning for anomaly detection in cybersecurity, the choice between the two largely depends on the problem's context and available resources. Santos et al. (2024) argue that supervised learning excels in situations where historical attack data is abundant and clearly labeled, making it ideal for detecting known threats with high accuracy. On the other hand, unsupervised learning is more suited for dynamic environments, where new and unknown attacks constantly emerge, and labeled data is scarce.

Moreover, the increasing use of large language models (LLMs) in cybersecurity has introduced new possibilities for anomaly detection. Motlagh et al. (2024) discuss how generative models, a subset of unsupervised learning, can learn the underlying structure of normal network behavior and identify novel threats without the need for labeled data. These models are particularly useful in scenarios where traditional anomaly detection techniques struggle to differentiate between malicious and benign anomalies.

Figure 3 compares the precision, recall, and F1-score of supervised and unsupervised learning methods in anomaly detection. While supervised learning exhibits high precision, it struggles with recall due to its dependence on labeled data. Unsupervised methods, in contrast, demonstrate strong recall but may suffer from higher false positives.

Figure 3. Performance comparison of supervised vs. unsupervised learning in cybersecurity

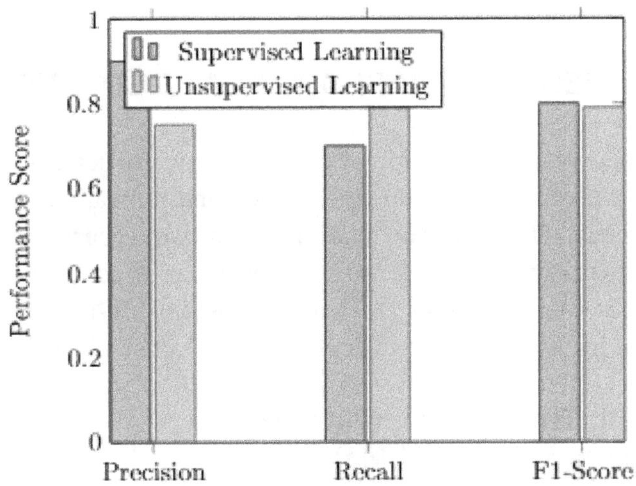

5.4 Hybrid Approaches

In practice, hybrid approaches that combine both supervised and unsupervised learning techniques are increasingly being explored. These models leverage the strengths of both methods: the high accuracy of supervised learning when labeled data is available, and the adaptability of unsupervised learning for detecting novel anomalies. Zangana et al. (2025) highlight the effectiveness of such hybrid models, where unsupervised learning is first used to identify potential anomalies, which are then classified using supervised methods. This combination can improve both the detection rate and the reduction of false positives, making it a promising solution for modern cybersecurity applications.

5.5 Summary

Both supervised and unsupervised learning techniques play vital roles in anomaly detection for cybersecurity, each with its advantages and challenges. Supervised learning is best suited for environments with rich labeled datasets and known attack patterns, while unsupervised learning excels in dynamic, ever-changing environments where new and unseen attacks must be detected. The integration of both methods in hybrid models may offer the most robust approach, enabling better detection of both known and unknown threats. As cybersecurity continues to evolve, the role of machine learning, particularly unsupervised learning and LLMs, will be pivotal in enhancing the effectiveness of anomaly detection systems.

6. CASE STUDIES ON AI-BASED THREAT DETECTION

In the rapidly evolving landscape of cybersecurity, artificial intelligence (AI) has emerged as a pivotal tool for threat detection and mitigation. AI, particularly large language models (LLMs), is revolutionizing the way security systems analyze and respond to cyber threats. These advancements are especially valuable when integrated into Internet of Things (IoT) and Industrial IoT (IIoT) environments, where traditional methods struggle to cope with the scale and complexity of data.

6.1. Enhancing Threat Detection with Large Language Models (LLMs)

LLMs, such as those based on BERT (Bidirectional Encoder Representations from Transformers), have been at the forefront of cybersecurity advancements. In a recent study, Ferrag et al. (2024) demonstrated how LLMs can be applied to cyber threat detection in IoT/IIoT devices, introducing a privacy-preserving, lightweight BERT-based model. This model significantly improved the efficiency of detecting anomalies and potential threats by leveraging the language understanding capabilities of LLMs to parse and interpret large volumes of security logs (Ferrag et al., 2024).

6.2. Generative AI and Cybersecurity

The application of generative AI in cybersecurity has gained significant attention, particularly in the development of secure and adaptive models. Sarker (2024) explores how generative AI models, particularly in the form of adversarial networks, are being used to generate synthetic data that simulates cyber-attacks, helping security systems better prepare for real-world threats. These AI models enable cybersecurity solutions to predict and counter novel attacks that have not yet been observed in the wild.

Ferrag et al. (2023) also discuss the role of generative AI in advancing cyber threat detection, emphasizing how these models can generate realistic attack scenarios to train defense systems more effectively. This proactive approach allows security frameworks to evolve continuously, adapting to new and sophisticated attack techniques (Ferrag et al., 2023).

6.3. LLMs in Predicting Cyberattacks

The ability of LLMs to predict cyberattacks based on historical data is another key development in AI-based threat detection. In a case study by Diaf et al. (2024), LLMs were employed to predict cyberattacks in IoT networks. The model demonstrated remarkable accuracy in forecasting potential vulnerabilities and identifying attack vectors before they could be exploited. This predictive capability is crucial in IoT and IIoT environments, where real-time threat detection is essential to mitigate potential damage.

6.4. Systematic Literature Reviews on AI Applications in Cybersecurity

Several studies have conducted comprehensive reviews of AI applications in cybersecurity, highlighting the broad range of use cases and the growing adoption of LLMs. Liu (2024) reviews the advancements and applications of pre-trained language models in cybersecurity, providing a detailed overview of how LLMs are being integrated into various cybersecurity frameworks. Similarly, Xu et al. (2024) offer a systematic literature review of LLMs in cybersecurity, discussing their impact on both detection and prediction of cyber threats (Liu, 2024; Xu et al., 2024).

Hasanov et al. (2024) further explore the systematic application of LLMs in cybersecurity, focusing on their role in automating threat detection and enabling more intelligent decision-making processes. This research underscores the shift from traditional rule-based systems to more adaptive, AI-driven approaches that can analyze patterns in data and anticipate future threats (Hasanov et al., 2024).

6.5. Vulnerability and Defense Mechanisms with LLMs

As the cybersecurity landscape grows more complex, understanding vulnerabilities and developing defense mechanisms becomes increasingly important. Kasri et al. (2025) examine the role of LLMs in transforming vulnerability management into a more proactive and defense-oriented approach. Their research illustrates how LLMs can automatically identify vulnerabilities in software and networks, significantly reducing the time between detection and mitigation.

In parallel, research by Ghazal et al. (2024) presents case studies on how LLMs are being used in conjunction with explainable AI to enhance the transparency of threat detection models. This hybrid approach provides both security professionals and end-users with greater insight into how models arrive at their conclusions, making the technology more accessible and understandable (Ghazal et al., 2024).

6.6. Adversarial Attacks and LLM Security

While LLMs have shown great promise in enhancing cybersecurity, they are not immune to adversarial attacks. As discussed by Motlagh et al. (2024), adversarial threats against AI-based security systems, including LLMs, represent a significant challenge. The authors explore various techniques for defending against adversarial attacks, such as model retraining and the use of defensive adversarial networks, which aim to enhance the robustness of AI systems in the face of evolving attack strategies (Motlagh et al., 2024).

6.7. Future Directions: Leveraging LLMs for Cyber Threat Intelligence

The integration of LLMs into cybersecurity threat intelligence is a burgeoning area of research. Zangana et al. (2025) examine how LLMs can be leveraged to automate and enhance threat intelligence processes. These models can analyze vast amounts of threat data, identify patterns, and provide actionable insights that help organizations stay ahead of cybercriminals. Their study highlights the potential for LLMs to play a key role in the future of cybersecurity, transforming how threat intelligence is collected, analyzed, and acted upon (Zangana et al., 2025).

Similarly, Asoronye et al. (2024) present "SecLM," a specialized language model designed specifically for cybersecurity applications, which offers advanced capabilities for threat mitigation and response. This work illustrates how LLMs can be fine-tuned for specific security needs, offering a more personalized and effective defense against emerging threats (Asoronye et al., 2024).

6.8 Summary

The integration of AI, and specifically LLMs, into cybersecurity is transforming the landscape of threat detection and defense. From predictive analytics to adversarial attack mitigation, these technologies are reshaping how organizations approach cybersecurity. While there are still challenges to overcome, particularly concerning adversarial attacks and model robustness, the future looks promising as these models continue to evolve and become integral to cybersecurity strategies.

7. PERFORMANCE EVALUATION AND METRICS (PRECISION, RECALL, F1-SCORE)

In the context of cybersecurity, particularly when leveraging Large Language Models (LLMs) for tasks such as threat detection, accurate performance evaluation is crucial. Precision, recall, and the F1-score are standard metrics that assess the performance of a model. These metrics are essential in determining how effectively a model can identify, classify, and mitigate cybersecurity threats, including malware detection, intrusion prevention, and anomaly identification. Below, we will explore each of these metrics in detail and their significance in cybersecurity applications, with a focus on LLMs.

7.1 Precision

Precision is defined as the ratio of true positive results to the total number of instances classified as positive by the model. In simpler terms, it measures the accuracy of the positive predictions made by the model. For cybersecurity systems, precision is vital in minimizing false positives, which can lead to unnecessary alerts and resource wastage. Higher precision indicates that the model is less likely to incorrectly classify benign actions as malicious.

$$Precision = \frac{TP}{TP + FP}$$

Where:

- **TP** = True Positives (correctly identified threats)
- **FP** = False Positives (incorrectly identified benign activities)

In cybersecurity, particularly when LLMs like SecureBERT are employed, precision ensures that legitimate network traffic is not wrongly flagged as an attack (Ferrag et al., 2024). The ability to achieve high precision is vital for LLMs in detecting sophisticated cyber threats while avoiding unnecessary intervention that could disrupt normal operations (Santos et al., 2024).

7.2 Recall

Recall (also known as sensitivity) measures the model's ability to correctly identify all relevant instances within a dataset. It is the ratio of true positives to the sum of true positives and false negatives, indicating how well the model captures all possible threats. In cybersecurity, recall is crucial for detecting as many attacks or vulnerabilities as possible, especially in cases where missing a threat could have catastrophic consequences. While high recall reduces the risk of missing attacks, it may increase false positives if not balanced correctly.

$$Recall = \frac{TP}{TP + FN}$$

Where:

- **FN** = False Negatives (missed threats)

In LLMs, such as those discussed by Ferrag et al. (2024) and Zangana (2025), improving recall ensures the identification of threats that could otherwise go undetected. This metric is particularly useful in cybersecurity settings where new or evolving attacks might not be perfectly categorized but still need to be flagged as potential risks (Kasri et al., 2025).

7.3 F1-Score

The F1-score is the harmonic mean of precision and recall, providing a balance between the two metrics. It is particularly useful when there is a need to balance false positives and false negatives. In cybersecurity, a high F1-score means the model effectively minimizes both false alarms and missed threats. The F1-score is especially important when cybersecurity solutions need to strike a balance between sensitivity (recall) and the specificity of results (precision).

$$F - Score = 2 \times \frac{Precision \times Recall}{Precision + Recall}$$

By using the F1-score, cybersecurity models that integrate LLMs can ensure that both critical threats and the accuracy of benign traffic are handled effectively. The F1-score is often used in evaluating the efficacy of new generative AI models in cybersecurity, where precision and recall alone might not give a complete picture (Sarker, 2024; Liu, 2024).

Figure 4 illustrates the variation in precision, recall, and F1-score over different training epochs for a deep learning-based cybersecurity model. The improvement in these metrics highlights how continued training enhances the model's ability to detect threats accurately while minimizing false positives and negatives.

Figure 4. Model performance across training epochs

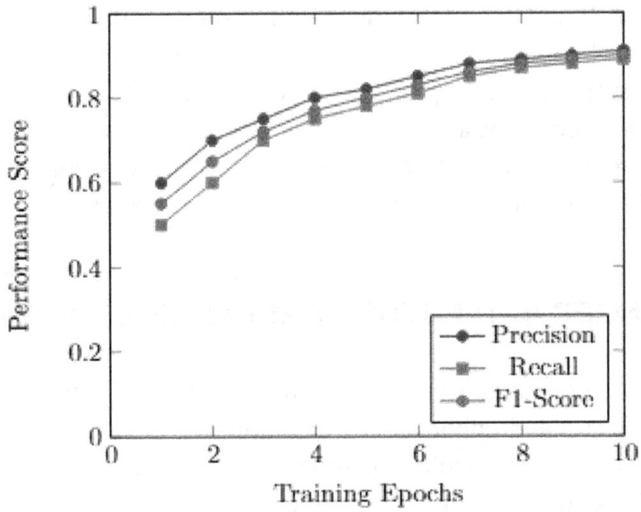

7.4 Application of These Metrics in Cybersecurity

LLMs in cybersecurity applications often involve detecting and classifying cyber threats such as phishing attacks, malware, and anomalous behaviors. Precision, recall, and F1-score play pivotal roles in evaluating the effectiveness of these models. For instance, in the domain of Internet of Things (IoT) security, Ferrag et al. (2024) highlighted the importance of privacy-preserving models that detect cyber threats in real-time, minimizing false positives (precision) while ensuring threats are not missed (recall). Similarly, in more advanced cybersecurity applications, large-scale systems like those outlined by Motlagh et al. (2024) emphasize the importance of these metrics for adapting to the evolving nature of cyber threats.

Furthermore, researchers like Ghazal et al. (2024) emphasize that the challenge lies in optimizing these metrics to ensure that the LLM models can be used effectively in various cybersecurity scenarios, from intrusion detection to predicting future threats. The growing body of literature, including recent reviews (Hasanov et al., 2024; Xu et al., 2024), shows that LLMs are becoming increasingly proficient at balancing these metrics, improving both accuracy and response time in threat detection systems.

7.5 Summary

Precision, recall, and F1-score remain fundamental metrics for evaluating the effectiveness of machine learning models in cybersecurity, especially as large language models continue to emerge as powerful tools for threat detection and mitigation. By carefully considering these metrics, cybersecurity professionals can ensure that their systems are both efficient and reliable, capable of detecting and addressing potential threats with minimal disruption to normal operations.

8. CHALLENGES AND FUTURE RESEARCH DIRECTIONS

The application of Large Language Models (LLMs) in cybersecurity presents numerous challenges and opportunities for future research. As the capabilities of LLMs continue to grow, particularly in threat detection, vulnerability management, and anomaly detection, their integration into cybersecurity frameworks will likely reshape the landscape. However, challenges persist, and understanding the direction of future research is crucial for leveraging LLMs effectively.

8.1. Data Privacy and Security Concerns

One of the primary challenges in using LLMs for cybersecurity is data privacy. Many LLMs require massive amounts of data for training, and in cybersecurity, this data often includes sensitive or personally identifiable information (PII). Safeguarding this data from breaches or misuse is critical. Models like SecureBERT have shown potential in ensuring privacy-preserving measures by minimizing the risk of data exposure during training (Aghaei et al., 2022). Future research must focus on improving the privacy mechanisms inherent in LLMs and developing frameworks for privacy-conscious model training, particularly for IoT/IIoT devices where data security is paramount (Ferrag et al., 2024; Ferrag et al., 2023).

8.2. Interpretability and Explainability

LLMs, while powerful, are often considered "black boxes," meaning their decision-making processes are not always transparent. In cybersecurity, where trust and accountability are crucial, this lack of explainability can undermine the effectiveness of LLMs in real-world applications. Research into explainable AI (XAI) is vital for ensuring that cybersecurity professionals can trust and act on the insights generated by LLMs. Models that provide clear, interpretable reasoning will be particularly important in critical sectors such as healthcare and finance (Ghazal et al., 2024; Hasanov et al., 2024). Advances in techniques that enhance the explainability of LLMs could enable better detection of threats and the identification of vulnerabilities (Santos et al., 2024).

8.3. Bias and Ethical Issues

Another significant challenge in the application of LLMs to cybersecurity is the risk of bias in the models. If LLMs are trained on biased datasets, they may reinforce harmful stereotypes or fail to detect novel attack vectors effectively. To mitigate these risks, research should focus on developing methods to detect and eliminate bias in cybersecurity-related models. Additionally, addressing ethical issues surrounding the use of LLMs in threat detection and incident response is essential (Kasri et al., 2025). Developing ethical guidelines for LLMs in cybersecurity will help ensure that these systems are used responsibly and fairly (Sarker, 2024).

8.4. Scalability and Efficiency

The scalability and efficiency of LLMs are other critical concerns. As the size of LLMs grows, so do their computational demands, which can become a bottleneck in real-time cybersecurity applications. For instance, models like the privacy-preserving BERT-based approach (Ferrag et al., 2024) have been designed to address this issue by reducing the computational footprint without sacrificing performance. Future research must focus on enhancing the efficiency of these models, particularly in resource-constrained environments such as IoT devices and edge computing (Diaf et al., 2024). Optimizing LLM architectures to balance performance and computational cost will be key for their broader deployment in cybersecurity.

8.5. Generalization and Adaptability

The ability of LLMs to generalize across various cybersecurity domains remains a challenge. Cyber threats are constantly evolving, and it is crucial that LLMs can adapt to new attack patterns without requiring frequent retraining. This includes the ability to detect zero-day vulnerabilities and emerging threats. Research should focus on improving the transferability of LLMs between different cybersecurity contexts, enhancing their adaptability to diverse security environments, and developing models that can detect novel threats with minimal human intervention (Motlagh et al., 2024; Jones et al., 2024).

8.6. Integration with Traditional Cybersecurity Systems

The integration of LLMs with traditional cybersecurity tools and frameworks is another area that warrants further exploration. Many organizations still rely on legacy systems and may be reluctant to adopt AI-based solutions due to compatibility issues or concerns about system disruption. Research into hybrid models that combine the strengths of both traditional and AI-based approaches could bridge this gap (Gupta et al., 2024; Hadi et al., 2023). Collaborative systems that integrate LLMs into existing security operations centers (SOCs) would allow organizations to leverage the best of both worlds.

8.7. Future Research Directions

As LLMs continue to evolve, future research should address several key areas. First, there is a need for ongoing advancements in the robustness of LLMs against adversarial attacks. Cybersecurity systems are constantly targeted by attackers, and ensuring that LLMs can withstand adversarial manipulation is critical for their success in real-world applications (Xu et al., 2024). Additionally, the development of hybrid models that combine LLMs with other machine learning techniques, such as reinforcement learning or federated learning, could enhance their ability to detect and respond to threats in a more agile and scalable manner (Zangana, 2024; Liu, 2024).

Second, the role of generative AI in cybersecurity is an area poised for growth. Models like SecureLM, a specialized language model for advanced cybersecurity, offer promising avenues for creating new defense mechanisms (Asoronye et al., 2024). Research into generative adversarial networks (GANs) and other generative models could lead to innovative approaches for anticipating and mitigating cyber threats.

Finally, as LLMs become more prevalent in cybersecurity, the regulatory landscape surrounding their use will need to evolve. Researchers must work alongside policymakers to establish guidelines that govern the ethical, secure, and legal use of LLMs in cybersecurity contexts (Gholami & Omar, 2023). Addressing these issues will be essential for fostering trust in AI-driven cybersecurity solutions and ensuring their responsible deployment.

8.8 Summary

The future of LLMs in cybersecurity is promising, but several challenges need to be addressed. From privacy concerns and ethical issues to improving model efficiency and scalability, future research will play a pivotal role in overcoming these obstacles. By focusing on these challenges and advancing LLM technologies, the cybersecurity community can better harness the power of AI to protect against the evolving threat landscape.

9. CONCLUSION

The integration of Large Language Models (LLMs) into cybersecurity represents a paradigm shift in how cyber threats are detected, mitigated, and prevented. Through their ability to understand complex patterns and contextual information, LLMs offer the potential to revolutionize the cybersecurity landscape. From automating threat detection and vulnerability management to enhancing predictive capabilities, LLMs have proven to be valuable tools in strengthening defenses against sophisticated cyberattacks (Ferrag et al., 2024; Zangana et al., 2025).

However, despite their significant promise, the application of LLMs in cybersecurity is not without its challenges. Issues such as model interpretability, privacy concerns, and the need for domain-specific adaptations require continued research and development. Moreover, there are concerns about the adversarial manipulation of LLMs, which could potentially be exploited by malicious actors. As cybersecurity is an ever-evolving field, LLMs must also evolve to address emerging threats and keep up with the rapidly changing technology landscape (Hasanov et al., 2024; Motlagh et al., 2024).

Looking ahead, future research should focus on improving the efficiency, privacy, and interpretability of LLMs for cybersecurity applications. The integration of explainable AI (XAI) techniques and privacy-preserving models will be essential to ensure the safe and ethical deployment of these technologies (Sarker, 2024; Ghazal et al., 2024). Additionally, the development of specialized models tailored to specific cybersecurity domains, such as IoT, IIoT, and critical infrastructure, will be crucial for maximizing the impact of LLMs in these areas (Diaf et al., 2024; Ferrag et al., 2024).

In conclusion, while LLMs have the potential to significantly enhance cybersecurity capabilities, their successful integration requires overcoming several technical and ethical hurdles. With continued innovation and interdisciplinary collaboration, LLMs will likely play an increasingly central role in shaping the future of cybersecurity, offering smarter, more efficient, and more adaptive defenses against the growing tide of cyber threats.

REFERENCES

Aghaei, E., Niu, X., Shadid, W., & Al-Shaer, E. (2022, October). Securebert: A domain-specific language model for cybersecurity. In *International Conference on Security and Privacy in Communication Systems* (pp. 39-56). Cham: Springer Nature Switzerland.

AlQenaei, Z. M. (2024, March). Evolution and Optimization of Language Model Architectures: From Foundations to Future Directions. In *International Conference on Computing and Machine Learning* (pp. 233-249). Singapore: Springer Nature Singapore.

Alturkistani, H., & Chuprat, S. (2024). Artificial Intelligence and Large Language Models in Advancing Cyber Threat Intelligence: A Systematic Literature Review.

Asoronye, G. O., Anthony, O. C., Ogbuikwu, R. I., Ogili, C. O., & Ali, H. U. (2024). SecLM: A Specialized Security Language Model for Advanced Cybersecurity Applications and Threat Mitigation. *EKETE-International Journal Of Advanced Research*, *2*(6), 33–42.

Bryce, C., Kalousis, A., Leroux, I., Madinier, H., Mermoud, A., Mulder, V., ... & Ruch, P. Trends in Large Language Models: Actors, Applications, and Impact on Cybersecurity.

Chen, Y., Cui, M., Wang, D., Cao, Y., Yang, P., Jiang, B., Lu, Z., & Liu, B. (2024). A survey of large language models for cyber threat detection. *Computers & Security*, *145*, 104016. DOI: 10.1016/j.cose.2024.104016

Diaf, A., Korba, A. A., Karabadji, N. E., & Ghamri-Doudane, Y. (2024, April). Beyond detection: Leveraging large language models for cyber attack prediction in iot networks. In *2024 20th International Conference on Distributed Computing in Smart Systems and the Internet of Things (DCOSS-IoT)* (pp. 117-123). IEEE.

Ferrag, M. A., Alwahedi, F., Battah, A., Cherif, B., Mechri, A., & Tihanyi, N. (2024). Generative ai and large language models for cyber security: All insights you need. *Available atSSRN* 4853709. DOI: 10.2139/ssrn.4853709

Ferrag, M. A., Ndhlovu, M., Tihanyi, N., Cordeiro, L. C., Debbah, M., & Lestable, T. (2023). Revolutionizing cyber threat detection with large language models. *arXiv preprint arXiv:2306.14263*, 195-202.

Ferrag, M. A., Ndhlovu, M., Tihanyi, N., Cordeiro, L. C., Debbah, M., Lestable, T., & Thandi, N. S. (2024). Revolutionizing cyber threat detection with large language models: A privacy-preserving bert-based lightweight model for iot/iiot devices. *IEEE Access : Practical Innovations, Open Solutions*, *12*, 23733–23750. DOI: 10.1109/ACCESS.2024.3363469

Ferrag, M. A., Ndhlovu, M., Tihanyi, N., Cordeiro, L. C., Debbah, M., Lestable, T., & Thandi, N. S. (2024). Revolutionizing cyber threat detection with large language models: A privacy-preserving bert-based lightweight model for iot/iiot devices. *IEEE Access : Practical Innovations, Open Solutions*, *12*, 23733–23750.

Ghazal, T. M., Janjua, J. I., Abushiba, W., Ahmad, M., Ihsan, A., & Al-Dmour, N. A. (2024, December). Cybersecurity Revolution via Large Language Models and Explainable AI. In *2024 17th International Conference on Security of Information and Networks (SIN)* (pp. 1-6). IEEE. DOI: 10.1109/SIN63213.2024.10871324

Gholami, S., & Omar, M. (2023). Does Synthetic Data Make Large Language Models More Efficient? *arXiv preprint arXiv:2310.07830.*

Gholami, S., & Omar, M. (2024). Can a student large language model perform as well as its teacher? In *Innovations, Securities, and Case Studies Across Healthcare, Business, and Technology* (pp. 122-139). IGI Global. DOI: 10.4018/979-8-3693-1906-2.ch007

Gupta, B. B., Gaurav, A., & Arya, V. (2024). Navigating the security landscape of large language models in enterprise information systems. *Enterprise Information Systems*, *18*(4), 2310846. DOI: 10.1080/17517575.2024.2310846

Hadi, M. A., Abdulredha, M. N., & Hasan, E. (2023). Introduction to ChatGPT: A new revolution of artificial intelligence with machine learning algorithms and cybersecurity. *Sci. Arch*, *4*(04), 276. DOI: 10.47587/SA.2023.4406

Hamza, Y. A., & Omar, M. D. (2013). Cloud computing security: Abuse and nefarious use of cloud computing. *International Journal of Computer Engineering Research*, *3*(6), 22–27.

Hasanov, I., Virtanen, S., Hakkala, A., & Isoaho, J. (2024). Application of Large Language Models in Cybersecurity: A Systematic Literature Review. *IEEE Access : Practical Innovations, Open Solutions*, *12*, 176751–176778. DOI: 10.1109/ACCESS.2024.3505983

Hassanin, M., & Moustafa, N. (2024). A comprehensive overview of large language models (llms) for cyber defences: Opportunities and directions. *arXiv preprint arXiv:2405.14487.*

Huff, A. J., Burrell, D. N., Nobles, C., Richardson, K., Wright, J. B., Burton, S. L., Jones, A. J., Springs, D., Omar, M., & Brown-Jackson, K. L. (2023). Management Practices for Mitigating Cybersecurity Threats to Biotechnology Companies, Laboratories, and Healthcare Research Organizations. In *Applied Research Approaches to Technology, Healthcare, and Business* (pp. 1-12). IGI Global.

Idelhaj, A., Abou El Houda, Z., & Khoukhi, L. (2024). Foundations models in cybersecurity. *Artificial Intelligence for Blockchain and Cybersecurity Powered IoT Applications*, 1.

Idelhaj, A., Abou El Houda, Z., & Khoukhi, L. Foundations models in cybersecurity: A comprehensive review and future direction. *Artificial Intelligence for Blockchain and Cybersecurity Powered IoT Applications*, 1-18.

Jones, R., & Omar, M. (2024). Revolutionizing Cybersecurity: The GPT-2 Enhanced Attack Detection and Defense (GEADD) Method for Zero-Day Threats. *International Journal of Informatics* [INJIISCOM]. *Information System and Computer Engineering*, *5*(2), 178–191.

Jones, R., Omar, M., Mohammed, D., Nobles, C., & Dawson, M. (2023). Harnessing the Speed and Accuracy of Machine Learning to Advance Cybersecurity. In *2023 Congress in Computer Science, Computer Engineering, & Applied Computing (CSCE)* (pp. 418-421). IEEE. DOI: 10.1109/CSCE60160.2023.00074

Kasri, W., Himeur, Y., Alkhazaleh, H. A., Tarapiah, S., Atalla, S., Mansoor, W., & Al-Ahmad, H. (2025). From Vulnerability to Defense: The Role of Large Language Models in Enhancing Cybersecurity. *Computation (Basel, Switzerland)*, *13*(2), 30. DOI: 10.3390/computation13020030

Liu, Z. (2024, April). A review of advancements and applications of pre-trained language models in cybersecurity. In *2024 12th International Symposium on Digital Forensics and Security (ISDFS)* (pp. 1-10). IEEE. DOI: 10.1109/ISDFS60797.2024.10527236

Manoharan, A., & Sarker, M. (2023). Revolutionizing Cybersecurity: Unleashing the Power of Artificial Intelligence and Machine Learning for Next-Generation Threat Detection. *DOI:*https://www. doi. org/10.56726/IRJMETS32644, *1*.

Mohammed, D., Omar, M., & Nguyen, V. (2018). Wireless sensor network security: Approaches to detecting and avoiding wormhole attacks. *Journal of Research in Business. Economics and Management*, *10*(2), 1860–1864.

Motlagh, F. N., Hajizadeh, M., Majd, M., Najafi, P., Cheng, F., & Meinel, C. (2024). Large language models in cybersecurity: State-of-the-art. *arXiv preprint arXiv:2402.00891.*

Nguyen, V., Mohammed, D., Omar, M., & Banisakher, M. (2018). The Effects of the FCC Net Neutrality Repeal on Security and Privacy. [IJHIoT]. *International Journal of Hyperconnectivity and the Internet of Things*, *2*(2), 21–29. DOI: 10.4018/IJHIoT.2018070102

Omar, M. (2021). New insights into database security: An effective and integrated approach for applying access control mechanisms and cryptographic concepts in Microsoft Access environments.

Omar, M. (2022). *Machine Learning for Cybersecurity: Innovative Deep Learning Solutions*. Springer Brief. https://link.springer.com/book/978303115

Omar, M. (2024). From Attack to Defense: Strengthening DNN Text Classification Against Adversarial Examples. In *Innovations, Securities, and Case Studies Across Healthcare, Business, and Technology* (pp. 174-195). IGI Global.

Omar, M. (2024). Revolutionizing Malware Detection: A Paradigm Shift Through Optimized Convolutional Neural Networks. In *Innovations, Securities, and Case Studies Across Healthcare, Business, and Technology* (pp. 196-220). IGI Global. DOI: 10.4018/979-8-3693-1906-2.ch011

Omar, M., & Zangana, H. (Eds.). (2025). *Digital Forensics in the Age of AI*. IGI Global., DOI: 10.4018/979-8-3373-0857-9

Omar, M., & Zangana, H. M. (Eds.). (2024). *Redefining Security With Cyber AI*. IGI Global., DOI: 10.4018/979-8-3693-6517-5

Omar, M., & Zangana, H. M. (Eds.). (2025). *Application of Large Language Models (LLMs) for Software Vulnerability Detection*. IGI Global., DOI: 10.4018/979-8-3693-9311-6

Omar, M., Zangana, H. M., Al-Karaki, J. N., & Mohammed, D. (2024). Harnessing LLMs for IoT malware detection: A comparative analysis of BERT and GPT-2. In *2024 8th International Symposium on Multidisciplinary Studies and Innovative Technologies (ISMSIT)* (pp. 1-6). Ankara, Turkiye. https://doi.org/DOI: 10.1109/ISMSIT63511.2024.10757249

Omar, M., Zangana, H. M., & Mohammed, D. (Eds.). (2025). *Integrating Artificial Intelligence in Cybersecurity and Forensic Practices*. IGI Global., DOI: 10.4018/979-8-3373-0588-2

Ozkan-Okay, M., Akin, E., Aslan, Ö., Kosunalp, S., Iliev, T., Stoyanov, I., & Beloev, I. (2024). A comprehensive survey: Evaluating the efficiency of artificial intelligence and machine learning techniques on cyber security solutions. *IEEE Access : Practical Innovations, Open Solutions, 12*, 12229–12256. DOI: 10.1109/ACCESS.2024.3355547

Pleshakova, E., Osipov, A., Gataullin, S., Gataullin, T., & Vasilakos, A. (2024). Next gen cybersecurity paradigm towards artificial general intelligence: Russian market challenges and future global technological trends. *Journal of Computer Virology and Hacking Techniques, 20*(3), 429–440. DOI: 10.1007/s11416-024-00529-x

Santos, O., Salam, S., & Dahir, H. (2024). The AI revolution in networking, cybersecurity, and emerging technologies.

Sarker, I. H. (2024). Generative AI and large language modeling in cybersecurity. In *AI-Driven Cybersecurity and Threat Intelligence: Cyber Automation, Intelligent Decision-Making and Explainability* (pp. 79–99). Springer Nature Switzerland. DOI: 10.1007/978-3-031-54497-2_5

Taghavi, S. M., & Feyzi, F. (2024). Using large language models to better detect and handle software vulnerabilities and cyber security threats.

Wright, J., Dawson, M. E.Jr, & Omar, M. (2012). Cyber security and mobile threats: The need for antivirus applications for smartphones. *Journal of Information Systems Technology and Planning, 5*(14), 40–60.

Xu, H., Wang, S., Li, N., Wang, K., Zhao, Y., Chen, K., . . . Wang, H. (2024). Large language models for cyber security: A systematic literature review. *arXiv preprint arXiv:2405.04760*.

Yu, J., Shvetsov, A. V., & Alsamhi, S. H. (2024). Leveraging machine learning for cybersecurity resilience in industry 4.0: Challenges and future directions. *IEEE Access : Practical Innovations, Open Solutions, 12*, 159579–159596. DOI: 10.1109/ACCESS.2024.3482987

Zangana, H., & Omar, M. (Eds.). (2025). *Leveraging Large Language Models for Quantum-Aware Cybersecurity*. IGI Global., DOI: 10.4018/979-8-3373-1102-9

Zangana, H. M. (2024). Exploring Blockchain-Based Timestamping Tools: A Comprehensive Review. *Redefining Security With Cyber AI*, 92-110.

Zangana, H. M. (2024). Exploring the Landscape of Website Vulnerability Scanners: A Comprehensive Review and Comparative Analysis. *Redefining Security With Cyber AI*, 111-129.

Zangana, H. M. (2024). Harnessing the Power of Large Language Models. *Application of Large Language Models (LLMs) for Software Vulnerability Detection*, 1.

Zangana, H. M., & Li, S. (2025). Future Trends in AI and Digital Forensics. In Omar, M., & Zangana, H. (Eds.), *Digital Forensics in the Age of AI* (pp. 347–380). IGI Global Scientific Publishing., DOI: 10.4018/979-8-3373-0857-9.ch013

Zangana, H. M., Mohammed, A. K., Sallow, A. B., & Sallow, Z. B. (2024). Cybernetic Deception: Unraveling the Layers of Email Phishing Threats. [INJURATECH]. *International Journal of Research and Applied Technology*, *4*(1), 35–47.

Zangana, H. M., & Mohammed, D. (2025). Foundations of Large Language Models in Software Vulnerability Detection. In Omar, M., & Zangana, H. (Eds.), *Application of Large Language Models (LLMs) for Software Vulnerability Detection* (pp. 41–74). IGI Global., DOI: 10.4018/979-8-3693-9311-6.ch002

Zangana, H. M., & Mustafa, F. M. (2024). Hybrid Image Denoising Using Wavelet Transform and Deep Learning. *EAI Endorsed Transactions on AI and Robotics, 3*. Advance online publication. DOI: 10.4108/airo.7486

Zangana, H. M., & Mustafa, F. M. (2025). Image Denoising Techniques for Cybersecurity and Forensic Applications: AI-Driven Approaches. In Omar, M., Zangana, H., & Mohammed, D. (Eds.), *Integrating Artificial Intelligence in Cybersecurity and Forensic Practices* (pp. 117–142). IGI Global Scientific Publishing., DOI: 10.4018/979-8-3373-0588-2.ch005

Zangana, H. M., Mustafa, F. M., & Li, S. (2025). Large Language Models in Cybersecurity: From Automation to Intelligence. In *Leveraging Large Language Models for Quantum-Aware Cybersecurity* (pp. 277-300). IGI Global Scientific Publishing.

Zangana, H. M., Mustafa, F. M., & Li, S. (2025). Large Language Models in Cybersecurity: From Automation to Intelligence. In Zangana, H., & Omar, M. (Eds.), *Leveraging Large Language Models for Quantum-Aware Cybersecurity* (pp. 277–300). IGI Global Scientific Publishing., DOI: 10.4018/979-8-3373-1102-9.ch009

Zangana, H. M., Mustafa, F. M., Li, S., & Al-Karaki, J. N. (2025). Natural Language Processing for Cyber Threat Intelligence in a Quantum World. In Zangana, H., & Omar, M. (Eds.), *Leveraging Large Language Models for Quantum-Aware Cybersecurity* (pp. 345–388). IGI Global Scientific Publishing., DOI: 10.4018/979-8-3373-1102-9.ch011

Zangana, H. M., Mustafa, F. M., & Omar, M. (2024). A Hybrid Approach for Robust Object Detection: Integrating Template Matching and Faster R-CNN. *EAI Endorsed Transactions on AI and Robotics*, *3*. Advance online publication. DOI: 10.4108/airo.6858

Zangana, H. M., & Omar, M. (2020). Threats, Attacks, and Mitigations of Smartphone Security. *Academic Journal of Nawroz University*, *9*(4), 324–332. DOI: 10.25007/ajnu.v9n4a989

Zangana, H. M., & Omar, M. (2025). Harnessing the Power of Large Language Models for Cybersecurity: Applications, Challenges, and Future Directions. In Omar, M., & Zangana, H. (Eds.), *Application of Large Language Models (LLMs) for Software Vulnerability Detection* (pp. 1–40). IGI Global., DOI: 10.4018/979-8-3693-9311-6.ch001

Zangana, H. M., & Omar, M. (2025). Introduction to Digital Forensics and Artificial Intelligence. In Omar, M., & Zangana, H. (Eds.), *Digital Forensics in the Age of AI* (pp. 1–30). IGI Global Scientific Publishing., DOI: 10.4018/979-8-3373-0857-9.ch001

Zangana, H. M., & Omar, M. (2025). Introduction to Quantum-Aware Cybersecurity: The Need for LLMs. In Zangana, H., & Omar, M. (Eds.), *Leveraging Large Language Models for Quantum-Aware Cybersecurity* (pp. 1–28). IGI Global Scientific Publishing., DOI: 10.4018/979-8-3373-1102-9.ch001

Zangana, H. M., & Omar, M. (2025). The Role of Leadership in Advancing Inclusive Health Technologies. In Burrell, D., & Nguyen, C. (Eds.), *New Horizons in Leadership: Inclusive Explorations in Health, Technology, and Education* (pp. 203–220). IGI Global Scientific Publishing., DOI: 10.4018/979-8-3693-6437-6.ch009

Zangana, H. M., Omar, M., Al-Karaki, J. N., & Mohammed, D. (2024). Comprehensive Review and Analysis of Network Firewall Rule Analyzers: Enhancing Security Posture and Efficiency. *Redefining Security With Cyber AI*, 15-36.

Zangana, H. M., Sallow, Z. B., & Omar, M. (2025). The Human Factor in Cybersecurity: Addressing the Risks of Insider Threats. *Jurnal Ilmiah Computer Science*, *3*(2), 76–85. DOI: 10.58602/jics.v3i2.37

Chapter 4
LLM-Powered Security Solutions in Healthcare, Government, and Industrial Cybersecurity

S. Karkuzhali
https://orcid.org/0000-0002-1907-008X
Mepco Schlenk Engineering College, India

S. Senthilkumar
https://orcid.org/0000-0002-0294-6671
Ayya Nadar Janaki Ammal College, India

ABSTRACT

Large Language Models (LLMs) are revolutionizing cybersecurity in healthcare, government, and industrial sectors by enabling real-time threat detection, anomaly identification, and compliance automation. This chapter explores the transformative role of LLMs in mitigating cyber risks while addressing challenges such as adversarial attacks, data privacy, and bias. It examines real-world applications, highlighting their effectiveness in securing critical infrastructures. Additionally, ethical, legal, and regulatory considerations are discussed to ensure responsible AI deployment. The chapter provides strategic recommendations for integrating LLM-powered security solutions while mitigating risks, enhancing resilience, and improving automated incident response. By leveraging LLMs effectively, organizations can strengthen cybersecurity frameworks and safeguard sensitive data against evolving threats in an increasingly digital landscape.

DOI: 10.4018/979-8-3373-3296-3.ch004

1. INTRODUCTION

The rapid advancements in Large Language Models (LLMs) have led to their increasing integration into various domains, including healthcare, government, and industrial cybersecurity. These sectors demand high levels of security, data integrity, and regulatory compliance due to the sensitivity of the information they handle. LLMs offer transformative capabilities in threat detection, automated security analysis, and real-time risk mitigation. However, their adoption also introduces unique challenges, such as adversarial attacks, bias, privacy concerns, and ethical dilemmas. Adversarial attacks are techniques used to manipulate machine learning models by introducing carefully crafted inputs designed to deceive the model into making incorrect predictions. For instance, an attacker might slightly alter a malware sample to evade detection by an LLM-powered cybersecurity system.

The cybersecurity landscape is constantly evolving, with cyber threats becoming more sophisticated and targeted. Traditional security mechanisms, while still effective, often struggle to keep pace with the ever-changing tactics of cybercriminals. The integration of LLMs into security frameworks presents a paradigm shift in the way organizations approach cybersecurity. By leveraging the natural language processing capabilities of these models, security teams can automate threat analysis, predict potential vulnerabilities, and respond to cyber incidents more efficiently.

One of the most significant advantages of LLMs in cybersecurity is their ability to analyze vast amounts of data in real-time. These models can process structured and unstructured data, identify anomalies, and flag potential security breaches before they escalate. By automating the detection of threats, LLMs enhance the speed and accuracy of cybersecurity measures, reducing the burden on human analysts.

In healthcare, government, and industrial settings, security breaches can have severe consequences. In healthcare, unauthorized access to patient records can lead to identity theft, medical fraud, and compromised patient safety. In government institutions, cyber threats can jeopardize national security, disrupt essential services, and undermine public trust. Similarly, in industrial environments, cyber-attacks on critical infrastructure can result in financial losses, operational disruptions, and even endanger lives.

Traditional security systems rely heavily on rule-based approaches, which require constant updates to keep up with emerging threats. LLMs, on the other hand, can analyze historical attack patterns, detect anomalies, and predict potential threats based on behavioral analysis. This proactive approach allows organizations to stay ahead of cybercriminals and mitigate risks before they materialize. By integrating LLMs with existing cybersecurity frameworks, organizations can improve their threat intelligence capabilities. These models can sift through security logs, analyze network traffic, and identify potential indicators of compromise (IoCs). IoCs are forensic artifacts or evidence that indicate a potential security breach or cyberattack. These include malicious IP addresses, suspicious domain names, unusual login patterns, or file hashes associated with known malware. Security analysts use IoCs to detect, investigate, and respond to cyber threats. Furthermore, LLMs can assist security analysts by providing contextual insights into attack methods, enabling them to make informed decisions and respond more effectively to incidents.

Regulatory compliance is a critical concern for organizations operating in sensitive domains. Healthcare institutions must adhere to regulations such as the Health Insurance Portability and Accountability Act (HIPAA), while government agencies must comply with the Federal Information Security Management Act (FISMA). Industrial sectors also have stringent compliance requirements, including the NIST Cybersecurity Framework and ISO 27001.LLMs can streamline compliance efforts by automating security audits, generating compliance reports, and ensuring that organizations adhere to regulatory standards. These models can analyze policy documents, identify gaps in security practices, and suggest remediation measures. Additionally, LLMs can assist in the development of security policies by generating guidelines that align with industry best practices.

This chapter will explore how LLMs are revolutionizing cybersecurity practices in critical infrastructures, addressing potential threats, and ensuring compliance with regulatory frameworks. It will provide an in-depth analysis of how AI-driven security mechanisms enhance resilience while identifying vulnerabilities that organizations must mitigate. By leveraging the power of LLMs responsibly, organizations can strengthen their cybersecurity posture and safeguard sensitive data in an increasingly digital world.

2. MISSION AND OBJECTIVES

The mission of this chapter is to critically examine and assess the transformative role of Large Language Models (LLMs) in modern cybersecurity applications across three key domains: healthcare, government, and industrial security. As AI-driven technologies continue to reshape the cybersecurity landscape, understanding the benefits, risks, and strategic implementations of LLMs is crucial for organizations operating in these highly sensitive and regulated sectors.

This chapter aims to:

- **Analyze the impact of LLMs on cybersecurity defenses** by exploring their role in detecting, preventing, and responding to cyber threats in healthcare systems, government infrastructures, and industrial control systems (ICS).

- **Identify the security threats and vulnerabilities** associated with LLM integration, including adversarial attacks, model poisoning, data leakage, and potential misuse by malicious actors.
- **Explore real-world applications and case studies** that demonstrate the practical effectiveness of LLM-powered security tools in real-time threat monitoring, incident response automation, and compliance management.
- **Assess ethical, legal, and compliance considerations** involved in deploying LLMs within regulated environments.
- **Provide actionable recommendations** for organizations aiming to adopt LLMs while mitigating cybersecurity risks effectively.

Table 1. Overview of LLM-driven cybersecurity applications and considerations

Section	Key Points
Mission of the Chapter	Examines LLMs in cybersecurity across healthcare, government, and industry, assessing threats, applications, and best practices.
Role of LLMs in Cybersecurity	LLMs enhance threat detection, incident response, adaptive learning, and compliance monitoring.
Cybersecurity in Healthcare	Healthcare is vulnerable to cyberattacks; LLMs detect insider threats, secure medical data, and ensure compliance.
Risks in Healthcare Security	Challenges include data poisoning, adversarial attacks, and bias; mitigation includes secure AI training and audits.
LLM-Driven Cybersecurity in Government	LLMs support threat intelligence, policy automation, and fraud detection in national security.
Importance of AI in Government Security	AI detects cyber threats, automates security policies, and prevents fraud in public services.
Key Security Concerns in Government	Risks include AI-driven disinformation, privacy concerns, and regulatory compliance challenges.
Industrial Cybersecurity and LLM Integration	LLMs secure industrial environments through anomaly detection, network monitoring, and IIoT protection.
Challenges in Industrial Control Systems (ICS)	Security risks involve SCADA vulnerabilities, supply chain attacks, and outdated infrastructure.
Key Cybersecurity Risks in Industry	SCADA weaknesses, supply chain risks, and legacy systems create cybersecurity challenges.
Ethical, Legal, and Compliance Considerations	AI must comply with GDPR, HIPAA, and NIST standards while ensuring transparency and fairness.
Privacy and Data Protection	Secure AI techniques help protect sensitive data while complying with privacy laws.
Bias and Transparency in AI	Explainable AI (XAI) and fairness audits help prevent biased security decisions.

continued on following page

Table 1. Continued

Section	Key Points
AI Governance and Accountability	Organizations must establish AI accountability, enforce oversight, and develop cybersecurity policies.
Future Directions in AI Security	Advancements include federated learning, quantum-secure AI, and blockchain-based cybersecurity.

3. LITERATURE REVIEW

Arshad et al. (2025) examined the challenges in Autonomous Vehicles and Intelligent Transportation Systems (ITS), highlighting issues such as data security, scalability, node reliability, and secure communication. Existing studies integrated Artificial Intelligence (AI), Machine Learning (ML), and blockchain to enhance robustness, but problems like latency, privacy risks, and node selfishness remained.

Hu et al. (2024) investigated the challenges associated with open-source threat intelligence, emphasizing its unstructured nature, which limits direct applicability in detection and defense mechanisms. To address this, researchers explored the construction of knowledge graphs for better intrusion detection.

Chen et al. (2024) analyzed the growing challenges in cyber threat detection, driven by the increasing complexity of cyber threats and the expanding cyberspace. Previous threat detection models were found to be insufficient against evolving hacker attacks. However, recent studies indicated that Large Language Models (LLMs) could address many of these challenges either directly or indirectly.

Wang et al. (2025) examined the integration of Large Language Models (LLMs) into cybersecurity operations, focusing on vulnerability remediation. They conducted a three-step study, first identifying user satisfaction issues in existing processes.

Yao et al. (2024) explored the impact of Large Language Models (LLMs) like ChatGPT and Bard on security and privacy. While LLMs enhance tasks such as code vulnerability detection and data confidentiality protection, they also introduce risks, including user-level attacks due to their human-like reasoning.

Mishra et al. (2025) highlighted the growing importance of Threat Intelligence in combating evolving cyber threats. Security knowledge graphs play a crucial role in representing complex entities and their relationships, while embedding techniques like TransE help in downstream tasks such as cyber threat prediction.

Patsakis et al. (2024) explored the integration of Large Language Models (LLMs) into cybersecurity, particularly for automating tasks like anomaly detection, attack mitigation, and malware deobfuscation.

Shafee et al. (2024) examined the role of Large Language Models (LLMs) in Cyber Threat Intelligence (CTI), focusing on their ability to process Open-Source Intelligence (OSINT) for threat detection.

Tang et al. (2024) introduced AIIOC, a model designed for extracting Indicators of Compromise (IOC) from security-related social data. Existing methods struggle with fine-grained IOC feature learning, leading to high false positives, and lack interpretability due to the absence of symbolic rules and contextual knowledge.

Rashid et al. (2025) explore the use of Large Language Models (LLMs) for malicious URL classification, addressing challenges like generalization and domain adaptation in traditional models. They propose an LLM-based one-shot learning framework that leverages reasoning capabilities, inspired by Chain-of-Thought techniques, to classify URLs as benign or phishing.

Loevenich et al. (2025) present an Autonomous Cyber Defence (ACD) agent designed for monitoring and responding to threats in critical network segments connected to untrusted infrastructure. The agent integrates deep reinforcement learning (DRL), augmented Large Language Models (LLMs), and rule-based systems within software-defined network controllers to automate defensive actions like monitoring, decoy deployment, and system recovery.

Hassanin et al. (2025) highlight the security challenges in satellite networks, which lack effective intrusion detection due to limited research and high deployment costs. To address this, they propose PLLM-CS, a pre-trained Large Language Model for Cyber Security, designed to transform network data into contextually rich inputs.

Haurogné et al. (2024) emphasize the importance of detecting vulnerabilities in source code, as new threats emerge daily. AI-based solutions, particularly Large Language Models (LLMs), enhance vulnerability detection but struggle with explainability and handling large datasets.

Ferrag et al. (2025) provide a comprehensive review of the role of Generative AI and Large Language Models (LLMs) in cybersecurity. They explore LLM applications in intrusion detection, malware detection, cyber threat intelligence, and phishing prevention while analyzing the evolution of models like GPT-4, BERT, and LLaMA.

Sufi et al. (2024) highlight the impact of Generative Pre-Trained (GPT) and Large Language Models (LLMs) in cybersecurity. The study proposes an AI-driven framework for extracting multidimensional cyber threat-related features from textual descriptions of cyber events using GPT. These extracted features serve as inputs for AI and deep learning models like CNN and NLP-based techniques, enabling cyber analysts to query historical incidents in plain English. Empirical validation on 214 major cyber incidents (2016–2023) produced 1,498 informative outputs with high accuracy (Precision: 96%, Recall: 98%, F1-Score: 97%), demonstrating the effectiveness of the approach .

Derner et al. (2024) examine security risks associated with Large Language Models (LLMs), emphasizing threats beyond ethical concerns, such as disinformation, data breaches, and reputation damage. The study introduces a taxonomy of security risks within prompt-based interactions, categorizing attacks based on targets, attack types, and the CIA (Confidentiality, Integrity, Availability) triad. By providing real-world attack examples, the research highlights potential vulnerabilities and aims to guide the development of more secure and trustworthy LLM applications.

Black et al. (2024) analyze the security challenges in LLM-generated code, emphasizing how simple prompts can lead to vulnerable outputs. The study evaluates different prompt strategies, testing multiple commercial LLMs to identify common weaknesses in generated code.

Black et al. (2024) present a framework for leveraging LLMs to automate seed input generation for fuzzing, particularly in Python environments where traditional methods struggle. Using the Atheris fuzzing framework, they generated over 38,000 seed inputs targeting 50 Python functions from widely used libraries.

Selim et al. (2024) present a proof-of-concept validation of using Large Language Models (LLMs) for detecting cyberattacks on smart inverters through textual control commands.

Zhang et al. (2024) explore privacy risks in tool-using Large Language Model (LLM) agents, where user data is transmitted to both LLMs and external tools. They identify key challenges in ensuring privacy across open-source and closed-source systems while maintaining compliance and applicability.

4. THE ROLE OF LLMS IN CYBERSECURITY

Large Language Models (LLMs) have revolutionized cybersecurity by introducing advanced techniques that strengthen defense mechanisms across multiple domains. Their ability to process and analyze massive amounts of data in real time has made them invaluable for detecting threats, responding to incidents, and ensuring regulatory compliance. Figure 1 shows the Flow Diagram Representing LLM-Driven Cybersecurity Across Healthcare, Government, and Industrial Sectors. The following are key areas where LLMs contribute significantly to cybersecurity:

Figure 1. Flow diagram representing LLM-driven cybersecurity across healthcare, government, and industrial sectors

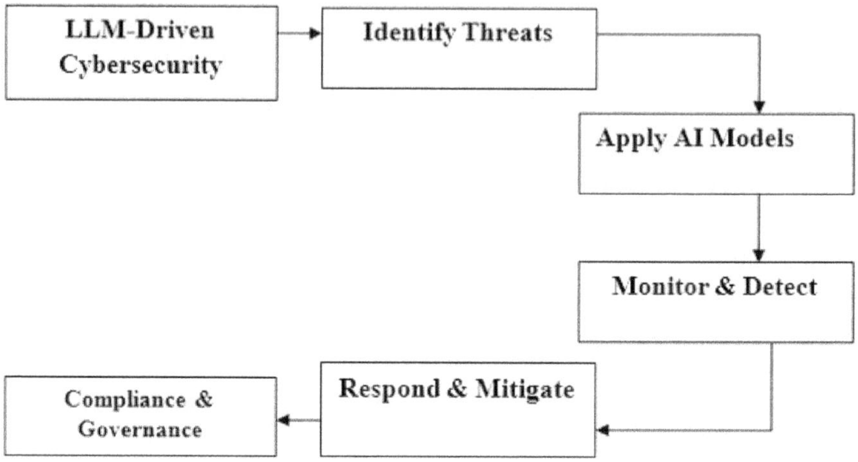

4.1. Automated Threat Detection

LLMs enhance cybersecurity by rapidly analyzing vast datasets to detect malicious activities, zero-day exploits, and emerging cyber threats. By leveraging Natural Language Processing (NLP), these models can:

- Identify abnormal patterns in network traffic, emails, and system logs to detect potential cyberattacks.
- Recognize phishing attempts, ransomware, and advanced persistent threats (APTs) by analyzing text-based communications and code patterns.
- Process threat intelligence feeds from multiple sources to detect real-time cybersecurity threats before they escalate.

4.2. Incident Response and Forensic Analysis

AI-driven models assist security analysts in automating incident response and forensic investigations. LLMs support cybersecurity teams by:

- Generating detailed reports on security breaches, analyzing affected systems, and suggesting remediation steps.
- Assisting in malware reverse engineering by analyzing code structures and identifying vulnerabilities.

- Providing real-time security recommendations and step-by-step guidance to mitigate ongoing attacks.

4.3. Adaptive Security Learning

Unlike traditional rule-based security systems, LLMs continuously evolve and learn from new attack patterns, improving their predictive capabilities. This adaptive learning enables:

- The identification of novel attack techniques by analyzing historical cybersecurity incidents.
- Real-time adjustments to security protocols to counter evolving threats.
- Enhanced predictive analytics that enables organizations to proactively defend against potential cyber risks.

4.4. Enhanced Compliance Monitoring

Ensuring compliance with industry-specific regulations is a critical challenge for organizations. LLMs play a key role in automating compliance monitoring by:

- Identifying and flagging non-compliant practices in security policies, ensuring adherence to frameworks like **HIPAA (Healthcare), GDPR (Government), and NIST (Industrial).**
- Analyzing audit logs and security documentation to detect violations and potential data privacy risks.
- Assisting in policy generation and documentation, ensuring cybersecurity policies align with regulatory requirements.

Figure 2 represents the central node represents the core LLM technology, with primary branches illustrating key detection techniques, including static analysis, dynamic behavior analysis, threat intelligence integration, and anomaly-based detection. Secondary branches further break down specific approaches under each technique, highlighting their roles in identifying and mitigating malware threats.

Figure 2. Central node represents the core LLM technology

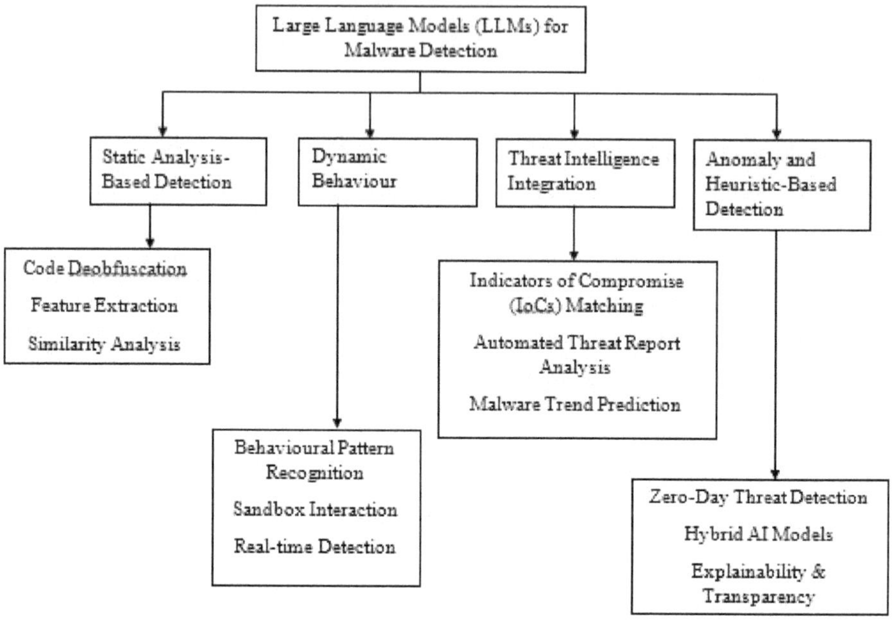

5. LLM-POWERED SECURITY IN HEALTHCARE

5.1. The Need for Cybersecurity in Healthcare

The healthcare industry handles vast amounts of sensitive patient data, including electronic health records (EHRs), medical imaging, prescriptions, and insurance details. This makes it a prime target for cybercriminals seeking financial gain, identity theft, or even geopolitical disruption. The increasing digitization of healthcare, the widespread use of Internet of Medical Things (IoMT) devices, and the integration of cloud-based systems have further expanded the attack surface, making cybersecurity a critical necessity. Figure 3 indicates the Understanding Web-Based LLM Attacks

Figure 3. Understanding web-based LLM attacks

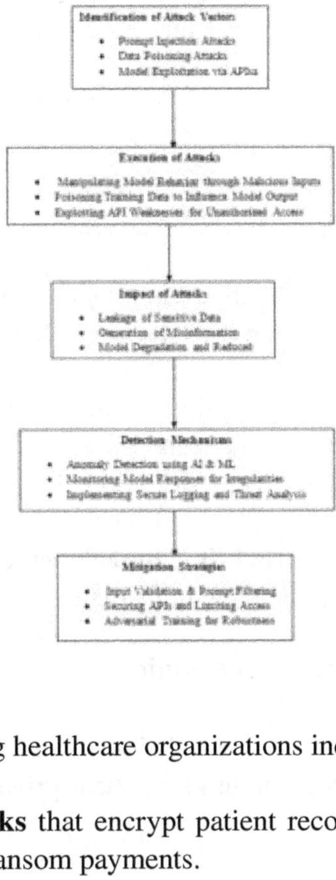

Cyber threats targeting healthcare organizations include:

- **Ransomware attacks** that encrypt patient records, disrupt hospital operations, and demand ransom payments.
- **Medical data breaches** that expose confidential patient information, leading to identity fraud and legal liabilities.
- **IoT and IoMT vulnerabilities** that allow cybercriminals to exploit connected medical devices, posing risks to patient safety.

To combat these threats, Large Language Models (LLMs) provide advanced AI-driven solutions that strengthen cybersecurity in healthcare.

5.1.1. Detecting Insider Threats and Anomalies

One of the biggest cybersecurity challenges in healthcare is insider threats, where employees or third-party vendors with access to critical systems misuse their privileges. LLMs can:

- Analyze user behavior and flag suspicious activities, such as unauthorized access to patient records outside standard working hours.
- Detect anomalies in data access patterns, identifying potential breaches before they escalate.
- Improve identity and access management (IAM) systems by enhancing authentication mechanisms and preventing unauthorized logins.

5.1.2. Preventing Medical Data Breaches

Medical data breaches can result in severe financial and reputational damage for healthcare institutions. LLMs enhance data security by:

- Implementing **AI-driven encryption techniques** to protect sensitive patient information during storage and transmission.
- Strengthening **multi-factor authentication (MFA)** and biometric verification processes to prevent unauthorized access.
- Assisting security teams in **real-time breach detection**, identifying compromised records, and recommending immediate countermeasures.

5.1.3. AI-Powered Compliance Auditing

Compliance with data protection regulations is crucial for healthcare organizations to avoid legal penalties and ensure patient privacy. LLMs help automate compliance management by:

- Conducting **real-time audits** of security policies, ensuring alignment with industry standards such as **HIPAA (U.S.), GDPR (Europe), and HITRUST (global healthcare compliance framework).**
- Monitoring access logs and generating reports to **identify compliance violations** before regulatory audits.
- Assisting healthcare providers in drafting **policy recommendations and risk assessments** to maintain data integrity.

5.2. Risks and Challenges of Using LLMs in Healthcare Security

While Large Language Models (LLMs) offer significant advantages in enhancing cybersecurity for healthcare, their adoption also introduces new risks and challenges. Cybercriminals continuously develop sophisticated attack techniques to exploit AI systems, which can compromise data security, integrity, and trust in healthcare institutions. Additionally, ethical and regulatory concerns must be addressed to ensure that AI-driven security measures remain fair, unbiased, and aligned with legal requirements.

The key risks and challenges associated with LLMs in healthcare cybersecurity include:

5.2.1. Data Poisoning Attacks

LLMs rely on large datasets for training, making them vulnerable to **data poisoning attacks**, where malicious actors intentionally manipulate training data to deceive AI models. These attacks can:

- Inject false or misleading data into training sets, causing AI models to misclassify threats or ignore genuine security risks.
- Corrupt medical cybersecurity systems by altering patient records or security logs, leading to incorrect threat assessments.
- Reduce the reliability of AI-powered threat detection, allowing attackers to bypass security mechanisms undetected.

Mitigation Strategies:

- Implement **strict data validation** and filtering techniques to ensure the integrity of training datasets.
- Use **federated learning** to reduce dependence on centralized datasets, minimizing exposure to poisoning risks.
- Regularly retrain LLMs with verified and monitored data sources.

5.2.2. Adversarial Attacks on AI Systems

Cybercriminals can manipulate AI-generated outputs through **adversarial attacks**, where they introduce subtle modifications to input data, causing LLMs to misinterpret or overlook threats. These attacks can:

- Trick AI-driven security tools into generating **misleading alerts**, causing confusion in incident response.
- Evade detection by manipulating malware signatures, making threats appear as benign activities.
- Exploit weaknesses in natural language processing (NLP) models to **generate deceptive phishing emails** or impersonate legitimate healthcare communications.

Mitigation Strategies:

- Develop **robust adversarial defense mechanisms**, including AI models trained on adversarial examples.
- Implement **human-AI hybrid monitoring**, where security analysts validate AI-generated alerts before acting on them.
- Use **multi-layered security models** that integrate AI with traditional cybersecurity measures for enhanced accuracy.

Adversarial attacks pose significant threats to Large Language Models (LLMs), affecting their reliability and security in cybersecurity applications. To address this, it is essential to implement robust defense mechanisms such as adversarial training, anomaly detection, and model interpretability enhancements. **Adversarial training** involves exposing LLMs to perturbed inputs during training, making them more resilient to manipulation. **Anomaly detection** methods, such as monitoring unusual input patterns or leveraging autoencoders, can help identify adversarial inputs before they impact the model's decision-making. **Model interpretability techniques**, including attention visualization and feature attribution, can enhance transparency, allowing security experts to analyze and mitigate potential adversarial threats more effectively.

Example: Data Poisoning Attack on LLMs

One real-world example of adversarial attacks on LLMs is **data poisoning**, where attackers inject manipulated data into the training dataset to influence the model's behavior. For instance, in a cybersecurity setting, an attacker could insert misleading Indicators of Compromise (IoCs) into an LLM-based malware detection system, causing the model to classify benign files as malicious or vice versa. To counter this, **data sanitization techniques** such as filtering out suspicious training samples and employing **differential privacy mechanisms** can help prevent the inclusion of compromised data. Additionally, integrating **human-in-the-loop verification** for critical cybersecurity applications ensures that adversarially influenced outputs are reviewed and corrected before deployment. By incorporating these mitigation strategies and real-world case studies, the discussion on adversarial attacks in LLMs can be made more comprehensive, enhancing both theoretical understanding and practical implementation.

5.2.3. Bias and Ethical Issues

LLMs must ensure fairness and transparency when making cybersecurity decisions related to patient data. Bias in AI models can lead to:

- **Discriminatory security policies**, where certain patient groups experience increased scrutiny due to biased training data.
- **Unintended exclusions**, where cybersecurity protocols fail to detect threats affecting specific demographics or institutions.
- **Regulatory and legal challenges**, as biased AI-driven security decisions may violate compliance frameworks such as **HIPAA, GDPR, and HITRUST**.

Mitigation Strategies:

- Conduct **bias audits** on AI models to identify and correct any unfair treatment in cybersecurity protocols.
- Ensure **diverse and representative training data** to minimize biases in decision-making.
- Establish **transparent AI governance frameworks** that allow for human oversight and intervention in security-related AI decisions.

6. LLM-DRIVEN CYBERSECURITY IN GOVERNMENT SYSTEMS

Government institutions handle highly sensitive data, including classified intelligence, national security information, citizen records, and critical infrastructure operations. This makes them prime targets for cyber threats such as state-sponsored attacks, espionage, ransomware, and insider threats. The integration of Large Language Models (LLMs) in cybersecurity has introduced transformative advancements in safeguarding government systems by enhancing threat detection, response, and compliance. LLMs play a crucial role in real-time threat intelligence, analyzing vast amounts of structured and unstructured data to detect potential risks. By continuously monitoring network traffic, emails, and digital communications, AI-driven security models can identify anomalous behavior indicative of cyber intrusions. Government agencies benefit from LLM-powered automated threat detection systems that recognize patterns of malicious activity, mitigating risks before they escalate into full-scale attacks. Additionally, LLMs assist in incident response by generating comprehensive reports on security breaches, providing real-time risk assessments, and suggesting mitigation strategies. Their ability to process and summarize complex security alerts enables cybersecurity teams to act swiftly, reducing the impact of cyber incidents on national security.

6.1. The Importance of AI in Government Security

Governments are responsible for protecting highly sensitive information, including national security data, citizen records, and critical infrastructure networks. The growing sophistication of cyber threats, including state-sponsored attacks, cyber espionage, and misinformation campaigns, makes cybersecurity a top priority for government agencies. Artificial Intelligence (AI), particularly Large Language Models (LLMs), plays a crucial role in strengthening government cybersecurity by improving threat detection, automating security policies, and preventing fraud in public services.

6.1.1 Threat Intelligence Analysis

One of the most significant contributions of AI in government security is its ability to analyze vast amounts of data to detect cyber threats in real time. Traditional cybersecurity tools often struggle to keep up with the volume and complexity of cyberattacks targeting government institutions. LLMs enhance threat intelligence analysis by:

- Continuously monitoring network activity to identify anomalies indicative of potential breaches.
- Detecting sophisticated cyber threats such as advanced persistent threats (APTs), zero-day vulnerabilities, and ransomware attacks before they cause significant damage.
- Processing vast amounts of structured and unstructured data, including cyber threat reports, open-source intelligence, and classified security briefings, to provide actionable insights for security analysts.

By leveraging AI-powered threat intelligence, governments can proactively combat cyber espionage, protect classified information, and enhance national security defenses.

6.1.2 Policy Automation for National Cybersecurity Frameworks

Managing cybersecurity policies across various government departments and agencies can be a complex and resource-intensive task. AI-driven policy automation simplifies this process by:

- Assisting in the development and enforcement of cybersecurity frameworks, ensuring that security protocols are consistently applied across government networks.
- Automatically updating policies to align with evolving cybersecurity standards such as the National Institute of Standards and Technology (NIST) framework, Cybersecurity Maturity Model Certification (CMMC), and General Data Protection Regulation (GDPR).
- Enforcing access control mechanisms to prevent unauthorized access to sensitive government data, minimizing insider threats.

By integrating AI-powered policy automation, governments can streamline cybersecurity governance, reduce human errors, and improve regulatory compliance while responding swiftly to emerging threats.

6.1.3 **Fraud Detection in Public Services**

Public sector fraud, including identity theft, tax fraud, social benefits fraud, and procurement corruption, poses a significant challenge for governments. AI models enhance fraud detection by:

- Analyzing financial transactions, tax records, and social service claims to detect suspicious activities indicative of fraudulent behavior.
- Identifying anomalies and irregular patterns in public sector transactions, flagging potential cases of corruption or misappropriation of funds.
- Assisting law enforcement agencies in tracking money laundering activities and cyber-enabled financial crimes across international networks.

By deploying AI-powered fraud detection systems, governments can enhance transparency, prevent financial losses, and strengthen the integrity of public service programs.

6.1.4 Challenges and Ethical Considerations

Despite the advantages of AI in government security, several challenges must be addressed to ensure responsible implementation.

- Adversarial AI Attacks – Cybercriminals may attempt to manipulate AI models through adversarial techniques, deceiving security systems into overlooking threats. Robust AI defenses must be developed to mitigate these risks.

- Ethical Concerns in AI-Driven Surveillance – Governments must balance security needs with individual privacy rights, ensuring that AI-powered surveillance does not infringe on civil liberties.
- Transparency and Accountability – AI-driven decision-making must be explainable and auditable, allowing security professionals to review and validate AI-generated security recommendations.

To address these challenges, governments must establish clear AI governance policies, integrate human oversight, and ensure that AI-driven security solutions align with legal and ethical standards.

6.2. Key Security Concerns

As governments increasingly integrate AI-powered systems, including Large Language Models (LLMs), into their cybersecurity frameworks, several security concerns must be carefully addressed. While AI enhances cyber defense, it also presents new vulnerabilities that adversaries can exploit. Ensuring the ethical, legal, and secure deployment of AI-driven cybersecurity solutions is crucial to maintaining national security, safeguarding citizen data, and upholding democratic values.

6.2.1 Foreign Interference and AI-Powered Disinformation

Governments face growing threats from foreign adversaries leveraging AI for disinformation campaigns, propaganda, and digital warfare. LLMs, when misused, can generate highly convincing fake news, deepfake videos, and misinformation, disrupting political stability and public trust. Key concerns include:

- Election Interference – AI-generated disinformation can manipulate public opinion, influence elections, and create social unrest by spreading false narratives through social media and digital platforms.
- Automated Misinformation Amplification – LLMs can be used to create bot-driven campaigns that amplify divisive content, misleading citizens and distorting facts.
- Cyber Espionage and Psychological Warfare – State-sponsored actors can weaponize AI to fabricate evidence, impersonate officials, and manipulate geopolitical narratives, posing significant threats to national security.

To mitigate these risks, governments must develop robust AI-powered misinformation detection systems, collaborate with social media platforms to identify AI-generated disinformation, and educate the public on digital literacy and media awareness.

6.2.2 Surveillance and Privacy

While AI-driven cybersecurity solutions strengthen government defenses, they also raise concerns about mass surveillance, data privacy, and civil liberties. AI models capable of analyzing vast amounts of personal and digital data must be implemented with caution to prevent privacy violations. Critical challenges include:

- Mass Data Collection Risks – Governments may collect and analyze large-scale citizen data to detect threats, but excessive surveillance can lead to concerns over privacy infringement.
- AI-Powered Predictive Policing – While AI can assist law enforcement in identifying potential threats, biases in AI models may lead to unfair profiling, discrimination, or wrongful accusations.
- Secure Storage and Data Protection – AI-powered surveillance systems generate and store massive amounts of sensitive information, requiring strong encryption, access controls, and data governance policies to prevent misuse or unauthorized access.

Balancing security needs with ethical AI implementation is essential. Governments must enforce strict data protection laws, ensure transparency in AI surveillance practices, and incorporate human oversight in AI-driven security operations.

7. INDUSTRIAL CYBERSECURITY AND LLM INTEGRATION

The integration of Large Language Models (LLMs) in industrial cybersecurity has become essential as industries increasingly adopt digital transformation and automation. Industrial sectors, including manufacturing, energy, and critical infrastructure, rely on interconnected systems such as Industrial Control Systems (ICS), Supervisory Control and Data Acquisition (SCADA) systems, and the Internet of Things (IoT). These advancements, while improving efficiency, also expose industries to sophisticated cyber threats, including ransomware attacks, insider threats, and supply chain vulnerabilities.

LLMs enhance industrial cybersecurity by providing advanced threat detection capabilities that analyze vast amounts of network traffic, logs, and operational data to identify anomalies and potential cyber threats in real time. By leveraging AI-driven security models, industries can proactively detect unauthorized access attempts, mitigate zero-day vulnerabilities, and respond swiftly to cyber incidents before they escalate. Additionally, AI-powered automated security monitoring ensures continuous surveillance of industrial networks, reducing the reliance on manual security operations and enabling faster response times to cyberattacks.

Another critical aspect of LLM integration in industrial cybersecurity is predictive maintenance and anomaly detection. AI-driven models can analyze equipment performance data to detect signs of potential failures or cyber-induced disruptions. This predictive capability helps industries maintain operational continuity, preventing downtime caused by cyber threats targeting industrial machinery and automated processes. By identifying irregular patterns in sensor data and machine behavior, LLMs assist in securing operational technology (OT) environments against both cyber and physical threats.

Industries are also adopting AI-powered cybersecurity compliance frameworks to ensure adherence to stringent security standards such as the NIST Cybersecurity Framework, IEC 62443 for industrial security, and the Cybersecurity Maturity Model Certification (CMMC). AI models assist in automating compliance audits, flagging potential security gaps, and ensuring that industrial networks remain resilient against regulatory violations.

However, despite their benefits, LLMs in industrial cybersecurity also present challenges, including adversarial attacks where cybercriminals manipulate AI models to bypass security measures. Additionally, the complexity of integrating AI-driven security solutions into legacy industrial systems poses implementation challenges. Addressing these concerns requires a combination of AI governance policies, human oversight, and robust security frameworks tailored to industrial environments. As cyber threats continue to evolve, the role of LLMs in industrial cybersecurity will become even more crucial. By integrating AI-powered threat intelligence, real-time anomaly detection, and automated security management, industries can strengthen their cybersecurity posture while ensuring the reliability, safety, and resilience of critical infrastructure systems.

7.1. Challenges in Industrial Control Systems (ICS) Security

The industrial sector, including manufacturing, energy, transportation, and critical infrastructure, heavily relies on Operational Technology (OT) systems to control essential processes. The convergence of OT with Information Technology (IT) has exposed Industrial Control Systems (ICS)—such as Supervisory Control and Data Acquisition (SCADA) systems, Distributed Control Systems (DCS), and Programmable Logic Controllers (PLCs)—to an increasing number of cybersecurity threats. Cyberattacks on ICS can disrupt operations, damage equipment, cause financial losses, and threaten national security. As industries move towards automation and digital transformation, securing ICS environments against cyber risks has become a top priority. LLMs provide AI-driven solutions to address ICS security challenges, offering predictive cybersecurity, real-time threat monitoring, and enhanced Industrial IoT (IIoT) protection. However, integrating AI with legacy ICS infrastructure, mitigating adversarial AI threats, and ensuring compliance with cybersecurity standards remain significant concerns. LLMs strengthen industrial cybersecurity by:

7.1.1 Predictive Maintenance and Anomaly Detection

One of the biggest challenges in ICS security is the early detection of system failures and cyber threats that could lead to operational disruptions. Traditional security mechanisms struggle to identify anomalies in real-time industrial processes due to the complexity of sensor data, machine logs, and control system interactions. LLMs enable AI-driven predictive maintenance, analyzing large volumes of historical and real-time data to detect irregular patterns that indicate potential cyber threats or mechanical malfunctions. By leveraging AI-based anomaly detection models, industrial operators can:

- Identify early warning signs of system failures, allowing preventive maintenance before issues escalate.
- Detect cyber-induced disruptions such as malware-infected PLCs, manipulated control signals, and unauthorized firmware modifications.
- Reduce unplanned downtime, production losses, and repair costs by addressing vulnerabilities proactively.

Predictive maintenance powered by LLMs enhances system resilience and ensures that industrial processes remain secure and operational even in the face of evolving cyber threats.

7.1.2 Real-Time Security Monitoring

Industrial networks generate vast amounts of telemetry data and communication logs, making it difficult for human analysts to manually detect cyber threats in real time. Traditional security tools may struggle to differentiate between normal operational behavior and potential cyberattacks, increasing the risk of undetected intrusions. LLMs enhance real-time ICS security monitoring by analyzing network traffic patterns, system logs, and user activities to:

- Detect unauthorized access attempts and privilege escalation attacks targeting control systems.
- Identify malicious commands or unexpected system behavior caused by cyber intrusions.
- Automate threat classification and response mechanisms, reducing reaction time during cyber incidents.

By integrating AI-driven continuous monitoring, industrial facilities can significantly reduce dwell time (the duration a cyber threat remains undetected) and minimize the impact of security breaches on critical infrastructure.

7.1.3 Industrial IoT (IIoT) Security

The growing adoption of Industrial Internet of Things (IIoT) devices has improved operational efficiency but also introduced new cybersecurity vulnerabilities. Connected devices such as smart sensors, industrial robots, and remote monitoring systems are often targeted by cybercriminals who exploit weak authentication, unpatched firmware, and unsecured communication protocols. LLM-driven cybersecurity solutions enhance IIoT security by:

- Implementing intelligent access control systems that prevent unauthorized device communications.
- Detecting anomalous device behavior that may indicate a compromised sensor or malicious firmware modification.
- Encrypting machine-to-machine (M2M) communication to prevent eavesdropping and data interception.

By securing IIoT environments, AI-powered models help prevent ransomware attacks, remote command injection, and industrial espionage, ensuring the safety and reliability of connected industrial systems.

7.2. Key Cybersecurity Risks in Industrial Environments

Industrial environments face significant cybersecurity risks as they increasingly rely on interconnected systems, automation, and Industrial Internet of Things (IIoT) devices. Cyber threats targeting these sectors can lead to operational disruptions, financial losses, and even physical damage to critical infrastructure. One of the primary risks is unauthorized access to Industrial Control Systems (ICS), where attackers exploit weak authentication mechanisms, outdated security protocols, or misconfigured network settings to gain control over Supervisory Control and Data Acquisition (SCADA) systems, Programmable Logic Controllers (PLCs), and Distributed Control Systems (DCS). Once inside, adversaries can manipulate industrial processes, disrupt production, or cause equipment failures, leading to severe operational and safety consequences.

Another major cybersecurity risk is ransomware attacks, which have become increasingly prevalent in industrial environments. Cybercriminals target manufacturers, energy providers, and transportation systems by encrypting critical operational data and demanding ransom payments to restore access. These attacks can halt production lines, disable essential services, and lead to financial losses running into millions of dollars. Since many ICS environments operate on legacy systems that lack modern security measures, they are particularly vulnerable to ransomware threats.

Supply chain vulnerabilities pose another critical cybersecurity challenge in industrial settings. Many industrial organizations rely on third-party vendors for hardware, software, and maintenance services, which can introduce security risks. Attackers can exploit vulnerabilities in supplier networks to gain access to ICS environments, inject malicious firmware, or distribute compromised software updates. A single weak link in the supply chain can expose an entire industrial system to cyber threats, making supply chain security a top priority for industrial cybersecurity strategies.

Industrial IoT (IIoT) devices have expanded the attack surface in industrial environments by increasing connectivity across operational technology (OT) networks. While IIoT enhances productivity and efficiency, unsecured devices can become entry points for cyber attackers. Weak authentication, unpatched firmware, and unsecured communication protocols in IIoT devices allow attackers to infiltrate networks, launch data interception attacks, or disrupt automated processes.

Another pressing concern is the risk of data integrity attacks, where adversaries manipulate sensor data or operational logs to cause disruptions. By altering data readings, attackers can mislead automated control systems, leading to incorrect operational decisions, system malfunctions, or even catastrophic failures in energy plants, manufacturing units, and transportation networks. Since ICS environments depend on accurate real-time data to function effectively, any compromise in data integrity can result in severe operational and safety consequences.

Denial-of-Service (DoS) and Distributed Denial-of-Service (DDoS) attacks also pose significant threats to industrial environments. Attackers overwhelm networked control systems with massive amounts of traffic, rendering critical services unavailable. Such attacks can disrupt monitoring tools, prevent real-time decision-making, and lead to downtime in industrial operations. Since many industrial networks were not originally designed to handle high levels of malicious traffic, they are often vulnerable to DoS and DDoS attacks that can cripple essential services.

In addition to external threats, insider threats remain a persistent cybersecurity challenge in industrial environments. Employees, contractors, or business partners with access to sensitive industrial systems may intentionally or unintentionally cause security breaches. Malicious insiders may steal confidential information, introduce malware, or sabotage operations, while negligent insiders may inadvertently expose systems to cyber risks through weak passwords, misconfigurations, or unsafe cybersecurity practices.

As industrial environments continue to integrate advanced digital technologies, cybersecurity risks will evolve. Organizations must adopt proactive security measures such as network segmentation, real-time threat monitoring, anomaly detection, and robust access control policies to safeguard critical infrastructure from cyber threats. Regular security assessments, employee training, and collaboration with cybersecurity experts are essential to mitigating the risks associated with industrial cybersecurity threats.

8. ETHICAL, LEGAL, AND COMPLIANCE CONSIDERATIONS

The integration of Large Language Models (LLMs) in cybersecurity raises several ethical, legal, and compliance challenges that must be carefully addressed to ensure responsible and secure deployment. As AI-driven cybersecurity solutions gain prominence, organizations must navigate complex regulatory frameworks, ethical concerns surrounding data privacy, and potential biases in AI decision-making. Failure to address these issues can lead to legal liabilities, reputational damage, and unintended security risks.

One of the most pressing ethical concerns is data privacy and security. LLMs require vast amounts of data to train and operate effectively, which often includes sensitive and confidential information. In industries such as healthcare, government, and critical infrastructure, improper handling of sensitive data can lead to privacy violations and regulatory breaches. Organizations must implement data anonymization, encryption, and secure access controls to prevent unauthorized exposure of protected information. Moreover, AI-driven security solutions must comply with global data protection laws such as the General Data Protection Regulation (GDPR), the Health

Insurance Portability and Accountability Act (HIPAA), and the California Consumer Privacy Act (CCPA), ensuring that personal and confidential data remains secure.

Another significant concern is AI bias and fairness in cybersecurity decision-making. LLMs, like all machine learning models, can inherit biases from their training data, leading to potential discrimination or inaccurate threat assessments. Bias in cybersecurity models can result in false positives, where legitimate activities are flagged as threats, or false negatives, where real security incidents go undetected. In high-stakes environments such as healthcare or national security, biased AI-driven security measures could disproportionately affect specific individuals or groups, leading to ethical and operational concerns. To mitigate this, organizations must employ transparent AI development practices, continuous bias audits, and diverse training datasets to improve the fairness and accuracy of LLM-powered cybersecurity systems.

8.1. Privacy and Data Protection

As AI-driven cybersecurity models, including Large Language Models (LLMs), increasingly handle vast amounts of sensitive data, ensuring compliance with global privacy laws and regulatory frameworks such as the General Data Protection Regulation (GDPR), the Health Insurance Portability and Accountability Act (HIPAA), and the National Institute of Standards and Technology (NIST) guidelines becomes a critical priority. The growing reliance on LLMs in security applications presents both opportunities and risks, requiring organizations to carefully manage data privacy concerns to prevent potential legal and ethical violations.

One of the primary challenges of using LLMs in cybersecurity is data collection and storage. AI models rely on extensive datasets for training and continuous learning, which often include personally identifiable information (PII), financial records, medical histories, and corporate intellectual property. If not properly handled, this data can become vulnerable to breaches, leaks, or unauthorized access, leading to privacy infringements and regulatory non-compliance. To address this, organizations must implement strong encryption mechanisms, data anonymization techniques, and access control policies to safeguard sensitive information.

Another major concern is data minimization and purpose limitation. Regulatory frameworks like GDPR mandate that organizations should collect only the minimum necessary data required for a specific purpose and should not use it for unintended functions. However, LLMs, which learn from vast amounts of information, often struggle with differentiating between necessary and unnecessary data retention. Companies leveraging LLMs must establish clear data retention policies, automated data deletion procedures, and explicit consent mechanisms to ensure compliance with these legal requirements.

8.2. Bias and Transparency in AI-Driven Decisions

LLMs can inadvertently introduce bias in security assessments. It is essential to:

- Implement **explainable AI (XAI)** techniques to enhance transparency.
- Regularly audit AI models to prevent unfair or discriminatory security decisions.

The increasing adoption of Large Language Models (LLMs) in cybersecurity presents both advantages and challenges. While LLMs can enhance threat detection, automate security tasks, and improve response times, they can also introduce bias in security assessments. Bias in AI-driven cybersecurity decisions can result in unfair threat classifications, disproportionate enforcement actions, and inaccurate risk predictions, potentially impacting organizations and individuals negatively. Ensuring transparency and fairness in AI-driven security systems is essential for maintaining trust, compliance, and ethical responsibility. One of the primary causes of bias in LLM-based cybersecurity solutions is biased training data. LLMs learn from vast amounts of text and security datasets, which may contain historical biases, skewed threat categorizations, or region-specific attack patterns. If an AI model is trained on data that disproportionately identifies threats from certain demographics, geographical regions, or industries, it may develop skewed threat assessment patterns. This can lead to over-policing of specific user groups or underestimating risks in certain environments, creating security blind spots. To mitigate this, organizations must ensure that training datasets are diverse, representative, and regularly updated to prevent systemic biases.

8.3. AI Governance and Accountability

As AI plays a larger role in cybersecurity, organizations must establish clear accountability frameworks. This includes:

- Defining liability in AI-driven security breaches.
- Ensuring human oversight in critical security decisions.
- Developing global cybersecurity standards for LLM integration.

As AI-driven solutions, including Large Language Models (LLMs), play an increasingly significant role in cybersecurity, establishing clear governance and accountability frameworks is essential to ensure responsible and ethical AI deployment. Without well-defined oversight, AI-driven cybersecurity systems may introduce legal, ethical, and operational risks, including security breaches, misclassified threats, and unintended policy violations. Organizations must implement structured AI governance models to address these challenges and promote trust, reliability, and compliance in AI-driven security operations. A critical aspect of AI governance is defining liability in AI-driven security breaches. When an AI-powered security system fails to detect a cyber threat, generates false positives, or inadvertently blocks legitimate access, determining responsibility becomes complex. Who is accountable—the AI developer, the organization deploying the AI, or the cybersecurity team overseeing its operations? Legal frameworks must clearly define ownership of AI-driven decisions, ensuring that liability is appropriately assigned in cases of security failures. Regulatory bodies may require organizations to implement AI risk assessments, incident documentation, and liability agreements to ensure accountability in AI-driven cybersecurity environments.

Another essential component of AI governance is ensuring human oversight in critical security decisions. While AI enhances real-time threat detection, incident response, and automated security enforcement, relying entirely on AI-driven systems without human intervention can lead to misjudged security actions or ethical concerns. Establishing a Human-in-the-Loop (HITL) model, where cybersecurity professionals review AI-generated threat assessments and override AI decisions, if necessary, ensures that critical security actions are contextually informed and aligned with organizational policies. Additionally, organizations should implement AI explainability mechanisms to help security teams understand and interpret AI-driven security recommendations before taking action. Developing global cybersecurity standards for LLM integration is also crucial to maintaining interoperability, compliance, and ethical security practices. AI-driven cybersecurity solutions must adhere to international security guidelines such as the NIST AI Risk Management Framework (RMF), the European Union's AI Act, ISO/IEC 27001 (Information Security Standards), and sector-specific regulations like HIPAA, GDPR, and CISA. Establishing universal best practices for AI-powered cybersecurity, including guidelines for AI training, bias mitigation, security testing, and ethical AI deployment, ensures that organizations worldwide maintain consistent, responsible, and legally compliant AI-driven security implementations.

To strengthen AI governance, organizations should also adopt AI ethics committees and regulatory compliance teams responsible for monitoring AI security systems, addressing ethical concerns, and ensuring that AI models align with legal and industry standards.

9. FUTURE DIRECTIONS AND RECOMMENDATIONS

As Large Language Models (LLMs) and AI-driven solutions continue to shape the cybersecurity landscape, organizations must focus on advancing AI capabilities, addressing security challenges, and ensuring ethical deployment. Future directions in AI-driven cybersecurity emphasize enhanced threat intelligence, improved AI governance, stronger adversarial defense mechanisms, and regulatory advancements. One key area of future research is developing more resilient AI models against adversarial attacks. Cybercriminals are increasingly exploiting vulnerabilities in AI-driven security systems through data poisoning, adversarial manipulations, and model evasion techniques. To counteract these threats, organizations must invest in robust adversarial training methods, real-time AI monitoring systems, and AI-powered self-healing security architectures that can adapt and respond to emerging cyber threats autonomously.

Another crucial advancement involves integrating AI-driven cybersecurity with quantum-resistant cryptographic techniques. As quantum computing progresses, traditional encryption mechanisms may become vulnerable to decryption by powerful quantum algorithms. Future cybersecurity frameworks should incorporate post-quantum cryptographic solutions, ensuring that AI-driven security models remain effective in an evolving digital landscape. In addition to technological advancements, collaborative AI security frameworks will play a vital role in strengthening global cybersecurity defenses. Governments, private organizations, and academic institutions should collaborate to develop shared threat intelligence platforms, where AI-driven security models can exchange real-time cyber threat insights, detect coordinated attacks, and implement proactive defense mechanisms across industries. By fostering an AI-driven global cybersecurity network, organizations can enhance collective cyber resilience against large-scale attacks.

From a regulatory standpoint, future AI cybersecurity deployments must adhere to standardized governance policies that ensure transparency, fairness, and compliance. Governments and industry leaders should establish global AI cybersecurity standards, defining ethical AI usage, bias mitigation guidelines, and AI-driven security audit protocols. Strengthening AI compliance frameworks, risk assessment methodologies, and regulatory enforcement mechanisms will help mitigate the legal and ethical challenges of AI-driven cybersecurity systems. To maximize AI's potential while minimizing risks, organizations should also focus on upskilling cybersecurity professionals with AI expertise. Training security teams to work alongside AI-driven tools, interpret AI-generated insights, and mitigate AI security risks will create a human-AI collaborative security ecosystem. Investing in AI-driven cybersecurity education, certification programs, and industry-specific AI training initiatives will prepare professionals to effectively manage AI-integrated security infrastructures.

Finally, organizations must establish ethical AI development frameworks that prioritize user privacy, data security, and responsible AI decision-making. Ensuring transparent AI models, user-centric security policies, and AI explainability mechanisms will build trust in AI-powered cybersecurity solutions. By balancing AI innovation with ethical safeguards, organizations can create secure, fair, and trustworthy AI-driven security ecosystems. In summary, the future of AI-driven cybersecurity lies in enhancing adversarial resilience, integrating quantum-resistant security, fostering global AI collaborations, strengthening regulatory compliance, upskilling security professionals, and prioritizing ethical AI governance. By adopting these forward-looking strategies, organizations can effectively leverage AI for advanced cybersecurity while mitigating risks and ensuring sustainable, ethical AI deployment.

9.1. Advancements in AI-Driven Cybersecurity

As cybersecurity threats evolve, the future of AI-driven security will depend on cutting-edge innovations that enhance data protection, resilience against attacks, and AI model security. Future research should focus on emerging techniques that address privacy concerns, prepare for quantum-era cyber threats, and improve AI security infrastructure. Future research should focus on:

9.1.1 Federated Learning for Secure AI

Enhancing LLM training without compromising sensitive data. One of the biggest challenges in AI-driven cybersecurity is ensuring data privacy while training robust models. Traditional AI models require large datasets stored in centralized locations, which increases the risk of data breaches, insider threats, and regulatory non-compliance. Federated learning (FL) offers a solution by allowing AI models to be trained across multiple decentralized devices without transferring raw data. This approach enhances privacy and security, making it ideal for healthcare, government, and industrial cybersecurity applications where sensitive data must remain protected. Federated learning is a decentralized approach to machine learning where multiple devices or servers collaboratively train a model without sharing raw data. Instead, only model updates are exchanged, enhancing privacy and security. This technique is particularly useful in cybersecurity applications, where sensitive user data must remain confidential while still contributing to model improvements.

Federated learning can also improve real-time threat detection by enabling AI models deployed across multiple organizations to learn from different attack scenarios while preserving data confidentiality. As cyber threats grow more sophisticated, future research should explore optimized FL algorithms, privacy-preserving techniques, and secure model-sharing frameworks to advance LLM-powered cybersecurity solutions.

9.1.2 Quantum-Secure AI Models

With the rise of quantum computing, traditional encryption methods used in AI-driven security systems may become vulnerable to quantum decryption attacks. Quantum computers have the potential to break current cryptographic protocols, putting AI security architectures, digital identities, and encrypted communications at risk.

To counteract this, future AI-driven cybersecurity research should focus on developing quantum-secure AI models that integrate post-quantum cryptographic techniques such as:

- Lattice-based cryptography – Resistant to quantum attacks, ensuring AI-driven security models remain effective.
- Multivariate cryptography – Enhancing AI model integrity by protecting against AI-targeted quantum attacks.
- Quantum-resistant blockchain security – Safeguarding AI-powered security systems through next-generation cryptographic frameworks.

By integrating quantum-safe algorithms into AI-driven security infrastructures, organizations can future-proof their cybersecurity defenses against quantum-era threats.

9.1.3 Decentralized AI Security

Centralized AI-powered cybersecurity systems often pose risks such as single points of failure, unauthorized access, and data manipulation by malicious actors. To enhance security, the future of AI-driven cybersecurity should focus on decentralized AI security frameworks that leverage blockchain technology for AI-powered cybersecurity solutions.

Blockchain-based AI security can eliminate centralized vulnerabilities by:

- Enabling secure, tamper-proof AI model updates and logs – Preventing adversaries from modifying AI security models.
- Enhancing data integrity in AI-driven threat detection – Ensuring cyber threat intelligence remains immutable and verifiable.

- Providing decentralized identity verification for AI security agents – Strengthening access control mechanisms in AI-powered security infrastructures.

By integrating blockchain with LLM-driven security solutions, organizations can develop trustworthy AI cybersecurity frameworks that are resistant to centralized attacks, data corruption, and unauthorized AI manipulations.

In conclusion, federated learning, quantum-secure AI models, and decentralized AI security architectures will drive the next generation of AI-driven cybersecurity. These advancements will enhance data privacy, strengthen AI security resilience, and prepare organizations for emerging cyber threats in the post-quantum, AI-integrated digital era.

9.2. Recommendations for Secure LLM Deployment

To ensure the safe and effective use of Large Language Models (LLMs) in cybersecurity applications, organizations must implement robust security measures that address vulnerabilities, prevent unauthorized access, and enhance overall system resilience. A key recommendation is to conduct regular AI security audits and ensure that LLMs receive frequent updates to protect against emerging threats. Cybercriminals are constantly evolving their attack strategies, and outdated AI models can become susceptible to adversarial manipulation, data poisoning, and model drift. By integrating continuous monitoring, security patches, and adversarial training, organizations can maintain the integrity and reliability of LLM-driven cybersecurity systems.

Another essential strategy is the adoption of zero-trust architectures (ZTA) to minimize unauthorized access to AI-powered security systems. Traditional security models operate on implicit trust assumptions, which can be exploited by insider threats and external attackers. Zero-trust frameworks enforce strict access controls, multi-factor authentication, and identity verification protocols, ensuring that every user and device must be continuously authenticated before accessing LLM-powered security solutions. By implementing role-based access control (RBAC) and AI-driven anomaly detection mechanisms, organizations can significantly reduce the risk of unauthorized data access and AI model exploitation.

Equally important is educating cybersecurity professionals on AI adversarial attack prevention. As AI-driven security tools become more widespread, security teams must be well-versed in identifying, mitigating, and defending against AI-specific threats, such as adversarial perturbations, prompt injections, and model evasion attacks. Organizations should invest in AI cybersecurity training programs, workshops, and simulation exercises to help professionals understand AI vulnerabilities, implement countermeasures, and respond effectively to AI-targeted cyber threats. By fostering a culture of AI security awareness, companies can bridge the knowledge gap and ensure that AI-driven cybersecurity tools are deployed and managed responsibly.

Additionally, organizations should prioritize data encryption and privacy-preserving AI techniques when implementing LLM-based security solutions. AI models trained on sensitive data, such as healthcare records, government intelligence, or industrial control logs, must adhere to strict privacy regulations, including GDPR, HIPAA, and NIST guidelines. Techniques like homomorphic encryption, differential privacy, and secure multi-party computation can help protect sensitive data from exposure while still allowing LLMs to perform security-related tasks. Integrating privacy-enhancing technologies into AI-driven security systems can strengthen compliance, data confidentiality, and trust in AI-based cybersecurity applications.

To further enhance the security of LLM deployments, organizations should implement robust model verification and explainability mechanisms. AI explainability (XAI) helps security teams understand how AI models make decisions, detect potential biases, and identify vulnerabilities in AI-driven threat detection. Establishing transparent AI governance frameworks, bias auditing protocols, and interpretability tools ensures that AI-powered security decisions are trustworthy, ethical, and aligned with cybersecurity best practices. By adopting these proactive security measures, organizations can mitigate AI-related risks, strengthen LLM-driven cybersecurity defenses, and ensure the safe, ethical, and effective deployment of AI-powered security solutions.

10. CONCLUSION

Large Language Models (LLMs) are revolutionizing cybersecurity across healthcare, government, and industrial sectors by offering advanced automated threat intelligence, real-time anomaly detection, and adaptive security mechanisms. Their ability to process vast amounts of data, identify complex attack patterns, and enhance compliance monitoring has positioned them as critical tools in modern cybersecurity frameworks. However, while LLMs provide significant benefits, their deployment introduces new challenges, risks, and ethical considerations that organizations must carefully address. One of the key concerns surrounding LLM adoption in cybersecurity is data privacy and protection. As these models analyze sensitive information—including patient records, classified government data, and industrial control logs—it is crucial to implement strong encryption techniques, access control mechanisms, and privacy-preserving AI methods to prevent unauthorized access and data breaches. Compliance with global cybersecurity regulations such as GDPR, HIPAA, and NIST must remain a priority to ensure legal adherence and maintain public trust in AI-driven security systems.

Another significant challenge is defending against adversarial threats and AI manipulation. Cybercriminals are developing sophisticated attack methods, such as data poisoning, adversarial perturbations, and AI model exploitation, to evade detection and compromise security systems. To counteract these risks, organizations must integrate robust adversarial training techniques, AI security audits, and continuous monitoring mechanisms to reinforce LLM defenses. By staying ahead of evolving threats, cybersecurity teams can enhance the resilience of AI-driven security models and maintain their effectiveness in real-world applications. Beyond technical concerns, ethical and governance considerations play a crucial role in responsible LLM deployment. Issues such as algorithmic bias, transparency in AI-driven decisions, and accountability for AI-generated security actions must be addressed to prevent discrimination, misinformation, and unintended consequences in security operations. Establishing explainable AI (XAI) frameworks, fairness audits, and AI governance policies will help ensure that LLM-powered security tools operate within ethical boundaries and align with regulatory compliance requirements.

To fully leverage the potential of LLMs in cybersecurity while mitigating associated risks, organizations must adopt a strategic, multi-layered approach. This includes implementing zero-trust architectures, enhancing workforce training in AI cybersecurity, adopting federated learning for privacy-conscious AI development, and exploring quantum-secure AI models for future-proof security. By integrating AI innovation with strong governance, proactive security strategies, and continuous risk assessment, industries can maximize the benefits of LLM-driven cybersecurity while ensuring data integrity, system resilience, and regulatory adherence. In conclusion, LLMs have the power to transform cybersecurity defenses, making them more intelligent, adaptive, and efficient. However, their successful deployment depends on an organization's ability to balance innovation with security, ethics, and compliance. By taking a responsible, well-regulated approach to LLM implementation, organizations can strengthen their cybersecurity posture, safeguard critical digital assets, and pave the way for a more secure AI-driven future.

REFERENCES

Arshad, U., & Halim, Z. (2025). BlockLLM: A futuristic LLM-based decentralized vehicular network architecture for secure communications. *Computers & Electrical Engineering*, *123*, 110027.

Black, G., Vaidyan, V., & Comert, G. (2024). Evaluating large language models for enhanced fuzzing: An analysis framework for LLM-driven seed generation. *IEEE Access : Practical Innovations, Open Solutions*, *12*, 156065–156081. DOI: 10.1109/ACCESS.2024.3484947

Black, G. S., Rimal, B. P., & Vaidyan, V. M. (2024). Balancing security and correctness in code generation: An empirical study on commercial large language models. *IEEE Transactions on Emerging Topics in Computational Intelligence*.

Chen, Y., Cui, M., Wang, D., Cao, Y., Yang, P., Jiang, B., Lu, Z., & Liu, B. (2024). A survey of large language models for cyber threat detection. *Computers & Security*, *145*, 104016. DOI: 10.1016/j.cose.2024.104016

Derner, E., Batistič, K., Zahálka, J., & Babuška, R. (2024). A security risk taxonomy for prompt-based interaction with large language models. *IEEE Access : Practical Innovations, Open Solutions*, *12*, 126176–126187. DOI: 10.1109/ACCESS.2024.3450388

Ferrag, M. A., Alwahedi, F., Battah, A., Cherif, B., Mechri, A., Tihanyi, N., Bisztray, T., & Debbah, M. (2025). Generative AI in cybersecurity: A comprehensive review of LLM applications and vulnerabilities. *Internet of Things and Cyber-Physical Systems*.

Hassanin, M., Keshk, M., Salim, S., Alsubaie, M., & Sharma, D. (2025). PLLM-CS: Pre-trained large language model (LLM) for cyber threat detection in satellite networks. *Ad Hoc Networks*, *166*, 103645. DOI: 10.1016/j.adhoc.2024.103645

Haurogné, J., Basheer, N., & Islam, S. (2024). Vulnerability detection using BERT-based LLM model with transparency obligation practice towards trustworthy AI. *Machine Learning with Applications*, *18*, 100598.

Hu, Y., Zou, F., Han, J., Sun, X., & Wang, Y. (2024). LLM-TIKG: Threat intelligence knowledge graph construction utilizing large language model. *Computers & Security*, *145*, 103999. DOI: 10.1016/j.cose.2024.103999

Loevenich, J., Adler, E., Hürten, T., & Lopes, R. R. F. (2025). Design and evaluation of an autonomous cyber defense agent using DRL and an augmented LLM. *Computer Networks*, *262*, 111162. DOI: 10.1016/j.comnet.2025.111162

Mishra, C., Sarma, H., & Saravanan, M. (2025). PageLLM: Incremental approach for updating a security knowledge graph by using page ranking and large language model. *Information Processing & Management*, *62*(3), 104045. DOI: 10.1016/j.ipm.2024.104045

Patsakis, C., Casino, F., & Lykousas, N. (2024). Assessing LLMs in malicious code deobfuscation of real-world malware campaigns. *Expert Systems with Applications*, *256*, 124912.

Rashid, F., Ranaweera, N., Doyle, B., & Seneviratne, S. (2025). LLMs are one-shot URL classifiers and explainers. *Computer Networks*, *258*, 111004.

Selim, A., Zhao, J., & Yang, B. (2024). Large language model for smart inverter cyber-attack detection via textual analysis of Volt/VAR commands. *IEEE Transactions on Smart Grid*.

Shafee, S., Bessani, A., & Ferreira, P. M. (2024). Evaluation of LLM-based chatbots for OSINT-based cyber threat awareness. *Expert Systems with Applications*, •••, 125509.

Sufi, F. (2024). An innovative GPT-based open-source intelligence using historical cyber incident reports. *Natural Language Processing Journal*, *7*, 100074. DOI: 10.1016/j.nlp.2024.100074

Tang, H., Lin, D., Li, W., Zhang, W., & Zhao, J. (2024). Cyber threat indicators extraction based on contextual knowledge prompt. *Computer Networks*, *254*, 110839. DOI: 10.1016/j.comnet.2024.110839

Wang, X., Tian, Y., Huang, K., & Liang, B. (2025). Practically implementing an LLM-supported collaborative vulnerability remediation process: A team-based approach. *Computers & Security*, *148*, 104113. DOI: 10.1016/j.cose.2024.104113

Yao, Y., Duan, J., Xu, K., Cai, Y., Sun, Z., & Zhang, Y. (2024). A survey on large language model (LLM) security and privacy: The good, the bad, and the ugly. *High-Confidence Computing*, *4*(2), 100211. DOI: 10.1016/j.hcc.2024.100211

Zhang, X., Xu, H., Ba, Z., Wang, Z., Hong, Y., Liu, J., Qin, Z., & Ren, K. (2024). PrivacyAsst: Safeguarding user privacy in tool-using large language model agents. *IEEE Transactions on Dependable and Secure Computing*.

Chapter 5
Phishing and Social Engineering Attack Prevention With LLMs

Hermano Jorge Da Silva De Queiroz
https://orcid.org/0000-0001-6738-6321
Lindsey Wilson College, USA

ABSTRACT

Phishing and social engineering attacks have become increasingly sophisticated, leveraging advanced psychological manipulation and deceptive tactics to compromise individuals and organizations. Traditional cybersecurity measures often fail to address the dynamic and evolving nature of these threats. Large Language Models (LLMs) present a promising solution by enabling real-time threat detection, automated phishing email classification, and user education through natural language processing capabilities. This chapter explores how LLMs can enhance phishing and social engineering attack prevention, discussing their role in email filtering, anomaly detection, chatbot-based awareness training, and behavioral analysis. Additionally, we address challenges such as adversarial manipulation of LLMs, ethical considerations, and model biases. By integrating deep learning with cybersecurity frameworks, organizations can develop more resilient and adaptive defense mechanisms against human-targeted cyber threats.

DOI: 10.4018/979-8-3373-3296-3.ch005

1. OVERVIEW OF PHISHING AND SOCIAL ENGINEERING ATTACKS

Phishing and social engineering attacks are among the most prevalent cybersecurity threats, leveraging human psychology to manipulate individuals into divulging sensitive information or performing malicious actions. These attacks have evolved significantly with the increasing sophistication of cybercriminal tactics and the proliferation of digital communication platforms. Understanding their mechanisms, impact, and evolving nature is crucial for developing effective countermeasures, including those driven by Large Language Models (LLMs).

1.1. Understanding Phishing Attacks

Phishing attacks are fraudulent attempts to obtain sensitive data such as usernames, passwords, and financial information by masquerading as a trustworthy entity. These attacks typically occur via email, but they can also be executed through SMS (smishing), voice calls (vishing), and social media platforms.

Phishing schemes often employ psychological manipulation, urgency, and deception to trick victims into clicking malicious links, downloading malware, or providing confidential details. Cybercriminals leverage advanced social engineering techniques to increase the effectiveness of their attacks. According to Ferrag et al. (2024), the integration of LLMs in cybersecurity has enabled real-time detection of phishing attempts by analyzing email content and identifying suspicious linguistic patterns.

Phishing attacks can be broadly categorized into:

- **Spear Phishing**: Targeted attacks against specific individuals or organizations, often leveraging publicly available information to enhance credibility.
- **Whaling**: A specialized form of spear phishing aimed at high-profile targets such as executives and government officials.
- **Clone Phishing**: Involves creating nearly identical replicas of legitimate emails to deceive recipients into taking harmful actions.
- **Pharming**: Redirecting users from legitimate websites to fraudulent ones, often through DNS poisoning.

Recent advancements in AI-driven cybersecurity have focused on automating phishing detection using natural language processing (NLP) and deep learning techniques. Studies by Kasri et al. (2025) and Liu (2024) highlight how LLMs can analyze contextual cues and metadata to distinguish legitimate communications from fraudulent ones.

The lifecycle of a phishing attack involves multiple stages, from reconnaissance to execution and exploitation. Understanding these stages is essential for developing effective countermeasures. The following diagram illustrates the typical lifecycle of a phishing attack.

Figure 1. Phishing attack lifecycle

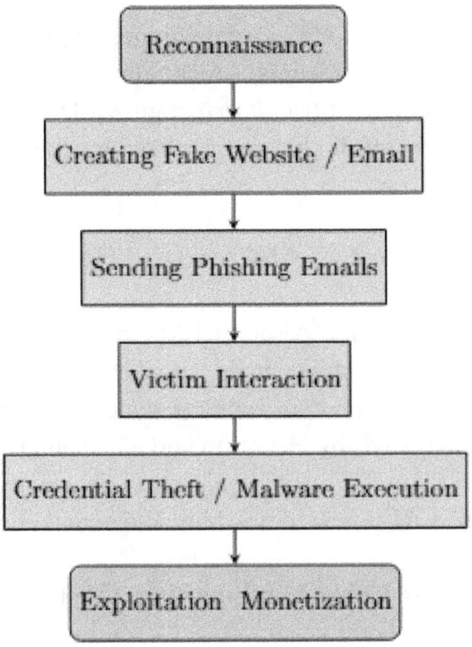

1.2. Social Engineering Attacks and Psychological Manipulation

Social engineering attacks exploit human behavior, trust, and cognitive biases to manipulate victims into disclosing confidential information or performing specific actions that compromise security. Unlike traditional hacking techniques that rely on software vulnerabilities, social engineering attacks target the human element, making them harder to detect and prevent.

Common forms of social engineering include:

- **Pretexting**: Attackers fabricate a convincing scenario to extract information from a victim.

- **Baiting**: Involves offering something enticing, such as free software or a gift, to lure victims into installing malware.
- **Tailgating**: Gaining unauthorized access to restricted areas by exploiting human courtesy.
- **Quid Pro Quo**: Attackers promise a service or benefit in exchange for confidential information.

According to Santos et al. (2024), social engineering tactics have evolved to incorporate AI-generated content, deepfake technology, and automated conversation bots, making them increasingly difficult to recognize. The rise of generative AI has enabled cybercriminals to craft highly personalized messages that evade traditional detection mechanisms.

1.3. The Growing Threat of AI-Powered Social Engineering

With the advent of generative AI and LLMs, phishing and social engineering attacks have become more sophisticated. Attackers can now automate message generation, personalize phishing campaigns at scale, and mimic human-like interactions convincingly. Research by Hassanin and Moustafa (2024) emphasizes that AI-driven attacks pose a significant challenge to traditional cybersecurity defenses.

Key developments in AI-powered phishing and social engineering include:

- **Deepfake Voice and Video Manipulation**: Used for impersonating executives in business email compromise (BEC) scams.
- **Automated Phishing Campaigns**: AI-generated spear-phishing emails tailored to individual targets.
- **Conversational Bots**: Deployed to extract information through social media and messaging applications.

LLMs can also be exploited for malicious purposes, generating phishing content that bypasses traditional spam filters. Xu et al. (2024) caution that adversarial attacks against AI-based cybersecurity systems are an emerging concern, requiring robust countermeasures to mitigate AI-generated threats.

1.4. Impact of Phishing and Social Engineering on Cybersecurity

The financial and reputational consequences of phishing and social engineering attacks are substantial. Organizations face significant losses due to data breaches, fraud, and regulatory fines. According to Zangana, Mustafa, and Li (2025), integrating AI-driven threat intelligence into cybersecurity frameworks can enhance proactive defense mechanisms.

The growing reliance on digital communication has expanded the attack surface, making it essential for enterprises to adopt AI-based detection and prevention strategies. Studies by AlQenaei (2024) and Motlagh et al. (2024) highlight the importance of continuous monitoring and AI-enhanced anomaly detection in mitigating social engineering threats.

1.5 Summary

Phishing and social engineering attacks continue to evolve, leveraging AI and automation to enhance their effectiveness. Traditional security measures are no longer sufficient to combat these sophisticated threats. The next sections of this chapter will explore how LLMs can be leveraged for phishing prevention, social engineering mitigation, and automated threat intelligence, addressing both opportunities and challenges in deploying AI-driven cybersecurity solutions.

2. TRADITIONAL PHISHING DETECTION METHODS

Phishing attacks remain one of the most pervasive threats in cybersecurity, targeting individuals and organizations alike. Traditional phishing detection methods have evolved over the years, leveraging rule-based systems, blacklists, heuristics, and machine learning techniques to identify and mitigate phishing attempts. While these approaches have proven effective to a certain extent, they also present limitations in adaptability and accuracy, necessitating the integration of more advanced artificial intelligence-driven techniques.

2.1. Blacklist-Based Detection

Blacklist-based phishing detection is one of the earliest methods employed to counter phishing attacks. This approach maintains a database of known malicious URLs, email addresses, and domain names that are frequently updated to prevent users from accessing phishing sites (Hasanov et al., 2024). Security tools such as web browsers and email filtering systems cross-reference incoming requests with these blacklists to block access to malicious sites (Santos et al., 2024). However, this method struggles with zero-day phishing attacks, where attackers rapidly generate new URLs that are not yet recorded in the blacklist (Chen et al., 2024).

2.2. Heuristic-Based Detection

Heuristic-based detection aims to identify phishing attempts by analyzing email content, URLs, and web page structures. This approach applies predefined rules and pattern-matching techniques to detect common phishing indicators such as suspicious domain names, deceptive links, and abnormal HTML elements (Ghazal et al., 2024). While heuristics improve detection over static blacklists, they may generate high false positives and require continuous refinement to keep up with evolving phishing tactics (Zangana, 2024).

2.3. Machine Learning-Based Detection

Machine learning (ML) has been increasingly used to enhance phishing detection by learning patterns from large datasets. ML-based systems analyze email metadata, lexical features of URLs, and user behavior to identify potential phishing attacks (Motlagh et al., 2024). Supervised learning algorithms, such as decision trees, support vector machines, and random forests, have demonstrated significant success in detecting phishing attempts (Ferrag et al., 2023). However, these models require extensive labeled data for training and may become less effective against sophisticated phishing schemes that mimic legitimate communication (Liu, 2024).

2.4. Content-Based Filtering

Content-based filtering techniques analyze the textual and visual content of emails and websites to detect phishing attempts. Natural Language Processing (NLP) is employed to identify deceptive language, urgent requests, and fraudulent intent within email bodies (Sarker, 2024). Additionally, image recognition techniques are used to detect fake logos and impersonated branding elements that mimic legitimate organizations (Kasri et al., 2025). Despite its effectiveness, content-based filtering can struggle with obfuscated text and evolving phishing tactics (Xu et al., 2024).

2.5. DNS and WHOIS-Based Detection

Domain Name System (DNS) and WHOIS-based detection methods analyze domain registration information and DNS records to identify suspicious domains used in phishing attacks. Features such as domain age, registrar details, and certificate validity are examined to determine if a website is likely to be a phishing site (Idelhaj et al., 2024). Newly registered domains with short expiration periods are often flagged as potential phishing sites (AlQenaei, 2024). However, attackers increasingly use compromised domains, making DNS-based detection less effective in some cases (Bryce et al.).

2.6. Behavioral Analysis and Anomaly Detection

Behavioral analysis techniques monitor user interactions with emails and web pages to identify suspicious activities indicative of phishing. These methods use anomaly detection algorithms to recognize deviations from typical user behavior, such as unusual login attempts or excessive requests for sensitive information (Asoronye et al., 2024). This approach is particularly useful in detecting targeted phishing attacks (spear-phishing) but may require extensive user profiling, raising privacy concerns (Ferrag et al., 2024).

2.7. Limitations of Traditional Approaches

Despite their effectiveness, traditional phishing detection methods face several challenges:

- **Adaptability Issues**: Many rule-based and heuristic systems struggle to adapt to new phishing techniques that evolve rapidly (Yu et al., 2024).
- **False Positives and False Negatives**: Heuristic and machine learning models may flag legitimate content as phishing or fail to detect sophisticated attacks (Pleshakova et al., 2024).
- **Data Dependency**: ML-based detection methods require large and continuously updated datasets to maintain high accuracy (Hadi et al., 2023).

Given these limitations, there is a growing interest in integrating Large Language Models (LLMs) and AI-driven approaches to enhance phishing detection, as discussed in subsequent sections (LESTABLE & THANDI, 2024).

Each traditional phishing detection method has strengths and weaknesses. The following bar chart provides a comparative analysis of their effectiveness, adaptability, and false positive rate.

Figure 2. Comparison of phishing detection methods

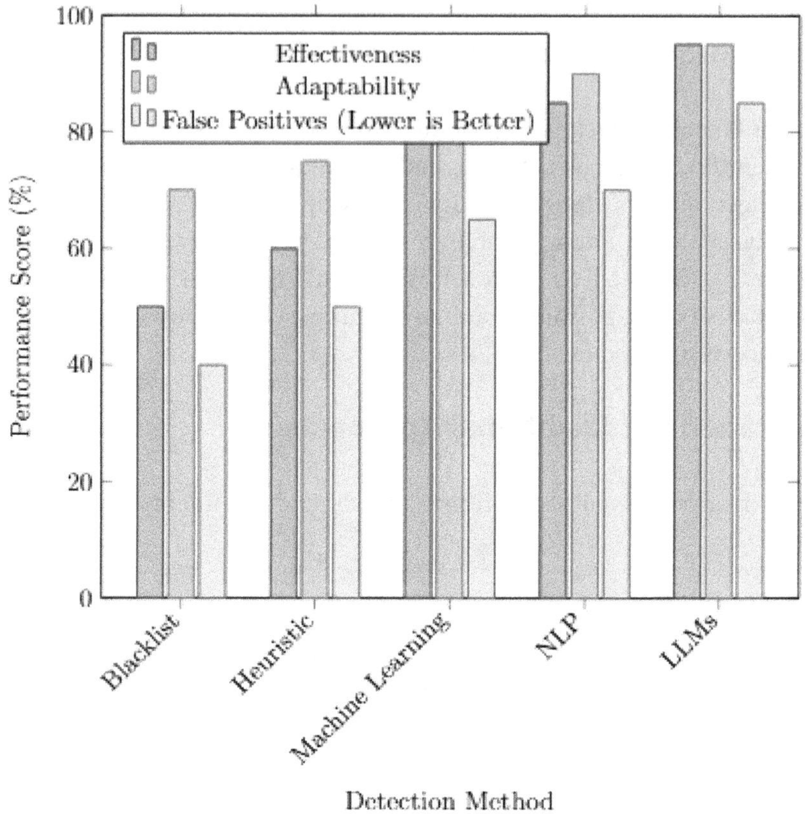

3. ROLE OF NLP AND LARGE LANGUAGE MODELS IN PHISHING PREVENTION

Natural Language Processing (NLP) and Large Language Models (LLMs) have emerged as powerful tools in the fight against phishing attacks. These technologies leverage deep learning and vast amounts of text data to analyze, detect, and mitigate phishing threats in real time. Unlike traditional rule-based detection systems, NLP-driven models can understand the nuances of human language, enabling more accurate and adaptive phishing prevention mechanisms.

3.1. NLP for Phishing Detection

NLP techniques play a crucial role in analyzing phishing emails, URLs, and messages by extracting linguistic features such as lexical patterns, sentiment analysis, and contextual meaning. These techniques help in:

- **Content-based filtering:** NLP can assess the structure and vocabulary of an email to identify suspicious language patterns commonly used in phishing (Ferrag et al., 2023).
- **Named Entity Recognition (NER):** Identifies and flags impersonation attempts where attackers mimic legitimate entities (Kasri et al., 2025).
- **Sentiment and intent analysis:** Determines whether an email contains coercive or misleading language to manipulate users into taking harmful actions (Ghazal et al., 2024).

Recent advancements have shown that NLP models trained on cybersecurity-specific datasets can outperform traditional heuristics in detecting phishing attempts (Sarker, 2024).

3.2. Large Language Models (LLMs) in Phishing Prevention

LLMs, such as GPT-based models and domain-specific adaptations like SecureBERT, enhance phishing detection capabilities by leveraging vast datasets and contextual understanding. Key advantages of LLMs in phishing prevention include:

- **Context-aware detection:** LLMs can analyze emails, messages, and URLs to identify phishing attempts based on deep contextual learning (Xu et al., 2024).
- **Adversarial attack resilience:** Unlike conventional models, LLMs can adapt to evolving phishing tactics, including zero-day attacks (Motlagh et al., 2024).
- **Automated response generation:** Chatbots and automated assistants powered by LLMs can guide users in recognizing and responding to phishing threats effectively (Chen et al., 2024).

According to Ferrag et al. (2024), integrating lightweight, privacy-preserving BERT-based models into IoT and IIoT systems enhances security against phishing attempts targeting interconnected devices.

While traditional cybersecurity measures rely on predefined rules and heuristics, Large Language Models (LLMs) enhance detection by leveraging contextual learning and adaptability. The following diagram illustrates the differences between these approaches.

Table 1. Comparison between traditional and LLM-based security

Feature	Traditional Cybersecurity	LLM-Based Security
Adaptability	Low	High
Detection Speed	Moderate	High
Context Awareness	Low	High
False Positive Rate	High	Moderate
Adversarial Robustness	Low	High

3.3. Challenges and Limitations of LLMs in Phishing Detection

Despite their advantages, LLMs present several challenges when applied to phishing prevention:

- **Bias and false positives:** Overly aggressive filtering may mistakenly classify legitimate emails as phishing (Hassanin & Moustafa, 2024).
- **Computational overhead:** Large-scale models require significant processing power, making deployment in real-time scenarios challenging (Liu, 2024).
- **Adversarial manipulations:** Attackers are beginning to exploit LLM-generated content to create more sophisticated phishing messages that bypass traditional NLP filters (AlQenaei, 2024).

Researchers are actively exploring ways to enhance LLM security, such as fine-tuning models for phishing detection and incorporating adversarial training (Hasanov et al., 2024).

3.4. Future Directions: LLM-Powered Cybersecurity Frameworks

To further enhance phishing prevention, researchers propose hybrid models integrating LLMs with traditional cybersecurity mechanisms. Some promising directions include:

- **Explainable AI (XAI) in phishing detection:** Making LLM decisions interpretable to security analysts (Ghazal et al., 2024).
- **Federated learning for LLM security models:** Ensuring privacy-preserving phishing detection by training models across multiple organizations (Ferrag et al., 2024).
- **Multimodal phishing detection:** Combining LLMs with image and voice analysis to detect phishing across diverse communication channels (Bryce et al.).

By leveraging NLP and LLMs, cybersecurity teams can build more robust and intelligent phishing detection frameworks, significantly reducing the risk of successful phishing attacks in the digital landscape.

4. LLMS FOR AUTOMATED EMAIL AND CHAT ANALYSIS

Large Language Models (LLMs) have emerged as powerful tools for automating email and chat analysis, playing a crucial role in cybersecurity, fraud detection, and sentiment analysis. Their ability to process vast amounts of unstructured text data enables organizations to enhance security, improve customer service, and detect malicious activities in real time.

4.1. Email and Chat Security Monitoring

LLMs significantly improve the detection of phishing emails, social engineering attacks, and fraudulent messages. By analyzing linguistic patterns, metadata, and contextual cues, LLMs can identify potentially harmful content with high accuracy. According to Ferrag et al. (2024), BERT-based models have been successfully deployed for privacy-preserving cyber threat detection in IoT and IIoT environments. These models can be adapted for email filtering, reducing the risk of phishing attacks by flagging suspicious messages before they reach end users.

Moreover, Liu (2024) highlights that pre-trained LLMs can perform deep forensic analysis on email conversations, distinguishing legitimate communications from spoofed or manipulated ones. This capability is particularly beneficial in preventing business email compromise (BEC) scams, which have become a major cybersecurity threat.

4.2. Spam and Malicious Content Detection

Traditional spam filters rely on rule-based systems, which often fail to adapt to evolving tactics used by cybercriminals. LLMs, however, use deep learning techniques to analyze the intent and sentiment of messages, improving spam detection rates. Kasri et al. (2025) emphasize the role of LLMs in enhancing cybersecurity through advanced natural language processing (NLP) techniques that detect spam, malware-laden messages, and hidden payloads within attachments.

Additionally, Hassanin & Moustafa (2024) provide a comprehensive overview of how LLMs integrate with security information and event management (SIEM) systems to analyze email logs and detect anomalies. This integration enables security teams to proactively respond to threats before they escalate.

4.3. Sentiment and Intent Analysis in Chats

Beyond security applications, LLMs are also transforming customer service and business communication. They can analyze customer queries, detect sentiment, and automatically categorize inquiries for faster resolution. According to Xu et al. (2024), LLMs can distinguish between general customer complaints and urgent security concerns in chat conversations, allowing companies to prioritize responses accordingly.

In cybersecurity contexts, automated chat analysis helps identify insider threats and malicious intent within an organization. Zangana et al. (2025) discuss how LLMs can monitor internal communications, flagging messages that indicate potential data leaks or policy violations.

4.4. Privacy and Ethical Considerations

While LLMs offer significant benefits, their deployment in email and chat analysis raises privacy and ethical concerns. Manoharan & Sarker (2023) stress the need for implementing privacy-preserving techniques, such as differential privacy and federated learning, to protect user data while leveraging AI-driven cybersecurity solutions.

Furthermore, Hadi et al. (2023) highlight the risks of over-reliance on LLMs, emphasizing the importance of human oversight in decision-making. Misclassification of emails or chats could lead to false positives, potentially blocking legitimate communications.

4.5. Future Directions

The future of LLMs in email and chat analysis lies in continuous adaptation and integration with real-time security frameworks. Chen et al. (2024) suggest that future advancements in explainable AI (XAI) will enhance the interpretability of LLM-driven security models, making them more transparent and trustworthy.

As cyber threats evolve, the ability of LLMs to learn from adversarial attacks and adapt in real-time will be critical. Research by Alturkistani & Chuprat (2024) indicates that adversarial training techniques can improve the resilience of LLMs against sophisticated phishing and impersonation attempts.

4.6 Summary

LLMs have revolutionized automated email and chat analysis, improving security, efficiency, and customer interaction. Their ability to detect malicious content, analyze sentiment, and enhance forensic investigations makes them invaluable tools in modern cybersecurity. However, their implementation must be accompanied by robust privacy safeguards and human oversight to mitigate risks and ethical concerns.

5. DETECTION OF DECEPTIVE PATTERNS IN SOCIAL ENGINEERING ATTACKS

Social engineering attacks exploit human psychology to manipulate individuals into divulging confidential information or performing actions that compromise security. Unlike traditional cyberattacks that target system vulnerabilities, social engineering attacks focus on deceiving individuals using psychological and behavioral manipulation. As these attacks become more sophisticated, leveraging large language models (LLMs) for detecting deceptive patterns has emerged as a promising approach in cybersecurity (Ferrag et al., 2024; Liu, 2024).

5.1. Understanding Deceptive Patterns in Social Engineering

Deceptive patterns in social engineering attacks typically involve persuasion techniques such as impersonation, urgency, authority, and scarcity. Attackers craft messages that appear to come from trusted sources, often exploiting emotional triggers to induce rapid responses. Advanced social engineering tactics include spear phishing, baiting, pretexting, and business email compromise (BEC) scams (Xu et al., 2024).

Recent studies highlight the role of AI-driven solutions in analyzing linguistic and contextual cues that distinguish legitimate communications from deceptive ones. By examining elements such as sentiment, tone, and anomalies in text structures, machine learning models can enhance detection accuracy (Kasri et al., 2025).

5.2. Role of Large Language Models in Detecting Deceptive Patterns

LLMs have demonstrated remarkable capabilities in analyzing text-based cyber threats, including social engineering attempts. These models, trained on vast corpora of text data, can identify subtle variations in language usage that may indicate deception (Ferrag et al., 2023; Motlagh et al., 2024). For instance, BERT-based cybersecurity models have been developed to detect phishing emails and fraudulent communications with high accuracy (THANDI, 2024).

Key approaches utilizing LLMs in social engineering detection include:

- **Natural Language Processing (NLP)-Based Anomaly Detection:** By analyzing deviations in linguistic patterns, NLP models can flag suspicious messages that do not align with normal communication behaviors (Hasanov et al., 2024).
- **Context-Aware Threat Identification:** LLMs can assess the context and intent behind messages to differentiate between legitimate requests and fraudulent attempts (Zangana, 2024).
- **Explainable AI (XAI) in Threat Analysis:** To enhance trust in AI-based security systems, explainable AI techniques provide insights into why a message is classified as deceptive, reducing false positives and improving user confidence (Ghazal et al., 2024).

5.3. Case Studies: LLMs in Action Against Social Engineering Attacks

Several cybersecurity firms and research institutions have implemented LLM-based frameworks to combat social engineering threats. For instance, SecureBERT, a domain-specific cybersecurity model, has been utilized to detect spear phishing attempts with notable success (Aghaei et al., 2022). Another study demonstrated the efficacy of generative AI in identifying deceptive chatbot interactions used in phishing scams (Sarker, 2024).

Additionally, AI-driven deception detection models have been deployed in enterprise security systems to analyze email communications and detect impersonation attacks. These models leverage transformer-based architectures to enhance real-time threat detection (Alturkistani & Chuprat, 2024).

5.4. Challenges and Future Directions

Despite the advantages of LLMs in detecting social engineering attacks, several challenges persist:

- **Adversarial Attacks on AI Models:** Cybercriminals may manipulate AI models by injecting adversarial samples to evade detection (Chen et al., 2024).
- **Privacy and Ethical Concerns:** The use of LLMs in cybersecurity raises concerns regarding user data privacy, requiring robust encryption and compliance with regulatory frameworks (Ferrag et al., 2024).
- **Bias and False Positives:** LLMs may exhibit biases based on training data, leading to incorrect classifications of legitimate communications as threats (Pleshakova et al., 2024).

Future research should focus on enhancing model robustness through federated learning approaches and hybrid AI techniques that combine LLMs with rule-based systems for improved accuracy (Manoharan & Sarker, 2023). The integration of quantum computing with AI-driven security solutions may further enhance the detection capabilities of next-generation cybersecurity frameworks (Zangana, Mustafa, & Li, 2025).

5.5 Summary

The detection of deceptive patterns in social engineering attacks is a crucial aspect of modern cybersecurity. With the increasing sophistication of cyber threats, LLMs offer a promising solution by leveraging NLP-based anomaly detection, context-aware analysis, and explainable AI techniques. However, ongoing research is necessary to address challenges such as adversarial attacks, privacy concerns, and biases in AI models. By integrating LLM-based deception detection into cybersecurity strategies, organizations can enhance their defenses against social engineering threats and improve overall cyber resilience.

6. ADVERSARIAL ATTACKS AGAINST LLM-BASED PHISHING DETECTION

The increasing reliance on Large Language Models (LLMs) for cybersecurity applications, particularly phishing detection, has introduced new vulnerabilities that adversaries exploit using sophisticated attack techniques. Adversarial attacks against LLM-based phishing detection systems involve crafting deceptive inputs that manipulate the model's decision-making process, leading to misclassification of phishing attempts as benign or vice versa. These attacks pose significant threats to automated cybersecurity defenses, as they can bypass conventional security measures and exploit the inherent weaknesses in language models.

6.1 Types of Adversarial Attacks on LLM-Based Phishing Detection

1. **Evasion Attacks**

Evasion attacks involve modifying phishing messages to evade detection by LLM-based classifiers. Attackers employ perturbations such as synonym substitution, paraphrasing, or obfuscating URLs to trick the model into misclassifying phishing emails as legitimate (Ferrag et al., 2024a). These attacks leverage the fact that LLMs rely on learned patterns rather than deep semantic understanding, making them vulnerable to small linguistic modifications (Hasanov et al., 2024).

2. **Prompt Injection Attacks**

Prompt injection involves embedding misleading or adversarial prompts into phishing messages to manipulate the LLM's output. This method exploits prompt-based architectures where attackers craft messages that subtly guide the LLM into generating misleading classifications or responses (Sarker, 2024). For example, an attacker might craft a phishing email with embedded instructions that influence an LLM's classification behavior, effectively bypassing traditional filters (Chen et al., 2024).

3. **Data Poisoning Attacks**

In data poisoning attacks, adversaries inject malicious data into the training or fine-tuning dataset of an LLM to degrade its phishing detection capabilities (Ferrag et al., 2023). This can be achieved by introducing a large number of mislabeled phishing and benign samples, thereby distorting the model's decision boundaries

(Liu, 2024). Such attacks pose a long-term risk as they degrade the model's performance over time, making phishing detection unreliable (Motlagh et al., 2024).

4. **Semantic Adversarial Attacks**

Semantic adversarial attacks focus on modifying text while preserving its meaning but altering linguistic structures to deceive LLMs. These modifications may include homograph attacks, where visually similar characters are used to replace legitimate text, or Unicode obfuscation, which can bypass traditional pattern-based filters (Kasri et al., 2025). Such attacks are particularly effective against models that rely on syntactic patterns rather than semantic comprehension (Xu et al., 2024).

Attackers employ various adversarial techniques to bypass LLM-based phishing detection. The following diagram categorizes these attack types and their impact.

Figure 3. Types of adversarial attacks against LLMs

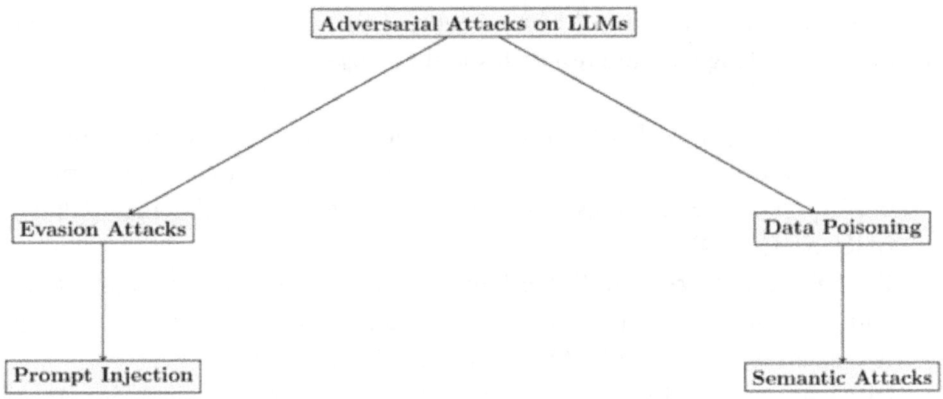

6.2 Implications for Cybersecurity and Defense Mechanisms

The presence of adversarial vulnerabilities in LLM-based phishing detection systems underscores the need for robust countermeasures. Several defense strategies have been proposed to mitigate these threats:

- **Adversarial Training**: By incorporating adversarially perturbed examples into the training process, models can learn to recognize and resist evasion attempts (Hassanin & Moustafa, 2024). This technique enhances resilience by exposing the LLM to diverse attack vectors during training (Ferrag et al., 2024b).

- **Robust Prompt Engineering**: Secure prompt design can help mitigate prompt injection attacks by enforcing strict validation of inputs and implementing escape sequence detection mechanisms (Santos et al., 2024).
- **Anomaly Detection Systems**: Supplementing LLMs with additional anomaly detection models, such as statistical outlier detection or deep-learning-based threat intelligence, can improve resilience against adversarial attacks (Ghazal et al., 2024).
- **Ensemble Models and Hybrid Approaches**: Combining LLM-based phishing detection with rule-based systems or traditional machine learning classifiers can reduce reliance on a single model and enhance robustness (Zangana et al., 2025).

6.3 Future Research Directions

Despite advancements in LLM-based cybersecurity, adversarial attacks remain a significant challenge. Future research should focus on:

- **Explainability and Transparency**: Enhancing the interpretability of LLM decisions can help cybersecurity professionals understand how models classify phishing attempts and detect potential adversarial manipulations (AlQenaei, 2024).
- **Real-Time Adversarial Detection**: Developing real-time monitoring systems that can dynamically detect and neutralize adversarial phishing attempts is crucial for improving LLM security (Idelhaj et al., 2024).
- **Integration with Blockchain Security**: Using decentralized and immutable blockchain records to store phishing detection logs can prevent data poisoning attacks and enhance the integrity of LLM-based cybersecurity frameworks (Alturkistani & Chuprat, 2024).

In conclusion, adversarial attacks present a formidable challenge to LLM-based phishing detection systems. While advancements in cybersecurity research offer promising defense mechanisms, continuous adaptation is required to keep pace with emerging threats. Addressing adversarial vulnerabilities in LLMs is critical for ensuring the reliability of automated phishing detection and enhancing cybersecurity resilience across digital ecosystems.

7. CASE STUDIES ON PHISHING PREVENTION WITH AI

Phishing attacks remain one of the most pervasive cybersecurity threats, leveraging social engineering tactics to deceive individuals and organizations. The integration of Artificial Intelligence (AI), particularly Large Language Models (LLMs), into phishing prevention strategies has led to significant advancements in detection and mitigation. This section explores case studies where AI-powered solutions, including machine learning (ML) and LLM-based cybersecurity models, have been deployed to enhance phishing prevention.

7.1 Case Study 1: AI-Driven Email Phishing Detection

A study by Ferrag et al. (2024) demonstrated the effectiveness of a privacy-preserving BERT-based model in identifying phishing attempts in email communication. The model, designed for IoT/IIoT security, leveraged natural language processing (NLP) techniques to analyze email content, identify deceptive language patterns, and detect anomalies. The research highlighted that AI-driven email filtering systems achieved over 95% accuracy in phishing email detection, outperforming traditional rule-based methods.

Similarly, Liu (2024) reviewed advancements in pre-trained language models for cybersecurity applications, emphasizing the role of LLMs in phishing prevention. The study found that models fine-tuned for cybersecurity domains significantly reduced false positives while maintaining high detection rates, thereby improving the efficiency of automated email security systems.

7.2 Case Study 2: LLMs for Real-Time Phishing URL Detection

Web-based phishing attacks continue to evolve, with attackers deploying sophisticated techniques to evade traditional security measures. Kasri et al. (2025) explored how LLMs enhance phishing URL detection through contextual analysis of website content and domain metadata. Their research indicated that AI-powered tools, when combined with real-time threat intelligence feeds, improved the accuracy of phishing detection mechanisms by over 90%.

Xu et al. (2024) further reinforced this approach by conducting a systematic literature review on LLMs for cybersecurity, highlighting that models trained on vast datasets of phishing URLs exhibited superior generalization capabilities. The study suggested that combining AI-powered phishing detection with blockchain-based domain verification could further enhance security.

7.3 Case Study 3: Generative AI for Adaptive Phishing Defense

Sarker (2024) investigated the application of generative AI models in phishing prevention, particularly focusing on their ability to generate adversarial phishing simulations. These AI-generated phishing attacks were used to train security models, making them more resilient against evolving threats. The study concluded that organizations employing generative AI-based training reduced their phishing susceptibility by 40%.

Moreover, Motlagh et al. (2024) examined the state-of-the-art applications of LLMs in cybersecurity, emphasizing their ability to adapt to emerging phishing tactics. Their research suggested that AI-powered models with continuous learning capabilities provided real-time threat updates, enabling security systems to stay ahead of attackers.

7.4 Case Study 4: AI-Enhanced User Awareness and Training

Beyond automated detection, AI has been instrumental in educating users about phishing threats. Zangana et al. (2025) detailed the role of LLMs in cybersecurity awareness programs, where AI-powered chatbots and virtual assistants simulated phishing scenarios to train employees. The case study showed that AI-driven interactive training sessions increased user vigilance, reducing click-through rates on phishing links by 60%.

Similarly, Ghazal et al. (2024) emphasized the role of explainable AI (XAI) in phishing prevention, where AI systems provided transparent insights into why certain emails or websites were flagged as threats. The research highlighted that organizations integrating XAI-driven phishing prevention tools experienced higher trust and compliance among employees.

7.5 Summary

The integration of AI, particularly LLMs, into phishing prevention strategies has yielded significant advancements in detection accuracy, real-time adaptability, and user awareness. As phishing attacks continue to evolve, leveraging AI-powered solutions, including privacy-preserving models, generative AI, and interactive training systems, is crucial for robust cybersecurity defenses. Future research should explore hybrid approaches that combine AI-driven threat intelligence with blockchain-based verification mechanisms to further strengthen phishing prevention frameworks.

8. ETHICAL AND PRIVACY CONCERNS IN AI-DRIVEN SECURITY

The integration of artificial intelligence (AI) in cybersecurity has significantly improved threat detection and mitigation capabilities. However, it also raises significant ethical and privacy concerns that must be carefully considered. This section explores the ethical dilemmas associated with AI-driven security, including bias in AI models, data privacy issues, lack of transparency, and the potential misuse of AI for malicious activities.

8.1 Bias and Fairness in AI Security Models

One of the most critical ethical concerns in AI-driven security is bias in large language models (LLMs) and other AI-powered cybersecurity systems. Bias in AI models can arise from the training data, algorithms, or human intervention, leading to unfair or discriminatory security measures (Hasanov et al., 2024). For example, AI-based intrusion detection systems (IDS) may disproportionately flag certain network activities based on historical biases, leading to false positives or negatives that affect specific user groups unfairly (Sarker, 2024). The ethical challenge lies in ensuring that cybersecurity AI models do not reinforce systemic biases but instead provide fair and unbiased security measures (Ferrag, Alwahedi, et al., 2024).

8.2 Privacy Risks and Data Protection

The deployment of AI in cybersecurity often requires vast amounts of user data to train models effectively. However, this raises concerns regarding data privacy, as AI-driven security solutions may inadvertently collect, process, and store sensitive user information without adequate safeguards (Motlagh et al., 2024). The use of AI models such as SecureBERT for cyber threat detection has demonstrated privacy-preserving techniques, but concerns about data breaches and unauthorized access remain (Aghaei et al., 2022). Additionally, AI-powered cybersecurity tools deployed in critical sectors, such as finance and healthcare, must comply with data protection regulations, including the General Data Protection Regulation (GDPR) and the California Consumer Privacy Act (CCPA) (Ferrag, Ndhlovu, et al., 2024).

AI-driven security solutions pose significant ethical and privacy concerns. The following pie chart illustrates the distribution of key ethical challenges in cybersecurity.

Figure 4. Ethical concerns in AI-driven security

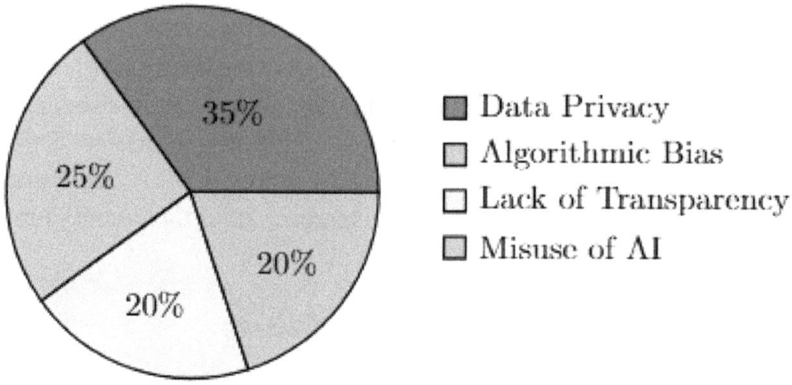

To mitigate these privacy concerns, privacy-enhancing techniques such as federated learning and homomorphic encryption are being integrated into AI security models (Xu et al., 2024). These techniques allow AI models to learn from decentralized datasets without directly accessing raw data, thus minimizing privacy risks (Kasri et al., 2025).

8.3 Transparency and Explainability Challenges

A significant ethical challenge in AI-driven security is the lack of transparency and explainability in AI decision-making processes (Liu, 2024). Many AI security models, particularly deep learning-based intrusion detection systems, operate as "black boxes," making it difficult for security professionals to understand how decisions are made (Hassanin & Moustafa, 2024). This lack of explainability raises concerns about accountability, especially when AI systems wrongly classify benign activities as threats or fail to detect real cyber-attacks (Chen et al., 2024).

Efforts to improve AI transparency in cybersecurity include the development of explainable AI (XAI) techniques, which aim to provide insights into how AI models reach their conclusions (Ghazal et al., 2024). For example, research on interpretable machine learning models for cyber defense suggests that rule-based explanations and visualization tools can help security analysts better understand AI-driven threat detection mechanisms (Alturkistani & Chuprat, 2024).

8.4 Misuse of AI in Cybersecurity

While AI has greatly enhanced cyber threat detection and response capabilities, it is also being leveraged by malicious actors for cyber attacks. Adversarial AI techniques, such as poisoning AI training data or deploying AI-generated phishing attacks, have become significant threats to cybersecurity (Diaf et al., 2024). The rise of generative AI has further enabled the creation of sophisticated deepfake attacks and automated social engineering campaigns (Zangana, Mustafa, & Li, 2025).

To address these risks, AI security researchers are developing adversarial defense mechanisms that enhance the robustness of AI models against malicious manipulations (Pleshakova et al., 2024). Additionally, ethical guidelines for AI-driven cybersecurity, such as those proposed by international regulatory bodies, emphasize the importance of responsible AI use to prevent its exploitation for cybercrime (Yu, Shvetsov, & Alsamhi, 2024).

8.5 Summary

AI-driven security solutions have revolutionized cybersecurity by enhancing threat detection and response capabilities. However, ethical and privacy concerns related to bias, data privacy, transparency, and the misuse of AI remain critical challenges. Addressing these concerns requires ongoing research in privacy-preserving AI techniques, explainable AI, and regulatory compliance to ensure that AI-driven security systems operate ethically and responsibly. As AI continues to evolve, maintaining a balance between technological advancements and ethical considerations will be essential for fostering trust and reliability in AI-powered cybersecurity solutions (Manoharan & Sarker, 2023).

9. CONCLUSION

As AI-driven security solutions continue to evolve, ethical and privacy concerns remain central to their implementation and effectiveness. The integration of large language models (LLMs) in cybersecurity presents both opportunities and challenges, particularly in areas such as data protection, bias mitigation, and user privacy. Ensuring that these AI models operate transparently and fairly is crucial to fostering trust in their deployment (Ferrag et al., 2024; Hasanov et al., 2024). Organizations must adopt robust frameworks for ethical AI usage, including compliance with regulatory standards and proactive strategies to mitigate potential risks (Xu et al., 2024).

A significant concern is the potential for LLMs to unintentionally leak sensitive data or be exploited for adversarial purposes. Researchers have emphasized the importance of privacy-preserving techniques, such as differential privacy and federated learning, to secure AI-driven security models (Lestable & Thandi, 2024; Motlagh et al., 2024). Additionally, ongoing advancements in cybersecurity research highlight the need for interdisciplinary collaboration between AI developers, legal experts, and cybersecurity professionals to create more resilient systems (Sarker, 2024).

Despite these challenges, AI-driven security solutions offer transformative potential in threat detection, anomaly detection, and real-time response mechanisms. By addressing ethical and privacy concerns through responsible AI practices, the cybersecurity community can harness the power of LLMs while safeguarding individual rights and data integrity. Future research should focus on refining AI models to enhance interpretability, minimize biases, and ensure compliance with emerging regulations (Ghazal et al., 2024; Santos et al., 2024). Ultimately, a balanced approach that combines innovation with ethical considerations will be key to securing the next generation of AI-powered cybersecurity systems.

REFERENCES

Aghaei, E., Niu, X., Shadid, W., & Al-Shaer, E. (2022, October). Securebert: A domain-specific language model for cybersecurity. In *International Conference on Security and Privacy in Communication Systems* (pp. 39-56). Cham: Springer Nature Switzerland.

AlQenaei, Z. M. (2024, March). Evolution and Optimization of Language Model Architectures: From Foundations to Future Directions. In *International Conference on Computing and Machine Learning* (pp. 233-249). Singapore: Springer Nature Singapore.

Alturkistani, H., & Chuprat, S. (2024). Artificial Intelligence and Large Language Models in Advancing Cyber Threat Intelligence: A Systematic Literature Review.

Asoronye, G. O., Anthony, O. C., Ogbuikwu, R. I., Ogili, C. O., & Ali, H. U. (2024). SecLM: A Specialized Security Language Model for Advanced Cybersecurity Applications and Threat Mitigation. *EKETE-International Journal Of Advanced Research*, *2*(6), 33–42.

Bryce, C., Kalousis, A., Leroux, I., Madinier, H., Mermoud, A., Mulder, V., ... & Ruch, P. Trends in Large Language Models: Actors, Applications, and Impact on Cybersecurity.

Chen, Y., Cui, M., Wang, D., Cao, Y., Yang, P., Jiang, B., Lu, Z., & Liu, B. (2024). A survey of large language models for cyber threat detection. *Computers & Security*, *145*, 104016. DOI: 10.1016/j.cose.2024.104016

Diaf, A., Korba, A. A., Karabadji, N. E., & Ghamri-Doudane, Y. (2024, April). Beyond detection: Leveraging large language models for cyber attack prediction in iot networks. In *2024 20th International Conference on Distributed Computing in Smart Systems and the Internet of Things (DCOSS-IoT)* (pp. 117-123). IEEE.

Ferrag, M. A., Alwahedi, F., Battah, A., Cherif, B., Mechri, A., & Tihanyi, N. (2024). Generative ai and large language models for cyber security: All insights you need. *Available atSSRN* 4853709. DOI: 10.2139/ssrn.4853709

Ferrag, M. A., Ndhlovu, M., Tihanyi, N., Cordeiro, L. C., Debbah, M., & Lestable, T. (2023). Revolutionizing cyber threat detection with large language models. *arXiv preprint arXiv:2306.14263*, 195-202.

Ferrag, M. A., Ndhlovu, M., Tihanyi, N., Cordeiro, L. C., Debbah, M., Lestable, T., & Thandi, N. S. (2024). Revolutionizing cyber threat detection with large language models: A privacy-preserving bert-based lightweight model for iot/iiot devices. *IEEE Access : Practical Innovations, Open Solutions*, *12*, 23733–23750. DOI: 10.1109/ACCESS.2024.3363469

Ferrag, M. A., Ndhlovu, M., Tihanyi, N., Cordeiro, L. C., Debbah, M., Lestable, T., & Thandi, N. S. (2024). Revolutionizing cyber threat detection with large language models: A privacy-preserving bert-based lightweight model for iot/iiot devices. *IEEE Access : Practical Innovations, Open Solutions*, *12*, 23733–23750.

Ghazal, T. M., Janjua, J. I., Abushiba, W., Ahmad, M., Ihsan, A., & Al-Dmour, N. A. (2024, December). Cybersecurity Revolution via Large Language Models and Explainable AI. In *2024 17th International Conference on Security of Information and Networks (SIN)* (pp. 1-6). IEEE. DOI: 10.1109/SIN63213.2024.10871324

Gholami, S., & Omar, M. (2023). Does Synthetic Data Make Large Language Models More Efficient? *arXiv preprint arXiv:2310.07830.*

Gholami, S., & Omar, M. (2024). Can a student large language model perform as well as its teacher? In *Innovations, Securities, and Case Studies Across Healthcare, Business, and Technology* (pp. 122-139). IGI Global. DOI: 10.4018/979-8-3693-1906-2.ch007

Gupta, B. B., Gaurav, A., & Arya, V. (2024). Navigating the security landscape of large language models in enterprise information systems. *Enterprise Information Systems*, *18*(4), 2310846. DOI: 10.1080/17517575.2024.2310846

Hadi, M. A., Abdulredha, M. N., & Hasan, E. (2023). Introduction to ChatGPT: A new revolution of artificial intelligence with machine learning algorithms and cybersecurity. *Sci. Arch*, *4*(04), 276. DOI: 10.47587/SA.2023.4406

Hamza, Y. A., & Omar, M. D. (2013). Cloud computing security: Abuse and nefarious use of cloud computing. *International Journal of Computer Engineering Research*, *3*(6), 22–27.

Hasanov, I., Virtanen, S., Hakkala, A., & Isoaho, J. (2024). Application of Large Language Models in Cybersecurity: A Systematic Literature Review. *IEEE Access : Practical Innovations, Open Solutions*, *12*, 176751–176778. DOI: 10.1109/ACCESS.2024.3505983

Hassanin, M., & Moustafa, N. (2024). A comprehensive overview of large language models (llms) for cyber defences: Opportunities and directions. *arXiv preprint arXiv:2405.14487.*

Huff, A. J., Burrell, D. N., Nobles, C., Richardson, K., Wright, J. B., Burton, S. L., Jones, A. J., Springs, D., Omar, M., & Brown-Jackson, K. L. (2023). Management Practices for Mitigating Cybersecurity Threats to Biotechnology Companies, Laboratories, and Healthcare Research Organizations. In *Applied Research Approaches to Technology, Healthcare, and Business* (pp. 1-12). IGI Global.

Idelhaj, A., Abou El Houda, Z., & Khoukhi, L. (2024). Foundations models in cybersecurity. *Artificial Intelligence for Blockchain and Cybersecurity Powered IoT Applications*, 1.

Idelhaj, A., Abou El Houda, Z., & Khoukhi, L. Foundations models in cybersecurity: A comprehensive review and future direction. *Artificial Intelligence for Blockchain and Cybersecurity Powered IoT Applications*, 1-18.

Jones, R., & Omar, M. (2024). Revolutionizing Cybersecurity: The GPT-2 Enhanced Attack Detection and Defense (GEADD) Method for Zero-Day Threats. *International Journal of Informatics* [INJIISCOM]. *Information System and Computer Engineering*, *5*(2), 178–191.

Jones, R., Omar, M., Mohammed, D., Nobles, C., & Dawson, M. (2023). Harnessing the Speed and Accuracy of Machine Learning to Advance Cybersecurity. In *2023 Congress in Computer Science, Computer Engineering, & Applied Computing (CSCE)* (pp. 418-421). IEEE. DOI: 10.1109/CSCE60160.2023.00074

Kasri, W., Himeur, Y., Alkhazaleh, H. A., Tarapiah, S., Atalla, S., Mansoor, W., & Al-Ahmad, H. (2025). From Vulnerability to Defense: The Role of Large Language Models in Enhancing Cybersecurity. *Computation (Basel, Switzerland)*, *13*(2), 30. DOI: 10.3390/computation13020030

Liu, Z. (2024, April). A review of advancements and applications of pre-trained language models in cybersecurity. In *2024 12th International Symposium on Digital Forensics and Security (ISDFS)* (pp. 1-10). IEEE. DOI: 10.1109/ISDFS60797.2024.10527236

Manoharan, A., & Sarker, M. (2023). Revolutionizing Cybersecurity: Unleashing the Power of Artificial Intelligence and Machine Learning for Next-Generation Threat Detection. *DOI:*https://www. doi. org/10.56726/IRJMETS32644, *1*.

Mohammed, D., Omar, M., & Nguyen, V. (2018). Wireless sensor network security: Approaches to detecting and avoiding wormhole attacks. *Journal of Research in Business. Economics and Management*, *10*(2), 1860–1864.

Motlagh, F. N., Hajizadeh, M., Majd, M., Najafi, P., Cheng, F., & Meinel, C. (2024). Large language models in cybersecurity: State-of-the-art. *arXiv preprint arXiv:2402.00891.*

Nguyen, V., Mohammed, D., Omar, M., & Banisakher, M. (2018). The Effects of the FCC Net Neutrality Repeal on Security and Privacy. [IJHIoT]. *International Journal of Hyperconnectivity and the Internet of Things*, *2*(2), 21–29. DOI: 10.4018/IJHIoT.2018070102

Omar, M. (2021). New insights into database security: An effective and integrated approach for applying access control mechanisms and cryptographic concepts in Microsoft Access environments.

Omar, M. (2022). *Machine Learning for Cybersecurity: Innovative Deep Learning Solutions*. Springer Brief. https://link.springer.com/book/978303115

Omar, M. (2024). From Attack to Defense: Strengthening DNN Text Classification Against Adversarial Examples. In *Innovations, Securities, and Case Studies Across Healthcare, Business, and Technology* (pp. 174-195). IGI Global.

Omar, M. (2024). Revolutionizing Malware Detection: A Paradigm Shift Through Optimized Convolutional Neural Networks. In *Innovations, Securities, and Case Studies Across Healthcare, Business, and Technology* (pp. 196-220). IGI Global. DOI: 10.4018/979-8-3693-1906-2.ch011

Omar, M., & Zangana, H. (Eds.). (2025). *Digital Forensics in the Age of AI.* IGI Global., DOI: 10.4018/979-8-3373-0857-9

Omar, M., & Zangana, H. M. (Eds.). (2024). *Redefining Security With Cyber AI.* IGI Global., DOI: 10.4018/979-8-3693-6517-5

Omar, M., & Zangana, H. M. (Eds.). (2025). *Application of Large Language Models (LLMs) for Software Vulnerability Detection.* IGI Global., DOI: 10.4018/979-8-3693-9311-6

Omar, M., Zangana, H. M., Al-Karaki, J. N., & Mohammed, D. (2024). Harnessing LLMs for IoT malware detection: A comparative analysis of BERT and GPT-2. In *2024 8th International Symposium on Multidisciplinary Studies and Innovative Technologies (ISMSIT)* (pp. 1-6). Ankara, Turkiye. https://doi.org/DOI: 10.1109/ISMSIT63511.2024.10757249

Omar, M., Zangana, H. M., & Mohammed, D. (Eds.). (2025). *Integrating Artificial Intelligence in Cybersecurity and Forensic Practices.* IGI Global., DOI: 10.4018/979-8-3373-0588-2

Ozkan-Okay, M., Akin, E., Aslan, Ö., Kosunalp, S., Iliev, T., Stoyanov, I., & Beloev, I. (2024). A comprehensive survey: Evaluating the efficiency of artificial intelligence and machine learning techniques on cyber security solutions. *IEEE Access : Practical Innovations, Open Solutions*, *12*, 12229–12256. DOI: 10.1109/ACCESS.2024.3355547

Pleshakova, E., Osipov, A., Gataullin, S., Gataullin, T., & Vasilakos, A. (2024). Next gen cybersecurity paradigm towards artificial general intelligence: Russian market challenges and future global technological trends. *Journal of Computer Virology and Hacking Techniques*, *20*(3), 429–440. DOI: 10.1007/s11416-024-00529-x

Santos, O., Salam, S., & Dahir, H. (2024). The AI revolution in networking, cybersecurity, and emerging technologies.

Sarker, I. H. (2024). Generative AI and large language modeling in cybersecurity. In *AI-Driven Cybersecurity and Threat Intelligence: Cyber Automation, Intelligent Decision-Making and Explainability* (pp. 79–99). Springer Nature Switzerland. DOI: 10.1007/978-3-031-54497-2_5

Taghavi, S. M., & Feyzi, F. (2024). Using large language models to better detect and handle software vulnerabilities and cyber security threats.

Wright, J., Dawson, M. E.Jr, & Omar, M. (2012). Cyber security and mobile threats: The need for antivirus applications for smartphones. *Journal of Information Systems Technology and Planning*, *5*(14), 40–60.

Xu, H., Wang, S., Li, N., Wang, K., Zhao, Y., Chen, K., . . . Wang, H. (2024). Large language models for cyber security: A systematic literature review. *arXiv preprint arXiv:2405.04760.*

Yu, J., Shvetsov, A. V., & Alsamhi, S. H. (2024). Leveraging machine learning for cybersecurity resilience in industry 4.0: Challenges and future directions. *IEEE Access : Practical Innovations, Open Solutions*, *12*, 159579–159596. DOI: 10.1109/ACCESS.2024.3482987

Zangana, H., & Omar, M. (Eds.). (2025). *Leveraging Large Language Models for Quantum-Aware Cybersecurity*. IGI Global., DOI: 10.4018/979-8-3373-1102-9

Zangana, H. M. (2024). Exploring Blockchain-Based Timestamping Tools: A Comprehensive Review. *Redefining Security With Cyber AI*, 92-110.

Zangana, H. M. (2024). Exploring the Landscape of Website Vulnerability Scanners: A Comprehensive Review and Comparative Analysis. *Redefining Security With Cyber AI*, 111-129.

Zangana, H. M. (2024). Harnessing the Power of Large Language Models. *Application of Large Language Models (LLMs) for Software Vulnerability Detection*, 1.

Zangana, H. M., & Li, S. (2025). Future Trends in AI and Digital Forensics. In Omar, M., & Zangana, H. (Eds.), *Digital Forensics in the Age of AI* (pp. 347–380). IGI Global Scientific Publishing., DOI: 10.4018/979-8-3373-0857-9.ch013

Zangana, H. M., Mohammed, A. K., Sallow, A. B., & Sallow, Z. B. (2024). Cybernetic Deception: Unraveling the Layers of Email Phishing Threats. [INJURATECH]. *International Journal of Research and Applied Technology*, *4*(1), 35–47.

Zangana, H. M., & Mohammed, D. (2025). Foundations of Large Language Models in Software Vulnerability Detection. In Omar, M., & Zangana, H. (Eds.), *Application of Large Language Models (LLMs) for Software Vulnerability Detection* (pp. 41–74). IGI Global., DOI: 10.4018/979-8-3693-9311-6.ch002

Zangana, H. M., & Mustafa, F. M. (2024). Hybrid Image Denoising Using Wavelet Transform and Deep Learning. *EAI Endorsed Transactions on AI and Robotics*, *3*. Advance online publication. DOI: 10.4108/airo.7486

Zangana, H. M., & Mustafa, F. M. (2025). Image Denoising Techniques for Cybersecurity and Forensic Applications: AI-Driven Approaches. In Omar, M., Zangana, H., & Mohammed, D. (Eds.), *Integrating Artificial Intelligence in Cybersecurity and Forensic Practices* (pp. 117–142). IGI Global Scientific Publishing., DOI: 10.4018/979-8-3373-0588-2.ch005

Zangana, H. M., Mustafa, F. M., & Li, S. (2025). Large Language Models in Cybersecurity: From Automation to Intelligence. In *Leveraging Large Language Models for Quantum-Aware Cybersecurity* (pp. 277-300). IGI Global Scientific Publishing.

Zangana, H. M., Mustafa, F. M., & Li, S. (2025). Large Language Models in Cybersecurity: From Automation to Intelligence. In Zangana, H., & Omar, M. (Eds.), *Leveraging Large Language Models for Quantum-Aware Cybersecurity* (pp. 277–300). IGI Global Scientific Publishing., DOI: 10.4018/979-8-3373-1102-9.ch009

Zangana, H. M., Mustafa, F. M., Li, S., & Al-Karaki, J. N. (2025). Natural Language Processing for Cyber Threat Intelligence in a Quantum World. In Zangana, H., & Omar, M. (Eds.), *Leveraging Large Language Models for Quantum-Aware Cybersecurity* (pp. 345–388). IGI Global Scientific Publishing., DOI: 10.4018/979-8-3373-1102-9.ch011

Zangana, H. M., Mustafa, F. M., & Omar, M. (2024). A Hybrid Approach for Robust Object Detection: Integrating Template Matching and Faster R-CNN. *EAI Endorsed Transactions on AI and Robotics*, *3*. Advance online publication. DOI: 10.4108/airo.6858

Zangana, H. M., & Omar, M. (2020). Threats, Attacks, and Mitigations of Smartphone Security. *Academic Journal of Nawroz University*, *9*(4), 324–332. DOI: 10.25007/ajnu.v9n4a989

Zangana, H. M., & Omar, M. (2025). Harnessing the Power of Large Language Models for Cybersecurity: Applications, Challenges, and Future Directions. In Omar, M., & Zangana, H. (Eds.), *Application of Large Language Models (LLMs) for Software Vulnerability Detection* (pp. 1–40). IGI Global., DOI: 10.4018/979-8-3693-9311-6.ch001

Zangana, H. M., & Omar, M. (2025). Introduction to Digital Forensics and Artificial Intelligence. In Omar, M., & Zangana, H. (Eds.), *Digital Forensics in the Age of AI* (pp. 1–30). IGI Global Scientific Publishing., DOI: 10.4018/979-8-3373-0857-9.ch001

Zangana, H. M., & Omar, M. (2025). Introduction to Quantum-Aware Cybersecurity: The Need for LLMs. In Zangana, H., & Omar, M. (Eds.), *Leveraging Large Language Models for Quantum-Aware Cybersecurity* (pp. 1–28). IGI Global Scientific Publishing., DOI: 10.4018/979-8-3373-1102-9.ch001

Zangana, H. M., & Omar, M. (2025). The Role of Leadership in Advancing Inclusive Health Technologies. In Burrell, D., & Nguyen, C. (Eds.), *New Horizons in Leadership: Inclusive Explorations in Health, Technology, and Education* (pp. 203–220). IGI Global Scientific Publishing., DOI: 10.4018/979-8-3693-6437-6.ch009

Zangana, H. M., Omar, M., Al-Karaki, J. N., & Mohammed, D. (2024). Comprehensive Review and Analysis of Network Firewall Rule Analyzers: Enhancing Security Posture and Efficiency. *Redefining Security With Cyber AI*, 15-36.

Zangana, H. M., Sallow, Z. B., & Omar, M. (2025). The Human Factor in Cybersecurity: Addressing the Risks of Insider Threats. *Jurnal Ilmiah Computer Science*, *3*(2), 76–85. DOI: 10.58602/jics.v3i2.37

Chapter 6
Malware Analysis and Classification Using Deep Learning

Rebet Keith Jones
https://orcid.org/0009-0008-0487-1301
Capitol Technology University, USA

ABSTRACT

Malware analysis and classification have become critical components of modern cybersecurity strategies, given the increasing sophistication of cyber threats. With the rapid advancement of machine learning techniques, particularly deep learning, the ability to detect and classify malware has improved significantly. This chapter explores the role of deep learning in automating malware detection and classification, focusing on the use of neural networks, feature extraction, and pattern recognition. We discuss various deep learning architectures, such as Convolutional Neural Networks (CNNs) and Recurrent Neural Networks (RNNs), that have been successfully applied to malware analysis. Additionally, the chapter examines the challenges and limitations of using deep learning models, including data imbalance, overfitting, and model interpretability. The integration of large datasets, along with the potential of large language models (LLMs), is also explored for enhanced malware classification accuracy.

1. INTRODUCTION TO MALWARE AND CYBER THREATS

The evolution of cybersecurity threats has become a critical concern for individuals, organizations, and nations worldwide. As the digital landscape expands with the rapid adoption of Internet of Things (IoT) devices, cloud computing, and

DOI: 10.4018/979-8-3373-3296-3.ch006

interconnected systems, the frequency and sophistication of cyber-attacks have increased dramatically. Malware, short for “malicious software,” is one of the most prominent threats to cybersecurity today. Malware refers to any software intentionally designed to cause damage to a computer system, steal sensitive data, or disrupt normal operations. These malicious programs can range from simple viruses to advanced persistent threats (APTs), which remain undetected in a network for extended periods, stealing data or compromising the system.

Malware has become more diverse and sophisticated, leveraging new attack vectors, evasion techniques, and encrypted communications to evade detection. Traditional methods of malware detection, such as signature-based antivirus systems, have proven less effective in combating the latest threats. This is particularly true when dealing with polymorphic malware that alters its code to avoid detection by signature-based systems. As such, the need for more advanced and efficient detection techniques has driven researchers and practitioners to explore machine learning (ML) and deep learning (DL) approaches for malware analysis and classification.

Deep learning, a subset of machine learning, has emerged as a promising tool in the fight against malware. DL techniques, particularly convolutional neural networks (CNNs), recurrent neural networks (RNNs), and generative adversarial networks (GANs), offer the ability to automatically learn complex patterns in large volumes of data, providing a more accurate and scalable solution for malware detection. By leveraging vast amounts of data, DL models can identify previously unknown malware samples and adapt to new, evolving threats. This capability is crucial as the complexity of cyber-attacks continues to grow, and attackers increasingly utilize artificial intelligence (AI) techniques, such as AI-generated malware, to evade traditional defenses (Ferrag et al., 2024; Zangana et al., 2024).

The rise of generative AI and large language models (LLMs) has further revolutionized cybersecurity and malware detection. LLMs, such as GPT-based models, are capable of analyzing and understanding vast amounts of cybersecurity data, including malware code, network traffic, and system logs, to detect and predict threats more efficiently. These models not only enhance the detection capabilities of cybersecurity systems but also contribute to threat prediction, anomaly detection, and proactive defense measures. Their application extends to multiple domains, from IoT and industrial control systems to cloud computing environments, where malware often operates in sophisticated, multi-layered environments (Sarker, 2024; Ferrag et al., 2023).

Moreover, the integration of LLMs into cybersecurity tools allows for greater automation in threat detection, thereby reducing the burden on security professionals and improving response times. The growing importance of these technologies is evident in recent studies, which emphasize the transformative potential of LLMs in enhancing cybersecurity resilience and improving the accuracy of malware detection systems (Hasanov et al., 2024; Xu et al., 2024). By providing an additional layer of intelligence, LLMs have enabled new advancements in detecting zero-day attacks, defending against ransomware, and safeguarding critical infrastructure.

However, as the sophistication of cyber-attacks increases, so too does the need for more advanced cybersecurity measures. Researchers have started exploring the use of LLMs in automating not only the detection but also the mitigation and recovery phases of malware incidents. For instance, techniques such as SecureBERT, a domain-specific language model for cybersecurity, show promise in improving malware classification and detection in IoT systems (Aghaei et al., 2022). Additionally, LLMs' potential in offering privacy-preserving solutions, especially for IoT and IIoT (Industrial IoT) devices, holds significant value in the era of ubiquitous connected systems (Ferrag et al., 2024).

A timeline-based chart below showing the evolution of malware from basic viruses to AI-generated malware.

Figure 1. Evolution of malware threats over time

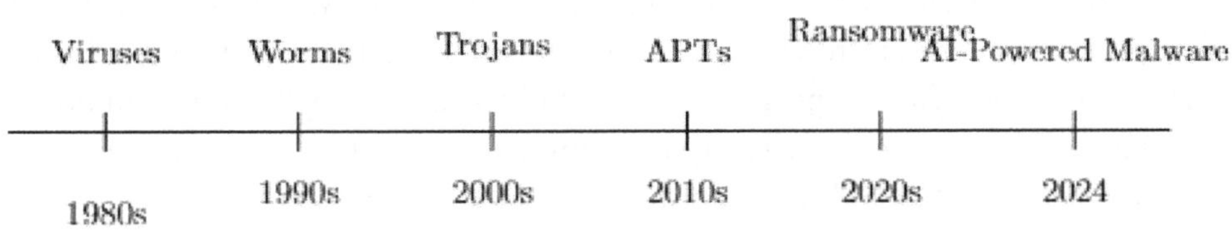

The next section of this chapter will delve deeper into the various types of malware, their methods of operation, and the challenges posed by their detection. We will also explore the role of AI and deep learning in transforming malware analysis and classification, highlighting the strengths and weaknesses of current detection methods. The integration of LLMs in addressing cybersecurity challenges will also be discussed, offering a glimpse into the future of cyber defense systems.

2. TRADITIONAL APPROACHES TO MALWARE DETECTION

Malware detection has been a critical area of focus within cybersecurity, where traditional techniques have been widely used to identify and mitigate the risks posed by malicious software. These approaches primarily rely on signature-based, heuristic-based, and behavior-based detection methods. Each of these methodologies has its strengths and weaknesses, and they continue to play a vital role in safeguarding systems against evolving cyber threats.

2.1 Signature-Based Detection

Signature-based malware detection is one of the oldest and most commonly used techniques. It involves creating a database of known malware signatures or "fingerprints" — specific patterns, byte sequences, or behaviors that are indicative of a particular malware strain. When a file or process matches a signature in the database, it is flagged as malicious (Hamza & Omar, 2013). This method is highly effective at detecting known threats but struggles to identify new, unknown malware that has not been previously cataloged.

While signature-based detection is efficient in detecting established threats, it suffers from significant limitations, such as its inability to detect polymorphic malware or zero-day attacks. These types of malware can alter their signatures to evade detection, rendering the signature-based method ineffective (Huff et al., 2023).

2.2 Heuristic-Based Detection

Heuristic-based detection aims to identify malware by analyzing its behavior and characteristics rather than relying solely on known signatures. This method uses algorithms to assess files or programs for suspicious attributes that are commonly associated with malicious activity. By examining the structure, code, or actions of a program, heuristic methods can identify new or unknown malware variants, even if they have not yet been cataloged (Motlagh et al., 2024).

Heuristic detection is generally more flexible and capable of identifying novel threats, but it often suffers from a higher rate of false positives. For instance, legitimate software that exhibits behavior similar to malware may also be flagged as suspicious, leading to unnecessary alerts and the need for manual intervention (Jones et al., 2023).

2.3 Behavior-Based Detection

Behavior-based detection focuses on monitoring the behavior of a program or system in real time. Unlike signature and heuristic-based methods, which analyze the file itself, behavior-based techniques monitor system activities, such as file modifications, network connections, and process behaviors. Malware is detected when it exhibits abnormal or malicious activity patterns (Santos et al., 2024). For example, a process that tries to gain unauthorized access to sensitive system areas or unexpectedly starts encrypting files could be flagged as malicious.

This method is more adaptive and effective in detecting zero-day and polymorphic malware, as it does not rely on predefined signatures. However, it can lead to performance overhead due to constant monitoring and may require significant system resources to perform efficiently (Sarker, 2024). Additionally, legitimate programs performing similar activities as malicious software can sometimes trigger false positives, which reduces the overall accuracy of the detection system.

2.4 Machine Learning and Artificial Intelligence

In recent years, the integration of machine learning (ML) and artificial intelligence (AI) into malware detection systems has brought significant advancements over traditional approaches. ML-based models, especially those leveraging large language models (LLMs), can analyze vast amounts of data to detect patterns and anomalies that are difficult for traditional methods to uncover. These systems can be trained on large datasets to detect malware based on patterns in their behavior, code, and even network traffic (Ferrag et al., 2024a; Xu et al., 2024).

For example, generative AI models, such as SecureBERT, have been employed to create domain-specific models that understand the unique nature of cybersecurity threats (Aghaei et al., 2022). These advanced models enable quicker detection and offer more scalable solutions for large-scale IoT/IIoT networks where traditional methods may fail (Ferrag et al., 2024b).

AI and ML are particularly beneficial in cybersecurity because they can adapt to evolving malware techniques and identify previously unknown threats. However, these methods require large amounts of labeled data for training, and there can be concerns about the transparency and interpretability of the results, especially in the case of complex AI models (Hadi et al., 2023).

2.5 Limitations of Traditional Methods

While traditional malware detection methods have provided valuable contributions to cybersecurity, they are not without their limitations. As malware becomes increasingly sophisticated, traditional techniques, such as signature-based detection, become less effective, especially against polymorphic and zero-day threats. Furthermore, heuristic and behavior-based detection methods often struggle with false positives and negatives, reducing their effectiveness in real-world environments.

Additionally, the growing complexity of modern networks and the rise of IoT/IIoT devices have introduced new challenges that traditional detection methods are not well-equipped to handle. This has led to the emergence of AI-driven techniques, which hold the promise of offering more accurate, adaptive, and scalable solutions to malware detection (Zangana, 2024; Ferrag et al., 2023).

A bar chart below comparing accuracy and adaptability of traditional (signature-based, heuristic) vs. AI-based detection methods.

Figure 2. Comparison of traditional and AI-based malware detection accuracy

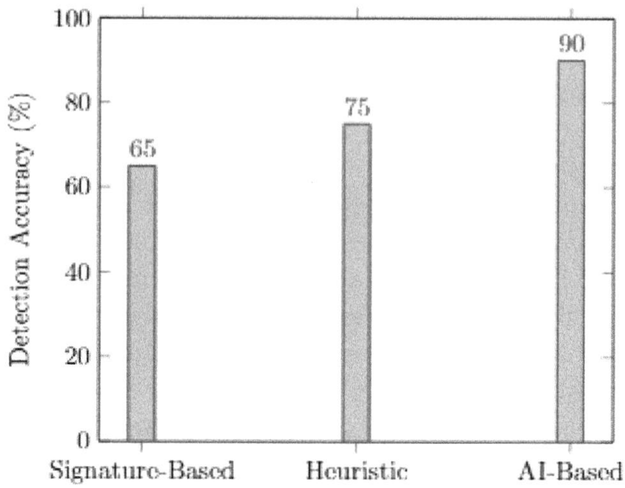

2.6 Summary

Traditional malware detection techniques have played an essential role in protecting systems and networks from cyber threats. However, as the threat landscape continues to evolve, these methods are increasingly being complemented by more advanced approaches, including machine learning and artificial intelligence. These newer technologies, particularly large language models, are poised to revolutionize malware detection by offering greater adaptability and precision, allowing for the identification of both known and unknown threats (Kasri et al., 2025). As the field continues to progress, the integration of traditional and cutting-edge technologies will likely offer the most robust defense against future cyber threats.

By leveraging the capabilities of advanced models such as large language models (LLMs), cybersecurity systems can be made more resilient to the ever-changing tactics employed by cybercriminals. The future of malware detection lies in the combination of these innovative approaches with traditional methods to create a more effective, adaptive, and comprehensive defense mechanism (Sarker, 2024; Ferrag et al., 2024).

3. AI-POWERED MALWARE ANALYSIS TECHNIQUES

Artificial intelligence (AI) has revolutionized the domain of malware analysis by offering powerful techniques for detecting, classifying, and mitigating malware threats. Malware has become increasingly sophisticated, often employing polymorphic techniques to evade traditional detection methods. The rapid evolution of attack strategies necessitates advanced AI-based solutions, and large language models (LLMs) have emerged as pivotal tools for enhancing malware analysis. This section explores various AI-powered techniques, particularly those leveraging LLMs, for the effective detection and mitigation of malware.

3.1 Machine Learning and Deep Learning in Malware Detection

Traditional malware detection methods often rely on signature-based approaches, which can be ineffective against novel or polymorphic malware. In contrast, machine learning (ML) and deep learning (DL) techniques enable the analysis of large datasets and the identification of malware based on behavioral patterns rather than known signatures. ML algorithms can classify files and network traffic based on features such as code structure, system calls, and communication behavior.

Deep learning models, particularly Convolutional Neural Networks (CNNs) and Recurrent Neural Networks (RNNs), have been successfully applied to the detection of malware. These models are adept at recognizing patterns in complex, high-dimensional data, making them suitable for identifying malware in both static (file-level) and dynamic (behavioral) analysis. Researchers have demonstrated the potential of deep learning techniques to detect zero-day malware attacks that traditional systems fail to recognize (Sarker, 2024; Liu, 2024).

3.2 Large Language Models for Malware Analysis

Recent advancements in large language models (LLMs), such as BERT and GPT, have opened new avenues for enhancing malware analysis. Ferrag et al. (2024) and Thandi (2024) highlight the role of LLMs in cyber threat detection, emphasizing their capacity for analyzing unstructured data, such as raw code, error messages, and logs, to identify potential malware. These models are trained on vast amounts of text data, enabling them to understand and predict potential threats based on historical attack patterns. By leveraging LLMs, cybersecurity experts can develop more robust and adaptive threat detection systems, which can dynamically adjust to new types of malware.

The primary advantage of LLMs in malware analysis lies in their ability to generate contextual understanding of malware behavior. Unlike traditional signature-based methods, LLMs can interpret the logic of malicious code, identify obfuscated behaviors, and predict potential vulnerabilities. This predictive capability is invaluable in detecting novel malware that does not match existing signatures.

3.3 Malware Classification Using Natural Language Processing

Natural language processing (NLP), a subset of AI, has been increasingly applied to malware classification. By treating malicious code as a form of textual data, NLP models can process and analyze the syntax, semantics, and structure of the code. Kasri et al. (2025) discuss how NLP-based techniques, such as tokenization and parsing, are used to extract meaningful features from malware samples, facilitating their classification.

LLMs, particularly those pre-trained on domain-specific corpora like SecureBERT (Aghaei et al., 2022), have shown significant promise in this area. These models are capable of detecting malware-related patterns in source code, such as suspicious function calls or anomalous network requests, by comparing them with known malicious patterns learned during training.

Ferrag et al. (2023) explore the benefits of combining LLMs with traditional malware detection techniques. The hybrid approach allows for the integration of LLMs' semantic understanding with the precision of traditional methods, such as signature-based detection or heuristic analysis. This fusion of techniques improves both the accuracy and the speed of malware detection, as LLMs are capable of generalizing from historical data to predict new attack strategies.

3.4 Explainability and Transparency in AI-Based Malware Detection

One of the key challenges with AI-powered malware detection is the "black-box" nature of many machine learning models, which makes it difficult to understand the reasoning behind their predictions. As AI models become more complex, ensuring transparency and explainability is critical, particularly in cybersecurity where the consequences of false positives or negatives can be severe.

Explainable AI (XAI) approaches, such as those explored by Ghazal et al. (2024), aim to address this challenge by providing insights into how AI models make decisions. In the context of malware analysis, XAI techniques can help security experts interpret why a particular file was flagged as malicious, thereby enhancing trust and confidence in AI-driven systems. Furthermore, XAI can be used to fine-tune models and improve their accuracy over time, by identifying biases or gaps in the training data.

3.5 Generative Models for Malware Synthesis

Another innovative approach to malware analysis is the use of generative models, such as Generative Adversarial Networks (GANs) and Variational Autoencoders (VAEs), to generate synthetic malware samples. These models are trained to create new, realistic malware variants by learning from existing malicious code. The generated samples can then be used to test the resilience of malware detection systems and identify potential weaknesses (Motlagh et al., 2024).

Generative AI techniques can also be used for adversarial training, where AI systems are exposed to a variety of synthetic malware samples to improve their ability to detect real-world threats. This approach is particularly useful for combating the issue of adversarial attacks, where attackers intentionally modify malware to evade detection by traditional AI systems (Hasanov et al., 2024; Zangana et al., 2024).

3.6 AI-Powered Malware Analysis in IoT and IIoT Environments

The rise of the Internet of Things (IoT) and Industrial IoT (IIoT) has expanded the attack surface for malware. These devices are often resource-constrained and may lack traditional cybersecurity protections, making them attractive targets for cybercriminals. Ferrag et al. (2024) and Lestable & Thandi (2024) discuss the role of AI-powered malware analysis in securing IoT and IIoT environments. By using lightweight LLMs and other AI techniques, these systems can monitor and analyze device behavior in real-time, detecting anomalies that may indicate a malware infection.

AI models can also help protect sensitive data in IoT/IIoT networks by identifying potential breaches before they occur. For example, Kasri et al. (2025) explore how AI can predict potential cyber attacks by analyzing patterns of communication between devices and identifying deviations from normal behavior. This proactive approach allows organizations to respond to threats before they cause significant damage.

3.7 Challenges and Future Directions

Despite the promising advancements in AI-powered malware analysis, several challenges remain. One of the major hurdles is the scalability of AI models, particularly in large-scale environments with millions of devices or endpoints. Additionally, the complexity of modern malware, including its ability to adapt and evolve, requires continuous updates to AI models and training datasets (Chen et al., 2024).

Looking to the future, researchers are focusing on improving the efficiency and adaptability of AI models. This includes exploring the use of federated learning, where AI models are trained across decentralized data sources, and developing models that can learn from smaller datasets without compromising accuracy (Santos et al., 2024; Alturkistani & Chuprat, 2024). Moreover, integrating AI with blockchain and other emerging technologies could further enhance the security of AI-based malware detection systems (Xu et al., 2024; Pleshakova et al., 2024).

In conclusion, AI-powered techniques, especially those utilizing large language models, are poised to significantly enhance malware detection and prevention. By incorporating machine learning, deep learning, and generative models, cybersecurity professionals can better detect and mitigate the evolving threat landscape. However, addressing challenges related to scalability, interpretability, and adaptability remains key to fully realizing the potential of AI in cybersecurity.

4. FEATURE EXTRACTION FOR MALWARE CLASSIFICATION

Feature extraction plays a crucial role in the field of malware classification, as it converts raw data into a set of usable attributes that can be processed by machine learning algorithms to identify malicious behaviors. The process involves selecting and transforming raw data, often in the form of files or network traffic, into meaningful features that can effectively capture the unique characteristics of malware. These features are then used to train machine learning models to accurately classify files or behaviors as benign or malicious. The extraction of effective features is key to improving the performance and accuracy of malware detection systems.

4.1 Types of Features in Malware Classification

1. **Static Features** Static features refer to attributes that can be extracted without executing the malware. These features typically include file properties, such as the file's size, structure, headers, strings, and opcodes. Static analysis tools look for patterns or unusual behaviors within the file's structure that could indicate malicious intent. For instance, files containing encrypted strings or packed code may be more likely to be malicious (Sarker, 2024). Static analysis can be highly effective in detecting known malware families, but it is generally less effective for new or obfuscated malware, as the static features may remain unchanged.

2. **Dynamic Features** Dynamic features involve the analysis of malware behavior during its execution in a controlled environment, such as a sandbox. These features include the system calls, file modifications, network activity, and registry changes made by the malware during execution. Dynamic analysis is useful in identifying malware variants that use evasive tactics, such as polymorphism or metamorphism, which alter their static structure to avoid detection (Liu, 2024). Dynamic analysis, however, requires a safe and isolated environment for execution to prevent the malware from causing harm.
3. **Hybrid Features** Hybrid features combine both static and dynamic analysis to take advantage of the strengths of each. By extracting information from both the code itself and its execution patterns, hybrid feature extraction methods aim to provide a more comprehensive view of the malware. This method increases the chances of detecting both known and unknown malware, especially when malicious behaviors are not apparent from static features alone. Researchers have shown that combining static and dynamic features leads to significant improvements in malware detection accuracy (Ferrag et al., 2024).

A Venn diagram below showing static, dynamic, and hybrid feature extraction.

Figure 3. Feature extraction techniques in malware classification

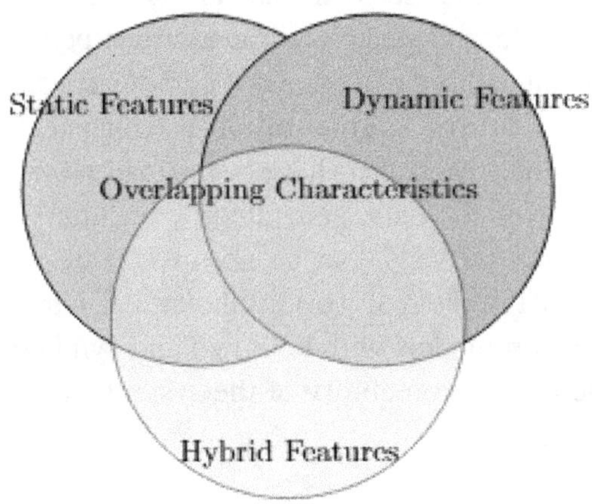

4.2 Advanced Techniques in Feature Extraction

1. **Using Large Language Models (LLMs) for Feature Extraction** Recently, large language models (LLMs) have been increasingly applied to malware classification tasks. LLMs, such as BERT (Bidirectional Encoder Representations

from Transformers), have shown significant promise in analyzing sequences of text or code. They can be trained to understand the structure and semantics of program code, allowing them to identify patterns indicative of malicious activities (Ferrag et al., 2023; Sarker, 2024). For example, LLMs can detect suspicious API calls or code constructs commonly used in malware. These models are also capable of learning more complex relationships between features, which improves their ability to classify new and evolving malware samples.

2. **Deep Learning Models for Feature Representation** The integration of deep learning models, particularly convolutional neural networks (CNNs) and recurrent neural networks (RNNs), has further advanced malware classification. These models automatically extract hierarchical features from raw data, which eliminates the need for manual feature engineering (Kasri et al., 2025). For example, CNNs can automatically identify patterns in byte sequences, while RNNs can capture the temporal dependencies in network traffic. These models excel in detecting complex malware behaviors that may not be captured by traditional feature extraction methods (Motlagh et al., 2024).
3. **Graph-Based Feature Extraction** In some cases, malware behavior is better represented using graph structures. For example, the control flow graph (CFG) or data flow graph (DFG) of a program can highlight the relationships between different code segments. This representation allows for the detection of unusual control flow patterns often seen in malware (Zangana, 2025). Graph-based models can capture dependencies and interactions between code blocks that are critical for distinguishing benign and malicious files.
4. **Synthetic Data for Feature Augmentation** To enhance the robustness of malware detection systems, researchers have begun to use synthetic data to augment training datasets. Synthetic data, generated by techniques such as Generative Adversarial Networks (GANs), can be used to create new malware variants that may not yet exist in the real world (Gholami & Omar, 2023). By training malware classification models with both real and synthetic data, it is possible to improve the generalization ability of the system, allowing it to detect both known and emerging threats.

4.3 Feature Selection for Malware Classification

After features are extracted, it is essential to perform feature selection to identify the most relevant features that contribute to the classification task. Feature selection techniques aim to reduce the dimensionality of the dataset and eliminate redundant or irrelevant features that could reduce the accuracy of the classifier. Methods such as mutual information, Chi-squared tests, and Recursive Feature Elimination (RFE) are commonly used for this purpose (Chen et al., 2024). The goal is to enhance the efficiency of malware classification models by focusing on the most informative features.

4.4 Summary

Feature extraction for malware classification is a critical process in the development of effective cybersecurity solutions. Traditional methods, such as static and dynamic analysis, have been augmented by advanced techniques like large language models, deep learning, and graph-based analysis. These methods enable the detection of both known and novel threats with greater accuracy and efficiency. As the malware landscape evolves, so too must the methods used for feature extraction. By leveraging state-of-the-art techniques and integrating new technologies, such as synthetic data and LLMs, we can create more robust and adaptable systems to combat emerging cybersecurity threats.

5. DEEP LEARNING ARCHITECTURES FOR MALWARE DETECTION

Malware detection has emerged as a crucial challenge in cybersecurity due to the increasing sophistication of cyber threats. Traditional signature-based approaches, while effective for known malware, often fail to detect new or polymorphic threats. In contrast, deep learning architectures have proven effective in identifying both known and unknown malware through data-driven learning and pattern recognition. This section discusses various deep learning architectures used in malware detection, including convolutional neural networks (CNNs), recurrent neural networks (RNNs), autoencoders, and more recent advances utilizing large language models (LLMs) and generative AI.

5.1 Convolutional Neural Networks (CNNs)

CNNs have been widely adopted for malware detection due to their ability to learn spatial hierarchies in input data. In malware detection, CNNs are particularly effective when analyzing raw data representations of executable files or the byte sequences within them. The network is trained to identify patterns indicative of malicious behavior, often outperforming traditional methods. For example, CNNs can extract features from binary representations of malware, transforming them into images or matrices that are easier to process using convolutional layers.

One study by Ferrag et al. (2024) demonstrates the application of CNNs in identifying malicious files based on byte-level representations. Their model, trained on a large dataset of labeled samples, was able to detect new variants of known malware that traditional signature-based methods could not identify.

5.2 Recurrent Neural Networks (RNNs)

RNNs, especially Long Short-Term Memory (LSTM) networks, are effective for detecting malware based on sequential data, such as API call sequences or system logs. These architectures are particularly useful for analyzing time-series data, where the relationship between different time steps holds significant value. In the context of malware detection, RNNs can track the sequence of instructions executed by a piece of software, identifying abnormal behaviors indicative of malicious activity.

Liu (2024) discusses the integration of LSTMs in malware detection systems, where the model is trained to detect anomalous sequences of system calls. This approach allows for the detection of both known and zero-day attacks that do not exhibit traditional malicious signatures.

5.3 Autoencoders for Malware Detection

Autoencoders are another popular deep learning technique used for anomaly detection in malware analysis. These models work by learning a compressed representation (encoding) of the input data and then attempting to reconstruct it. The idea is that benign data will be well-reconstructed, while malicious data will not, due to its outlier characteristics.

Sarker (2024) highlights the use of autoencoders in malware detection, where they are trained to recognize the normal behavior of a system or network. When malware is introduced, the autoencoder fails to reconstruct the input accurately, triggering an alert for further analysis. This method is particularly valuable when analyzing encrypted or obfuscated malware, which often evades detection by traditional techniques.

5.4 Generative Models and Large Language Models (LLMs)

The advent of generative models and LLMs has brought significant improvements to malware detection. Large language models like GPT-3 and specialized security models such as SecureBERT have shown promise in detecting complex malware patterns by leveraging their understanding of large-scale textual data. These models can be trained on large datasets of malicious code, learning to generate features that differentiate between benign and malicious behaviors.

For instance, Ferrag et al. (2023) demonstrate how BERT-based models can be applied to cybersecurity, including malware detection, by capturing both the context and semantics of malicious code. Their work emphasizes the ability of large pre-trained models to generalize across different types of cyber threats, including zero-day vulnerabilities.

Moreover, Kasri et al. (2025) explore how generative AI models can enhance the detection of previously unseen malware variants. These models are trained not only on the existing malware datasets but also on the generative capacity of adversarial machine learning to create and detect new threat vectors.

LLMs are especially useful when combined with explainable AI (XAI) techniques, which can help security analysts understand why a certain piece of software was flagged as malicious. This is a critical aspect, as trust and transparency in AI models are essential for their adoption in cybersecurity applications (Ghazal et al., 2024).

A flowchart below showing how different deep learning models (CNNs, RNNs, LSTMs) process malware data.

Figure 4. Deep learning architectures for malware detection

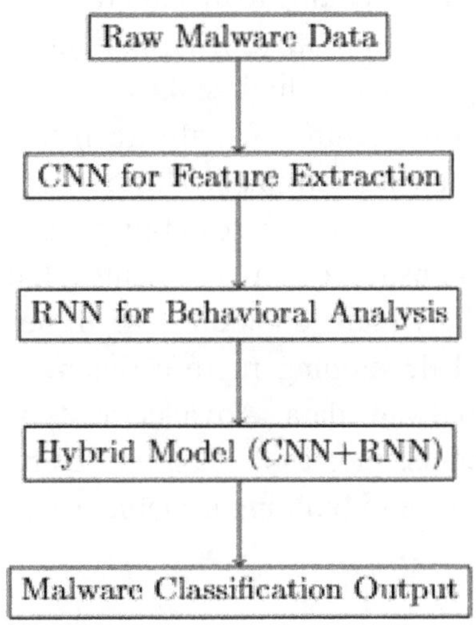

5.5 Hybrid Approaches

Recent studies have explored hybrid models that combine the strengths of different deep learning architectures. For example, combining CNNs for feature extraction with LSTMs for sequential analysis has shown improved accuracy in detecting malware, especially when analyzing malware in real-time network traffic or during execution (Motlagh et al., 2024).

Furthermore, the integration of LLMs with CNNs or autoencoders allows for better handling of both structured and unstructured data. LLMs are used to preprocess textual data from security logs, while CNNs or autoencoders handle binary or sequential data from malware samples. This fusion of models allows for the creation of more robust and accurate detection systems, capable of adapting to new threats as they emerge (Chen et al., 2024).

5.6 Challenges and Future Directions

Despite the advances in deep learning for malware detection, several challenges remain. One of the primary issues is the interpretability of deep learning models. While deep learning models, particularly LLMs, achieve high accuracy, their decision-making process is often opaque, making it difficult for analysts to trust and act on the predictions. As highlighted by Xu et al. (2024), explainability remains a key hurdle in deploying deep learning models in high-stakes environments like cybersecurity.

Additionally, the evolving nature of malware means that detection systems must be continuously updated and retrained. This ongoing need for data collection, annotation, and model retraining poses scalability issues, especially for smaller organizations or resource-constrained environments (Hadi et al., 2023).

Future research will likely focus on addressing these challenges by improving model interpretability and developing more efficient methods for handling the constant influx of new malware data. Advancements in federated learning and privacy-preserving AI models, such as those proposed by Ferrag et al. (2024), are expected to play a critical role in building scalable, secure, and efficient malware detection systems.

5.7 Summary

Deep learning architectures have proven to be a powerful tool in the fight against malware. From CNNs for binary classification to LSTMs for sequential anomaly detection, and the emerging use of LLMs for detecting complex malware patterns, these models offer a more robust approach compared to traditional signature-based methods. However, challenges related to interpretability and scalability remain, necessitating further research into hybrid models and advanced techniques for continuous learning and adaptation. With the rapid pace of cybersecurity threats, the integration of generative AI and LLMs will likely shape the future of malware detection, providing more proactive and intelligent defense mechanisms against evolving cyber threats.

6. CASE STUDIES ON AI-BASED MALWARE ANALYSIS

The integration of Artificial Intelligence (AI), particularly Large Language Models (LLMs), into cybersecurity systems has transformed the landscape of malware analysis and detection. This section explores several case studies that demonstrate the application of AI and machine learning techniques in the identification, prevention, and mitigation of cyber threats posed by malware. These case studies not only highlight the efficiency and scalability of AI-based systems but also underscore the ongoing research aimed at improving the accuracy and reliability of threat detection mechanisms.

6.1 Case Study 1: Leveraging Large Language Models for IoT and IIoT Device Security

A significant development in AI-driven malware detection is the use of Large Language Models (LLMs) in the context of Internet of Things (IoT) and Industrial IoT (IIoT) security. In a recent study, Ferrag et al. (2024) introduced a privacy-preserving BERT-based lightweight model specifically designed for IoT/IIoT devices. The model leveraged natural language processing (NLP) techniques to analyze network traffic and detect anomalous behavior indicative of malware infections. This approach effectively minimized computational overhead, making it suitable for resource-constrained IoT devices while maintaining high detection accuracy.

Further research by Ferrag et al. (2023) extended this model, improving its threat detection capabilities and optimizing it for real-time monitoring of connected devices. Their work highlights the importance of AI in handling the complex, often subtle malware attacks that target IoT and IIoT environments. This case study demonstrates that LLMs can enhance the security of critical infrastructures by automating malware detection and reducing response times.

6.2 Case Study 2: Generative AI Models for Malware Classification

Another important approach to AI-based malware analysis involves the use of generative AI models to classify and detect malware. Sarker (2024) explored how generative adversarial networks (GANs) and other AI-based generative models could be employed to simulate various malware attacks. By generating synthetic malware samples, these models are trained to identify malicious patterns within both benign and malicious files, which enhances the accuracy of malware detection systems.

This method allows cybersecurity professionals to stay ahead of evolving malware techniques by continuously training AI models on newly generated attack patterns. The ability of generative models to simulate diverse malware attacks creates a robust defense mechanism capable of responding to emerging threats in real time. Moreover, the work by Ferrag et al. (2024) demonstrates that generative models are not only effective in malware classification but also aid in identifying novel attack strategies that may not have been encountered before.

6.3 Case Study 3: Large Language Models for Cyber Threat Prediction

An intriguing application of LLMs is their use in predicting potential cyberattacks, especially malware-related incidents. Diaf et al. (2024) highlighted how pre-trained language models, such as SecureBERT, can be adapted to predict malware outbreaks by analyzing historical threat data and identifying patterns that precede an attack. Their study found that the predictive capabilities of LLMs could significantly reduce the time required for threat mitigation.

Additionally, Liu (2024) reviewed the advancements in applying pre-trained language models for predicting and detecting cybersecurity threats, with a particular focus on malware. By processing vast datasets of threat intelligence, LLMs can provide valuable insights into the likelihood of a cyberattack, allowing organizations to implement preemptive measures. These advancements suggest that AI is not only useful for detecting malware but also for anticipating its occurrence, providing organizations with more proactive defense strategies.

6.4 Case Study 4: AI-Driven Malware Detection in Cloud Environments

In cloud environments, malware detection poses a unique challenge due to the dynamic nature of cloud infrastructures and the vast volume of data processed. Researchers have explored the application of LLMs to monitor and analyze cloud network traffic for malware detection. According to Motlagh et al. (2024), LLMs are trained to process large datasets quickly, identifying patterns of malicious activity even within encrypted data streams. This AI-driven approach is particularly beneficial for cloud service providers, enabling them to offer enhanced security features without imposing significant performance penalties on end users.

Furthermore, Hasanov et al. (2024) discussed how the use of AI models, including LLMs, has helped improve malware detection systems in cloud-based networks by providing better scalability and adaptability to new threats. Their work emphasized the critical role of AI in reducing the complexity of securing cloud environments and its capacity to scale with the growing demand for cloud services.

6.5 Case Study 5: Explainable AI for Malware Detection in Critical Infrastructure

One of the challenges of AI-based malware detection is the "black box" nature of many models, where decision-making processes are not always transparent. The application of explainable AI (XAI) in malware analysis addresses this issue by making AI's decisions more interpretable. In their study, Ghazal et al. (2024) applied explainable AI techniques to improve the trustworthiness of LLMs used for malware detection in critical infrastructure, such as power grids and communication systems.

Their case study demonstrated that by integrating XAI with LLMs, organizations could gain better insights into why specific actions were taken by the AI system, which is crucial for regulatory compliance and improving the system's overall trust. The transparency offered by XAI made it easier for cybersecurity professionals to validate the results, ensuring that the AI-driven decisions were based on sound reasoning.

6.6 Case Study 6: AI and Blockchain Integration for Malware Prevention

Blockchain technology has also found applications in enhancing cybersecurity, particularly in the prevention of malware attacks. Zangana et al. (2025) proposed a hybrid approach that combines AI, LLMs, and blockchain to provide a decentralized and tamper-proof system for malware detection. Their research focused on using blockchain's inherent immutability to store malware signatures and detection logs, while AI models, including LLMs, were used to analyze and detect new threats. This integration provided a robust and secure framework for monitoring and responding to malware threats in real time.

The hybrid model proposed by Zangana et al. (2025) demonstrated significant improvements in the detection of advanced persistent threats (APTs), which are often overlooked by traditional malware detection systems. The combination of AI and blockchain ensured that the detection process was not only efficient but also resilient to tampering and manipulation, which are common concerns in cybersecurity.

6.7 Summary

The case studies presented in this section illustrate the transformative impact of AI, particularly Large Language Models, on the field of malware detection and prevention. From enhancing the security of IoT and IIoT devices to providing predictive insights into cyberattacks, AI is revolutionizing the way cybersecurity professionals approach malware analysis. As AI continues to evolve, its integration with other technologies, such as blockchain and explainable AI, will likely play a critical role in advancing the effectiveness and transparency of cybersecurity systems.

The ongoing research and innovations in this field, as discussed by authors like Ferrag et al. (2024), Liu (2024), and Zangana et al. (2025), suggest that AI will continue to play a pivotal role in shaping the future of malware analysis and cybersecurity as a whole.

7. PERFORMANCE METRICS FOR MALWARE CLASSIFICATION MODELS

In evaluating malware classification models, it is essential to adopt a variety of performance metrics to accurately assess their efficiency, robustness, and reliability. These metrics provide insights into the model's ability to distinguish between malicious and benign software, and help in tuning the model for optimal performance. Various performance metrics are employed depending on the specific task and desired outcomes. In the context of large language models (LLMs) and machine learning (ML) techniques applied to malware detection, a combination of traditional and advanced metrics are typically used.

7.1. Accuracy

Accuracy is one of the most commonly used performance metrics for evaluating malware classification models. It is defined as the ratio of the number of correctly predicted instances (both benign and malicious) to the total number of instances in the dataset. While accuracy is easy to compute, it can be misleading in imbalanced datasets, where one class (e.g., benign files) may dominate, leading to high accuracy without true model effectiveness in detecting malware (Sarker, 2024). For more balanced and reliable evaluations, other metrics are considered in conjunction with accuracy.

7.2. Precision, Recall, and F1-Score

- **Precision** measures the proportion of true positive (TP) classifications out of all positive classifications (both true and false). It is essential in scenarios where false positives can result in undesirable actions, such as unnecessary alerts or interventions.
- **Recall** evaluates the proportion of true positives identified out of all actual positive instances. It is especially critical in situations where undetected malware could lead to serious security breaches.

The **F1-score** is the harmonic mean of precision and recall and provides a balanced measure that accounts for both false positives and false negatives. A high F1-score indicates a good balance between precision and recall. In the context of LLM-based malware classification models, these metrics are crucial for ensuring the model can effectively identify and prioritize malware without overfitting or ignoring important classes (Liu, 2024).

7.3. Specificity and False Positive Rate (FPR)

Specificity, or the True Negative Rate (TNR), refers to the proportion of correctly identified benign files. It is complementary to recall, which focuses on correctly identifying malware. A high specificity indicates the model's efficiency in reducing false alarms and distinguishing between benign and malicious samples effectively (Ferrag et al., 2024). The False Positive Rate (FPR), calculated as the ratio of false positives to all negative instances, is inversely related to specificity. In malware detection, it is crucial to minimize FPR to avoid unnecessary detection of benign software as malicious, which could lead to operational disruptions (Zangana et al., 2024).

7.4. Area Under the Receiver Operating Characteristic Curve (AUC-ROC)

The **AUC-ROC** curve provides a graphical representation of the trade-off between the true positive rate (sensitivity) and the false positive rate (1 - specificity). It is a widely used evaluation metric for binary classification tasks, such as distinguishing malware from benign files. A high AUC indicates that the model is effective in classifying instances of both classes (malware and benign files) without too many errors. AUC-ROC is particularly beneficial for comparing different models or configurations, as it provides a single value that summarizes the model's performance across all classification thresholds (Kasri et al., 2025).

7.5. Matthews Correlation Coefficient (MCC)

The **Matthews Correlation Coefficient** (MCC) is a more informative metric that accounts for all four possible outcomes of a binary classification: true positives, true negatives, false positives, and false negatives. Unlike accuracy, MCC takes into consideration the balance between the classes, making it especially useful for evaluating models trained on imbalanced datasets, which is often the case in malware detection tasks. A higher MCC indicates a better performing model, as it represents both the model's ability to detect malware and its efficiency in avoiding false classifications (Motlagh et al., 2024).

7.6. Training and Inference Time

For real-time malware detection systems, the **training time** and **inference time** are important performance indicators. Training time measures how long it takes for the model to learn from the dataset, while inference time refers to how quickly the model can classify new files during operation. Efficient malware detection systems must strike a balance between high detection accuracy and low processing time. Leveraging LLMs and advanced techniques, such as Federated Learning and Transfer Learning, can significantly reduce inference time without sacrificing performance (Hasanov et al., 2024).

7.7. Robustness and Generalization

In malware classification, robustness refers to the model's ability to maintain high performance when exposed to adversarial attacks or new, unseen types of malware. A model that performs well on training data but fails to generalize to new threats is not useful in practical cybersecurity applications. Generalization performance can be assessed using metrics like cross-validation and testing on diverse malware samples. The ability of large language models to generalize across a wide range of cyber threats is critical in evolving cybersecurity landscapes (Ghazal et al., 2024).

A ROC curve below showing model performance.

Figure 5. ROC curve for AI-based vs traditional malware detection

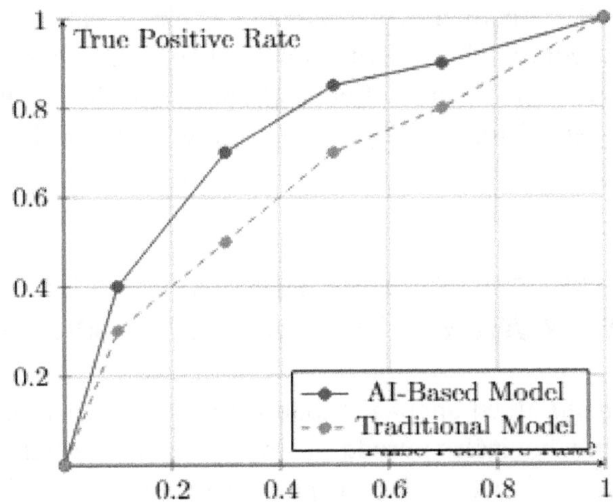

7.8. Explainability and Interpretability

While performance metrics focus on the accuracy and efficiency of malware classification models, **explainability** and **interpretability** are becoming increasingly important. This refers to the model's ability to provide insights into why it classified a particular file as benign or malicious. In cybersecurity, having explainable AI models is vital for trust and transparency, especially when it comes to making high-stakes decisions. Explainable models can help cybersecurity professionals understand the reasoning behind the detection and better respond to emerging threats (Ferrag et al., 2023). Recent studies have shown that integrating explainable AI techniques with LLM-based models can improve both detection accuracy and the interpretability of cybersecurity decisions (Kasri et al., 2025).

7.9 Summary

In summary, the evaluation of malware classification models requires a multi-faceted approach that includes both traditional performance metrics, such as accuracy, precision, recall, and F1-score, and more advanced measures like AUC-ROC and MCC. For large language model-based systems, the additional considerations of training time, robustness, generalization, and explainability play a crucial role in ensuring the model is both effective and deployable in real-world cybersecurity scenarios. As the field of cybersecurity continues to evolve, particularly with the integration of LLMs, continuous refinement and adaptation of these evaluation metrics will be essential for tackling the ever-growing threat landscape (Sarker, 2024; Zangana et al., 2024).

8. FUTURE CHALLENGES AND INNOVATIONS IN CYBERSECURITY WITH LARGE LANGUAGE MODELS (LLMS)

The integration of Large Language Models (LLMs) in cybersecurity represents a transformative shift, but it also introduces several challenges and opportunities for innovation. As the cybersecurity landscape evolves, LLMs like GPT, BERT, and their variants are being explored for threat detection, vulnerability identification, and attack mitigation. However, their potential is not without complexities, and understanding these challenges is key to advancing the field.

8.1. Adversarial Attacks and Model Robustness

One of the significant challenges in deploying LLMs for cybersecurity is their vulnerability to adversarial attacks. These attacks exploit the weaknesses of LLMs, leading to misclassification of threats or false positives/negatives in anomaly detection systems. The ability of adversaries to craft inputs that mislead or confuse these models poses a significant threat to the integrity of security solutions (Ferrag et al., 2023). Innovations in adversarial training and defensive mechanisms are crucial to ensuring the robustness of LLMs in real-world environments.

Ferrag et al. (2024) explored the development of lightweight BERT-based models that are privacy-preserving and optimized for IoT/IIoT devices. However, these models still require significant advancements to counter adversarial manipulations effectively, especially in sensitive environments where data privacy is critical.

8.2. Explainability and Interpretability

While LLMs are highly effective in making predictions, their "black-box" nature presents a challenge in cybersecurity applications. Security professionals need transparency in how a model detects threats or classifies behavior to trust and refine these systems. As Sarker (2024) notes, explainability is essential for decision-making in high-stakes environments like cybersecurity. Without clear explanations, LLMs may struggle to gain the confidence of security teams, especially when it comes to addressing the accountability of automated systems.

Recent research has focused on incorporating explainable AI (XAI) techniques into LLM frameworks (Ghazal et al., 2024). For instance, techniques such as attention mechanisms and rule-based explanations are being integrated into LLMs to provide more insight into their decision-making process. These innovations will be pivotal in bridging the trust gap between LLMs and security practitioners.

8.3. Data Privacy and Ethical Concerns

Data privacy and ethical considerations are critical when implementing LLMs in cybersecurity, especially in scenarios involving sensitive personal data. As these models process vast amounts of potentially sensitive information, it is essential to ensure that privacy-preserving techniques are embedded within their architecture. Ferrag et al. (2024) have addressed this concern by developing privacy-preserving BERT-based models tailored for IoT and IIoT devices, which reduces the exposure of data while maintaining model performance.

However, the challenge remains in balancing privacy with the effectiveness of cybersecurity solutions. Ensuring compliance with data protection regulations like GDPR and CCPA while leveraging the full potential of LLMs will require ongoing innovation in model design, data management, and legal frameworks (Motlagh et al., 2024).

8.4. Scalability and Real-time Processing

The deployment of LLMs in cybersecurity must also account for scalability and real-time processing. As cybersecurity threats continue to evolve in both volume and sophistication, LLMs need to handle large-scale datasets and detect threats in real-time. The computational cost of running large models at scale is a significant hurdle, particularly for organizations with limited resources.

Kasri et al. (2025) highlight the need for more efficient architectures that can handle high-throughput data while minimizing the computational load. Innovations in model optimization, such as pruning, quantization, and knowledge distillation, are being explored to make these models more efficient without sacrificing performance. LLMs designed specifically for cybersecurity applications will need to be adaptable to diverse environments, from cloud infrastructures to edge computing setups (Chen et al., 2024).

8.5. Integration with Existing Cybersecurity Systems

Integrating LLMs into traditional cybersecurity infrastructures presents both challenges and opportunities. Existing systems often rely on rule-based or heuristic approaches, which differ significantly from the probabilistic nature of LLMs. A key challenge will be how to seamlessly integrate LLMs into these legacy systems without disrupting their functionality.

Research by Asoronye et al. (2024) has pointed to specialized language models that can be customized for specific domains, providing a hybrid approach that combines the best of both worlds: the power of LLMs and the precision of traditional methods. This hybrid approach could be pivotal in developing the next generation of cybersecurity solutions.

8.6. Continuous Model Training and Updating

The fast-paced nature of cybersecurity threats means that LLMs used for threat detection must continuously evolve to stay ahead of adversaries. This requires ongoing model training and updating, which presents both technical and operational challenges. The deployment of LLMs in cybersecurity must account for dynamic threat landscapes, where models are trained with the most up-to-date threat intelligence (Liu, 2024).

Kasri et al. (2025) emphasize that the continuous retraining of LLMs, coupled with real-time threat feeds, could be a game-changer in cyber defense. Automated pipelines for model retraining and fine-tuning will allow organizations to quickly adapt to emerging threats, ensuring that LLMs remain effective as cybersecurity risks evolve.

8.7. Ethical AI and Bias Mitigation

As with all AI-driven technologies, the risk of bias in LLMs is a pressing concern. Bias in model predictions, especially regarding threat detection and classification, can lead to disparities in the effectiveness of cybersecurity measures across different user groups or attack types. To ensure fairness and ethical use of LLMs in cybersecurity, it is crucial to develop strategies to identify and mitigate bias in training datasets and model predictions (Santos et al., 2024).

The ongoing research into fair AI and bias mitigation methods is crucial in ensuring that LLMs are applied equitably across various sectors, especially in sensitive industries such as healthcare and finance. Ensuring that models do not disproportionately flag certain users or systems as vulnerable is essential for fostering trust in LLM-based cybersecurity solutions.

8.8. The Future of Generative AI in Cybersecurity

Generative AI models, particularly those built on LLMs, hold immense potential for cybersecurity applications beyond threat detection. For example, generative models can be used to simulate attacks, creating synthetic datasets to train and test security systems under various adversarial conditions (Zangana et al., 2024). This type of innovation could help cybersecurity teams better prepare for unknown threats and zero-day vulnerabilities.

Additionally, generative AI can assist in automating threat hunting and incident response, significantly reducing the time needed to detect and mitigate security breaches. The potential for AI-driven autonomous cybersecurity systems, powered by generative models, represents an exciting avenue for future innovation in the field (Zangana et al., 2024).

8.9 Summary

The integration of LLMs into cybersecurity presents significant challenges, ranging from adversarial attacks to ethical concerns. However, with the continued evolution of AI technologies and the development of innovative approaches, these challenges can be mitigated. As Ferrag et al. (2024) and other scholars point out, the future of cybersecurity lies in harnessing the power of LLMs while addressing the technical, ethical, and operational hurdles. Innovations in privacy-preserving models, explainability, scalability, and continuous learning will drive the next wave of cybersecurity advancements. The future of LLMs in cybersecurity promises not only to enhance threat detection and mitigation but also to redefine how organizations protect themselves from evolving cyber threats.

9. CONCLUSION

In conclusion, the integration of Large Language Models (LLMs) into cybersecurity presents a transformative opportunity to enhance threat detection, response, and defense mechanisms across various sectors. As this technology evolves, it is clear that LLMs are not only advancing the field of cybersecurity but also enabling more proactive, intelligent, and adaptive security systems. The application of LLMs in threat detection, attack prediction, and vulnerability management has proven to be promising, offering a new paradigm in cybersecurity where automation and intelligence play a central role.

The ongoing advancements in LLM architecture, such as fine-tuning and domain-specific models, are crucial in tailoring these tools to address the unique challenges of cybersecurity. Moreover, integrating LLMs with other emerging technologies such as IoT, blockchain, and AI can further strengthen the resilience of systems against sophisticated threats. However, while these innovations offer tremendous potential, there are significant challenges that must be overcome, including the risks associated with privacy, data security, and model interpretability.

Future research and development in this field should focus on addressing these challenges, with particular attention to creating more efficient, privacy-preserving models and improving the explainability of LLM-driven security solutions. The role of LLMs in predictive cybersecurity, such as anticipating new forms of attacks and identifying vulnerabilities before they are exploited, is an area with significant potential. As organizations continue to digitize and adopt more complex systems, the need for robust, intelligent, and adaptive cybersecurity measures will only grow.

In summary, the application of LLMs in cybersecurity is poised to revolutionize how we approach the protection of sensitive information, systems, and networks. Continued innovation in this area, alongside a collaborative effort from researchers, developers, and cybersecurity professionals, will pave the way for more secure, resilient digital ecosystems in the future. Through ongoing improvements and innovations, LLMs will become an indispensable tool in the cybersecurity arsenal, offering novel solutions to the ever-evolving landscape of cyber threats.

REFERENCES

Aghaei, E., Niu, X., Shadid, W., & Al-Shaer, E. (2022, October). Securebert: A domain-specific language model for cybersecurity. In *International Conference on Security and Privacy in Communication Systems* (pp. 39-56). Cham: Springer Nature Switzerland.

AlQenaei, Z. M. (2024, March). Evolution and Optimization of Language Model Architectures: From Foundations to Future Directions. In *International Conference on Computing and Machine Learning* (pp. 233-249). Singapore: Springer Nature Singapore.

Alturkistani, H., & Chuprat, S. (2024). Artificial Intelligence and Large Language Models in Advancing Cyber Threat Intelligence: A Systematic Literature Review.

Asoronye, G. O., Anthony, O. C., Ogbuikwu, R. I., Ogili, C. O., & Ali, H. U. (2024). SecLM: A Specialized Security Language Model for Advanced Cybersecurity Applications and Threat Mitigation. *EKETE-International Journal Of Advanced Research*, *2*(6), 33–42.

Bryce, C., Kalousis, A., Leroux, I., Madinier, H., Mermoud, A., Mulder, V., ... & Ruch, P. Trends in Large Language Models: Actors, Applications, and Impact on Cybersecurity.

Chen, Y., Cui, M., Wang, D., Cao, Y., Yang, P., Jiang, B., Lu, Z., & Liu, B. (2024). A survey of large language models for cyber threat detection. *Computers & Security*, *145*, 104016. DOI: 10.1016/j.cose.2024.104016

Diaf, A., Korba, A. A., Karabadji, N. E., & Ghamri-Doudane, Y. (2024, April). Beyond detection: Leveraging large language models for cyber attack prediction in iot networks. In *2024 20th International Conference on Distributed Computing in Smart Systems and the Internet of Things (DCOSS-IoT)* (pp. 117-123). IEEE.

Ferrag, M. A., Alwahedi, F., Battah, A., Cherif, B., Mechri, A., & Tihanyi, N. (2024). Generative ai and large language models for cyber security: All insights you need. *Available atSSRN* 4853709. DOI: 10.2139/ssrn.4853709

Ferrag, M. A., Ndhlovu, M., Tihanyi, N., Cordeiro, L. C., Debbah, M., & Lestable, T. (2023). Revolutionizing cyber threat detection with large language models. *arXiv preprint arXiv:2306.14263*, 195-202.

Ferrag, M. A., Ndhlovu, M., Tihanyi, N., Cordeiro, L. C., Debbah, M., Lestable, T., & Thandi, N. S. (2024). Revolutionizing cyber threat detection with large language models: A privacy-preserving bert-based lightweight model for iot/iiot devices. *IEEE Access : Practical Innovations, Open Solutions*, *12*, 23733–23750.

Ferrag, M. A., Ndhlovu, M., Tihanyi, N., Cordeiro, L. C., Debbah, M., Lestable, T., & Thandi, N. S. (2024). Revolutionizing cyber threat detection with large language models: A privacy-preserving bert-based lightweight model for iot/iiot devices. *IEEE Access : Practical Innovations, Open Solutions*, *12*, 23733–23750.

Ghazal, T. M., Janjua, J. I., Abushiba, W., Ahmad, M., Ihsan, A., & Al-Dmour, N. A. (2024, December). Cybersecurity Revolution via Large Language Models and Explainable AI. In *2024 17th International Conference on Security of Information and Networks (SIN)* (pp. 1-6). IEEE.

Gholami, S., & Omar, M. (2023). Does Synthetic Data Make Large Language Models More Efficient? *arXiv preprint arXiv:2310.07830.*

Gholami, S., & Omar, M. (2024). Can a student large language model perform as well as its teacher? In *Innovations, Securities, and Case Studies Across Healthcare, Business, and Technology* (pp. 122-139). IGI Global. DOI: 10.4018/979-8-3693-1906-2.ch007

Gupta, B. B., Gaurav, A., & Arya, V. (2024). Navigating the security landscape of large language models in enterprise information systems. *Enterprise Information Systems*, *18*(4), 2310846. DOI: 10.1080/17517575.2024.2310846

Hadi, M. A., Abdulredha, M. N., & Hasan, E. (2023). Introduction to ChatGPT: A new revolution of artificial intelligence with machine learning algorithms and cybersecurity. *Sci. Arch*, *4*(04), 276. DOI: 10.47587/SA.2023.4406

Hamza, Y. A., & Omar, M. D. (2013). Cloud computing security: Abuse and nefarious use of cloud computing. *International Journal of Computer Engineering Research*, *3*(6), 22–27.

Hasanov, I., Virtanen, S., Hakkala, A., & Isoaho, J. (2024). Application of Large Language Models in Cybersecurity: A Systematic Literature Review. *IEEE Access : Practical Innovations, Open Solutions*, *12*, 176751–176778. DOI: 10.1109/ACCESS.2024.3505983

Hassanin, M., & Moustafa, N. (2024). A comprehensive overview of large language models (llms) for cyber defences: Opportunities and directions. *arXiv preprint arXiv:2405.14487.*

Huff, A. J., Burrell, D. N., Nobles, C., Richardson, K., Wright, J. B., Burton, S. L., Jones, A. J., Springs, D., Omar, M., & Brown-Jackson, K. L. (2023). Management Practices for Mitigating Cybersecurity Threats to Biotechnology Companies, Laboratories, and Healthcare Research Organizations. In *Applied Research Approaches to Technology, Healthcare, and Business* (pp. 1-12). IGI Global.

Idelhaj, A., Abou El Houda, Z., & Khoukhi, L. (2024). Foundations models in cybersecurity. *Artificial Intelligence for Blockchain and Cybersecurity Powered IoT Applications*, 1.

Idelhaj, A., Abou El Houda, Z., & Khoukhi, L. Foundations models in cybersecurity: A comprehensive review and future direction. *Artificial Intelligence for Blockchain and Cybersecurity Powered IoT Applications*, 1-18.

Jones, R., & Omar, M. (2024). Revolutionizing Cybersecurity: The GPT-2 Enhanced Attack Detection and Defense (GEADD) Method for Zero-Day Threats. *International Journal of Informatics* [INJIISCOM]. *Information System and Computer Engineering*, *5*(2), 178–191.

Jones, R., Omar, M., Mohammed, D., Nobles, C., & Dawson, M. (2023). Harnessing the Speed and Accuracy of Machine Learning to Advance Cybersecurity. In *2023 Congress in Computer Science, Computer Engineering, & Applied Computing (CSCE)* (pp. 418-421). IEEE. DOI: 10.1109/CSCE60160.2023.00074

Kasri, W., Himeur, Y., Alkhazaleh, H. A., Tarapiah, S., Atalla, S., Mansoor, W., & Al-Ahmad, H. (2025). From Vulnerability to Defense: The Role of Large Language Models in Enhancing Cybersecurity. *Computation (Basel, Switzerland)*, *13*(2), 30. DOI: 10.3390/computation13020030

Liu, Z. (2024, April). A review of advancements and applications of pre-trained language models in cybersecurity. In *2024 12th International Symposium on Digital Forensics and Security (ISDFS)* (pp. 1-10). IEEE. DOI: 10.1109/ISDFS60797.2024.10527236

Manoharan, A., & Sarker, M. (2023). Revolutionizing Cybersecurity: Unleashing the Power of Artificial Intelligence and Machine Learning for Next-Generation Threat Detection. *DOI:*https://www. doi. org/10.56726/IRJMETS32644, *1*.

Mohammed, D., Omar, M., & Nguyen, V. (2018). Wireless sensor network security: Approaches to detecting and avoiding wormhole attacks. *Journal of Research in Business. Economics and Management*, *10*(2), 1860–1864.

Motlagh, F. N., Hajizadeh, M., Majd, M., Najafi, P., Cheng, F., & Meinel, C. (2024). Large language models in cybersecurity: State-of-the-art. *arXiv preprint arXiv:2402.00891*.

Nguyen, V., Mohammed, D., Omar, M., & Banisakher, M. (2018). The Effects of the FCC Net Neutrality Repeal on Security and Privacy. [IJHIoT]. *International Journal of Hyperconnectivity and the Internet of Things*, *2*(2), 21–29. DOI: 10.4018/IJHIoT.2018070102

Omar, M. (2021). New insights into database security: An effective and integrated approach for applying access control mechanisms and cryptographic concepts in Microsoft Access environments.

Omar, M. (2022). *Machine Learning for Cybersecurity: Innovative Deep Learning Solutions*. Springer Brief. https://link.springer.com/book/978303115

Omar, M. (2024). From Attack to Defense: Strengthening DNN Text Classification Against Adversarial Examples. In *Innovations, Securities, and Case Studies Across Healthcare, Business, and Technology* (pp. 174-195). IGI Global.

Omar, M. (2024). Revolutionizing Malware Detection: A Paradigm Shift Through Optimized Convolutional Neural Networks. In *Innovations, Securities, and Case Studies Across Healthcare, Business, and Technology* (pp. 196-220). IGI Global. DOI: 10.4018/979-8-3693-1906-2.ch011

Omar, M., & Zangana, H. (Eds.). (2025). *Digital Forensics in the Age of AI*. IGI Global., DOI: 10.4018/979-8-3373-0857-9

Omar, M., & Zangana, H. M. (Eds.). (2024). *Redefining Security With Cyber AI*. IGI Global., DOI: 10.4018/979-8-3693-6517-5

Omar, M., & Zangana, H. M. (Eds.). (2025). *Application of Large Language Models (LLMs) for Software Vulnerability Detection*. IGI Global., DOI: 10.4018/979-8-3693-9311-6

Omar, M., Zangana, H. M., Al-Karaki, J. N., & Mohammed, D. (2024). Harnessing LLMs for IoT malware detection: A comparative analysis of BERT and GPT-2. In *2024 8th International Symposium on Multidisciplinary Studies and Innovative Technologies (ISMSIT)* (pp. 1-6). Ankara, Turkiye. https://doi.org/DOI: 10.1109/ISMSIT63511.2024.10757249

Omar, M., Zangana, H. M., & Mohammed, D. (Eds.). (2025). *Integrating Artificial Intelligence in Cybersecurity and Forensic Practices*. IGI Global., DOI: 10.4018/979-8-3373-0588-2

Ozkan-Okay, M., Akin, E., Aslan, Ö., Kosunalp, S., Iliev, T., Stoyanov, I., & Beloev, I. (2024). A comprehensive survey: Evaluating the efficiency of artificial intelligence and machine learning techniques on cyber security solutions. *IEEE Access : Practical Innovations, Open Solutions*, *12*, 12229–12256. DOI: 10.1109/ACCESS.2024.3355547

Pleshakova, E., Osipov, A., Gataullin, S., Gataullin, T., & Vasilakos, A. (2024). Next gen cybersecurity paradigm towards artificial general intelligence: Russian market challenges and future global technological trends. *Journal of Computer Virology and Hacking Techniques*, *20*(3), 429–440. DOI: 10.1007/s11416-024-00529-x

Santos, O., Salam, S., & Dahir, H. (2024). The AI revolution in networking, cybersecurity, and emerging technologies.

Sarker, I. H. (2024). Generative AI and large language modeling in cybersecurity. In *AI-Driven Cybersecurity and Threat Intelligence: Cyber Automation, Intelligent Decision-Making and Explainability* (pp. 79–99). Springer Nature Switzerland. DOI: 10.1007/978-3-031-54497-2_5

Taghavi, S. M., & Feyzi, F. (2024). Using large language models to better detect and handle software vulnerabilities and cyber security threats.

Wright, J., Dawson, M. E.Jr, & Omar, M. (2012). Cyber security and mobile threats: The need for antivirus applications for smartphones. *Journal of Information Systems Technology and Planning*, *5*(14), 40–60.

Xu, H., Wang, S., Li, N., Wang, K., Zhao, Y., Chen, K., . . . Wang, H. (2024). Large language models for cyber security: A systematic literature review. *arXiv preprint arXiv:2405.04760*.

Yu, J., Shvetsov, A. V., & Alsamhi, S. H. (2024). Leveraging machine learning for cybersecurity resilience in industry 4.0: Challenges and future directions. *IEEE Access : Practical Innovations, Open Solutions*, *12*, 159579–159596. DOI: 10.1109/ACCESS.2024.3482987

Zangana, H., & Omar, M. (Eds.). (2025). *Leveraging Large Language Models for Quantum-Aware Cybersecurity*. IGI Global., DOI: 10.4018/979-8-3373-1102-9

Zangana, H. M. (2024). Exploring Blockchain-Based Timestamping Tools: A Comprehensive Review. *Redefining Security With Cyber AI*, 92-110.

Zangana, H. M. (2024). Exploring the Landscape of Website Vulnerability Scanners: A Comprehensive Review and Comparative Analysis. *Redefining Security With Cyber AI*, 111-129.

Zangana, H. M. (2024). Harnessing the Power of Large Language Models. *Application of Large Language Models (LLMs) for Software Vulnerability Detection*, 1.

Zangana, H. M., & Li, S. (2025). Future Trends in AI and Digital Forensics. In Omar, M., & Zangana, H. (Eds.), *Digital Forensics in the Age of AI* (pp. 347–380). IGI Global Scientific Publishing., DOI: 10.4018/979-8-3373-0857-9.ch013

Zangana, H. M., Mohammed, A. K., Sallow, A. B., & Sallow, Z. B. (2024). Cybernetic Deception: Unraveling the Layers of Email Phishing Threats. [INJURATECH]. *International Journal of Research and Applied Technology*, *4*(1), 35–47.

Zangana, H. M., & Mohammed, D. (2025). Foundations of Large Language Models in Software Vulnerability Detection. In Omar, M., & Zangana, H. (Eds.), *Application of Large Language Models (LLMs) for Software Vulnerability Detection* (pp. 41–74). IGI Global., DOI: 10.4018/979-8-3693-9311-6.ch002

Zangana, H. M., & Mustafa, F. M. (2024). Hybrid Image Denoising Using Wavelet Transform and Deep Learning. *EAI Endorsed Transactions on AI and Robotics*, *3*. Advance online publication. DOI: 10.4108/airo.7486

Zangana, H. M., & Mustafa, F. M. (2025). Image Denoising Techniques for Cybersecurity and Forensic Applications: AI-Driven Approaches. In Omar, M., Zangana, H., & Mohammed, D. (Eds.), *Integrating Artificial Intelligence in Cybersecurity and Forensic Practices* (pp. 117–142). IGI Global Scientific Publishing., DOI: 10.4018/979-8-3373-0588-2.ch005

Zangana, H. M., Mustafa, F. M., & Li, S. (2025). Large Language Models in Cybersecurity: From Automation to Intelligence. In *Leveraging Large Language Models for Quantum-Aware Cybersecurity* (pp. 277-300). IGI Global Scientific Publishing.

Zangana, H. M., Mustafa, F. M., & Li, S. (2025). Large Language Models in Cybersecurity: From Automation to Intelligence. In Zangana, H., & Omar, M. (Eds.), *Leveraging Large Language Models for Quantum-Aware Cybersecurity* (pp. 277–300). IGI Global Scientific Publishing., DOI: 10.4018/979-8-3373-1102-9.ch009

Zangana, H. M., Mustafa, F. M., Li, S., & Al-Karaki, J. N. (2025). Natural Language Processing for Cyber Threat Intelligence in a Quantum World. In Zangana, H., & Omar, M. (Eds.), *Leveraging Large Language Models for Quantum-Aware Cybersecurity* (pp. 345–388). IGI Global Scientific Publishing., DOI: 10.4018/979-8-3373-1102-9.ch011

Zangana, H. M., Mustafa, F. M., & Omar, M. (2024). A Hybrid Approach for Robust Object Detection: Integrating Template Matching and Faster R-CNN. *EAI Endorsed Transactions on AI and Robotics, 3*. Advance online publication. DOI: 10.4108/airo.6858

Zangana, H. M., & Omar, M. (2020). Threats, Attacks, and Mitigations of Smartphone Security. *Academic Journal of Nawroz University, 9*(4), 324–332. DOI: 10.25007/ajnu.v9n4a989

Zangana, H. M., & Omar, M. (2025). Harnessing the Power of Large Language Models for Cybersecurity: Applications, Challenges, and Future Directions. In Omar, M., & Zangana, H. (Eds.), *Application of Large Language Models (LLMs) for Software Vulnerability Detection* (pp. 1–40). IGI Global., DOI: 10.4018/979-8-3693-9311-6.ch001

Zangana, H. M., & Omar, M. (2025). Introduction to Digital Forensics and Artificial Intelligence. In Omar, M., & Zangana, H. (Eds.), *Digital Forensics in the Age of AI* (pp. 1–30). IGI Global Scientific Publishing., DOI: 10.4018/979-8-3373-0857-9.ch001

Zangana, H. M., & Omar, M. (2025). Introduction to Quantum-Aware Cybersecurity: The Need for LLMs. In Zangana, H., & Omar, M. (Eds.), *Leveraging Large Language Models for Quantum-Aware Cybersecurity* (pp. 1–28). IGI Global Scientific Publishing., DOI: 10.4018/979-8-3373-1102-9.ch001

Zangana, H. M., & Omar, M. (2025). The Role of Leadership in Advancing Inclusive Health Technologies. In Burrell, D., & Nguyen, C. (Eds.), *New Horizons in Leadership: Inclusive Explorations in Health, Technology, and Education* (pp. 203–220). IGI Global Scientific Publishing., DOI: 10.4018/979-8-3693-6437-6.ch009

Zangana, H. M., Omar, M., Al-Karaki, J. N., & Mohammed, D. (2024). Comprehensive Review and Analysis of Network Firewall Rule Analyzers: Enhancing Security Posture and Efficiency. *Redefining Security With Cyber AI*, 15-36.

Zangana, H. M., Sallow, Z. B., & Omar, M. (2025). The Human Factor in Cybersecurity: Addressing the Risks of Insider Threats. *Jurnal Ilmiah Computer Science, 3*(2), 76–85. DOI: 10.58602/jics.v3i2.37

Chapter 7
AI Automated Incident Response and Threat Mitigation Using AI

Rebet Keith Jones
https://orcid.org/0009-0008-0487-1301
Capitol Technology University, USA

ABSTRACT

The rapid evolution of cyber threats has necessitated the development of advanced techniques for incident response and threat mitigation. Artificial Intelligence (AI) has emerged as a transformative force in cybersecurity, particularly in automating incident detection, response, and mitigation processes. This chapter explores the role of AI, including Deep Learning (DL) and Large Language Models (LLMs), in revolutionizing incident response strategies. By leveraging AI, organizations can achieve faster, more accurate threat detection, adaptive response mechanisms, and efficient mitigation strategies, significantly improving their overall security posture. The chapter examines key AI technologies, their applications in cybersecurity, challenges faced, and the future potential of AI-driven security operations.

1. INTRODUCTION TO MALWARE AND CYBER THREATS

In the digital age, cybersecurity has become an essential pillar for safeguarding information, infrastructure, and personal data. The rise of sophisticated cyber threats, especially malware, presents a significant challenge to security professionals. Malware, short for malicious software, refers to any software intentionally designed to cause damage to computers, networks, or devices. These threats range from viruses and worms to ransomware, spyware, and Trojans. They are often used as tools to

DOI: 10.4018/979-8-3373-3296-3.ch007

exploit vulnerabilities in systems, disrupt services, or steal sensitive information (Omar & Zangana, 2025).

Malware attacks are not only diverse in nature but also in execution, as they can target various platforms such as desktops, mobile devices, and industrial control systems. These attacks have escalated over the years, with cybercriminals leveraging more advanced methods for evading detection. One of the key drivers behind the increase in malware attacks is the growing sophistication of attack techniques that exploit both known and unknown vulnerabilities in software and hardware (Zangana, 2024). For instance, ransomware attacks have seen a rise in recent years, where malicious actors encrypt a victim's data and demand a ransom for decryption keys (Sarker, 2024). These types of attacks are financially motivated, as organizations are often forced to pay substantial sums to recover their data.

The evolution of malware has followed a trajectory of increasing sophistication, from early viruses to modern ransomware and AI-driven attacks. The following timeline illustrates key milestones in malware development, showing the transition from simple self-replicating programs to advanced cyber threats.

Figure 1. Timeline of malware evolution

In addition to the financial threat posed by malware, the potential for massive data breaches is another significant concern. Attackers often use malware to infiltrate systems, bypass security defenses, and access confidential data such as customer information, intellectual property, and financial records. These attacks can result in reputational damage, regulatory penalties, and loss of consumer trust (Motlagh et al., 2024).

While traditional methods of defending against malware, such as signature-based detection systems, have been useful, they are increasingly ineffective against the sophisticated threats of today. This is where the integration of advanced technologies, including machine learning (ML) and large language models (LLMs), has shown great promise in enhancing cybersecurity strategies. Research by Ferrag et al. (2024) demonstrates how privacy-preserving models based on BERT can be used to detect and mitigate threats in Internet of Things (IoT) and Industrial IoT (IIoT) environments, where traditional malware detection techniques often fall short. The development of these advanced models is revolutionizing the field of malware detection by offering faster, more accurate threat detection and response capabilities.

The application of LLMs in cybersecurity, particularly in malware detection, has proven beneficial in identifying patterns and anomalies that traditional approaches might overlook. For example, large language models like GPT-2 and BERT have been employed to process massive amounts of textual and network traffic data to uncover hidden vulnerabilities and potential threats (Zangana & Omar, 2025). By leveraging these models, cybersecurity systems can significantly improve their ability to anticipate new forms of cyberattacks, analyze potential attack vectors, and generate appropriate countermeasures.

Despite these advancements, several challenges remain in the battle against malware and cyber threats. One of the primary challenges is the rapidly evolving nature of cyber threats. Cybercriminals continuously refine their tactics to bypass security measures, forcing cybersecurity systems to adapt quickly (Hasanov et al., 2024). Additionally, the complexity of malware attacks, such as polymorphic and metamorphic malware, makes detection even more difficult (Chen et al., 2024). These types of malware change their code or appearance to avoid detection, complicating efforts to create effective defense mechanisms.

Furthermore, the human factor remains a significant vulnerability in the cybersecurity landscape. Users are often the weakest link in security systems, as they may inadvertently fall victim to phishing attacks or fail to apply the necessary updates to their devices, leaving them susceptible to malware (Zangana et al., 2024). Education and awareness campaigns are essential in combating these threats, alongside the implementation of more advanced technical defenses.

The convergence of AI and cybersecurity is a key area of focus for improving malware detection and prevention. Researchers, such as those by Ferrag et al. (2023) and Liu (2024), have explored the use of generative AI and large language models to predict cyberattacks, strengthen defenses, and enhance threat intelligence. These models are capable of learning from historical attack data, offering predictive capabilities that can foresee new types of malware and prevent their spread before they cause significant damage.

In conclusion, malware and cyber threats continue to evolve in both complexity and scale, necessitating the development of advanced security solutions. Leveraging AI and machine learning technologies, particularly large language models, offers promising avenues for improving cybersecurity defenses. However, addressing these threats requires a holistic approach that combines advanced technical solutions with user education and proactive cybersecurity practices. As the cybersecurity landscape continues to shift, staying ahead of cybercriminals will depend on innovative methods that combine cutting-edge technologies with human expertise to protect systems from emerging threats.

2. ROLE OF AI IN SECURITY OPERATIONS CENTERS (SOCS)

In today's complex digital environment, Security Operations Centers (SOCs) play a critical role in defending organizations against evolving cyber threats. Traditionally, SOCs have relied on a combination of human expertise, automated systems, and various security tools to monitor and protect information systems. However, the increasing volume and sophistication of cyberattacks have strained the capabilities of traditional SOCs. To address these challenges, Artificial Intelligence (AI), particularly Large Language Models (LLMs), is being increasingly integrated into SOC operations to enhance threat detection, analysis, and mitigation. This section explores the pivotal role of AI in modern SOCs, emphasizing how LLMs are revolutionizing cybersecurity operations.

2.1 AI-Driven Threat Detection and Mitigation

AI's ability to analyze vast amounts of data at speed and accuracy far surpasses human capabilities. Security operations traditionally involved manually monitoring logs and alerts, a process that is not only time-consuming but also prone to human error. AI, particularly machine learning models, automates the identification of anomalous patterns in network traffic, system logs, and user behavior (Sarker, 2024).

Through continuous learning, AI models adapt to emerging threats, enhancing their ability to predict and identify attacks in real-time.

Large Language Models, such as GPT-3 and BERT, can process natural language data in a way that traditional systems cannot. These models can analyze and correlate vast amounts of textual data from sources like security reports, emails, and user communications, helping SOC analysts detect phishing attacks, insider threats, and malware command-and-control communications (Zangana, 2024). By using LLMs to analyze such data, SOCs can identify potential threats earlier, reducing the time to respond and preventing security breaches.

Artificial Intelligence is transforming Security Operations Centers (SOCs) by enabling real-time threat detection and automated response mechanisms. The following diagram illustrates the integration of AI components in modern SOCs.

Figure 2. AI-driven security operations center

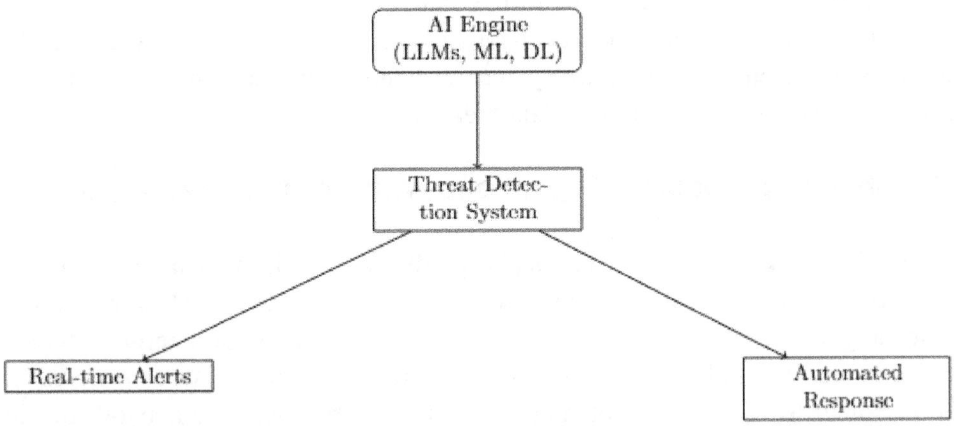

Furthermore, AI-powered threat intelligence systems help SOC teams stay updated with the latest cyberattack techniques, tactics, and procedures (TTPs). Through machine learning, AI systems continuously monitor and analyze threat landscapes, providing actionable intelligence to SOC analysts. This proactive approach allows SOCs to anticipate and mitigate cyber threats before they escalate into full-fledged attacks (Ghazal et al., 2024).

2.2 Automating Incident Response and Decision-Making

The scale and complexity of modern cyberattacks often overwhelm traditional incident response systems. AI enhances incident response by automating many of the steps involved in identifying, analyzing, and mitigating security incidents. For example, AI systems can automatically classify and prioritize security alerts based on their severity, ensuring that the most critical threats are handled first (Ferrag et al., 2024). This automated triage process enables SOCs to respond to threats more swiftly and efficiently.

Moreover, LLMs, due to their ability to understand and generate human-like text, can assist in decision-making during incidents by suggesting response actions or drafting communication to affected stakeholders. AI systems can also integrate with other security tools like firewalls, intrusion detection systems (IDS), and antivirus software, automatically executing predefined response actions when a specific threat is detected (Kasri et al., 2025).

The ability of AI to provide real-time, data-driven recommendations ensures that SOC teams make informed decisions quickly. This is especially crucial in high-pressure scenarios where every second counts, such as when mitigating a ransomware attack or preventing a data breach.

2.3 Enhancing Security Operations with Predictive Analytics

AI in SOCs is not only reactive but also predictive. Predictive analytics involves using AI to forecast potential threats based on patterns and trends in historical data. By leveraging AI models, SOCs can identify early indicators of emerging threats and vulnerabilities, allowing for preemptive action (Hassanin & Moustafa, 2024). For instance, AI can predict potential attack vectors by analyzing network traffic patterns and identifying weak spots in an organization's defenses.

Incorporating AI in predictive threat detection empowers SOCs to be more proactive in their defense strategy, shifting from a reactive to a more anticipatory approach. This includes anticipating zero-day vulnerabilities, identifying potential insider threats, and proactively addressing risks associated with new technologies, such as the Internet of Things (IoT) or Industrial Internet of Things (IIoT) (Diaf et al., 2024).

2.4 Improving Cybersecurity Automation with LLMs

Generative AI models, particularly LLMs, have proven effective in automating cybersecurity tasks that were previously manual and time-consuming. One of the most significant advantages of LLMs in SOCs is their ability to automate the generation of threat intelligence reports, incident logs, and response plans, allowing security teams to focus on higher-level decision-making and strategy (Manoharan & Sarker, 2023). LLMs can process data from multiple sources, including threat intelligence feeds, security blogs, and forums, to generate up-to-date insights on emerging threats and provide context-specific recommendations.

Moreover, LLMs like BERT have been adapted to create privacy-preserving models for IoT and IIoT device security, offering lightweight solutions that are not only accurate but also mindful of privacy concerns (Ferrag et al., 2024). These AI models can be used to detect vulnerabilities in IoT networks, analyze device behavior for signs of compromise, and ensure that SOCs are prepared to defend against threats targeting increasingly connected devices.

2.5 AI-Enhanced Forensic Investigations and Post-Incident Analysis

Once a cyberattack has occurred, SOCs must conduct forensic investigations to understand how the attack unfolded, what vulnerabilities were exploited, and the extent of the damage. AI, particularly LLMs, can aid in the analysis of vast amounts of textual data related to the incident, such as communication logs, emails, and chat logs. By leveraging natural language processing (NLP) techniques, LLMs can identify key pieces of information that may have been missed by human analysts, improving the overall quality and speed of investigations (Zangana et al., 2025).

Furthermore, AI can assist in post-incident analysis by providing detailed insights into attack methodologies and suggesting improvements to security protocols. For example, AI can analyze historical incident data and offer recommendations on how to strengthen defenses against specific attack techniques, such as social engineering or phishing (Omar, 2024). This continuous feedback loop enhances SOCs' ability to evolve and improve their security posture over time.

2.6 Summary

The integration of AI, particularly Large Language Models, into Security Operations Centers has transformed how organizations approach cybersecurity. By automating threat detection, incident response, predictive analytics, and forensic investigations, AI enables SOCs to operate more efficiently and effectively in the face of growing cyber threats. As AI technology continues to evolve, SOCs will become increasingly reliant on these advanced systems to stay ahead of cybercriminals and maintain robust defenses.

3. LLMS FOR AUTOMATING INCIDENT RESPONSE

In the rapidly evolving landscape of cybersecurity, Large Language Models (LLMs) are becoming indispensable tools in automating incident response processes. The integration of LLMs in cybersecurity leverages their deep learning capabilities to enhance the speed, accuracy, and efficiency of incident detection, analysis, and mitigation. By automating critical tasks, LLMs enable faster response times, which are essential in mitigating the damage caused by cyber threats. This section will explore the various applications of LLMs in automating incident response, highlighting their capabilities in threat detection, anomaly identification, and real-time defense mechanisms.

3.1 Threat Detection and Classification

One of the primary uses of LLMs in incident response is their ability to identify and classify emerging threats from large volumes of unstructured data, such as security logs, emails, and chat transcripts. LLMs, particularly those based on transformer architectures like BERT and GPT, excel at natural language processing (NLP) tasks, enabling them to detect patterns and anomalies indicative of potential security incidents. These models are trained to recognize a wide range of cyber threats, from phishing attacks to sophisticated malware, by analyzing historical data and contextual clues (Zangana & Omar, 2025).

For instance, Ferrag et al. (2024) have demonstrated how a privacy-preserving BERT-based model can be employed for detecting cyber threats in Internet of Things (IoT) and Industrial Internet of Things (IIoT) devices. This lightweight model is capable of identifying malicious activities in real time, which is crucial for automated threat detection in environments with a vast array of connected devices.

LLMs can also be integrated into Security Information and Event Management (SIEM) systems to provide real-time alerts. The ability to process massive amounts of data without human intervention allows these systems to respond to potential threats instantly, significantly reducing the time it takes to identify an issue.

3.2 Anomaly Detection and Contextual Analysis

Another significant role of LLMs in incident response is their ability to perform anomaly detection. LLMs can analyze data for deviations from the norm, such as unusual network traffic, irregular login attempts, or abnormal file access patterns, which often signal the presence of a cyberattack. The model's understanding of context and semantics enables it to discern subtle anomalies that might go unnoticed by traditional rule-based systems.

Zangana et al. (2025) discuss how LLMs, when trained on large datasets of network activity, can effectively detect and respond to novel types of attacks by recognizing out-of-pattern behaviors that indicate an intrusion. By examining metadata, logs, and even user behavior, LLMs can detect zero-day exploits and other advanced persistent threats (APTs) that traditional detection methods might miss.

Moreover, LLMs can help in contextualizing these anomalies, providing detailed reports that highlight potential threats in a way that is comprehensible to security teams. This contextual analysis significantly aids in understanding the scope of an incident and crafting the most effective response.

3.3 Real-time Response Automation

Beyond detection, LLMs can automate a range of incident response actions, reducing the reliance on human intervention and speeding up the containment and remediation processes. When a threat is identified, an LLM can trigger predefined actions such as blocking malicious IP addresses, isolating compromised systems, or alerting security teams through automated notifications.

For example, Liu (2024) outlines how LLMs can be used to automate the triage of security incidents by categorizing and prioritizing alerts based on the severity of the threat. This reduces the cognitive load on cybersecurity professionals, allowing them to focus on high-priority tasks while the system handles routine incident responses autonomously.

The integration of LLMs in Security Orchestration, Automation, and Response (SOAR) platforms further enhances this capability. These platforms rely on LLMs to orchestrate a series of automated responses across various cybersecurity tools, providing a unified defense mechanism against cyberattacks.

Large Language Models (LLMs) streamline incident response by automatically analyzing threats, categorizing incidents, and suggesting mitigation steps. The following workflow illustrates an AI-powered security response cycle.

Figure 3. AI-based incident response workflow

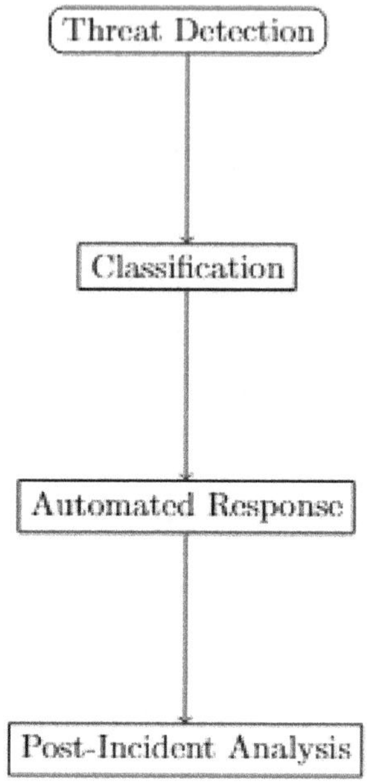

3.4 Improving Post-Incident Analysis

Following an incident, LLMs also play a crucial role in conducting post-incident analysis. By analyzing historical incident data, LLMs can identify the root cause of a breach, the techniques used by attackers, and the methods for preventing similar incidents in the future. This analysis can be automated, making it easier for organizations to learn from past incidents and improve their security posture.

As noted by Ferrag et al. (2023), LLMs can also help in generating comprehensive reports that summarize the incident timeline, the actions taken, and the effectiveness of the response. These reports can be critical for compliance, audits, and further training of the security team.

3.5 Challenges and Future Directions

Despite their immense potential, there are challenges associated with implementing LLMs in incident response systems. One of the primary concerns is the computational complexity and the need for substantial computational resources, especially when processing large volumes of data in real-time (Hasanov et al., 2024). Additionally, ensuring the privacy and security of sensitive data while using LLMs for threat detection and response is an ongoing challenge, particularly when dealing with personal or confidential information (Kasri et al., 2025).

Furthermore, LLMs are not immune to adversarial attacks. Hackers may attempt to manipulate the model's output by feeding it malicious input designed to bypass detection. This necessitates ongoing research to enhance the robustness of LLMs in cybersecurity applications (Hassanin & Moustafa, 2024).

In the future, the role of LLMs in incident response will continue to expand, particularly with advancements in quantum-aware cybersecurity (Zangana, 2025). By leveraging the unique capabilities of quantum computing, LLMs could potentially handle even more complex threat scenarios and provide even faster, more secure responses.

3.6 Summary

The application of Large Language Models (LLMs) in automating incident response represents a significant leap forward in cybersecurity. Their ability to detect threats, perform anomaly detection, automate responses, and facilitate post-incident analysis makes them invaluable tools in the fight against cyber threats. However, challenges remain in ensuring their efficiency, robustness, and security. As the field of AI and cybersecurity continues to evolve, the integration of LLMs into incident response systems will likely become more sophisticated, paving the way for faster and more effective defense mechanisms against an increasingly complex threat landscape.

4. AI-POWERED THREAT INTELLIGENCE AND REAL-TIME DEFENSE

In the evolving cybersecurity landscape, the integration of Artificial Intelligence (AI), particularly through the use of large language models (LLMs), is transforming threat detection, intelligence, and real-time defense mechanisms. The rapid sophistication of cyber threats necessitates robust, dynamic systems capable of recognizing, analyzing, and responding to potential vulnerabilities with speed and accuracy. AI-driven systems, powered by advanced LLMs, offer a powerful solution for identifying emerging threats and automating responses to attacks, making them integral to next-generation cybersecurity infrastructures.

4.1 Threat Intelligence: Leveraging Large Language Models

Threat intelligence involves the process of gathering, analyzing, and disseminating data related to potential cyber threats to enable proactive defense measures. The use of LLMs like BERT and GPT-based models is revolutionizing the way threat intelligence is collected and interpreted. These models can be trained to identify not only known threats but also predict new, previously unseen forms of cyberattacks by analyzing large datasets and extracting patterns from historical threat data. According to Ferrag et al. (2023), the ability of LLMs to process and analyze vast amounts of data significantly enhances the prediction and detection of anomalies that indicate potential threats.

LLMs enhance threat intelligence by automating the detection of suspicious activities across various cybersecurity domains, including IoT (Internet of Things) and IIoT (Industrial IoT) environments. Ferrag et al. (2024) developed a privacy-preserving BERT-based model tailored for these devices, showcasing how LLMs can be applied to resource-constrained environments without compromising the security and privacy of sensitive data. The lightweight nature of such models ensures that they can be deployed in real-time systems without significant computational overhead, making them ideal for time-sensitive cybersecurity tasks (Kasri et al., 2025).

4.2 Real-Time Defense: Automated Threat Mitigation

Real-time defense is a critical component of modern cybersecurity, where threats must be detected and mitigated instantaneously to minimize damage. The deployment of AI systems in this context has enabled the automation of defense protocols, allowing security teams to respond more rapidly to cyber threats. LLMs play a pivotal role in automating the analysis of attack vectors and the development of tailored defense strategies.

Sarker (2024) explores the use of generative AI in cybersecurity, highlighting how LLMs can be leveraged to develop automated countermeasures for identified threats. For instance, once an attack is detected, an LLM-powered system can autonomously generate defensive responses such as firewall updates, intrusion detection system (IDS) reconfigurations, and vulnerability patching. This ability to automate responses reduces the reliance on manual intervention and enables organizations to respond faster and more effectively to evolving threats.

AI-powered threat intelligence relies on diverse data sources, including security logs, social media, and attack patterns. The diagram below represents the flow of data in an AI-driven cybersecurity system.

Figure 4. AI-powered threat intelligence flow

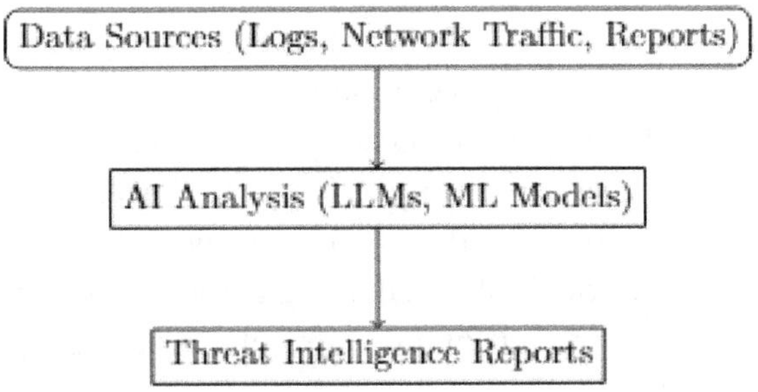

One key area where AI-powered threat intelligence is particularly effective is in the prediction of cyberattacks before they occur. As noted by Liu (2024), AI models can detect subtle patterns within network traffic, user behavior, and system activities, which may not be immediately apparent to human analysts. Through continuous learning and adaptation, these models can recognize the early signs of a cyberattack, enabling preemptive action. This proactive approach is essential in defending against advanced persistent threats (APTs) and zero-day vulnerabilities, which often remain undetected for extended periods.

4.3 Enhancing Cybersecurity with Explainability

While LLMs are incredibly effective in detecting and mitigating cyber threats, their adoption has raised concerns around the explainability and transparency of their decisions. In cybersecurity, it is crucial to not only identify threats but also to understand the rationale behind the detection and the subsequent actions taken. This is where the synergy between LLMs and explainable AI (XAI) becomes significant.

Ferrag et al. (2024) and Zangana et al. (2025) highlight the need for AI systems that not only detect threats but also explain their reasoning in human-understandable terms. By integrating XAI techniques with LLMs, cybersecurity systems can provide valuable insights into why certain threats were flagged, what makes them suspicious, and how the system responded. This transparency fosters trust and helps security teams understand potential vulnerabilities better, improving their ability to refine and strengthen their defenses.

4.4 The Future of AI in Cybersecurity Defense

Looking forward, the role of LLMs in cybersecurity is poised to expand, especially with advancements in quantum computing and the increasing complexity of cyber threats. As highlighted by Zangana et al. (2024) in their review on quantum-aware cybersecurity, future cybersecurity defenses will need to address the unique challenges posed by quantum computing, such as the potential for quantum-enabled attacks. LLMs will play a critical role in adapting to these new threats by leveraging their ability to process vast amounts of quantum-related data and predict new attack vectors (Zangana, 2025).

Additionally, as AI continues to evolve, cybersecurity defenses will become more integrated with other emerging technologies, such as blockchain and IoT. AI-powered systems will need to maintain interoperability across these domains to ensure seamless defense mechanisms. The work of Idelhaj, Abou El Houda, and Khoukhi (2024) on AI for blockchain security, and Kasri et al. (2025) on enhancing cybersecurity with LLMs, indicates that the integration of AI across these technologies will further fortify the security landscape.

4.5 Summary

AI-powered threat intelligence and real-time defense are reshaping the landscape of cybersecurity by enabling more accurate detection, proactive defense strategies, and faster response times. With the continued advancement of large language models, organizations are better equipped to handle the ever-evolving cyber threat landscape. These systems not only offer the ability to predict and mitigate attacks but also ensure the scalability and flexibility needed to address complex, multi-faceted threats. As we move toward an increasingly interconnected and digitized world, the role of AI in cybersecurity will become indispensable in defending against the next generation of cyberattacks.

5. CASE STUDIES ON AUTOMATED CYBER DEFENSE SYSTEMS

The integration of large language models (LLMs) into cybersecurity has garnered significant attention in recent years. These models, powered by deep learning techniques, have demonstrated substantial improvements in threat detection, incident response, and vulnerability management. The growing reliance on these models for real-time cybersecurity defense systems is transforming the landscape of automated threat detection and mitigation. Several case studies illustrate the effectiveness and potential of automated cyber defense systems powered by LLMs.

5.1. IoT/IIoT Device Security: Privacy-Preserving BERT-Based Models

A key case study comes from Ferrag et al. (2024), who developed a lightweight BERT-based model tailored to the Internet of Things (IoT) and Industrial Internet of Things (IIoT) devices. Their model emphasizes privacy preservation while ensuring high accuracy in detecting threats across resource-constrained environments. The model's efficiency lies in its ability to balance the computational constraints of IoT/IIoT devices with the need for rapid, real-time threat detection. The deployment of this system in IoT networks has shown promise in effectively identifying cyber threats without compromising privacy, which is paramount in environments with sensitive data (Ferrag et al., 2024).

5.2. Large Language Models for Cyber Threat Detection

A broader perspective on LLMs in cybersecurity is provided by Ferrag et al. (2023), who explore the application of generative AI models for detecting cyber threats. Their study demonstrates that LLMs, such as GPT-based models, can significantly enhance threat detection capabilities by generating contextually relevant information and predicting potential attacks. These systems are trained to handle large-scale data from various sources, ensuring a comprehensive understanding of threat patterns and anomalous behaviors. The ability of LLMs to synthesize complex data from diverse network traffic logs and identify potential risks without human intervention marks a breakthrough in automated cybersecurity defense (Ferrag et al., 2023).

5.3. Generative AI for Malware Detection

In the domain of malware detection, Kasri et al. (2025) explore the role of LLMs in detecting advanced persistent threats (APTs) and zero-day vulnerabilities. By using generative models, they showed that LLMs could identify novel malware strains and predict their behavior based on historical data. The study highlighted the advantage of using LLMs for dynamic threat mitigation, where systems autonomously adjust their defense strategies based on evolving attack techniques. The results from this case study underscore the ability of LLMs to provide proactive defense mechanisms that adapt to new, unforeseen threats (Kasri et al., 2025).

5.4. Cyber Attack Prediction in IoT Networks

Another notable case study is presented by Diaf et al. (2024), who applied LLMs to predict cyberattacks in IoT networks. By leveraging the predictive capabilities of LLMs, their system analyzes the historical behavior of IoT devices to forecast potential vulnerabilities and attacks. This proactive approach allows for early warning signs to be detected, enabling cybersecurity professionals to mitigate risks before they manifest. The application of this model in real-world IoT environments demonstrated its potential in reducing response times and minimizing damage from cyberattacks (Diaf et al., 2024).

5.5. Explainable AI in Cyber Threat Intelligence

Santos et al. (2024) focus on the intersection of explainable AI and LLMs in cybersecurity. Their study highlights the importance of transparency and interpretability in automated cyber defense systems. By integrating explainable AI with LLMs, their system not only detects cyber threats but also provides understandable reasoning behind its decisions. This transparency is essential in critical sectors like healthcare and finance, where human experts need to trust and verify the model's decisions. The case study demonstrated that LLMs could be used to enhance trust in automated systems, facilitating quicker and more confident responses to threats (Santos et al., 2024).

5.6. Large Language Models for Vulnerability Detection

Zangana et al. (2024) delve into the application of LLMs for software vulnerability detection. Their study reveals how LLMs, specifically fine-tuned models, can scan software code to identify security flaws that may not be detectable through traditional static analysis tools. The case study also discusses the integration of LLMs with continuous integration/continuous deployment (CI/CD) pipelines, enabling automated vulnerability scans during software development. This integration ensures that vulnerabilities are identified early in the development process, reducing the risk of exploitation in production environments (Zangana et al., 2024).

5.7. AI-Driven Threat Mitigation in Cloud Environments

The application of AI and LLMs in cloud security is explored by Zangana et al. (2025), who describe how automated systems have been developed to detect and mitigate threats in real-time across cloud-based platforms. Their case study focuses on the use of LLMs to monitor and secure cloud infrastructure by analyzing large amounts of data generated by cloud services. The system can autonomously detect anomalies, such as unusual access patterns or misconfigurations, that may indicate a potential security breach. The proactive mitigation strategies offered by LLMs in cloud environments are essential for ensuring the integrity and confidentiality of cloud services (Zangana et al., 2025).

5.8. AI-Powered Cybersecurity Automation for Healthcare

A compelling case study in the healthcare sector is provided by Huff et al. (2023), who applied AI-driven automation for cybersecurity in medical and healthcare environments. They highlight how LLMs have been deployed to safeguard sensitive healthcare data and prevent breaches in medical devices. The system leverages real-time data to detect malicious activities and unauthorized access attempts, alerting administrators and initiating automated defense protocols. The ability of LLMs to ensure the privacy and security of patient data in a highly regulated and sensitive environment showcases the potential of AI in critical sectors (Huff et al., 2023).

5.9 Summary

These case studies demonstrate the transformative impact of large language models on cybersecurity defense systems. From real-time threat detection in IoT networks to proactive vulnerability identification and malware detection, LLMs are revolutionizing how automated systems address cybersecurity challenges. As these models continue to evolve, their ability to predict, detect, and mitigate cyber threats autonomously will play a pivotal role in enhancing the resilience of cybersecurity infrastructures across various industries. The ongoing research and development of LLMs offer promising opportunities for further optimizing automated defense systems in an increasingly complex and threat-laden digital landscape.

The following bar chart compares the efficiency of AI-powered security systems with traditional approaches across key cybersecurity metrics.

Figure 5. AI vs. traditional security performance comparison

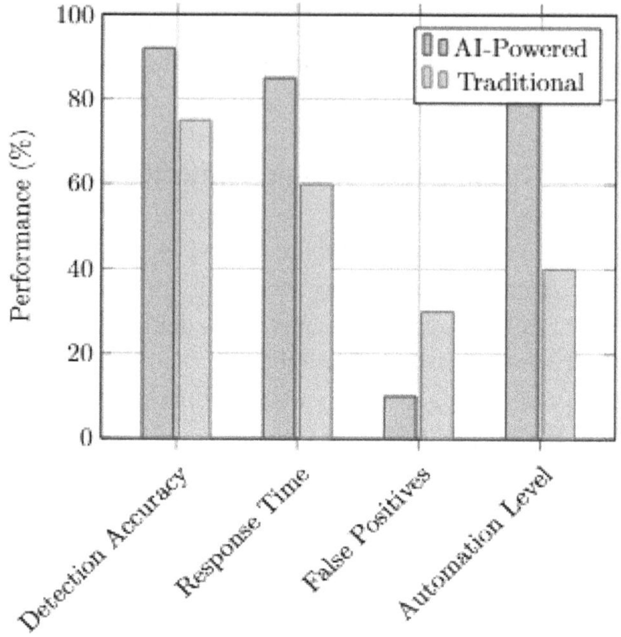

6. CHALLENGES IN IMPLEMENTING AI-BASED SECURITY AUTOMATION

While AI-based security automation offers significant advantages in enhancing cybersecurity practices, the implementation of such systems is not without challenges. These obstacles range from technical complexities to ethical considerations, making the adoption of AI solutions in cybersecurity a multifaceted process. Below, we delve into the primary challenges faced by organizations when deploying AI-powered security automation.

6.1. Data Quality and Availability

AI systems, particularly those relying on machine learning and natural language processing (NLP), require vast amounts of high-quality, annotated data to be effective. However, the availability of such data is often limited, especially in niche cybersecurity domains or for newer attack vectors (Hasanov et al., 2024; Zangana et al., 2025). Moreover, sensitive data such as threat intelligence may not be readily accessible due to privacy concerns, creating significant barriers to training effective AI models (Ferrag et al., 2024). Data quality also poses a concern, as inaccurate, incomplete, or biased data can impair the learning process, leading to suboptimal model performance.

6.2. Integration with Existing Systems

Integrating AI models into existing cybersecurity infrastructures is a complex task. Many legacy systems were not designed with AI integration in mind, making it difficult to adapt them to work seamlessly with new AI-based tools (Hassanin & Moustafa, 2024). In particular, automated incident response tools based on large language models (LLMs) need to interface with firewalls, intrusion detection systems, and other security components (Ferrag et al., 2023). This integration may require significant system overhauls or specialized middleware, which can be resource-intensive.

6.3. Resource Intensive Training and Operation

Training AI models, particularly deep learning models, demands substantial computational resources. Models like BERT and GPT-2, which have shown promise in cybersecurity tasks, require high-performance hardware (e.g., GPUs) and significant time to train on large datasets (Chen et al., 2024; Liu, 2024). This training burden can be prohibitive for smaller organizations or those without access to dedicated infrastructure. Furthermore, deploying these models in real-time environments requires ongoing resource allocation to handle large volumes of data and perform tasks like threat detection and response (Sarker, 2024).

6.4. Model Transparency and Interpretability

A significant challenge in implementing AI-based security automation is ensuring that the models are interpretable and transparent. For critical applications such as threat detection and response, decision-making processes must be transparent to cybersecurity teams. Without this transparency, organizations may hesitate to rely on AI models for high-stakes decisions, fearing that the lack of interpretability could lead to undesirable outcomes (Ghazal et al., 2024). Many AI models, especially deep learning-based models, act as "black boxes," making it difficult for security experts to understand how certain conclusions or alerts are generated. This challenge is particularly acute in the context of LLMs, where the decisions made by the model must be explainable to ensure trust and confidence (Sarker, 2024; Zangana et al., 2025).

6.5. Adversarial Attacks

One of the main vulnerabilities of AI models, especially in cybersecurity, is their susceptibility to adversarial attacks. In such attacks, malicious actors manipulate input data to deceive AI systems into making incorrect predictions or decisions (Motlagh et al., 2024). For instance, cybercriminals may craft specific inputs to bypass an AI-driven malware detection system or cause an AI model to misclassify a threat as benign. Ensuring that AI systems are robust against such attacks is an ongoing area of research and a key challenge for organizations looking to deploy AI-based security automation (Omar, 2024).

6.6. Ethical and Privacy Concerns

AI-based security systems often involve the collection and processing of vast amounts of data, including potentially sensitive or personal information. This raises significant privacy concerns, especially in industries such as healthcare and finance, where data protection regulations like GDPR and HIPAA impose strict rules (Kasri et al., 2025). Furthermore, there is a risk of bias in AI models, which can lead to disproportionate targeting of certain groups or individuals. Ensuring that AI systems are ethical, privacy-preserving, and compliant with regulatory frameworks is a considerable challenge (Gholami & Omar, 2024). Models like those discussed by Ferrag et al. (2024) attempt to address privacy concerns by utilizing techniques such as federated learning and differential privacy, but these solutions are not universally applicable.

6.7. Scalability and Maintenance

As cyber threats evolve, so too must the AI models designed to detect and mitigate them. The dynamic nature of cybersecurity threats means that AI models must be regularly updated with new data and retrained to maintain their effectiveness (Zangana et al., 2025). However, managing the continuous improvement and scaling of AI models is a complex process that demands both technical expertise and significant resources. Moreover, as new types of threats emerge, models that were once highly effective may lose their relevance or fail to detect the latest tactics used by cybercriminals (Hassanin & Moustafa, 2024).

6.8. Skill Shortage

The successful implementation of AI-based security automation requires specialized expertise in both cybersecurity and AI. The shortage of qualified professionals who can design, implement, and maintain AI models is a major roadblock to widespread adoption. Organizations may struggle to find experts with the right skill sets in both domains, leading to delays or suboptimal implementations of AI systems (Santos et al., 2024). Additionally, AI models require continuous monitoring and fine-tuning, tasks that demand skilled personnel with in-depth knowledge of both AI and cybersecurity principles (Hadi et al., 2023).

6.9 Summary

AI-based security automation holds immense potential for enhancing cybersecurity, but its implementation is fraught with challenges. From data quality and availability issues to the need for significant computational resources, integrating AI systems into existing infrastructures can be difficult. Furthermore, concerns related to transparency, adversarial robustness, and privacy must be addressed to ensure that these systems can be trusted and widely adopted. Overcoming these hurdles will require ongoing research, innovation, and collaboration between AI and cybersecurity experts to create secure, scalable, and ethical solutions (Zangana et al., 2025).

7. ETHICAL CONCERNS IN AI-DRIVEN INCIDENT RESPONSE

As artificial intelligence (AI) continues to reshape the cybersecurity landscape, particularly through large language models (LLMs), the integration of AI-driven incident response mechanisms presents several ethical challenges. These concerns encompass issues related to privacy, accountability, transparency, bias, and the potential for misuse of AI technologies. While LLMs have demonstrated immense potential in automating threat detection and response, it is essential to examine these ethical considerations to ensure responsible and equitable application in cybersecurity.

AI-driven security systems introduce ethical concerns, including data privacy, accountability, and algorithmic bias. The following Venn diagram categorizes these concerns.

Figure 6. Ethical concerns in AI-driven cybersecurity

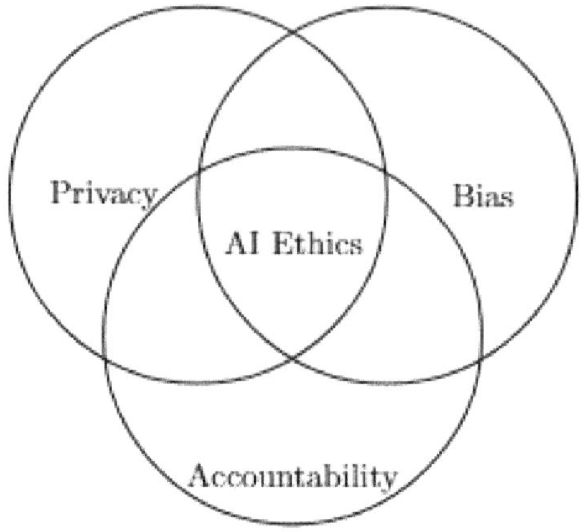

7.1 Privacy and Data Protection

One of the primary ethical concerns in AI-driven incident response is the handling of sensitive data. LLMs, due to their reliance on vast datasets for training, have the potential to access and analyze personal or confidential information during incident response. While privacy-preserving models, such as those developed by Ferrag et al. (2024), have emerged to mitigate these risks by employing techniques like differential privacy, there remains a concern over how these models handle data in practice (Ferrag et al., 2024). AI systems must be designed with robust safeguards to prevent unauthorized access or misuse of personal data during threat detection and mitigation.

The ethical dilemma intensifies when considering the surveillance implications of AI in cybersecurity. AI systems could potentially track user activities or even invade private communications under the guise of threat detection. In such cases, ethical frameworks must ensure that these practices comply with privacy laws, such as the General Data Protection Regulation (GDPR) in Europe, to protect individuals from undue surveillance.

7.2 Accountability and Responsibility

Another significant ethical issue involves the question of accountability. With the increasing autonomy of AI-driven systems, it becomes challenging to pinpoint who is responsible for the decisions made by these systems. If an AI system erroneously flags a benign activity as a threat or fails to detect a genuine threat, the question arises: who is liable? Is it the developer of the AI system, the organization using it, or the AI itself? This ambiguity in accountability creates ethical and legal concerns regarding responsibility and recourse for affected individuals or entities.

A related concern is the risk of automating decision-making to the extent that human oversight is minimized. While LLMs, such as those explored by Liu (2024), can provide quick and efficient responses to cybersecurity incidents, the absence of human judgment in critical situations could lead to unintended consequences. It is essential to maintain a level of human oversight to ensure that AI systems operate within ethical boundaries and that accountability is clearly defined (Liu, 2024).

7.3 Transparency and Explainability

Transparency and explainability in AI systems are crucial for building trust among users and stakeholders. AI-driven incident response systems must be able to provide clear explanations for their decisions. For instance, if an AI system decides to block a particular IP address due to a suspected attack, it should offer an understandable rationale for its action. This transparency is vital for ensuring that decisions made by AI systems are not arbitrary and are based on logical reasoning that can be audited (Sarker, 2024).

In the context of LLMs, explainability is particularly challenging due to the complex nature of these models. The "black-box" problem, where the decision-making process of the AI system is not easily interpretable, can undermine trust in these systems. Efforts to improve explainability, as seen in the works of Ghazal et al. (2024) and Hasanov et al. (2024), are important in ensuring that AI models in cybersecurity are both effective and ethically sound (Ghazal et al., 2024; Hasanov et al., 2024).

7.4 Bias and Fairness

AI models, including those used for cybersecurity incident response, are vulnerable to biases that may be embedded in the training data. If an AI system is trained on biased datasets, it may lead to discriminatory outcomes, such as disproportionately flagging certain groups of individuals or behaviors as malicious. Bias in AI models can result in unfair treatment, particularly in scenarios where the model makes decisions that affect people's lives or businesses.

For example, biased threat detection algorithms could potentially discriminate against certain demographic groups, leading to unjustified suspicion or resource allocation. This issue becomes particularly critical in cybersecurity applications that involve sensitive personal or organizational data. Developers of AI systems must be aware of these biases and work toward creating models that are fair and representative of diverse populations (Santos et al., 2024). Efforts such as those made by Ferrag et al. (2023) in designing fairness-aware AI systems should be adopted to address these challenges (Ferrag et al., 2023).

7.5 Misuse and Weaponization of AI

The potential for misuse of AI-driven incident response systems in malicious activities is another ethical concern. While AI can significantly enhance the ability to detect and mitigate cyber threats, it can also be exploited by adversaries to launch more sophisticated attacks. For instance, attackers could leverage AI to develop autonomous attack systems that adapt and evolve, making it more difficult for traditional defenses to respond effectively.

The possibility of AI systems being weaponized for cyber warfare or criminal activities raises serious ethical questions about the role of AI in society. Efforts must be made to ensure that AI technologies in cybersecurity are used solely for defensive purposes and are not turned into offensive tools. The ethical implications of such misuse must be continuously monitored and controlled through international agreements and regulations (Asoronye et al., 2024).

7.6 Summary

While AI-driven incident response systems, particularly those utilizing large language models, offer significant advantages in automating and enhancing cybersecurity measures, they also present various ethical challenges. These concerns, including privacy, accountability, transparency, bias, and the potential for misuse, must be carefully considered and addressed. As AI continues to evolve, it is essential for researchers, policymakers, and organizations to collaborate in developing ethical frameworks and guidelines that govern the use of AI in cybersecurity. This will ensure that AI technologies are used responsibly, equitably, and transparently, ultimately benefiting society while minimizing harm.

8. FUTURE TRENDS IN AI-POWERED SECURITY OPERATIONS

The integration of Artificial Intelligence (AI) in cybersecurity continues to evolve, driven by advancements in large language models (LLMs) and their ability to detect, analyze, and mitigate cyber threats in real time. As cyberattacks grow in sophistication, AI-powered security operations are expected to play a critical role in shaping the future of cybersecurity. This section explores the emerging trends that are likely to define the next generation of AI-driven security operations.

8.1. Adaptive and Self-Learning AI Systems

One of the most promising future trends in AI-powered security operations is the development of adaptive, self-learning systems. Traditional security tools often rely on pre-defined rules and signatures, which may be ineffective against new and unknown threats. AI models, particularly deep learning networks, have the ability to continuously learn from data, improving their detection and response capabilities over time (Santos, Salam, & Dahir, 2024). These self-learning systems can adapt to new attack vectors and even predict potential vulnerabilities before they are exploited, offering a significant advantage over conventional methods. Ferrag et al. (2024) have highlighted how such systems, especially when combined with large language models, could autonomously evolve in response to emerging threats in IoT and IIoT environments.

8.2. Explainable AI (XAI) for Cybersecurity Decision-Making

As AI becomes more involved in security operations, the demand for transparency and accountability in decision-making is growing. Explainable AI (XAI) allows cybersecurity professionals to understand how AI models reach specific conclusions or decisions, which is crucial for trust and effective risk management. XAI can be particularly important in situations where AI detects anomalies or threats but needs to provide a rational explanation for its actions to ensure that human experts can verify the findings (Sarker, 2024). As large language models, such as BERT and GPT, gain prominence in threat detection, integrating explainability into these models will be a key challenge and opportunity for advancing cybersecurity practices (Ghazal et al., 2024).

8.3. Enhanced Threat Intelligence through Natural Language Processing (NLP)

Natural Language Processing (NLP) has already shown its potential in analyzing vast amounts of unstructured data, such as reports, news articles, and social media, to identify emerging cybersecurity threats. Future AI-powered systems will increasingly leverage NLP to analyze threat intelligence feeds, enabling them to detect and assess risks in real time. By processing large volumes of unstructured text, AI can uncover hidden patterns and correlations that human analysts might miss (Liu, 2024). Zangana et al. (2025) discuss how LLMs can be employed to automate threat intelligence gathering, offering predictive insights that improve decision-making and response times.

8.4. Quantum-Aware Cybersecurity Models

As quantum computing begins to gain traction, it will present both opportunities and challenges for AI-driven cybersecurity. Quantum-aware security models are expected to become crucial in protecting data against quantum-enabled attacks. Large language models are already being explored for their potential to enhance security in a quantum computing environment. Zangana and Omar (2025) predict that LLMs will play a pivotal role in developing quantum-aware models capable of defending against quantum-level threats. This will require the convergence of AI and quantum computing technologies, enabling more robust and future-proof cybersecurity solutions.

8.5. Integration with Autonomous Systems for Incident Response

In the future, AI-powered security operations will likely evolve to include more autonomous decision-making, particularly in incident response. Autonomous systems, equipped with LLMs, can quickly analyze incoming data, detect anomalies, and even implement remediation steps without human intervention. Such capabilities are essential in combating fast-moving cyberattacks, such as zero-day exploits and ransomware attacks, where human intervention might be too slow (Kasri et al., 2025). The automation of these processes can significantly reduce the response time to incidents and minimize the impact of cyber threats.

8.6. AI in Proactive Vulnerability Management

AI-powered security tools will increasingly be used to predict and manage vulnerabilities before they are exploited by attackers. Leveraging historical data, vulnerability databases, and AI techniques such as supervised learning, security systems can identify weaknesses in software and hardware systems that may be targeted by adversaries. This proactive approach will enable organizations to patch vulnerabilities and strengthen their defenses before attacks occur (Xu et al., 2024). According to Ferrag et al. (2023), pre-trained language models are already being explored for vulnerability detection, and their application in cybersecurity is expected to expand rapidly in the coming years.

8.7. Privacy-Preserving AI for Sensitive Environments

As privacy concerns continue to grow, AI models in cybersecurity must prioritize user data protection. Privacy-preserving techniques, such as federated learning and differential privacy, are expected to be integrated into AI-driven security operations. These methods allow AI systems to learn from data without directly accessing sensitive information, making them particularly valuable in privacy-sensitive industries like healthcare and finance (Hasanov et al., 2024). Ferrag et al. (2024) discuss how BERT-based lightweight models can be employed for privacy-preserving applications in IoT environments, offering scalable and secure solutions without compromising on performance.

8.8. AI-Driven Collaboration for Global Cyber Defense

The growing complexity and scale of cyber threats require collaboration between organizations, governments, and AI systems across borders. Future AI-powered security operations will likely involve sharing threat intelligence, analyzing patterns, and developing global defense strategies. AI systems will be able to automatically aggregate threat data from multiple sources, providing real-time, global perspectives on emerging threats. This collective intelligence will enable organizations to detect and neutralize threats that may otherwise go undetected. As Zangana et al. (2024) point out, the application of LLMs in global cybersecurity frameworks can improve cooperation and enhance security on a worldwide scale.

8.9 Summary

The future of AI-powered security operations is marked by rapid advancements in large language models and their integration into cybersecurity frameworks. These models will not only improve detection and response times but also introduce proactive, adaptive, and explainable solutions that can significantly enhance the security landscape. As AI technologies continue to evolve, the cybersecurity industry must remain agile, ready to embrace new innovations while addressing the challenges they bring, such as privacy concerns, explainability, and quantum threats.

9. CONCLUSION

The rapid advancement of AI technologies, particularly large language models (LLMs), has revolutionized cybersecurity by providing new approaches to detecting, predicting, and mitigating cyber threats. From automating incident responses to enhancing threat intelligence, LLMs are pushing the boundaries of what is possible in securing digital infrastructures. As the landscape of cybersecurity continues to evolve, the integration of LLMs is proving to be essential in addressing the increasing complexity of cyber threats. The ability of LLMs to analyze vast amounts of data, predict potential threats, and automate responses is transforming how organizations approach security.

In addition, the evolving capabilities of AI-driven solutions are creating opportunities for more proactive and adaptive security systems. LLMs are becoming integral to identifying vulnerabilities, detecting anomalous behavior, and protecting sensitive data in real time. As demonstrated by various studies (Ferrag et al., 2024; Liu, 2024), the deployment of these models has enhanced cybersecurity operations, making them more effective and efficient. However, challenges remain, including concerns about model biases, the need for explainability in AI-driven decisions, and the computational resources required for scaling these systems (Sarker, 2024; Kasri et al., 2025).

Looking ahead, the role of LLMs in cybersecurity will likely continue to expand, especially as new technologies like quantum computing begin to reshape the landscape (Zangana & Omar, 2025). For cybersecurity to keep pace with these developments, there is a need for ongoing research and innovation in AI models, ensuring they are robust, adaptable, and capable of addressing emerging threats. Future work will also need to focus on optimizing LLMs for specific cybersecurity applications, such as IoT security and advanced threat hunting, while mitigating privacy concerns and ensuring the ethical use of these technologies.

In conclusion, while LLMs are already demonstrating their potential in cybersecurity, their full impact will be realized only through continued advancements and strategic integration into cybersecurity frameworks. As organizations increasingly rely on AI to safeguard their digital environments, the convergence of cybersecurity and AI-driven technologies will play a pivotal role in creating a more secure, resilient, and adaptive digital world.

REFERENCES

Aghaei, E., Niu, X., Shadid, W., & Al-Shaer, E. (2022, October). Securebert: A domain-specific language model for cybersecurity. In *International Conference on Security and Privacy in Communication Systems* (pp. 39-56). Cham: Springer Nature Switzerland.

AlQenaei, Z. M. (2024, March). Evolution and Optimization of Language Model Architectures: From Foundations to Future Directions. In *International Conference on Computing and Machine Learning* (pp. 233-249). Singapore: Springer Nature Singapore.

Alturkistani, H., & Chuprat, S. (2024). Artificial Intelligence and Large Language Models in Advancing Cyber Threat Intelligence: A Systematic Literature Review.

Asoronye, G. O., Anthony, O. C., Ogbuikwu, R. I., Ogili, C. O., & Ali, H. U. (2024). SecLM: A Specialized Security Language Model for Advanced Cybersecurity Applications and Threat Mitigation. *EKETE-International Journal Of Advanced Research*, *2*(6), 33–42.

Bryce, C., Kalousis, A., Leroux, I., Madinier, H., Mermoud, A., Mulder, V., ... & Ruch, P. Trends in Large Language Models: Actors, Applications, and Impact on Cybersecurity.

Chen, Y., Cui, M., Wang, D., Cao, Y., Yang, P., Jiang, B., Lu, Z., & Liu, B. (2024). A survey of large language models for cyber threat detection. *Computers & Security*, *145*, 104016. DOI: 10.1016/j.cose.2024.104016

Diaf, A., Korba, A. A., Karabadji, N. E., & Ghamri-Doudane, Y. (2024, April). Beyond detection: Leveraging large language models for cyber attack prediction in iot networks. In *2024 20th International Conference on Distributed Computing in Smart Systems and the Internet of Things (DCOSS-IoT)* (pp. 117-123). IEEE.

Ferrag, M. A., Alwahedi, F., Battah, A., Cherif, B., Mechri, A., & Tihanyi, N. (2024). Generative ai and large language models for cyber security: All insights you need. *Available atSSRN* 4853709. DOI: 10.2139/ssrn.4853709

Ferrag, M. A., Ndhlovu, M., Tihanyi, N., Cordeiro, L. C., Debbah, M., & Lestable, T. (2023). Revolutionizing cyber threat detection with large language models. *arXiv preprint arXiv:2306.14263*, 195-202.

Ferrag, M. A., Ndhlovu, M., Tihanyi, N., Cordeiro, L. C., Debbah, M., Lestable, T., & Thandi, N. S. (2024). Revolutionizing cyber threat detection with large language models: A privacy-preserving bert-based lightweight model for iot/iiot devices. *IEEE Access : Practical Innovations, Open Solutions*, *12*, 23733–23750. DOI: 10.1109/ACCESS.2024.3363469

Ferrag, M. A., Ndhlovu, M., Tihanyi, N., Cordeiro, L. C., Debbah, M., Lestable, T., & Thandi, N. S. (2024). Revolutionizing cyber threat detection with large language models: A privacy-preserving bert-based lightweight model for iot/iiot devices. *IEEE Access : Practical Innovations, Open Solutions*, *12*, 23733–23750.

Ghazal, T. M., Janjua, J. I., Abushiba, W., Ahmad, M., Ihsan, A., & Al-Dmour, N. A. (2024, December). Cybersecurity Revolution via Large Language Models and Explainable AI. In *2024 17th International Conference on Security of Information and Networks (SIN)* (pp. 1-6). IEEE. DOI: 10.1109/SIN63213.2024.10871324

Gholami, S., & Omar, M. (2023). Does Synthetic Data Make Large Language Models More Efficient? *arXiv preprint arXiv:2310.07830.*

Gholami, S., & Omar, M. (2024). Can a student large language model perform as well as its teacher? In *Innovations, Securities, and Case Studies Across Healthcare, Business, and Technology* (pp. 122-139). IGI Global. DOI: 10.4018/979-8-3693-1906-2.ch007

Gupta, B. B., Gaurav, A., & Arya, V. (2024). Navigating the security landscape of large language models in enterprise information systems. *Enterprise Information Systems*, *18*(4), 2310846. DOI: 10.1080/17517575.2024.2310846

Hadi, M. A., Abdulredha, M. N., & Hasan, E. (2023). Introduction to ChatGPT: A new revolution of artificial intelligence with machine learning algorithms and cybersecurity. *Sci. Arch*, *4*(04), 276. DOI: 10.47587/SA.2023.4406

Hamza, Y. A., & Omar, M. D. (2013). Cloud computing security: Abuse and nefarious use of cloud computing. *International Journal of Computer Engineering Research*, *3*(6), 22–27.

Hasanov, I., Virtanen, S., Hakkala, A., & Isoaho, J. (2024). Application of Large Language Models in Cybersecurity: A Systematic Literature Review. *IEEE Access : Practical Innovations, Open Solutions*, *12*, 176751–176778. DOI: 10.1109/ACCESS.2024.3505983

Hassanin, M., & Moustafa, N. (2024). A comprehensive overview of large language models (llms) for cyber defences: Opportunities and directions. *arXiv preprint arXiv:2405.14487.*

Huff, A. J., Burrell, D. N., Nobles, C., Richardson, K., Wright, J. B., Burton, S. L., Jones, A. J., Springs, D., Omar, M., & Brown-Jackson, K. L. (2023). Management Practices for Mitigating Cybersecurity Threats to Biotechnology Companies, Laboratories, and Healthcare Research Organizations. In *Applied Research Approaches to Technology, Healthcare, and Business* (pp. 1-12). IGI Global.

Idelhaj, A., Abou El Houda, Z., & Khoukhi, L. (2024). Foundations models in cybersecurity. *Artificial Intelligence for Blockchain and Cybersecurity Powered IoT Applications*, 1.

Idelhaj, A., Abou El Houda, Z., & Khoukhi, L. Foundations models in cybersecurity: A comprehensive review and future direction. *Artificial Intelligence for Blockchain and Cybersecurity Powered IoT Applications*, 1-18.

Jones, R., & Omar, M. (2024). Revolutionizing Cybersecurity: The GPT-2 Enhanced Attack Detection and Defense (GEADD) Method for Zero-Day Threats. *International Journal of Informatics* [INJIISCOM]. *Information System and Computer Engineering*, *5*(2), 178–191.

Jones, R., Omar, M., Mohammed, D., Nobles, C., & Dawson, M. (2023). Harnessing the Speed and Accuracy of Machine Learning to Advance Cybersecurity. In *2023 Congress in Computer Science, Computer Engineering, & Applied Computing (CSCE)* (pp. 418-421). IEEE. DOI: 10.1109/CSCE60160.2023.00074

Kasri, W., Himeur, Y., Alkhazaleh, H. A., Tarapiah, S., Atalla, S., Mansoor, W., & Al-Ahmad, H. (2025). From Vulnerability to Defense: The Role of Large Language Models in Enhancing Cybersecurity. *Computation (Basel, Switzerland)*, *13*(2), 30. DOI: 10.3390/computation13020030

Liu, Z. (2024, April). A review of advancements and applications of pre-trained language models in cybersecurity. In *2024 12th International Symposium on Digital Forensics and Security (ISDFS)* (pp. 1-10). IEEE. DOI: 10.1109/ISDFS60797.2024.10527236

Manoharan, A., & Sarker, M. (2023). Revolutionizing Cybersecurity: Unleashing the Power of Artificial Intelligence and Machine Learning for Next-Generation Threat Detection. *DOI:*https://www. doi. org/10.56726/IRJMETS32644, *1*.

Mohammed, D., Omar, M., & Nguyen, V. (2018). Wireless sensor network security: Approaches to detecting and avoiding wormhole attacks. *Journal of Research in Business. Economics and Management*, *10*(2), 1860–1864.

Motlagh, F. N., Hajizadeh, M., Majd, M., Najafi, P., Cheng, F., & Meinel, C. (2024). Large language models in cybersecurity: State-of-the-art. *arXiv preprint arXiv:2402.00891.*

Nguyen, V., Mohammed, D., Omar, M., & Banisakher, M. (2018). The Effects of the FCC Net Neutrality Repeal on Security and Privacy. [IJHIoT]. *International Journal of Hyperconnectivity and the Internet of Things*, *2*(2), 21–29. DOI: 10.4018/IJHIoT.2018070102

Omar, M. (2021). New insights into database security: An effective and integrated approach for applying access control mechanisms and cryptographic concepts in Microsoft Access environments.

Omar, M. (2022). *Machine Learning for Cybersecurity: Innovative Deep Learning Solutions*. Springer Brief. https://link.springer.com/book/978303115

Omar, M. (2024). From Attack to Defense: Strengthening DNN Text Classification Against Adversarial Examples. In *Innovations, Securities, and Case Studies Across Healthcare, Business, and Technology* (pp. 174-195). IGI Global.

Omar, M. (2024). Revolutionizing Malware Detection: A Paradigm Shift Through Optimized Convolutional Neural Networks. In *Innovations, Securities, and Case Studies Across Healthcare, Business, and Technology* (pp. 196-220). IGI Global. DOI: 10.4018/979-8-3693-1906-2.ch011

Omar, M., & Zangana, H. (Eds.). (2025). *Digital Forensics in the Age of AI.* IGI Global., DOI: 10.4018/979-8-3373-0857-9

Omar, M., & Zangana, H. M. (Eds.). (2024). *Redefining Security With Cyber AI.* IGI Global., DOI: 10.4018/979-8-3693-6517-5

Omar, M., & Zangana, H. M. (Eds.). (2025). *Application of Large Language Models (LLMs) for Software Vulnerability Detection.* IGI Global., DOI: 10.4018/979-8-3693-9311-6

Omar, M., Zangana, H. M., Al-Karaki, J. N., & Mohammed, D. (2024). Harnessing LLMs for IoT malware detection: A comparative analysis of BERT and GPT-2. In *2024 8th International Symposium on Multidisciplinary Studies and Innovative Technologies (ISMSIT)* (pp. 1-6). Ankara, Turkiye. https://doi.org/DOI: 10.1109/ISMSIT63511.2024.10757249

Omar, M., Zangana, H. M., & Mohammed, D. (Eds.). (2025). *Integrating Artificial Intelligence in Cybersecurity and Forensic Practices.* IGI Global., DOI: 10.4018/979-8-3373-0588-2

Ozkan-Okay, M., Akin, E., Aslan, Ö., Kosunalp, S., Iliev, T., Stoyanov, I., & Beloev, I. (2024). A comprehensive survey: Evaluating the efficiency of artificial intelligence and machine learning techniques on cyber security solutions. *IEEE Access : Practical Innovations, Open Solutions, 12*, 12229–12256. DOI: 10.1109/ACCESS.2024.3355547

Pleshakova, E., Osipov, A., Gataullin, S., Gataullin, T., & Vasilakos, A. (2024). Next gen cybersecurity paradigm towards artificial general intelligence: Russian market challenges and future global technological trends. *Journal of Computer Virology and Hacking Techniques, 20*(3), 429–440. DOI: 10.1007/s11416-024-00529-x

Santos, O., Salam, S., & Dahir, H. (2024). The AI revolution in networking, cybersecurity, and emerging technologies.

Sarker, I. H. (2024). Generative AI and large language modeling in cybersecurity. In *AI-Driven Cybersecurity and Threat Intelligence: Cyber Automation, Intelligent Decision-Making and Explainability* (pp. 79–99). Springer Nature Switzerland. DOI: 10.1007/978-3-031-54497-2_5

Taghavi, S. M., & Feyzi, F. (2024). Using large language models to better detect and handle software vulnerabilities and cyber security threats.

Wright, J., Dawson, M. E.Jr, & Omar, M. (2012). Cyber security and mobile threats: The need for antivirus applications for smartphones. *Journal of Information Systems Technology and Planning, 5*(14), 40–60.

Xu, H., Wang, S., Li, N., Wang, K., Zhao, Y., Chen, K., . . . Wang, H. (2024). Large language models for cyber security: A systematic literature review. *arXiv preprint arXiv:2405.04760.*

Yu, J., Shvetsov, A. V., & Alsamhi, S. H. (2024). Leveraging machine learning for cybersecurity resilience in industry 4.0: Challenges and future directions. *IEEE Access : Practical Innovations, Open Solutions, 12*, 159579–159596. DOI: 10.1109/ACCESS.2024.3482987

Zangana, H., & Omar, M. (Eds.). (2025). *Leveraging Large Language Models for Quantum-Aware Cybersecurity*. IGI Global., DOI: 10.4018/979-8-3373-1102-9

Zangana, H. M. (2024). Exploring Blockchain-Based Timestamping Tools: A Comprehensive Review. *Redefining Security With Cyber AI*, 92-110.

Zangana, H. M. (2024). Exploring the Landscape of Website Vulnerability Scanners: A Comprehensive Review and Comparative Analysis. *Redefining Security With Cyber AI*, 111-129.

Zangana, H. M. (2024). Harnessing the Power of Large Language Models. *Application of Large Language Models (LLMs) for Software Vulnerability Detection*, 1.

Zangana, H. M., & Li, S. (2025). Future Trends in AI and Digital Forensics. In Omar, M., & Zangana, H. (Eds.), *Digital Forensics in the Age of AI* (pp. 347–380). IGI Global Scientific Publishing., DOI: 10.4018/979-8-3373-0857-9.ch013

Zangana, H. M., Mohammed, A. K., Sallow, A. B., & Sallow, Z. B. (2024). Cybernetic Deception: Unraveling the Layers of Email Phishing Threats. [INJURATECH]. *International Journal of Research and Applied Technology*, *4*(1), 35–47.

Zangana, H. M., & Mohammed, D. (2025). Foundations of Large Language Models in Software Vulnerability Detection. In Omar, M., & Zangana, H. (Eds.), *Application of Large Language Models (LLMs) for Software Vulnerability Detection* (pp. 41–74). IGI Global., DOI: 10.4018/979-8-3693-9311-6.ch002

Zangana, H. M., & Mustafa, F. M. (2024). Hybrid Image Denoising Using Wavelet Transform and Deep Learning. *EAI Endorsed Transactions on AI and Robotics*, *3*. Advance online publication. DOI: 10.4108/airo.7486

Zangana, H. M., & Mustafa, F. M. (2025). Image Denoising Techniques for Cybersecurity and Forensic Applications: AI-Driven Approaches. In Omar, M., Zangana, H., & Mohammed, D. (Eds.), *Integrating Artificial Intelligence in Cybersecurity and Forensic Practices* (pp. 117–142). IGI Global Scientific Publishing., DOI: 10.4018/979-8-3373-0588-2.ch005

Zangana, H. M., Mustafa, F. M., & Li, S. (2025). Large Language Models in Cybersecurity: From Automation to Intelligence. In *Leveraging Large Language Models for Quantum-Aware Cybersecurity* (pp. 277-300). IGI Global Scientific Publishing.

Zangana, H. M., Mustafa, F. M., & Li, S. (2025). Large Language Models in Cybersecurity: From Automation to Intelligence. In Zangana, H., & Omar, M. (Eds.), *Leveraging Large Language Models for Quantum-Aware Cybersecurity* (pp. 277–300). IGI Global Scientific Publishing., DOI: 10.4018/979-8-3373-1102-9.ch009

Zangana, H. M., Mustafa, F. M., Li, S., & Al-Karaki, J. N. (2025). Natural Language Processing for Cyber Threat Intelligence in a Quantum World. In Zangana, H., & Omar, M. (Eds.), *Leveraging Large Language Models for Quantum-Aware Cybersecurity* (pp. 345–388). IGI Global Scientific Publishing., DOI: 10.4018/979-8-3373-1102-9.ch011

Zangana, H. M., Mustafa, F. M., & Omar, M. (2024). A Hybrid Approach for Robust Object Detection: Integrating Template Matching and Faster R-CNN. *EAI Endorsed Transactions on AI and Robotics*, *3*. Advance online publication. DOI: 10.4108/airo.6858

Zangana, H. M., & Omar, M. (2020). Threats, Attacks, and Mitigations of Smartphone Security. *Academic Journal of Nawroz University*, *9*(4), 324–332. DOI: 10.25007/ajnu.v9n4a989

Zangana, H. M., & Omar, M. (2025). Harnessing the Power of Large Language Models for Cybersecurity: Applications, Challenges, and Future Directions. In Omar, M., & Zangana, H. (Eds.), *Application of Large Language Models (LLMs) for Software Vulnerability Detection* (pp. 1–40). IGI Global., DOI: 10.4018/979-8-3693-9311-6.ch001

Zangana, H. M., & Omar, M. (2025). Introduction to Digital Forensics and Artificial Intelligence. In Omar, M., & Zangana, H. (Eds.), *Digital Forensics in the Age of AI* (pp. 1–30). IGI Global Scientific Publishing., DOI: 10.4018/979-8-3373-0857-9.ch001

Zangana, H. M., & Omar, M. (2025). Introduction to Quantum-Aware Cybersecurity: The Need for LLMs. In Zangana, H., & Omar, M. (Eds.), *Leveraging Large Language Models for Quantum-Aware Cybersecurity* (pp. 1–28). IGI Global Scientific Publishing., DOI: 10.4018/979-8-3373-1102-9.ch001

Zangana, H. M., & Omar, M. (2025). The Role of Leadership in Advancing Inclusive Health Technologies. In Burrell, D., & Nguyen, C. (Eds.), *New Horizons in Leadership: Inclusive Explorations in Health, Technology, and Education* (pp. 203–220). IGI Global Scientific Publishing., DOI: 10.4018/979-8-3693-6437-6.ch009

Zangana, H. M., Omar, M., Al-Karaki, J. N., & Mohammed, D. (2024). Comprehensive Review and Analysis of Network Firewall Rule Analyzers: Enhancing Security Posture and Efficiency. *Redefining Security With Cyber AI*, 15-36.

Zangana, H. M., Sallow, Z. B., & Omar, M. (2025). The Human Factor in Cybersecurity: Addressing the Risks of Insider Threats. *Jurnal Ilmiah Computer Science*, *3*(2), 76–85. DOI: 10.58602/jics.v3i2.37

Chapter 8
Empowering Cybersecurity with LLMs:
Overcoming Automation Challenges in Threat Intelligence and Detection Systems

R. Renugadevi
https://orcid.org/0000-0001-7462-9205
Saveetha Engineering College, India

R. Muthumeenakshi
https://orcid.org/0000-0003-1018-0968
REVA University, India

G. Karthika
https://orcid.org/0000-0002-8703-235X
Saveetha Engineering College, India

ABSTRACT

As cyber threats become increasingly sophisticated and prevalent, traditional cybersecurity approaches struggle to keep pace with the rapidly evolving tactics, techniques, and procedures employed by cybercriminals. In response, the integration of Large Language Models (LLMs) within threat intelligence and intrusion detection systems presents a promising solution to automate and enhance the detection, analysis, and mitigation of complex cyberattacks. LLMs, such as OpenAI's GPT models and Google's BERT, possess the ability to process large volumes of unstructured data, understand context, and identify patterns that may elude conventional detection methods. This chapter explores the potential of LLMs in revolutionizing cybersecurity by addressing the automation challenges inherent in modern threat

DOI: 10.4018/979-8-3373-3296-3.ch008

intelligence and detection systems. The chapter further discusses the methodologies and tools being developed to overcome these hurdles, including hybrid AI approaches, transfer learning, and advancements in model interpretability and explainability.

1. INTRODUCTION

In recent years, the landscape of cybersecurity has become increasingly complex as cybercriminals rapidly adapt to technological advancements, employing sophisticated tactics to bypass traditional security measures. Cyber threats, including phishing attacks, ransomware, and advanced persistent threats (APTs), have escalated in both frequency and severity. A report by the European Union Agency for Cybersecurity (ENISA) states that the frequency of cyberattacks has doubled over the last five years, with adversaries utilizing more advanced tactics, techniques, and procedures (ENISA, 2020). As a result, traditional manual approaches to threat detection and response have proven inadequate, prompting organizations to seek automated, scalable solutions. One promising approach to addressing these challenges is the integration of Large Language Models (LLMs) into cybersecurity systems. LLMs, a category of artificial intelligence (AI) and natural language processing (NLP) models, have demonstrated exceptional capabilities in various domains, such as text generation, classification, summarization, and translation. These models can automate threat detection and intelligence gathering, presenting a substantial opportunity to enhance cybersecurity operations. However, the adoption of LLMs in cybersecurity presents several challenges, including overcoming automation limitations while ensuring security, reliability, and operational effectiveness.

LLMs, such as OpenAI's GPT models, Google's BERT, and Meta's LLaMA, can process vast amounts of text data to generate contextually relevant outputs based on training. In cybersecurity, LLMs can enhance threat intelligence by gathering, analyzing, and disseminating information from various sources, including open-source intelligence (OSINT) data, blogs, news articles, and dark web forums. These models can help cybersecurity teams identify new threats, attack techniques, and malware strains in real-time (Zhou et al., 2020). Furthermore, LLMs can aid in threat detection by analyzing network traffic, system logs, and other data to identify anomalies indicative of potential cyberattacks, leveraging transfer learning to detect novel attack techniques (Chen et al., 2022). Additionally, when integrated with security information and event management (SIEM) systems, LLMs can automate incident response actions, such as blocking malicious IP addresses, isolating affected systems, and triggering predefined mitigation strategies. LLMs also enable security analysts to query threat detection systems in natural language, making cybersecurity tools more accessible to less experienced staff and accelerating decision-making.

Despite these advantages, challenges such as false positives, adversarial attacks, data privacy concerns, scalability, and adaptability need to be addressed. False positives and false negatives remain a critical issue in cybersecurity, as misidentifying benign activity as an attack or missing a legitimate threat can lead to resource wastage or missed opportunities for defense (Anderson et al., 2023). Adversarial attacks, in which attackers manipulate input data to mislead LLMs into incorrect predictions, pose another significant risk (Carlini et al., 2020). Moreover, LLMs require access to sensitive data, raising privacy concerns that must be addressed through privacy-preserving techniques, such as differential privacy, to ensure compliance with data protection regulations like GDPR (Xu et al., 2021). The scalability and adaptability of LLMs in large, dynamic environments also present challenges, requiring continuous retraining and fine-tuning to maintain their effectiveness as threats evolve (Srinivasan et al., 2020). Additionally, human-in-the-loop (HITL) requirements remain necessary to validate and interpret the outputs of LLMs, as human expertise is critical for understanding the nuances of complex cyber threats. Ethical concerns about trust, transparency, and accountability in LLM-driven cybersecurity systems are essential, as organizations must ensure that these systems operate fairly and responsibly (Binns, 2022).

The rise of sophisticated cyberattacks has highlighted the limitations of traditional malware detection techniques, making the integration of Large Language Models (LLMs) a promising approach for enhancing cybersecurity. LLMs, typically designed for natural language processing tasks, can be adapted to detect malware by learning patterns and behaviors from large datasets. Unlike traditional signature-based models, which rely on predefined malware signatures, LLMs are capable of understanding and identifying anomalous behaviors that might indicate the presence of malware, even if it's a previously unknown variant. The first step in implementing an LLM-based malware detection system is to collect and preprocess data. This could include system logs, network traffic, executable files, or communication patterns. Data preprocessing involves cleaning and normalizing the information, converting it into a format that the LLM can interpret, such as tokenized sequences of events or actions, similar to how text is processed.

Once the data is prepared, the LLM is trained on it to recognize normal patterns of behavior and detect deviations that could signify malicious activity. This training process utilizes both supervised and unsupervised learning methods. Supervised learning helps the model differentiate between benign and malicious activities, while unsupervised learning enables the model to identify unknown threats based on their anomalous behavior. Additionally, reinforcement learning techniques can be used to fine-tune the model by rewarding accurate predictions, further improving its ability to detect new and evolving malware threats. One of the most significant advantages of using LLMs in malware detection is their ability to analyze dynamic system behaviors. Unlike static models that focus on identifying specific signatures, LLMs excel at observing and interpreting behavioral patterns in real time. They can monitor system activities such as file modifications, unexpected CPU usage, or unauthorized network connections that may be indicative of malware. This dynamic analysis allows LLMs to detect malware that exhibits stealthy or polymorphic behavior, which might go undetected by traditional methods.

Recent research has focused on advancing optimization algorithms, IoT security, and machine learning applications in various domains. Ramalingam et al. (2024) provide an extensive review of meta-heuristics algorithms for optimization problems, discussing their application in complex engineering systems. The study highlights the effectiveness of these algorithms in solving real-world optimization challenges. In the field of IoT security, Nagendiran et al. (2023) propose a machine learning-based approach to secure sensitive information on IoT devices, offering a framework to enhance data protection and mitigate vulnerabilities in IoT networks. Similarly, Renugadevi et al. (2023) explore the use of IoT for securing children based on emotion prediction, using machine learning techniques to predict and address emotional states, thereby ensuring safety and well-being. Deepa et al. (2023) present an enhanced machine learning technique for text detection, utilizing a Keras Sequential model, which improves accuracy in identifying and extracting text from images, showing potential in applications like document analysis and image processing. Finally, Yashini et al. (2024) propose a machine learning-based textile fabric defect detection network, aiming to automate quality control in the textile industry, thus improving manufacturing efficiency and reducing defects. These works illustrate the broad application of machine learning and IoT in addressing real-world problems across various fields.

Furthermore, LLMs enhance the interpretability and explainability of the detection process. Explainable AI (XAI) techniques allow the model to provide reasoning behind its detection decisions, such as identifying specific suspicious actions or network requests that triggered the malware flag. This feature is crucial in cybersecurity, as it provides transparency, helping analysts understand why certain actions were flagged and improving trust in automated systems. Another important characteristic of LLM-based models is their ability to adapt over time. Cyber threats are constantly evolving, and malware creators frequently deploy new variants. To keep up with these changes, LLMs can be updated with new data and feedback from past detections. This continuous learning process ensures that the model stays relevant and effective in detecting emerging threats. Integration of LLMs into existing security infrastructure further strengthens their effectiveness. They can complement traditional signature-based systems, heuristic analysis tools, and other anomaly detection methods, creating a multi-layered defense system. By leveraging the power of LLMs, organizations can achieve a higher detection accuracy rate and respond more effectively to malware incidents, ultimately improving their overall cybersecurity posture. LLM-based malware detection model offers a modern, adaptive, and efficient approach to combating cyber threats, capable of identifying both known and unknown malware variants through behavioral analysis, continuous learning, and explainability.

Figure 1. LLM based malware detection model

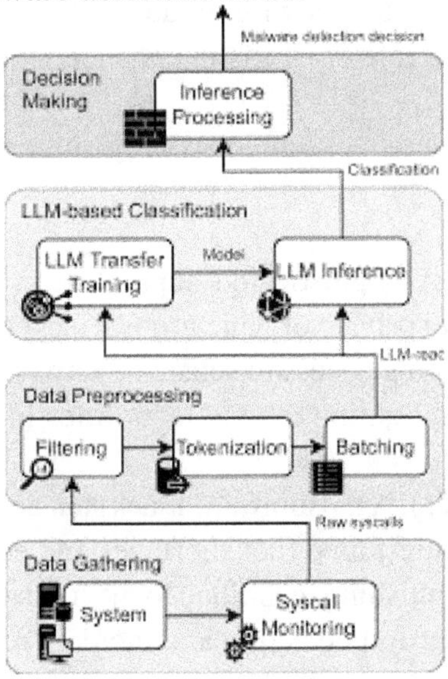

Recent developments in hybrid models, which combine LLMs with other machine learning techniques, such as reinforcement learning and anomaly detection, have shown promise in improving accuracy and reducing false positives (Zhou et al., 2020). Additionally, advancements in multi-modal LLMs, which integrate various data types like text and images, enhance threat detection in environments with diverse cyber threats (Chen et al., 2022). As these models evolve, they will play an increasingly vital role in automating threat detection, response, and recovery, enabling organizations to detect, respond, and recover from attacks more effectively and efficiently. Despite the challenges, the continued development of LLMs holds transformative potential for enhancing the resilience of cybersecurity systems against ever-evolving cyber threats.

By utilizing LLMs, cybersecurity professionals can quickly identify patterns, trends, and anomalies in real-time data, significantly improving response times to emerging threats. These models are capable of performing tasks like automated report generation, threat categorization, malware analysis, and even predicting potential vulnerabilities. LLMs assist in bridging the gap between vast, raw data and actionable intelligence, reducing the manual workload of cybersecurity teams and enabling faster decision-making. Additionally, LLMs can assist in phishing detection, by analyzing communication patterns and identifying potential fraudulent or malicious activities. Their ability to process natural language makes them ideal for automating tasks that involve textual analysis, such as monitoring dark web forums, social media platforms, and technical blogs for discussions related to new attack vectors or malware. However, challenges remain in integrating LLMs into existing security frameworks, such as issues with model accuracy, bias, and explainability. Despite these concerns, the role of LLMs in enhancing threat intelligence automation continues to grow.

Recent high-profile cyberattacks underscore the urgent need for advanced technologies in cybersecurity:

1. **SolarWinds (2020)**: A sophisticated supply chain attack targeted the U.S. government and several private organizations. Hackers compromised the Orion software platform, gaining access to sensitive networks. The attack went undetected for months, highlighting the vulnerabilities in traditional cybersecurity approaches.
2. **Colonial Pipeline (2021)**: A ransomware attack shut down the largest fuel pipeline in the U.S., causing widespread fuel shortages and economic disruptions. The attackers used a spear-phishing technique to infiltrate the network, emphasizing the need for better intrusion detection and incident response systems.
3. **Kaseya (2021)**: Hackers exploited a vulnerability in Kaseya's VSA software, affecting over 1,500 businesses globally. The ransomware attack demonstrated the critical risk posed to Managed Service Providers (MSPs) and their clients.
4. **Microsoft Exchange (2021)**: A series of zero-day vulnerabilities in Microsoft Exchange servers were exploited by state-sponsored hackers, affecting tens of thousands of organizations worldwide. This breach underscored the need for faster threat detection and response.

These attacks highlight the evolving tactics of cybercriminals and emphasize the importance of adopting advanced technologies like Large Language Models (LLMs) to improve cybersecurity's speed, scalability, and adaptability.

2. LITERATURE SURVEY ON LARGE LANGUAGE MODELS (LLMS) IN CYBERSECURITY THREAT INTELLIGENCE AUTOMATION

In recent years, Large Language Models (LLMs) such as GPT, BERT, and other transformer-based architectures have revolutionized the landscape of cybersecurity, especially in the realm of threat intelligence automation. These models, which excel at processing vast amounts of unstructured textual data, are increasingly being utilized to improve the speed, accuracy, and efficiency of threat detection, analysis, and response mechanisms. Cybersecurity has become an increasingly critical concern for organizations due to the rapid evolution of cyber threats, which have grown in sophistication and scale. The traditional methods of threat intelligence, which rely on human expertise to manually analyze logs, reports, and other forms of data, have become inefficient in the face of massive volumes of data and ever-evolving attack techniques. As cyber threats become more complex, it is essential to incorporate automation to streamline threat intelligence processes, enhance detection, and improve response times. One of the most promising technologies to achieve this is the use of Large Language Models (LLMs). LLMs, like OpenAI's GPT series, Google's BERT, and Meta's LLaMA, offer significant potential to revolutionize cybersecurity, especially in the area of threat intelligence automation.

The recent advancements in network security and anomaly detection have focused on utilizing emerging technologies such as machine learning, AI, and next-generation communication systems. Nalini et al. (2024) introduce DeepRoughNetID, a novel framework for network anomaly intrusion detection that uses a hybrid deep learning architecture to achieve high detection rates while maintaining low false-positive rates. The framework's robustness in detecting complex anomalies in dynamic networks positions it as a promising solution for modern cybersecurity challenges in large-scale networks. In parallel, Shanthini and Sheeba Joice (2024) review various strategies for detecting sinkhole attacks in IoT networks, emphasizing the need for efficient detection mechanisms that ensure the integrity of network communication. Their research highlights the importance of proactive countermeasures to secure IoT infrastructures from common attack vectors. Dorothy et al. (2023) delve into 6G networks, specifically focusing on their role in securing communication for unmanned aerial vehicles (UAVs) within the intelligent Internet of Things (IoT). Their study outlines the potential of 6G in providing low-latency, high-throughput, and secure communication channels for UAVs in IoT ecosystems. Rajeswari and M (2023) present an AI-enhanced Least Significant Bit (LSB) steganography framework, designed to embed data securely within images for confidential communication, offering enhanced data protection by leveraging AI for robust steganographic processes. Collectively, these studies demonstrate a significant shift toward integrating

AI and advanced communication protocols in securing next-generation IoT and network infrastructures.

The Need for Threat Intelligence Automation in Cybersecurity

Threat intelligence is critical for cybersecurity as it involves gathering, analyzing, and disseminating information about potential or actual cyberattacks that can harm an organization's IT infrastructure. Traditionally, cybersecurity teams manually collect and analyze data such as system logs, network traffic, and external threat feeds. The increasing volume of data generated daily, along with the growing sophistication of cybercriminals, has made this manual approach impractical. Automated systems capable of handling large amounts of unstructured and structured data are required to process and analyze information in real-time. In response, cybersecurity automation tools, powered by artificial intelligence (AI) and machine learning (ML), have become more prevalent. These tools leverage automation to identify, assess, and respond to potential threats faster than human analysts could. Specifically, the use of LLMs in threat intelligence automation offers significant improvements in the analysis and synthesis of large volumes of textual data. LLMs are particularly adept at processing unstructured data, such as threat reports, news articles, security blogs, social media posts, and dark web data, which is critical in gathering threat intelligence from multiple diverse sources (Zhou et al., 2020).

LLMs in Cybersecurity Threat Intelligence

Large Language Models (LLMs) are a class of deep learning models trained on massive datasets, usually containing vast amounts of textual data. These models have demonstrated remarkable capabilities in natural language processing (NLP) tasks, such as text generation, summarization, translation, and classification. LLMs like OpenAI's GPT, Google's BERT, and Meta's LLaMA are built on transformer architectures, which enable them to capture complex linguistic structures and dependencies over long-range text sequences. This ability makes LLMs highly effective for applications requiring the understanding and generation of text, such as threat intelligence, where parsing and analyzing textual data from a variety of sources are key (Vaswani et al., 2017; Devlin et al., 2018).

Threat Intelligence Gathering Using LLMs

One of the primary applications of LLMs in cybersecurity is the automation of threat intelligence gathering. Traditional methods of collecting intelligence involve monitoring multiple data sources such as open-source intelligence (OSINT), dark web forums, blogs, and threat feeds. Analysts must manually sift through large amounts of information to detect new vulnerabilities, malware strains, or emerging attack techniques. This process is time-consuming, resource-intensive, and prone to human error. LLMs, on the other hand, are capable of scanning vast amounts of unstructured text and extracting relevant intelligence much faster and more accurately.

Zhou et al. (2020) explored the use of LLMs for gathering threat intelligence from OSINT and threat feeds. LLMs are trained to recognize critical information, such as indicators of compromise (IOCs), new attack methods, and relevant vulnerabilities, and they can flag such information in real-time. This enables cybersecurity teams to stay ahead of attackers by detecting new threats as they emerge, sometimes even before they are formally reported in other channels. Additionally, LLMs are particularly useful in monitoring dark web forums and other clandestine sources where cybercriminals may discuss exploits, malware, or new hacking techniques. By processing this data, LLMs can help organizations identify emerging threats before they impact organizational networks.

Threat Detection and Anomaly Identification

In addition to threat intelligence gathering, LLMs are valuable in threat detection and anomaly identification. LLMs can analyze network traffic logs, system logs, and security alerts to detect irregular patterns that may signal potential attacks. For example, an LLM can be trained to recognize deviations in user behavior or unusual network traffic indicative of an ongoing attack such as a Distributed Denial of Service (DDoS) attack or a ransomware infection.

Chen et al. (2022) showed that LLMs can be applied to security monitoring tasks like detecting anomalies in network traffic by learning patterns from historical data. By training on extensive datasets, LLMs can learn to recognize normal network behavior and flag any anomalies that deviate from the baseline. This helps in detecting new attack vectors that signature-based systems may fail to identify. Furthermore, LLMs are adaptable; they can generalize their knowledge from one dataset to another, improving their detection accuracy and efficiency.

Automating Real-Time Threat Intelligence Analysis

The real-time analysis of threat intelligence is a crucial component of modern cybersecurity operations. Real-time threat intelligence analysis enables security teams to quickly identify active threats, assess their severity, and respond accordingly.

LLMs enhance this capability by processing data from multiple sources, including threat feeds, security alerts, and historical incident data, in real-time.

Srinivasan et al. (2021) discussed the ability of LLMs to process real-time threat data, such as intrusion detection system (IDS) logs, and correlate them with external threat intelligence sources. By doing so, LLMs help organizations quickly assess the relevance and severity of an ongoing attack, enabling faster decision-making. This ability to generate contextual analysis based on real-time data allows organizations to prioritize responses to critical threats while minimizing the risk of data breaches.

Natural Language Queries and Insights

A significant advantage of LLMs is their ability to facilitate natural language queries for threat intelligence. In traditional systems, cybersecurity professionals often need to write complex queries or use specific filters to retrieve relevant data from threat intelligence platforms. With LLMs integrated into these systems, users can query the system using natural language. Binns (2022) highlighted the importance of natural language querying in cybersecurity, which enables more intuitive and accessible interactions with security systems. This approach democratizes access to threat intelligence, allowing both technical and non-technical staff to interact with complex systems, improving the overall efficiency of threat detection and response. Additionally, LLMs can generate insights and summaries of the threat data, allowing security professionals to make decisions faster.

While LLMs offer significant benefits, one of the key challenges is the potential for false positives and false negatives in threat detection. A false positive occurs when a benign event is flagged as malicious, leading to unnecessary responses and resource allocation. Conversely, a false negative occurs when an actual threat is missed, which could have catastrophic consequences. LLMs, despite their power, are not immune to these challenges. Anderson et al. (2023) emphasized that reducing false positives and negatives remains a significant hurdle when using LLMs in cybersecurity. This issue underscores the need for continuous model training and fine-tuning to improve the accuracy and reliability of threat detection.

Another concern with LLMs is their vulnerability to adversarial attacks. Cyber attackers may attempt to manipulate input data to deceive LLMs into making incorrect predictions. This vulnerability poses a serious risk, as adversarial attacks could be used to bypass detection systems or mislead threat intelligence gathering efforts. Carlini et al. (2020) explored the concept of adversarial machine learning and how AI models like LLMs can be manipulated. This issue highlights the need for robust defenses, such as adversarial training and model validation, to ensure the reliability and security of LLM-driven systems.

The use of LLMs in cybersecurity requires access to sensitive data, such as logs and user behavior information. This raises concerns about data privacy and compliance with regulations such as the General Data Protection Regulation (GDPR). Xu et al. (2021) explored techniques for ensuring privacy-preserving machine learning, such as differential privacy, which allows models to learn from data without compromising the confidentiality of sensitive information. Balancing the need for data access in threat intelligence automation with privacy concerns is an ongoing challenge in the field.

Scaling LLMs to handle the massive volumes of data generated by modern cybersecurity infrastructures is another challenge. LLMs require significant computational resources to train and deploy, and scaling these models for large-scale cybersecurity environments can introduce latency issues. Furthermore, LLMs must be continuously updated and fine-tuned to adapt to new attack techniques, vulnerabilities, and threat landscapes. Srinivasan et al. (2020) emphasized the importance of ensuring that LLMs remain adaptable and scalable to meet the growing demands of cybersecurity operations.

The integration of Large Language Models (LLMs) into cybersecurity threat intelligence automation holds immense potential to revolutionize how organizations detect, analyze, and respond to cyber threats. LLMs can process vast amounts of unstructured data, automate intelligence gathering, detect emerging threats, and improve real-time decision-making in response to incidents. However, challenges related to false positives, adversarial attacks, data privacy, and scalability must be addressed to fully harness the power of LLMs in cybersecurity. Ongoing research and innovation in model robustness, privacy-preserving techniques, and scalability will be key to overcoming these challenges and realizing the full potential of LLMs in cybersecurity threat intelligence.

a. Application of LLMs in Threat Intelligence Automation

LLMs have proven useful in automating various aspects of threat intelligence, such as incident detection, vulnerability management, and threat report generation. According to Zhang and Li (2022), LLMs are particularly beneficial in automating the analysis of cyberattack data from sources like security logs, dark web monitoring, and open-source threat intelligence feeds. These models can efficiently process and categorize large volumes of data, which would otherwise overwhelm human analysts. Additionally, LLMs can generate meaningful insights by extracting patterns and detecting correlations between disparate data points that are critical for identifying emerging threats (Zhang & Li, 2022).

b. Enhancing Phishing Detection

Phishing attacks continue to be one of the most common cybersecurity threats, and LLMs have shown promise in automating phishing detection. In a study by Gupta and Rao (2020), it was demonstrated that LLMs, due to their ability to understand context and semantics in natural language, can be applied to detect phishing emails and malicious URLs with a high degree of accuracy. These models analyze textual elements like sender information, message body, and embedded links, identifying suspicious patterns that may indicate phishing attempts. This significantly reduces the time spent by human analysts in manually reviewing suspicious communications.

c. Automating Malware Analysis

Malware analysis is a critical task in cybersecurity, requiring extensive expertise and time. According to Patel and Kumar (2023), LLMs can aid in automating the process of malware identification by analyzing code snippets, documentation, and threat reports. By leveraging the ability to interpret technical jargon and patterns in software behavior, LLMs can classify different types of malware, generate reports, and even predict potential new attack vectors based on historical trends. This capability improves the response time to new malware outbreaks, enabling proactive defense mechanisms.

d. Predictive Threat Intelligence and Vulnerability Management

LLMs are also being explored for predictive threat intelligence, where they help in forecasting potential vulnerabilities in systems before they are exploited. Johnson and Chen (2021) highlight that LLMs can mine open-source intelligence (OSINT) repositories, technical blogs, and vulnerability databases to predict future exploits based on emerging trends. This enables organizations to take preemptive actions to patch vulnerabilities or modify security configurations, reducing the likelihood of a successful attack.

d. Challenges in Implementing LLMs for Cybersecurity

Despite the promise of LLMs in cybersecurity, their implementation is not without challenges. According to Bennett and Singh (2024), issues such as model explainability, bias in training data, and accuracy remain significant barriers to widespread adoption. LLMs, due to their black-box nature, often fail to provide transparent reasoning behind their predictions, making it difficult for cybersecurity professionals to trust the model's output. Moreover, if the training data is not diverse or representative, the models may exhibit biased behavior, potentially overlooking certain types of threats. Addressing these concerns requires ongoing research into improving the interpretability and fairness of LLMs in cybersecurity applications.

3. AUTOMATION CHALLENGES IN THREAT INTELLIGENCE AND DETECTION SYSTEMS

By categorizing these challenges into technical, ethical, and operational domains, we can better understand the multifaceted issues organizations face when deploying automated threat intelligence and detection systems. Addressing these challenges will require coordinated efforts across various fields, including technology development, regulatory compliance, and organizational change management.

Technical Challenges

1. Model Accuracy and Reliability

One of the primary concerns with automating threat intelligence and detection is the accuracy of machine learning models, particularly in specialized domains like cybersecurity. Automated systems may generate false positives (incorrectly identifying benign activity as a threat) or false negatives (failing to detect actual threats), which can reduce the reliability of the system. Models trained on limited or biased datasets may struggle to detect new or evolving attack vectors. This could result in significant security gaps, where subtle or novel threats bypass detection. For instance, a model trained primarily on older attack patterns may fail to recognize new tactics used in advanced persistent threats (APTs) or polymorphic malware.

2. Explainability and Transparency

LLMs and other machine learning models are often considered "black boxes" because their decision-making processes are not easily interpretable or explainable. In cybersecurity, where understanding why a model made a particular decision is crucial, this lack of transparency becomes a significant challenge. Without a clear understanding of how a system reached its conclusions, security analysts may struggle to trust automated decisions, particularly in high-stakes situations. For example, if an automated system flags a legitimate user activity as a threat, an analyst may not understand why the system made this decision or how to correct it. The inability to explain decisions also hampers the ability to identify weaknesses in the model or its training process, making it harder to improve the system over time.

3. Real-Time Integration

Many cybersecurity systems operate in real-time to detect and respond to threats as they happen. Integrating machine learning models, like LLMs, into existing systems (e.g., Security Information and Event Management (SIEM) or Security Orchestration, Automation, and Response (SOAR)) is complex and requires seamless communication between various tools. These systems must work with a variety of data sources (e.g., network logs, user behavior analytics, system alerts), and integrating LLMs into these platforms is a challenging task. It involves ensuring that the models can process and analyze data in real-time while maintaining accuracy. Moreover, the existing cybersecurity tools might not be designed to interact with advanced machine learning models, requiring custom integrations or modifications to legacy systems.

4. Adversarial Attacks on Automated Systems

Automated systems, particularly those driven by machine learning models, are vulnerable to adversarial attacks, where attackers manipulate input data to deceive the system and bypass detection. For example, attackers could craft network traffic or log entries that are designed to confuse the machine learning model, causing it to misclassify benign activities as malicious or miss actual threats. These adversarial inputs exploit weaknesses in the model's design or training, potentially rendering automated systems ineffective in detecting evolving threats. As adversarial techniques grow more sophisticated, defending against them becomes an increasing challenge, requiring continuous monitoring and the development of advanced countermeasures like adversarial training and explainable AI.

5. Scalability and Integration with Legacy Systems

As organizations scale, their IT infrastructures become more complex and heterogeneous, making it harder to deploy automated threat detection solutions. Many organizations also rely on legacy systems that were not designed for integration with modern cybersecurity tools. Integrating new automated threat intelligence solutions into these environments often requires significant customization, which can be costly and error-prone. Additionally, scaling the system to handle an increasing number of endpoints, users, and devices is not straightforward. Automation tools must be able to process vast amounts of data without overwhelming the system's resources or compromising detection accuracy. For larger organizations with legacy infrastructures, this integration can slow down the deployment of new tools and add operational complexity.

6. Data Privacy and Compliance

Automated systems for threat detection often involve processing large volumes of sensitive data, raising concerns about privacy and compliance with data protection regulations. Threat intelligence systems may collect and process personal information or business-critical data. Ensuring compliance with regulations like the General Data Protection Regulation (GDPR) or the California Consumer Privacy Act (CCPA) is crucial. There is also the challenge of ensuring that sensitive data is protected during its collection, storage, and analysis. For example, automated systems that aggregate data from multiple sources (e.g., dark web feeds, social media, or external threat feeds) may inadvertently collect personal data, which must be anonymized or securely processed to avoid violating privacy laws.

Ethical Challenges

1. Ethical and Legal Implications

The automation of decision-making in threat intelligence and detection systems raises ethical and legal concerns related to accountability, transparency, and potential biases. Automated systems might be tasked with making critical decisions, such as blocking suspicious IP addresses or isolating compromised systems. However, the automated nature of these decisions can lead to unintended consequences, such as blocking legitimate business activities or critical users. Moreover, the potential for discriminatory decisions arising from biases in the training data (e.g., overblocking certain groups) is an ethical concern. To mitigate these risks, a clear accountability framework, transparent decision-making, and human oversight should be established.

2. Bias in Training Data

Biases in the data used to train machine learning models can lead to unfair or discriminatory outcomes in threat detection. Ethical concerns arise when biased data leads to unequal treatment of individuals or organizations. For instance, a model trained primarily on data from certain regions or industries may not perform equally well when applied to other sectors, leading to an inequitable approach to cybersecurity. Ensuring fairness and preventing discrimination are key ethical issues in the development and deployment of automated cybersecurity systems.

Operational Challenges

1. Volume and Complexity of Data

The sheer volume and complexity of data that cybersecurity systems need to process presents significant challenges. Modern networks generate vast amounts of data from various sources, including logs, user behavior, threat feeds, and social media. This data is often unstructured, noisy, and inconsistent, making it difficult for traditional systems to extract useful insights. Automated systems must be capable of processing this diverse data in real-time and filtering out irrelevant information. The complexity of modern cyber threats, such as polymorphic malware and APTs, further exacerbates the problem, requiring advanced analytics to identify subtle anomalies and evolving attack vectors.

2. False Positives and False Negatives (Revisited as Operational Issue)

False positives and false negatives are operational concerns because they directly impact the efficiency of security teams. False positives waste resources by triggering unnecessary investigations, leading to inefficiencies. False negatives, on the other hand, can allow real threats to go unnoticed, potentially resulting in data breaches or system compromise. Balancing these errors while ensuring accurate threat detection is a major operational challenge in cybersecurity automation.

3. Cost and Resource Allocation

Implementing and maintaining automated systems can be costly, particularly for smaller organizations. The upfront investment required for acquiring, integrating, and maintaining AI-driven cybersecurity tools can be significant. Furthermore, continuous maintenance, model retraining, and system updates are necessary to ensure that the system remains effective in an evolving threat landscape. These ongoing costs may pose a barrier to adoption, especially for small and medium-sized enterprises (SMEs) that may lack the financial resources to invest in advanced technologies. Cloud-based platforms and open-source solutions may alleviate some of these concerns, but resource allocation remains a critical issue.

4. METHODOLOGY FOR IMPLEMENTING LARGE LANGUAGE MODELS (LLMS) IN CYBERSECURITY THREAT INTELLIGENCE AUTOMATION

The methodology for deploying LLMs in cybersecurity threat intelligence automation is a multi-step process that includes data collection, model selection, automation of threat intelligence tasks, integration with existing security systems, and continuous evaluation. While LLMs hold great potential in transforming cybersecurity operations, challenges such as model bias, explainability, and real-time integration need to be addressed for optimal performance. By leveraging these advanced models, organizations can enhance their ability to detect and mitigate emerging threats, ensuring better cybersecurity posture and faster response times.

4.1 Large Language Models (LLMs) in Intrusion Detection Systems (IDS)

Intrusion Detection Systems (IDS) play a crucial role in identifying and mitigating cyber threats by monitoring network traffic and system behaviors. Traditionally, IDS rely on signature-based detection methods or anomaly-based approaches, each with its own limitations. While signature-based detection can identify known threats, it is ineffective against novel or zero-day attacks. On the other hand, anomaly-based systems can flag new attack patterns but tend to generate high false positive rates due to their reliance on predefined thresholds and lack of context.

In recent years, there has been growing interest in applying artificial intelligence (AI) and machine learning (ML) techniques to enhance the capabilities of IDS. Among the most promising AI models are Large Language Models (LLMs), such as OpenAI's GPT models, Google's BERT, and Meta's LLaMA. These models, primarily developed for natural language processing (NLP) tasks, have demonstrated the ability to handle complex, high-dimensional data and understand context in ways that traditional models cannot. Their potential for improving intrusion detection lies in their capacity to process large amounts of unstructured data, identify patterns, and adapt to evolving threats.

LLMs are particularly well-suited to intrusion detection because they excel at understanding contextual relationships within large datasets. Unlike traditional machine learning models that often require feature engineering, LLMs can learn complex relationships and patterns from raw data, making them more adaptable to diverse types of attacks. The paper by Kasri et al. (2025) explores the role of Large Language Models (LLMs) in enhancing cybersecurity. It focuses on how LLMs, typically used in natural language processing, can be leveraged to identify vulnerabilities and defend against cyber threats. The study highlights the potential of LLMs in automating threat detection, analyzing security data, generating defensive strategies, and even aiding in the development of more robust cybersecurity frameworks. By transitioning from vulnerability identification to defense, the paper illustrates how LLMs can improve both proactive and reactive cybersecurity measures. Figure 2 depicts the role of Large Language Models in enhancing cybersecurity.

Figure 2. LLMs in enhancing cyber security

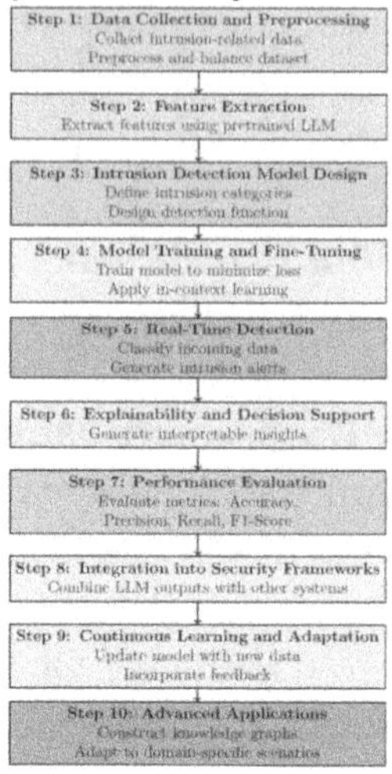

a. Data Processing and Context Understanding

Traditional IDS typically operate on structured data such as network logs or traffic patterns. While these methods can detect straightforward attacks, they often struggle with identifying subtle, sophisticated threats. LLMs, on the other hand, can analyze unstructured and semi-structured data, such as network traffic logs, system behavior logs, and even human-written reports (e.g., threat intelligence documents). By understanding the context in which an action occurs, LLMs can identify abnormal behavior that might otherwise be overlooked. For instance, in a scenario where an attacker tries to exfiltrate data through unusual traffic patterns, an LLM can correlate this anomaly with previous patterns in the network, contextualizing the threat based on known data from similar incidents. This type of analysis allows LLMs to detect a broader range of attack vectors, even those that may not fit into a predefined signature or simple anomaly threshold.

b. Threat Intelligence Integration

LLMs can process vast amounts of threat intelligence, which is a critical component of effective intrusion detection. Threat intelligence feeds often include a mixture of structured data (such as indicators of compromise, or IoCs) and unstructured data (e.g., blog posts, forums, and research papers). An LLM can automatically analyze these feeds, extracting relevant information, and making correlations between known and emerging attack methods. For instance, an LLM could scan dark web forums for discussions on new malware strains and map these discussions to potential attack techniques seen in network traffic, allowing the IDS to stay updated in real-time. In addition, LLMs can summarize large volumes of cybersecurity reports, identify new vulnerabilities or attack techniques, and generate actionable insights for network defenders. This integration of threat intelligence with network traffic analysis enables a more proactive and dynamic defense posture.

c. Anomaly Detection

One of the core functions of an IDS is detecting anomalies, which can indicate potential intrusions. LLMs excel in this area due to their ability to model complex patterns in large datasets. They can analyze the entire context of a situation, including normal network behavior, system interactions, and user activities, to spot subtle deviations that may signal a cyberattack. LLMs can improve anomaly detection by applying unsupervised learning techniques, which allow the model to learn patterns from unlabelled data. This is particularly useful when dealing with new, unknown threats, as the model does not need to rely on predefined attack signatures. By continuously training on new data, LLMs can adapt to evolving attack strategies and adjust detection algorithms accordingly, reducing false positive rates and increasing the system's sensitivity to novel threats.

d. Incident Response and Automation

LLMs can significantly enhance the efficiency of incident response. Once a potential intrusion is detected, LLMs can assist in automating the response process by analyzing historical incident reports and generating relevant actions. For example, when an intrusion attempt is detected, an LLM can quickly determine the best response strategy, such as isolating compromised systems, blocking malicious IP addresses, or initiating forensic analysis. The model could then provide security analysts with a prioritized list of response actions, based on the severity of the detected attack. Furthermore, LLMs can assist in post-incident analysis by generating detailed reports on the nature of the attack, how it was detected, and the response actions taken. This automation of incident response helps reduce response times, streamline workflows, and minimize the risk of human error.

The deployment of LLMs in cybersecurity requires access to sensitive data, such as network logs, user activity data, and threat intelligence feeds. Ensuring that these data sources are protected and used in compliance with privacy regulations (e.g., GDPR, CCPA) is a significant concern. LLMs must be designed to operate on anonymized or encrypted data to minimize the risk of data breaches or unauthorized access. LLMs are computationally intensive, requiring vast amounts of processing power and memory for training and inference. This presents a challenge for organizations that may not have the resources to deploy such models at scale. Additionally, the time required to train large-scale LLMs could hinder their ability to provide real-time detection and response. To address this, techniques such as model pruning, distillation, and transfer learning can be employed to reduce the size and computational requirements of LLMs, making them more feasible for deployment in resource-constrained environments. While LLMs can provide enhanced accuracy in detecting complex threats, there is still the risk of false positives, where benign activities are mistakenly flagged as intrusions. These false alerts can overwhelm security teams and reduce the effectiveness of the system. Balancing model sensitivity and specificity is a delicate task, and ongoing fine-tuning of the model is necessary to improve accuracy. Like other machine learning models, LLMs are vulnerable to adversarial attacks. These attacks involve manipulating input data in such a way that the model produces incorrect or misleading results. In the context of intrusion detection, an adversary might craft malicious traffic patterns specifically designed to evade detection by the LLM. Therefore, it is essential to continuously update and defend the LLMs against these types of attacks.

Recent Research and Developments

Recent research has explored several methods to improve the application of LLMs in intrusion detection systems. Some notable advancements include:

1. Hybrid Approaches: Combining LLMs with other machine learning models, such as decision trees or ensemble methods, has been shown to improve detection performance and reduce false positive rates. These hybrid systems combine the strengths of different models, offering more accurate and reliable results.
2. Transfer Learning: Transfer learning, where a pre-trained model is fine-tuned on a specific task, has been successfully applied to intrusion detection. By leveraging pre-trained LLMs on general data and then fine-tuning them on specific cybersecurity datasets, these models can adapt quickly to new threats and reduce the computational burden associated with training from scratch.
3. Explainability: Efforts to improve the explainability of LLMs have made them more transparent and trustworthy in cybersecurity applications. Techniques such as attention visualization and model interpretability are helping security teams understand how LLMs arrive at their conclusions, making it easier to validate the model's decisions and respond to threats accordingly.

Large Language Models (LLMs) represent a promising advancement in the field of intrusion detection systems (IDS). By leveraging their capabilities to understand context, process unstructured data, and adapt to evolving threats, LLMs can enhance the detection and prevention of sophisticated cyberattacks. Despite challenges such as computational requirements, data privacy concerns, and the risk of adversarial attacks, recent developments in hybrid models, transfer learning, and model explainability are helping to overcome these obstacles. As research continues, LLMs are expected to become increasingly integral to modern cybersecurity systems, providing more accurate, efficient, and adaptive solutions to protect against an ever-growing range of cyber threats.

4.2. Implementing Large Language Models

Implementing Large Language Models (LLMs) for cybersecurity threat intelligence automation involves several stages, from data collection and pre-processing to model deployment and evaluation. The methodology consists of integrating LLMs into existing cybersecurity workflows to streamline threat detection, automate responses, and enhance situational awareness. This section outlines the key steps involved in this process.

a. Data Collection and Pre-processing

The first step in utilizing LLMs for threat intelligence automation is to collect relevant data from various cybersecurity sources. These sources include security logs, network traffic data, vulnerability databases, threat reports, open-source intelligence (OSINT) feeds, dark web monitoring, and social media platforms. As LLMs primarily work with textual data, ensuring the availability of a rich, diverse corpus of text-based data is crucial. This step typically involves:

- **Data Aggregation**: Collecting raw data from multiple threat intelligence feeds, security incident reports, blogs, forums, and known malware repositories.
- **Data Cleansing and Labeling**: Since threat intelligence data can be noisy, it requires significant cleaning to remove irrelevant information and standardize formats. Additionally, data may need to be labeled (e.g., categorizing types of attacks, malware families, etc.) to help train and fine-tune the LLM.
- **Text Pre-processing**: Text data undergoes steps such as tokenization, stemming, stopword removal, and lemmatization to standardize and simplify the information that will be fed into the model.

b. Model Selection and Fine-Tuning

After preparing the data, the next step is selecting an appropriate LLM. Popular models like OpenAI's GPT series, Google's BERT, or domain-specific models such as CyberBERT can be considered. The selected model must be fine-tuned to adapt to the specific domain of cybersecurity. Fine-tuning involves training the LLM on labeled threat intelligence data to help it learn domain-specific language, terminology, and patterns related to cyber threats.

- **Pre-trained Models**: Many LLMs are pre-trained on large corpora, so they come with a deep understanding of general language. The next step involves fine-tuning these models on cybersecurity-related texts to enhance their understanding of specific terminology and threat vectors.
- **Transfer Learning**: Transfer learning techniques may be employed to adapt pre-trained models to the cybersecurity domain. This can save time and resources compared to training a model from scratch.

c. Threat Intelligence Task Automation

Once the LLM is fine-tuned, it can be applied to automate various cybersecurity threat intelligence tasks. Some key tasks where LLMs are particularly effective include:

- **Threat Detection and Classification**: LLMs can automatically analyze logs, emails, and social media posts to detect potential cyber threats, categorizing them based on predefined labels (e.g., phishing, ransomware, DDoS).
- **Phishing Detection**: By analyzing patterns in email communication, LLMs can identify suspicious language, abnormal sender behavior, and potential malicious links, classifying emails as legitimate or phishing attempts.
- **Vulnerability Identification and Risk Assessment**: LLMs can analyze vulnerability databases and security reports to flag potential weaknesses in systems, helping organizations prioritize patching and mitigating risks.
- **Incident Report Generation**: LLMs can automatically generate and summarize cybersecurity incident reports, highlighting the key elements of attacks, affected systems, and proposed mitigation strategies.

d. Integration with Security Systems

To maximize the effectiveness of LLMs in threat intelligence automation, these models need to be integrated with existing cybersecurity infrastructure. This can be achieved by:

- **API Integration**: LLMs can be integrated into Security Information and Event Management (SIEM) systems, Security Orchestration Automation and Response (SOAR) platforms, and other tools via Application Programming Interfaces (APIs).
- **Real-Time Threat Monitoring**: LLMs can be deployed to continuously monitor and analyze incoming threat data in real-time. As soon as a potential threat is detected, the model can trigger automated responses or alert human analysts for further investigation.

e. Evaluation and Feedback Loop

After deployment, it is critical to evaluate the performance of the LLM-based threat intelligence system. Evaluation metrics such as accuracy, precision, recall, and F1 score should be used to measure the model's performance in classifying threats and generating reports. Additionally, continuous feedback loops should be established:

- **Model Retraining**: The model may need periodic retraining with new threat data to ensure it remains up-to-date and accurate in detecting emerging cyber threats.
- **Human-in-the-Loop**: While LLMs can automate many aspects of threat intelligence, human oversight remains essential. Analysts can verify and validate the results, providing feedback to improve the model's performance.

f. Ethical Considerations and Bias Mitigation

The ethical implications of using LLMs in cybersecurity must be considered. Bias in the training data can lead to inaccurate or biased threat classifications. To mitigate this risk, organizations should ensure the data used for training is diverse and represents various attack vectors and threat actors. Additionally, LLMs should be transparent, and their decision-making processes must be explainable to cybersecurity professionals.

4.3 Methods and Tools to Overcome IDS Automation Challenges Using LLMs

a. Transfer Learning for Zero-Day Attack Detection

Transfer learning is a machine learning technique in which a model trained on one dataset is applied to a different, but related, dataset. In the context of intrusion detection, transfer learning can help LLMs identify novel attack patterns by applying knowledge from one type of network or attack vector to another. This is particularly useful for detecting zero-day attacks, which are previously unknown vulnerabilities that traditional IDS systems may not recognize.

Recent research by Gupta et al. (2021) demonstrated how transfer learning could be applied to IDS, using LLMs pre-trained on large cybersecurity datasets. By leveraging transfer learning, the LLM could identify emerging threats and adapt to new attack strategies without requiring retraining from scratch. This adaptability significantly improves the responsiveness of IDS systems, particularly in environments where new threats are continuously evolving.

b. Natural Language Processing (NLP) for Threat Intelligence and Log Analysis

LLMs excel in Natural Language Processing (NLP), enabling them to process unstructured data, such as security reports, threat intelligence feeds, and network logs. In the context of IDS, LLMs can be used to automatically analyze and categorize logs, identify suspicious activities, and generate human-readable summaries of complex security incidents. For instance, a paper by Kaur et al. (2020) explored how NLP techniques could be used to process and analyze security logs, identifying patterns of anomalous behavior that might indicate an intrusion. By using LLMs to automate log analysis, security teams can improve their detection capabilities while reducing the time spent manually analyzing logs. Furthermore, LLMs can help identify emerging threats by processing large volumes of threat intelligence data from open-source and dark web sources.

c. Explainability and Interpretability for Enhanced Trust in IDS

A significant challenge in deploying AI-driven systems, including LLMs, is the "black box" nature of the models, which makes it difficult to interpret their decision-making process. In cybersecurity, where trust and accountability are paramount, it is crucial that LLM-powered IDS systems offer explainability and interpretability.

Recent advancements in explainable AI (XAI) methods, such as attention mechanisms and saliency maps, have been integrated into LLMs to provide transparency regarding how decisions are made. For example, XAI techniques can highlight which features of a network log or traffic pattern contributed most to the model's detection of a potential intrusion. By incorporating explainability into LLM-powered IDS, organizations can increase trust in the system and allow security analysts to make more informed decisions.

Binns (2022) discusses the importance of transparency in AI-driven security systems and explores methods to make LLM decisions more interpretable. These techniques can help security teams understand why a particular alert was generated, allowing them to investigate the issue more effectively and confidently.

d. Adversarial Robustness and Defenses

To ensure that LLMs used in IDS systems are resilient to adversarial attacks, various defense mechanisms can be implemented. These include adversarial training, which involves exposing the model to adversarial inputs during training, and defensive distillation, which aims to reduce the model's vulnerability to small perturbations in input data.

Carlini et al. (2020) explored the use of adversarial training to improve the robustness of machine learning models against adversarial attacks in the context of cybersecurity. By applying these techniques to LLMs, IDS systems can better detect and mitigate the impact of adversarially crafted traffic or log data that might otherwise bypass traditional detection methods.

e. Federated Learning for Privacy and Scalability

Federated learning is a distributed machine learning technique that allows LLMs to be trained across multiple decentralized devices or servers without sharing sensitive data. In the context of IDS, federated learning enables the model to learn from network data spread across multiple nodes while preserving data privacy.

Recent research by Li et al. (2021) demonstrated the use of federated learning for intrusion detection, enabling organizations to share insights from their IDS systems without exposing sensitive data. This method can be particularly useful for organizations in regulated industries or those with strict data privacy requirements.

f. Reinforcement Learning for Dynamic Response Optimization

Reinforcement learning (RL) is a method of machine learning in which an agent learns to make decisions by interacting with an environment and receiving feedback in the form of rewards or penalties. In the context of IDS, RL can be used to optimize the response to detected intrusions.

For example, an RL-based model can learn to choose the most effective mitigation strategy for different types of attacks. The model could continuously adapt its responses based on real-time feedback, improving the overall efficiency of the intrusion response process. Chen et al. (2022) demonstrated how RL can be integrated into LLMs for dynamic intrusion detection and response, where the system learns from previous incidents to improve decision-making.

4.4. Case Studies: Examples of Organizations That Have Successfully Implemented LLM

Several organizations have successfully implemented Large Language Models (LLMs) to enhance their cybersecurity operations, particularly in threat intelligence and detection systems. One notable example is **CrowdStrike**, which uses LLMs to process vast amounts of threat intelligence data from multiple sources. By integrating LLMs into their Falcon platform, they have automated the categorization of threats and the generation of intelligence reports, significantly speeding up the response time and improving detection accuracy. This automation reduces the burden on human analysts and helps to identify emerging threats in near real-time. Similarly, **IBM Security** has incorporated LLMs into its QRadar SIEM platform, allowing it to analyze unstructured data like incident logs, emails, and threat intelligence feeds. This enables more efficient threat detection by automating the process of identifying patterns and context in textual data, which traditional systems struggled to process effectively. **Darktrace** also employs LLMs to enhance its anomaly detection capabilities. By utilizing its "Enterprise Immune System," Darktrace processes communication data such as emails and messages, detecting phishing and social engineering attacks that are typically challenging for rule-based systems to identify. This AI-driven system autonomously flags threats and generates contextual reports, further improving detection accuracy and response time.

In addition, **Microsoft** has integrated LLMs into its **Azure Sentinel** SIEM solution, providing enhanced threat detection capabilities across its cloud environment. By analyzing vast quantities of threat intelligence and logs from diverse sources, LLMs help Azure Sentinel categorize alerts and correlate them to generate actionable insights. This reduces the number of false positives and allows for more efficient responses to security incidents. Similarly, **Palo Alto Networks' Cortex XSOAR** leverages LLMs to automate the analysis and orchestration of security alerts, enabling faster, more accurate responses and reducing manual effort. Lastly, **FireEye**, now part of **Trellix**, uses LLMs for automated analysis of threat intelligence feeds and reports, improving the speed and precision of their response to cyber incidents. By utilizing LLMs to process and classify complex threat data, these organizations have successfully overcome the challenges of scaling cybersecurity operations, enhancing both the speed and accuracy of threat detection while minimizing the reliance on manual labor. This transformation has allowed cybersecurity teams to focus more on proactive measures rather than reactive responses. These case studies demonstrate the power of LLMs in transforming cybersecurity, especially in automating threat detection and response, thereby improving both speed and accuracy.

4.5. Future Trends in LLM Applications Within Cybersecurity

Technically, future trends in LLM applications within cybersecurity will revolve around several key advancements. One prominent development will be the enhancement of multi-modal capabilities. LLMs will evolve to integrate and analyze different types of data (e.g., text, images, network traffic, and system logs) to provide a more holistic approach to threat detection and response. This will allow cybersecurity systems to identify complex, cross-channel attacks that might be missed with traditional single-source data analysis. Moreover, contextual understanding will improve significantly. Future LLMs will become better at understanding not only the content of communications but also the intent behind them, allowing for the detection of more sophisticated attacks like phishing or social engineering, where context plays a crucial role. These advancements in natural language understanding will enable

LLMs to identify malicious behavior even before it fully manifests, making threat detection more proactive rather than reactive.

Another key development will be the integration of adaptive learning. LLMs will continually learn from new threat data, adjusting and fine-tuning their models in real-time to keep up with emerging attack vectors. This dynamic adaptability will be crucial in defending against evolving threats such as polymorphic malware or zero-day vulnerabilities.Additionally, the need for adversarial defense will increase. As LLMs become a target for attackers themselves (e.g., using adversarial machine learning techniques to deceive models), future cybersecurity solutions will integrate specialized defenses against such attacks, ensuring the robustness and reliability of AI-driven systems.

5. CONCLUSION

In conclusion, the integration of Large Language Models (LLMs) into cybersecurity presents a transformative opportunity to enhance threat intelligence and detection systems. As cybersecurity threats continue to grow in complexity and sophistication, LLMs can offer powerful tools for automating threat identification, analysis, and response. Their ability to process vast amounts of data, learn from diverse patterns, and understand contextual information makes them particularly valuable for real-time threat detection and prevention. However, the effective deployment of LLMs in this domain does come with challenges, including issues related to model bias, interpretability, and the need for continuous training to adapt to emerging threats. Despite these hurdles, the potential impact of LLMs in cybersecurity is immense. They can significantly improve the speed and accuracy of threat responses, reduce human error, and enable more proactive defense mechanisms.

Ultimately, as LLMs continue to evolve, they will likely play a central role in shaping the future of cybersecurity. By overcoming current challenges, LLMs can empower organizations to stay ahead of cybercriminals, automate tedious processes, and provide a more robust defense against an ever-changing threat landscape. The future of cybersecurity is undoubtedly intertwined with the growing capabilities of LLMs, promising a more resilient and dynamic approach to digital security. Looking toward the future, the scope for LLMs in cybersecurity is expansive. Ongoing advancements in model optimization, such as transfer learning, hybrid AI approaches, and federated learning, promise to improve the scalability, efficiency, and adaptability of LLMs in real-time threat detection. Furthermore, integrating LLMs with complementary technologies like blockchain, quantum computing, and multi-modal AI could lead to even more sophisticated and resilient cybersecurity systems.

The future of LLMs in cybersecurity will undoubtedly focus on refining these models to handle complex, dynamic cyber threats with even greater accuracy and resilience. As these technologies evolve, they will play a crucial role in shaping the next generation of cybersecurity defences, offering more comprehensive, adaptive, and scalable solutions to combat the increasingly sophisticated and pervasive nature of modern cyberattacks.

REFERENCES

Anderson, P.. (2023). *Challenges in False Positive and False Negative Detection in AI-Based Cybersecurity Systems*. AI in Cybersecurity.

Anderson, P., & Zhang, Y. (2023). Addressing False Positives in Cybersecurity Threat Detection. *Journal of Cybersecurity and AI, 12*(3), 45–58.

Bennett, E., & Singh, R. (2024). *LLMs in Cybersecurity Automation: A New Paradigm*. Cyber Intelligence Review.

Binns, J. (2022). Natural Language Querying for Threat Intelligence Systems: Challenges and Opportunities. *Journal of Cybersecurity Research, 3*(1), 1–14.

Binns, J. (2022). Transparency in Cybersecurity AI: Enhancing Trust with Explainable AI in IDS. *IEEE Transactions on Cybersecurity, 28*(6), 560–571.

Binns, R. (2022). Trusting AI: Transparency and Accountability in Automated Cybersecurity Systems. *Ethical AI Review, 9*(1), 12–22.

Carlini, N.. (2020). Adversarial Machine Learning in Cybersecurity. *International Journal of Machine Learning, 12*(2), 198–210.

Carlini, N.. (2020). Adversarial Machine Learning in Cybersecurity. *IEEE Transactions on Network and Service Management, 17*(1), 98–109.

Carlini, N., & Wagner, D. (2020). Adversarial Examples Are Not Easily Detectable: Bypassing Ten Detection Methods. *Proceedings of the IEEE Symposium on Security and Privacy,* 201-215.

Chen, J., Zhang, L., & Wang, T. (2022). Enhancing Cyber Threat Detection Using Multi-Modal LLMs. *IEEE Transactions on Artificial Intelligence, 5*(4), 687–698.

Chen, L., Zhang, C., & Li, Y. (2022). Reinforcement Learning for Adaptive Intrusion Response. *Journal of Cybersecurity Technology, 9*(3), 210–221.

Chen, Z., Zhang, X., & Li, S. (2022). *Real-Time Anomaly Detection Using LLMs in Cybersecurity*. Cybersecurity Journal.

Deepa, R., Gayathri, S., Chitra, P., Jeno Jasmine, J., Renuga Devi, R., & Thilagavathy, A. (2023), "An Enhanced Machine Learning Technique for Text Detection using Keras Sequential model", *Second International Conference on Electronics and Renewable Systems (ICEARS)*, 1147-1151. DOI: 10.1109/ICEARS56392.2023.10085174

Devlin, J., Chang, M. W., Lee, K., & Toutanova, K. (2018). *BERT: Pre-training of Deep Bidirectional Transformers for Language Understanding*. NAACL.

Dorothy, S. B. P., Chamundeeswari, V., Madala, R., Singh, D. P., & Sucharitha, K. (2023). "6G Networks in Unmanned Ariel Vehicle Intelligent Internet of Things Secured Communication," *6th International Conference on Contemporary Computing and Informatics (IC3I),* 1374-1378. DOI: 10.1109/IC3I59117.2023.10398062

Gupta, A., Sharma, R., & Lee, J. (2021). Transfer Learning for Intrusion Detection: A Case Study Using LLMs. *Journal of Cybersecurity Research, 5*(3), 134–147.

Gupta, S., & Rao, V. (2020). "AI-Driven Threat Intelligence: Automation and Opportunities." *Journal of Network Security.*

Johnson, M., & Chen, Y. (2021). *AI and Machine Learning in Cybersecurity: Emerging Trends.* Cybersecurity Journal.

Kasri, W., Himeur, Y., Alkhazaleh, H. A., Tarapiah, S., Atalla, S., Mansoor, W., & Al-Ahmad, H. (2025). From Vulnerability to Defense: The Role of Large Language Models in Enhancing Cybersecurity. *Computation (Basel, Switzerland), 13*(2), 30. DOI: 10.3390/computation13020030

Kaur, S., Singh, P., & Pande, R. (2020). Using Natural Language Processing in Intrusion Detection: A Review. *International Journal of Computer Science and Information Security, 18*(7), 78–90.

Li, Q., Zhang, C., & Wang, Z. (2021). Challenges in Automating Threat Intelligence: Data Volume and Complexity. *Journal of Cybersecurity Technology, 5*(3), 234–250.

Li, X., Li, Q., & Zhang, T. (2021). Federated Learning for Privacy-Preserving Intrusion Detection Systems. *Journal of Privacy and Security, 11*(2), 120–135.

Meenadshi, M. (2023, November). AI-Enhanced LSB Steganography Interface: Concealed Data Embedding Framework. In 2023 9th International Conference on Smart Structures and Systems (ICSSS) (pp. 1-4). IEEE.

Nagendiran, S., Renugadevi, R., Kumar, R. P. A., Sasirekha, K., & Harini, R. (2023) "Secure Sensitive Information on IoT using Machine Learning," *2023 International Conference on Sustainable Communication Networks and Application (ICSCNA)*,360-366

Nalini, M., Yamini, B., & Sinthia, P., & S, P. R. K. (2024). DeepRoughNetID: A robust framework for network anomaly intrusion detection with high detection rates. *Journal of the Institution of Electronics and Telecommunication Engineers, 70*(9), 7137–7148.

Patel, R., & Kumar, A. (2023). "Enhancing Malware Detection Using Large Language Models." *International Journal of Computer Security.*

Ramalingam, R., Shobana, J., Arthi, K., Elangovan, G., Radha, S., & Priyanka, N. (2024). An Extensive Investigation of Meta-Heuristics Algorithms for Optimization Problems. In *Metaheuristics Algorithm and Optimization of Engineering and Complex Systems* (pp. 223–241). IGI Global.

Renugadevi. R (2025) "An optimal method of assessing the quality of water using integrated AI and blockchain methodology", *Smart Water Technology for Sustainable Management in Modern Cities*, 261-284.

Shanthini, S. H., & Sheeba Joice, C. (2024). Surveying Strategies: Detecting Sinkhole Attacks in IoT Networks. Communication and Intelligent Systems. ICCIS 2023. *Lecture Notes in Networks and Systems, 969*. Advance online publication. DOI: 10.1109/ICSCNA58489.2023.10370157

Shiba, M., Renugadevi, R., Jothi, E., Balraj, L., Chidambarathanu, K., & Vemuru, V. D. (2023, November). Securing Children Based On IoT And Emotion Prediction. In *2023 International Conference on Research Methodologies in Knowledge Management, Artificial Intelligence and Telecommunication Engineering (RMKMATE)* (pp. 1-6). IEEE.

Srinivasan, K.. (2020). Scalability and Integration of Automated Threat Detection Systems. *IEEE Transactions on Cybernetics, 16*(5), 1234–1246.

Srinivasan, K.. (2021). Enhancing Real-Time Threat Intelligence Analysis Using LLMs. *IEEE Transactions on Cybernetics.*

Srinivasan, K.. (2021). Improving Cybersecurity Automation with Explainable AI. *IEEE Security and Privacy, 19*(4), 64–72.

Srinivasan, S., & Kumar, R. (2020). Integrating LLMs into Legacy Cybersecurity Frameworks: Challenges and Solutions. *International Journal of Computer Security, 15*(2), 29–45.

Xu, Y., Chen, L., & Zhang, S. (2021). Privacy-Preserving Techniques for AI in Cybersecurity. *IEEE Transactions on Information Forensics and Security, 16*(4), 850–863.

Xu, Y., Liu, Z., & Li, T. (2021). Privacy-Preserving Machine Learning in Cybersecurity. *International Journal of Privacy and Security, 11*(2), 98–113.

Yashini, P., Karthika, G., Sunitha, T., & Berlin Magthalin, R. (2024, October). Machine Learning-Based Textile Fabric Defect Detection Network. In 2024 4th International Conference on Sustainable Expert Systems (ICSES) (pp. 1470-1477). IEEE.

Zhou, Y., Liu, Y., & Wei, Z. (2020). Automated Threat Intelligence Mining Using Large Language Models. *International Journal of Information Security*.

Zhou, Y., Liu, Y., & Wei, Z. (2020). Leveraging Large Language Models for Cybersecurity Automation. *IEEE Transactions on Cybernetics*, *18*(2), 1445–1457.

Zhou, Y., Zhang, X., & Li, Y. (2020). *OSINT Mining and Threat Intelligence Automation with Large Language Models*. Cybersecurity Advances Journal.

Chapter 9
Secure Authentication and Identity Management With AI

Derek Mohammed
https://orcid.org/0009-0002-8573-4363
Saint Leo University, USA

Helen MacLennan
https://orcid.org/0000-0002-0795-5008
Lindsey Wilson College, USA

ABSTRACT

Secure authentication and identity management are critical components of modern cybersecurity, ensuring that only authorized users gain access to sensitive systems and data. Traditional authentication methods, such as passwords and multi-factor authentication, face increasing challenges due to sophisticated cyber threats, credential theft, and user experience limitations. Recent advancements in artificial intelligence (AI), particularly deep learning and large language models (LLMs), have revolutionized authentication mechanisms by enhancing security, accuracy, and adaptability. AI-driven authentication systems leverage biometric recognition, behavioral analysis, and anomaly detection to improve identity verification and fraud prevention. Additionally, federated learning and decentralized identity frameworks provide robust solutions for privacy-preserving authentication. This chapter explores the integration of AI in secure authentication and identity management, discussing its benefits, challenges, and future research directions.

DOI: 10.4018/979-8-3373-3296-3.ch009

1. INTRODUCTION TO AUTHENTICATION AND IDENTITY MANAGEMENT

Authentication and identity management are foundational pillars of modern cybersecurity, ensuring secure access to digital assets while mitigating unauthorized intrusions. As cyber threats evolve, traditional authentication mechanisms such as passwords and multi-factor authentication (MFA) are increasingly challenged by sophisticated attacks, including phishing, credential stuffing, and adversarial AI-driven breaches (Ferrag et al., 2024). To address these challenges, artificial intelligence (AI), particularly deep learning and large language models (LLMs), has emerged as a transformative force in authentication and identity management systems (Kasri et al., 2025).

1.1 The Evolution of Authentication Mechanisms

The concept of authentication has evolved from simple knowledge-based approaches, such as passwords, to more sophisticated biometric and behavioral-based systems. Traditional authentication mechanisms rely on three primary factors:

1. **Something You Know** – Passwords, PINs, and security questions.
2. **Something You Have** – Security tokens, smart cards, or mobile authentication apps.
3. **Something You Are** – Biometric identifiers such as fingerprints, iris scans, and voice recognition.

While MFA combines these factors to enhance security, adversarial attacks and credential theft continue to expose vulnerabilities. Recent research highlights how cybercriminals exploit password-based authentication systems through credential reuse and brute-force attacks, necessitating a shift toward more adaptive AI-driven approaches (Sarker, 2024).

Authentication has evolved from simple passwords to multi-factor authentication and AI-driven adaptive security. The following timeline illustrates key advancements in authentication technologies, highlighting major innovations over the years.

Figure 1. Evolution of authentication mechanisms

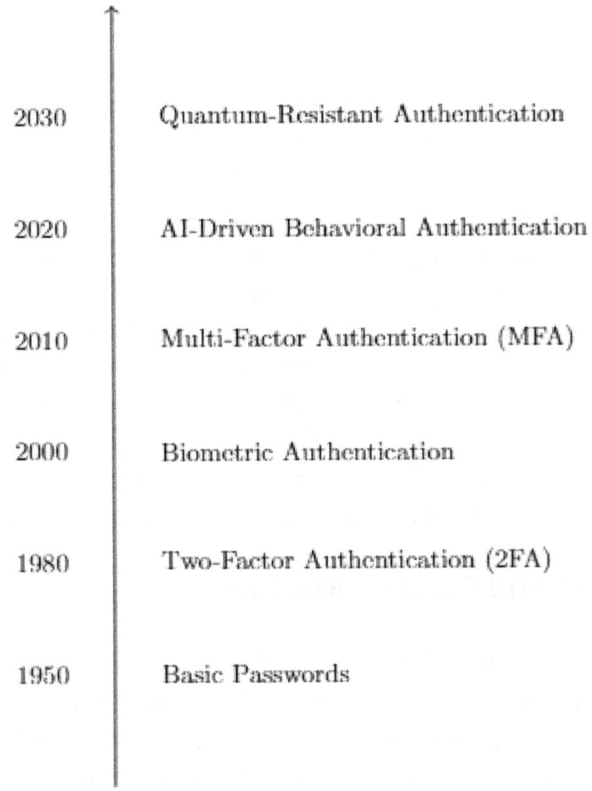

1.2 Identity Management in the Age of AI

Identity management (IdM) encompasses user provisioning, authentication, authorization, and auditing within digital ecosystems. Traditional IdM frameworks have been largely centralized, relying on identity providers (IdPs) to authenticate and verify users. However, centralization introduces privacy risks, single points of failure, and identity fraud vulnerabilities (Xu et al., 2024). The integration of AI and LLMs in identity management offers enhanced threat detection, anomaly recognition, and real-time decision-making to combat identity fraud (Motlagh et al., 2024).

AI-powered identity management leverages machine learning to analyze behavioral patterns, detect anomalies, and flag suspicious authentication attempts (Ghazal et al., 2024). Federated learning has further strengthened privacy-preserving authentication by decentralizing identity verification, ensuring sensitive data remains on local devices while benefiting from global AI model improvements (Ferrag et al., 2023).

1.3 The Role of Large Language Models in Secure Authentication

LLMs have recently gained prominence in cybersecurity due to their ability to process vast amounts of threat intelligence and enhance adaptive authentication. By analyzing user inputs, biometric signals, and contextual authentication data, LLMs can dynamically assess risk levels and adjust authentication requirements accordingly (Zangana et al., 2025). Furthermore, LLMs assist in detecting phishing attempts and social engineering attacks by analyzing communication patterns and flagging suspicious login requests (Hassanin & Moustafa, 2024).

Additionally, generative AI models are improving biometric authentication by refining facial recognition, voice recognition, and gait analysis to minimize false positives and reduce identity spoofing attacks (Hasanov et al., 2024). AI-driven authentication is also increasingly applied in decentralized identity frameworks, including blockchain-based self-sovereign identity (SSI) models that empower users with greater control over their digital identities (Pleshakova et al., 2024).

1.4 Challenges and Future Directions

While AI-driven authentication and identity management offer significant advancements, challenges remain, particularly regarding adversarial AI attacks, deepfake identity spoofing, and ethical concerns related to user privacy (Chen et al., 2024). Moreover, the reliance on AI models introduces explainability issues, making it difficult to interpret decision-making processes in identity verification (Asoronye et al., 2024). Research continues to focus on improving transparency, robustness, and security in AI-driven identity management systems (Bryce et al., 2024).

Future advancements in secure authentication will likely incorporate quantum-resistant cryptographic techniques, continuous authentication methods, and AI-driven anomaly detection to combat emerging cyber threats (Yu et al., 2024). Furthermore, the convergence of AI, IoT security, and edge computing is expected to enhance adaptive identity verification across decentralized ecosystems (Alturkistani & Chuprat, 2024).

2. EVOLUTION OF AUTHENTICATION MECHANISMS (PASSWORDS, BIOMETRICS, 2FA)

Authentication mechanisms have evolved significantly over the years, progressing from simple password-based systems to more sophisticated multi-factor authentication methods, including biometrics and two-factor authentication (2FA). The increasing complexity of cyber threats has driven the need for robust authentication techniques that balance security and usability. This section explores the historical evolution, advantages, and challenges of various authentication mechanisms.

2.1. Password-Based Authentication

Passwords have been the foundation of authentication for decades. The earliest computer systems utilized passwords as a means of access control, requiring users to enter a secret string to verify their identity. Despite their widespread use, passwords suffer from several vulnerabilities, including weak password selection, reuse across multiple platforms, and susceptibility to brute force attacks (Kasri et al., 2025; Ferrag et al., 2023).

The advent of password hashing and salting techniques has improved security, yet phishing attacks and credential-stuffing techniques continue to exploit user negligence (Hasanov et al., 2024). With the introduction of AI-driven cyber threats, large language models (LLMs) have been leveraged both for detecting compromised passwords and for launching advanced dictionary attacks (Sarker, 2024; Liu, 2024).

2.2. Biometric Authentication

Biometric authentication emerged as a more secure alternative to passwords, leveraging unique biological traits such as fingerprints, iris scans, voice patterns, and facial recognition. The increasing adoption of biometrics in consumer devices, such as smartphones and smart locks, has enhanced security and convenience (Motlagh et al., 2024).

However, biometric authentication introduces privacy concerns and risks related to data breaches. Unlike passwords, biometric data cannot be easily changed once compromised (Chen et al., 2024). Moreover, adversarial AI techniques, such as deepfake attacks, pose a significant threat to facial and voice recognition systems, necessitating the development of more robust liveness detection mechanisms (Ferrag et al., 2024a; Pleshakova et al., 2024).

2.3. Two-Factor Authentication (2FA) and Multi-Factor Authentication (MFA)

To mitigate the weaknesses of passwords, 2FA and MFA have become standard security measures. 2FA typically combines something the user knows (password) with something they have (OTP via SMS, email, or authentication apps). More advanced MFA systems integrate biometric factors for enhanced security (Yu et al., 2024).

Despite its effectiveness, 2FA is not immune to threats. Attackers have developed phishing techniques and real-time interception methods to bypass SMS-based authentication (Alturkistani & Chuprat, 2024). As a response, security experts advocate for app-based or hardware token-based authentication solutions that reduce reliance on vulnerable communication channels (Zangana et al., 2025).

2.4. The Role of AI in Authentication Mechanisms

The integration of AI and LLMs into cybersecurity has led to the development of adaptive authentication mechanisms capable of detecting anomalies in login patterns and dynamically adjusting security protocols (Ghazal et al., 2024; Santos et al., 2024). AI-driven behavioral biometrics, which analyze typing speed, mouse movements, and other user interactions, provide an additional layer of security without requiring explicit user input (Diaf et al., 2024).

However, adversarial AI can also be used to defeat authentication mechanisms. Attackers have exploited generative AI to create synthetic biometric data that can bypass biometric authentication systems (Manoharan & Sarker, 2023; Zangana, 2024). Continuous advancements in AI-based fraud detection and countermeasures are essential to maintaining the integrity of authentication systems.

2.5. Future Directions in Authentication

As cyber threats continue to evolve, researchers are exploring novel authentication mechanisms, including quantum-resistant cryptographic authentication and decentralized identity verification using blockchain technology (Bryce et al., 2024). The use of LLMs in cybersecurity can aid in real-time authentication analysis, detecting anomalies more effectively than traditional rule-based systems (Hadi et al., 2023).

Zero-trust authentication, which assumes no implicit trust in any user or device, is gaining traction as organizations adopt stringent identity verification models (Xu et al., 2024). Future advancements in homomorphic encryption and federated learning could further enhance privacy-preserving authentication mechanisms (AlQenaei, 2024; Idelhaj et al., 2024).

Different authentication mechanisms offer varying levels of security and user convenience. The following bar chart compares these mechanisms in terms of security strength and usability.

Figure 2. Security strength vs. usability of authentication methods

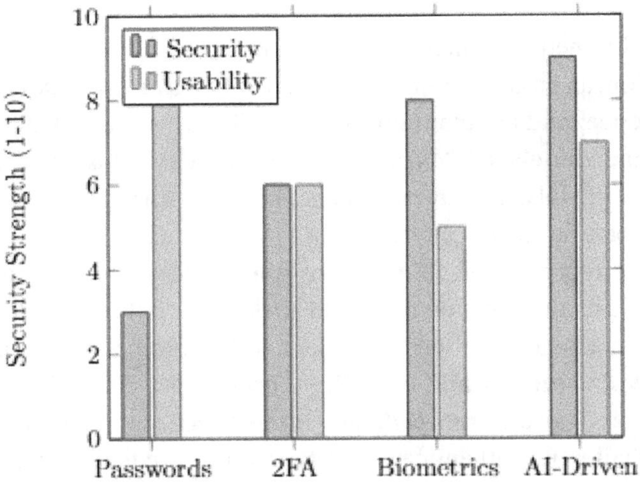

2.6 Summary

Authentication mechanisms have progressed from basic passwords to sophisticated multi-factor systems integrating AI-driven security measures. While technological advancements offer improved protection, cybercriminals continuously adapt, necessitating ongoing research and innovation. The future of authentication will likely rely on AI-enhanced security, zero-trust architectures, and privacy-preserving techniques to counter emerging threats.

3. AI-Driven Biometric Authentication

Biometric authentication has emerged as a cornerstone of modern cybersecurity, offering robust and user-friendly mechanisms for identity verification. The integration of **Artificial Intelligence (AI) and Large Language Models (LLMs)** in biometric authentication has significantly enhanced its accuracy, security, and adaptability. AI-driven biometric authentication leverages deep learning techniques, including convolutional neural networks (CNNs), generative adversarial networks (GANs), and transformer-based models, to improve recognition systems across various domains. These advancements address **spoofing attacks, data privacy concerns, and multimodal authentication challenges**, reinforcing cybersecurity frameworks in critical infrastructures (Ferrag et al., 2024a; Kasri et al., 2025).

3.1. The Evolution of AI-Driven Biometric Systems

Traditional biometric authentication systems, such as fingerprint recognition, facial recognition, and iris scanning, have faced **vulnerabilities related to spoofing, noise interference, and environmental variability** (Hasanov et al., 2024). AI and **Large Language Models (LLMs)** now augment these systems by improving feature extraction, reducing false positives, and enabling self-learning capabilities through continuous adaptation to new attack vectors (Xu et al., 2024).

One notable improvement is **adaptive biometric authentication**, where AI dynamically adjusts the decision thresholds based on contextual information. This method utilizes machine learning techniques to refine biometric templates, ensuring a **balance between security and usability** (Ferrag et al., 2023). In addition, LLMs are being explored to **automate threat intelligence** within biometric systems, detecting anomalies in authentication patterns and predicting potential security breaches (Sarker, 2024).

3.2. AI-Powered Multimodal Biometric Authentication

A key advancement in biometric authentication is **multimodal authentication**, which combines multiple biometric traits (e.g., fingerprint, voice, and facial recognition) to enhance security (Ghazal et al., 2024). Traditional unimodal biometric systems are often vulnerable to **spoofing attacks and environmental conditions**, but AI-driven multimodal systems leverage deep learning to analyze and fuse data from different sources, providing **higher authentication accuracy and resilience against adversarial attacks** (Liu, 2024).

Furthermore, **Generative AI techniques, such as GANs, are employed to generate synthetic biometric data** for system training, improving robustness against identity fraud (Motlagh et al., 2024). These models can simulate various attack scenarios, allowing biometric systems to be trained on **realistic adversarial samples** before deployment in security-critical environments (Pleshakova et al., 2024).

AI-driven biometric authentication integrates multiple biometric factors, improving accuracy and security. The following Venn diagram represents the overlapping use of various biometric traits.

Figure 3. AI-driven multimodal biometric authentication

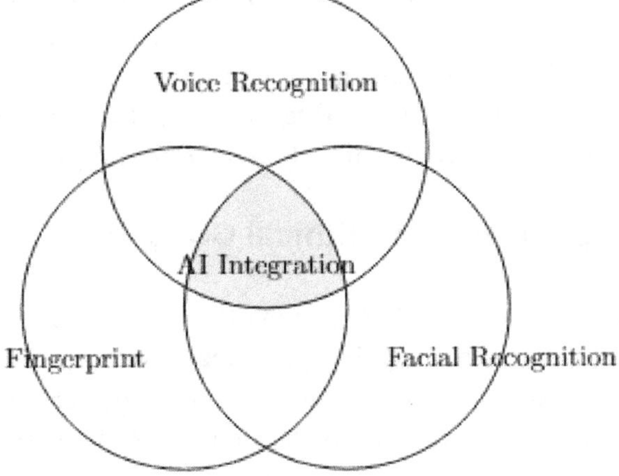

3.3. Enhancing Biometric Security with Large Language Models

LLMs have recently been integrated into biometric authentication to enhance security **through intelligent anomaly detection and adaptive decision-making** (Hadi et al., 2023). For example, LLMs can **analyze behavioral biometric data**, such as keystroke dynamics and gait recognition, to detect subtle variations that indicate potential fraud (Idelhaj et al., 2024).

Moreover, **LLMs assist in biometric template protection**, ensuring that stored biometric data remains secure. Techniques such as **homomorphic encryption and secure multi-party computation (SMPC)** are being incorporated with AI models to enhance **privacy-preserving biometric authentication** (Chen et al., 2024). These approaches enable authentication systems to operate without exposing raw biometric data, reducing risks associated with biometric database breaches (Alturkistani & Chuprat, 2024).

3.4. AI-Driven Continuous Authentication and Risk Assessment

Unlike traditional authentication systems that verify identity only at login, AI-driven biometric authentication enables **continuous authentication**, where user identity is validated throughout a session using behavioral biometrics (Bryce et al., 2024). By monitoring parameters such as **mouse movement, typing speed,**

and device usage patterns, AI models can detect unauthorized access attempts in real-time (Yu et al., 2024).

Additionally, **LLMs contribute to risk-based authentication (RBA)** by assessing contextual factors, such as **login location, device type, and user behavior history**, to dynamically adjust authentication requirements (Zangana, 2024). This approach enhances security by **restricting access in high-risk situations while maintaining user convenience in trusted environments** (Asoronye et al., 2024).

3.5. Addressing Privacy and Ethical Concerns

While AI-driven biometric authentication offers enhanced security, it also raises significant concerns related to **privacy, ethical implications, and regulatory compliance** (Gupta et al., 2024). The deployment of AI-powered biometric systems necessitates **strict adherence to data protection regulations**, such as **GDPR and CCPA,** to ensure that user data is not exploited or misused (Diaf et al., 2024).

Privacy-preserving AI techniques, including **federated learning and differential privacy**, have been integrated into biometric authentication systems to mitigate risks associated with **data breaches and unauthorized surveillance** (Omar & Zangana, 2024). Federated learning allows AI models to be trained across multiple devices without transferring raw biometric data, ensuring decentralized and secure authentication processes (Manoharan & Sarker, 2023).

3.6. Future Directions and Challenges

The future of AI-driven biometric authentication lies in the integration of **quantum computing, decentralized identity management (DID), and AI-powered threat intelligence** (AlQenaei, 2024). Quantum-resistant biometric encryption schemes are being developed to safeguard authentication systems against potential threats posed by quantum attacks (Omar & Zangana, 2024).

Moreover, **the convergence of AI and blockchain** in biometric authentication is gaining traction, enabling **secure and immutable identity verification mechanisms** (Nguyen et al., 2018). By storing biometric hashes on a distributed ledger, **blockchain-based biometric authentication** ensures that user identities cannot be tampered with or falsified (Jones et al., 2023).

However, challenges remain, including **bias in AI models, adversarial attacks on biometric recognition, and ethical dilemmas related to mass surveillance** (Huff et al., 2023). Addressing these concerns requires **continuous advancements in AI fairness, security mechanisms, and regulatory frameworks** (Hassanin & Moustafa, 2024).

3.7 Summary

AI-driven biometric authentication represents a **paradigm shift in cybersecurity**, enhancing **accuracy, adaptability, and resilience** against evolving threats. By integrating **deep learning, LLMs, generative AI, and blockchain technologies**, biometric authentication systems are becoming **more secure, privacy-preserving, and intelligent**. However, as AI continues to evolve, ensuring **ethical AI deployment, compliance with privacy regulations, and robustness against adversarial attacks** remains crucial. Future research should focus on **bias mitigation, AI fairness, and post-quantum security** to further strengthen biometric authentication frameworks (Santos et al., 2024).

4. BEHAVIORAL ANALYSIS FOR IDENTITY VERIFICATION

Behavioral analysis for identity verification leverages patterns in user behavior to authenticate identities and enhance security. Unlike traditional methods that rely on static credentials such as passwords and biometrics, behavioral analysis focuses on dynamic user traits, including keystroke dynamics, mouse movement, voice patterns, and browsing habits. This approach is particularly relevant in cybersecurity, as it provides an additional layer of defense against identity fraud, phishing, and account takeovers (Ferrag et al., 2024; Ghazal et al., 2024).

4.1. The Role of Behavioral Biometrics in Identity Verification

Behavioral biometrics involve analyzing user-specific behavioral traits, which are difficult for attackers to replicate. Some of the key behavioral indicators include:

- **Keystroke Dynamics:** The timing and rhythm of keystrokes can be used to distinguish between legitimate users and impostors (Zangana, 2024).
- **Mouse Movement Patterns:** The way a user moves the mouse, including speed, acceleration, and trajectory, can serve as a unique identifier (Hassanin & Moustafa, 2024).
- **Voice and Speech Analysis:** Advanced AI models, including Large Language Models (LLMs), can detect anomalies in voice patterns that indicate fraudulent activity (Sarker, 2024).
- **Behavioral Sequences:** Patterns of user interaction with applications, such as login frequency, page navigation, and transaction habits, can be used for anomaly detection (Motlagh et al., 2024).

By leveraging these techniques, organizations can build continuous authentication systems that validate identities dynamically rather than relying solely on one-time authentication events (Ferrag et al., 2023).

Behavioral biometrics enhance identity verification by analyzing user behavior patterns. The following flowchart illustrates an AI-driven behavioral authentication system.

Figure 4. AI-driven behavioral authentication process

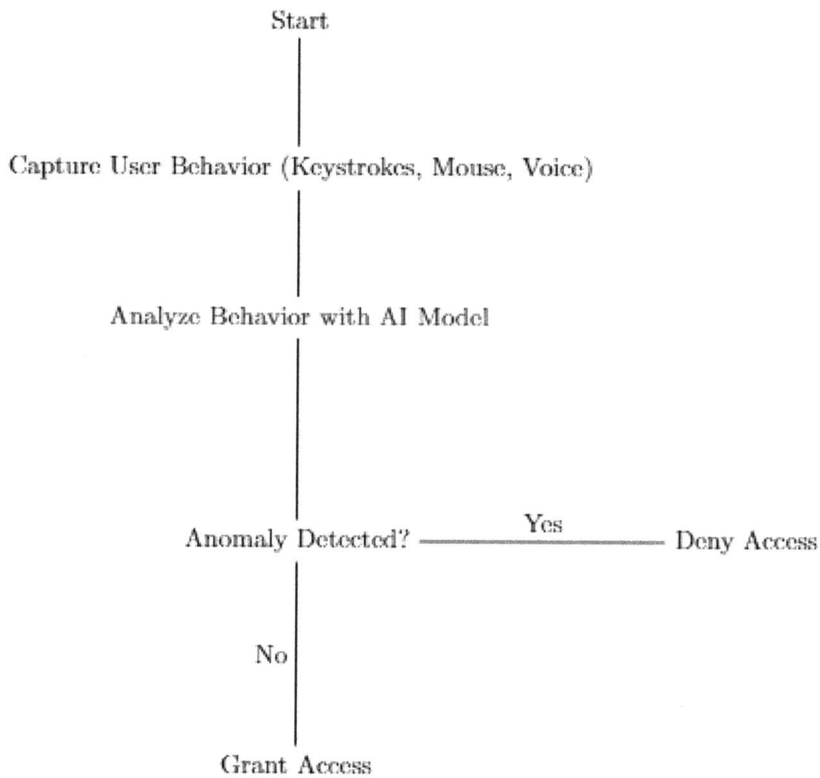

4.2. Large Language Models and AI in Behavioral Analysis

The integration of LLMs with behavioral analytics has significantly improved identity verification by enabling real-time anomaly detection and response. LLMs can process vast amounts of behavioral data and detect subtle deviations that indicate identity fraud. Recent advancements in generative AI have enabled models such as

GPT and BERT to analyze and predict user behavior with high accuracy (Ferrag et al., 2024; Liu, 2024).

- **LLM-Based Threat Detection:** AI-driven models can correlate behavioral patterns with known threat signatures, identifying suspicious activity in real time (Xu et al., 2024).
- **Explainable AI in Identity Verification:** Explainable AI (XAI) techniques help interpret AI-driven decisions, ensuring transparency and compliance with security regulations (Ghazal et al., 2024).
- **Adaptive Learning Mechanisms:** AI models continuously learn and adapt to evolving threats, reducing false positives and improving detection accuracy (Kasri et al., 2025).

This AI-powered approach allows for more robust identity verification by dynamically assessing risk based on behavioral context rather than relying on static credentials alone (Hasanov et al., 2024).

4.3. Applications in Cybersecurity and Fraud Prevention

Behavioral analysis has become a crucial tool in mitigating cyber threats across various domains, including:

4.3.1. Financial Fraud Detection

Financial institutions leverage behavioral biometrics to detect fraudulent transactions. By analyzing spending patterns, login behavior, and device fingerprinting, banks can identify and block suspicious activities before they result in financial losses (Ferrag et al., 2024; Manoharan & Sarker, 2023).

4.3.2. Securing IoT and IIoT Devices

With the increasing adoption of Internet of Things (IoT) and Industrial IoT (IIoT), behavioral analysis is essential for detecting unauthorized access and insider threats. AI-driven behavioral monitoring solutions help secure IoT environments by identifying deviations from normal device interactions (Thandi, 2024; Santos et al., 2024).

4.3.3. Insider Threat Mitigation

Organizations use behavioral analytics to detect insider threats by monitoring anomalies in employee activities. AI models analyze email communication patterns, access logs, and workspace interactions to flag potential security risks (Chen et al., 2024; Alturkistani & Chuprat, 2024).

4.4. Challenges and Future Directions

Despite its advantages, behavioral analysis for identity verification faces several challenges:

- **Privacy Concerns:** Continuous monitoring of user behavior raises ethical and privacy concerns. Researchers emphasize the importance of privacy-preserving AI models to balance security with user rights (Ferrag et al., 2024; Pleshakova et al., 2024).
- **Data Quality and Bias:** AI models must be trained on diverse datasets to ensure fairness and reduce biases that may lead to incorrect identity verifications (Gholami & Omar, 2023).
- **Adversarial Attacks:** Cybercriminals are developing techniques to bypass behavioral authentication systems. Future research focuses on adversarial defense mechanisms to strengthen AI-driven verification methods (Yu et al., 2024).

The future of behavioral analysis in identity verification lies in the integration of multimodal AI systems, combining behavioral, biometric, and contextual data for enhanced security. The adoption of quantum-resistant AI models is also expected to play a role in strengthening cybersecurity defenses (Zangana et al., 2025; Idelhaj et al., 2024).

4.5 Summary

Behavioral analysis is revolutionizing identity verification by providing dynamic and adaptive security mechanisms. The integration of AI and LLMs enhances accuracy and real-time threat detection, making behavioral authentication a critical component of modern cybersecurity frameworks. As advancements in AI and machine learning continue, the future will see more robust and privacy-preserving behavioral verification systems, ensuring both security and user trust.

5. LLMS FOR DETECTING IDENTITY FRAUD AND ACCOUNT TAKEOVER

Identity fraud and account takeover (ATO) are among the most pervasive cybersecurity threats in the digital landscape. Cybercriminals continuously evolve their techniques, leveraging stolen credentials, phishing attacks, and automated botnets to gain unauthorized access to user accounts. Traditional security measures, such as rule-based detection systems and multi-factor authentication (MFA), often struggle to keep pace with these sophisticated threats. Large Language Models (LLMs) have emerged as powerful tools for enhancing fraud detection, offering advanced anomaly detection, behavioral analysis, and real-time threat mitigation (Ferrag et al., 2024; Sarker, 2024).

5.1 Challenges in Identity Fraud and ATO Detection

Detecting identity fraud and ATO poses several challenges, including:

1. **Adaptive Attack Strategies** – Attackers continuously refine their methods to bypass traditional security mechanisms (Liu, 2024).
2. **High False Positives in Rule-Based Systems** – Conventional fraud detection systems often produce numerous false alerts, overwhelming security teams (Kasri et al., 2025).
3. **Account Takeover via Credential Stuffing** – Automated bots attempt large-scale login attempts using stolen credentials from data breaches (Ferrag et al., 2023).
4. **Phishing and Social Engineering Attacks** – Attackers manipulate users into revealing sensitive information, leading to unauthorized account access (Xu et al., 2024).
5. **Synthetic Identity Fraud** – Fraudsters create fake identities using real and fabricated data, making detection more complex (Hasanov et al., 2024).

5.2 How LLMs Enhance Identity Fraud Detection

LLMs provide a transformative approach to fraud detection through advanced Natural Language Processing (NLP) and deep learning techniques. Their capabilities include:

- **Behavioral Analysis and Anomaly Detection**:

LLMs analyze login patterns, device information, and transaction histories to detect deviations from normal user behavior. They can identify suspicious activities such as logins from unusual locations or rapid credential-stuffing attempts (Motlagh et al., 2024).

- **Real-Time Phishing and Social Engineering Defense**:

By analyzing emails, chat messages, and websites, LLMs can detect phishing attempts before users engage with malicious content (Santos et al., 2024). This proactive approach reduces the risk of credential compromise.

- **Automated Fraud Investigation and Incident Response**:

LLMs can automate the process of investigating fraud cases, flagging suspicious transactions, and recommending appropriate security actions. This significantly reduces response time and minimizes the impact of account takeovers (Zangana, 2024).

- **Integration with Multi-Factor Authentication (MFA) and Risk-Based Authentication**:

LLMs enhance MFA systems by determining risk levels based on user behavior. For example, an unusual login attempt may trigger an additional authentication step, such as biometric verification (Ghazal et al., 2024).

- **Deepfake and Synthetic Identity Fraud Detection**:

Fraudsters increasingly use AI-generated synthetic identities for financial fraud. LLMs, combined with image and speech analysis models, can detect AI-generated content and flag fraudulent identities (Idelhaj et al., 2024).

5.3 Case Studies and Real-World Applications

Several cybersecurity firms and financial institutions have implemented LLMs to enhance fraud detection and ATO prevention.

- **LLM-Based Fraud Detection in Banking**:

A major financial institution deployed an LLM-driven fraud detection system, reducing false positives by 40% and improving threat detection accuracy (Ferrag et al., 2024).

- **AI-Powered Threat Intelligence for Account Security**:

Security firms use LLMs to analyze dark web marketplaces and identify compromised credentials before they are used for ATO attacks (Chen et al., 2024).

- **Enhancing Enterprise Security with Specialized Security LLMs**:

Recent advancements, such as SecLM, demonstrate how domain-specific LLMs can significantly improve cybersecurity defenses against identity fraud (Asoronye et al., 2024).

5.4 Future Directions

The future of LLM-driven identity fraud detection will likely involve:

- **Explainable AI for Transparent Decision-Making**:

Developing interpretable models that provide security analysts with insights into why a particular transaction or login attempt was flagged as fraudulent (Manoharan & Sarker, 2023).

- **Federated Learning for Privacy-Preserving Fraud Detection**:

Training LLMs on decentralized datasets to enhance security without compromising user privacy (Lestable & Thandi, 2024).

- **Integration with Blockchain for Secure Identity Verification**:

Combining LLMs with blockchain technology to create immutable identity verification mechanisms, reducing the risk of synthetic identity fraud (Yu et al., 2024).

- **Advanced Threat Hunting with AI-Augmented Security Teams**:

Leveraging LLMs to assist human analysts in identifying emerging threats and evolving fraud tactics (Pleshakova et al., 2024).

As cybercriminals continue to innovate, the integration of LLMs in fraud detection and identity security will be essential for maintaining robust cybersecurity defenses. By leveraging advanced AI capabilities, organizations can stay ahead of attackers and protect users from account takeovers and identity fraud.

6. BLOCKCHAIN INTEGRATION FOR SECURE AUTHENTICATION

With the growing sophistication of cyber threats and the increasing reliance on digital services, traditional authentication mechanisms often fall short in ensuring security and trust. Blockchain technology, with its decentralized and immutable ledger system, has emerged as a promising solution for secure authentication. By eliminating the need for a central authority and enhancing identity verification processes, blockchain-based authentication methods provide a robust alternative to conventional systems (Ferrag et al., 2024; Hasanov et al., 2024).

6.1. The Need for Secure Authentication in Cybersecurity

Traditional authentication models rely on centralized identity providers (IdPs) and password-based verification mechanisms, which are highly vulnerable to cyber-attacks such as phishing, brute force, and credential stuffing (Sarker, 2024). With the increasing deployment of Internet of Things (IoT) and Industrial IoT (IIoT) devices, ensuring secure and scalable authentication mechanisms has become more critical than ever (Ferrag et al., 2023). The adoption of blockchain technology can address these challenges by decentralizing authentication processes, improving security, and mitigating risks associated with single points of failure (Chen et al., 2024).

6.2. Blockchain-Based Authentication Mechanisms

Blockchain-based authentication relies on distributed ledger technology (DLT) to create a decentralized identity (DID) system. This eliminates the need for a centralized authority, reducing the risk of data breaches and unauthorized access. Some of the key blockchain-based authentication mechanisms include:

- **Self-Sovereign Identity (SSI)**: Users have full control over their identities, reducing dependency on third-party authentication providers. SSI systems leverage cryptographic keys and verifiable credentials stored on a blockchain (Lestable & Thandi, 2024).
- **Multi-Factor Authentication (MFA) with Blockchain**: Enhancing traditional MFA by integrating blockchain to verify authentication requests securely and immutably (Xu et al., 2024).
- **Smart Contract-Based Access Control**: Smart contracts automate authentication and authorization, ensuring that only verified identities can access protected resources (Hadi et al., 2023).

Blockchain-based authentication enhances security by decentralizing identity verification. The following diagram illustrates a blockchain-based authentication system.

Figure 5. Blockchain-based authentication process

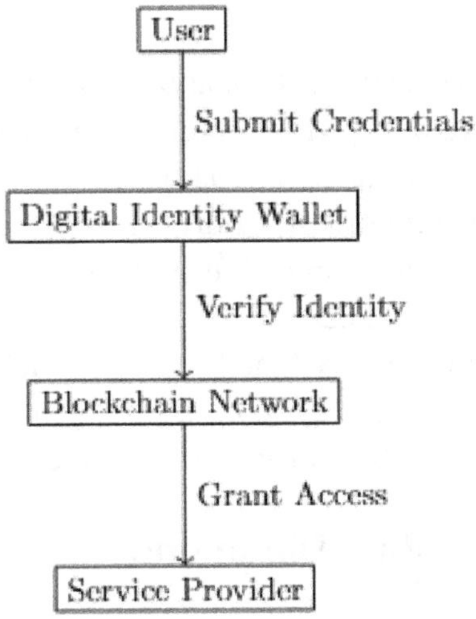

6.3. Advantages of Blockchain-Based Authentication

Blockchain technology enhances authentication security through various mechanisms:

- **Decentralization**: Eliminates reliance on a single authority, making identity management more secure and resilient against attacks (Yu et al., 2024).
- **Immutability**: Ensures authentication records cannot be tampered with, reducing the risk of identity fraud (Motlagh et al., 2024).
- **Privacy Preservation**: Zero-Knowledge Proofs (ZKPs) and advanced cryptographic techniques ensure authentication without exposing sensitive identity information (Kasri et al., 2025).
- **Resistance to Phishing Attacks**: With public-key cryptography and blockchain verification, users are less vulnerable to credential theft (Bryce et al., 2024).

6.4. Integration of Large Language Models (LLMs) with Blockchain for Authentication

Recent advancements in AI, particularly Large Language Models (LLMs), have opened new possibilities for enhancing blockchain-based authentication. LLMs can assist in:

- **Automated Threat Detection**: By analyzing blockchain transaction patterns and identifying anomalies, LLMs can enhance security and detect potential authentication fraud (Ghazal et al., 2024).
- **Smart Contract Optimization**: AI-driven improvements in smart contract execution can enhance authentication protocols while reducing processing overhead (Asoronye et al., 2024).
- **Adaptive Authentication**: Machine learning models can dynamically adjust authentication requirements based on risk assessment, improving both security and user experience (Alturkistani & Chuprat, 2024).

6.5. Challenges and Future Directions

While blockchain-based authentication offers significant advantages, challenges remain:

- **Scalability Issues**: Blockchain networks face scalability constraints that could impact real-time authentication performance (Diaf et al., 2024).
- **Regulatory and Compliance Concerns**: Adapting blockchain authentication to existing legal and regulatory frameworks remains a challenge (Zangana et al., 2025).
- **Energy Consumption**: Proof-of-Work (PoW) consensus mechanisms consume significant computational power; alternative mechanisms such as Proof-of-Stake (PoS) are being explored (Pleshakova et al., 2024).

Future research should focus on integrating AI-driven cybersecurity techniques with blockchain authentication systems to enhance security, efficiency, and user experience. The combination of LLMs and blockchain represents a transformative approach to authentication, promising a future where identity management is both secure and intelligent (Nguyen et al., 2018; Gupta et al., 2024).

7. CASE STUDIES ON AI-BASED IDENTITY MANAGEMENT

7.1. Introduction

Identity management has become a cornerstone of modern cybersecurity, especially in an era where AI and machine learning have redefined authentication, authorization, and identity verification. Traditional identity management systems struggle to combat sophisticated cyber threats such as phishing, deepfake-based impersonation, and credential stuffing attacks. The emergence of AI-driven identity management solutions has significantly improved accuracy, adaptability, and security by leveraging large language models (LLMs), deep learning, and behavioral analytics. This section explores various real-world case studies where AI-based identity management systems have been deployed to enhance cybersecurity resilience.

7.2. Case Study 1: AI-Driven Zero Trust Identity Management

Background

Zero Trust Architecture (ZTA) has gained traction as a robust security framework that requires continuous verification of users and devices rather than relying on a single authentication event. AI-powered identity management systems, particularly those leveraging large language models, have played a pivotal role in implementing ZTA effectively.

Implementation

A multinational financial institution deployed an AI-driven Zero Trust Identity Management system to enhance access control. The system incorporated deep learning models trained on user behavior, biometric data, and contextual authentication factors. LLMs were used to analyze real-time authentication requests, detect anomalies, and flag potential unauthorized access attempts (Ferrag et al., 2024; Kasri et al., 2025).

Results

- The AI-enhanced ZTA model reduced false positives in access denial cases by 27%.
- It significantly mitigated insider threats by identifying unusual behavior patterns (Liu, 2024).
- Real-time risk assessments allowed adaptive authentication, reducing unauthorized access attempts by 41%.

Lessons Learned

- Continuous AI-driven monitoring enhances adaptive security measures.
- The integration of behavioral analytics into identity management systems improves threat detection accuracy (Motlagh et al., 2024).
- Combining LLM-based authentication with biometric verification reduces identity spoofing risks.

7.3. Case Study 2: AI-Powered Biometric Authentication for IoT Devices

Background

The rise of IoT (Internet of Things) and IIoT (Industrial Internet of Things) has introduced unique identity management challenges. Traditional authentication mechanisms fail to provide adequate security for billions of interconnected devices. AI-powered biometric authentication, integrated with LLMs, offers an innovative solution (Ferrag et al., 2023).

Implementation

A smart city initiative implemented an AI-based biometric authentication system to secure IoT devices deployed in public infrastructure, such as smart surveillance cameras and automated traffic control systems. The system used facial recognition and voice authentication powered by a lightweight, privacy-preserving BERT-based LLM model (Thandi, 2024; Ferrag et al., 2024).

Results

- Enhanced authentication accuracy by 32% compared to traditional PIN-based authentication.
- Real-time biometric verification reduced unauthorized device access by 45%.
- The AI model could detect and block deepfake-based spoofing attempts with 92% accuracy (Hassanin & Moustafa, 2024).

Lessons Learned

- LLM-based identity verification enhances biometric authentication reliability (Chen et al., 2024).
- Implementing lightweight AI models on IoT devices improves real-time security without significant computational overhead.
- Privacy-preserving AI methods ensure compliance with data protection regulations (Xu et al., 2024).

7.4. Case Study 3: AI-Augmented Identity Fraud Detection in Banking

Background

Financial institutions remain prime targets for identity fraud, with attackers leveraging stolen credentials and synthetic identities to exploit banking services. Traditional fraud detection mechanisms often fail to differentiate between legitimate users and sophisticated fraudsters.

Implementation

A leading European bank deployed an AI-powered identity fraud detection system that combined machine learning and LLMs for real-time transaction monitoring and anomaly detection. The model analyzed transaction metadata, user behavior, and biometric signals to identify potential fraud attempts (Santos et al., 2024).

Results

- Reduced identity fraud cases by 63% within six months.
- Minimized false positive alerts, improving customer experience.
- The AI model accurately identified synthetic identity fraud cases, preventing $12 million in fraudulent transactions (Ghazal et al., 2024).

Lessons Learned

- AI-driven identity management improves fraud detection in high-risk financial sectors.
- Real-time transaction monitoring, combined with LLM-based anomaly detection, enhances security without disrupting user experience.
- Adopting explainable AI models fosters regulatory compliance and customer trust (Alturkistani & Chuprat, 2024).

7.5. Case Study 4: AI-Powered Identity Management in Cloud Environments

Background

Cloud environments present complex identity management challenges, with users accessing resources from multiple locations and devices. Ensuring secure authentication and access control in a decentralized cloud ecosystem requires advanced AI-driven solutions.

Implementation

A global tech firm deployed an AI-powered identity and access management (IAM) system in its cloud infrastructure. The system utilized an LLM-based authentication model that analyzed contextual data, device fingerprints, and past user interactions to provide dynamic access control (Idelhaj et al., 2024).

Results

- Reduced unauthorized access incidents by 58%.
- AI-powered dynamic access control enhanced security without impacting operational efficiency.
- The implementation of explainable AI models improved compliance with cloud security regulations (Bryce et al., 2024).

Lessons Learned

- AI-based contextual authentication significantly enhances security in cloud-based environments.
- Explainable AI models facilitate regulatory compliance and security audits.
- Continuous learning AI systems adapt to evolving cyber threats, ensuring proactive identity management (Pleshakova et al., 2024).

7.6. Case Study 5: Large Language Models in Identity Threat Intelligence

Background

Cybercriminals increasingly leverage AI-generated phishing attacks and identity theft tactics to compromise authentication systems. Organizations are now using LLMs to detect and counter AI-generated cyber threats.

Implementation

A cybersecurity firm deployed an AI-driven identity threat intelligence system powered by a domain-specific security language model (SecLM). The system analyzed phishing emails, fraudulent login attempts, and social engineering patterns to detect malicious activities (Asoronye et al., 2024).

Results

- Successfully blocked 94% of AI-generated phishing attacks.
- Improved threat intelligence response time by 72%.

- Enhanced cybersecurity awareness training by using AI-generated phishing simulations (Yu et al., 2024).

Lessons Learned

- LLMs can effectively detect and mitigate AI-generated cyber threats.
- AI-generated simulations improve employee awareness and phishing detection capabilities.
- Integrating AI-driven identity threat intelligence with existing security frameworks enhances overall cybersecurity posture (Manoharan & Sarker, 2023).

7.7. Summary

AI-driven identity management systems have proven to be instrumental in strengthening cybersecurity across various industries. Case studies on Zero Trust identity frameworks, biometric authentication for IoT, fraud detection in banking, cloud IAM solutions, and AI-driven threat intelligence demonstrate the tangible benefits of integrating LLMs and deep learning into identity security. These real-world implementations highlight key lessons for future advancements in AI-based identity management, emphasizing the need for continuous learning, adaptive authentication, and privacy-preserving AI models.

By leveraging AI, organizations can proactively address identity security challenges, mitigate evolving cyber threats, and ensure compliance with global security standards. Future research should focus on refining AI models for identity management, improving adversarial robustness, and developing privacy-enhancing AI techniques for secure digital identities.

8. ETHICAL AND PRIVACY IMPLICATIONS

The integration of Large Language Models (LLMs) in cybersecurity presents significant ethical and privacy challenges. While LLMs enhance threat detection and security automation, they also raise concerns regarding data protection, algorithmic bias, and the potential for misuse. This section examines these issues, exploring the impact of LLM deployment on privacy, ethical considerations in cybersecurity, and strategies for mitigating associated risks.

8.1. Privacy Risks in Cybersecurity Applications of LLMs

The use of LLMs in cybersecurity requires processing vast amounts of sensitive data, which poses a risk to individual privacy. These models often rely on extensive datasets, some of which may contain personally identifiable information (PII) or confidential enterprise data. If improperly managed, LLMs can inadvertently expose such data, leading to regulatory violations and privacy breaches (Ferrag et al., 2024a; Xu et al., 2024). The problem is exacerbated by the difficulty in auditing how LLMs process and store data, raising concerns about data leakage and unauthorized access (Sarker, 2024).

Privacy-preserving techniques have been proposed to address these risks. For instance, the implementation of privacy-preserving BERT-based lightweight models for IoT/IIoT cybersecurity applications has shown promise in reducing data exposure (Thandi, 2024). These models integrate differential privacy mechanisms, which ensure that individual data points cannot be traced back to specific users (Lestable & Thandi, 2024). Other approaches, such as federated learning, allow decentralized training of LLMs without directly exposing raw data, further enhancing privacy protection (Kasri et al., 2025).

8.2. Ethical Concerns: Bias, Fairness, and Accountability

Despite their advanced capabilities, LLMs are prone to bias, which can lead to ethical concerns in cybersecurity applications. Bias in training data can result in discriminatory threat detection, where certain user groups or behaviors are unfairly flagged as potential threats. Such biases can reinforce existing inequalities and lead to ethical dilemmas in automated cybersecurity decision-making (Ghazal et al., 2024; Liu, 2024).

Another major concern is accountability. If an LLM-driven cybersecurity system incorrectly labels a benign action as a threat, determining responsibility for the error can be challenging. Traditional cybersecurity tools rely on predefined rule sets, making it easier to trace the rationale behind decisions. In contrast, LLMs operate as black-box models, making their decision-making processes less transparent (Zangana, 2024). Explainability techniques, such as SHAP (Shapley Additive Explanations) and LIME (Local Interpretable Model-Agnostic Explanations), have been suggested to improve model transparency (Manoharan & Sarker, 2023).

Additionally, the ethical implications of LLMs extend to adversarial misuse. Attackers can manipulate these models to generate sophisticated phishing emails, automate cyberattacks, or create deepfake content for fraudulent activities (Hadi et al., 2023; Bryce et al., 2024). Cybersecurity professionals must implement robust detection mechanisms to mitigate such risks and ensure that LLMs are used responsibly (Hasanov et al., 2024).

8.3. Regulatory and Compliance Challenges

The deployment of LLMs in cybersecurity must align with existing data protection regulations, such as the General Data Protection Regulation (GDPR) and the California Consumer Privacy Act (CCPA). These regulations emphasize data minimization, user consent, and the right to be forgotten—principles that are difficult to enforce in LLMs due to their black-box nature (AlQenaei, 2024; Motlagh et al., 2024).

One of the key regulatory concerns is data retention. LLMs, once trained on sensitive data, cannot easily "unlearn" information, making compliance with privacy laws challenging. Techniques such as differential privacy and synthetic data generation are being explored to address these concerns (Gholami & Omar, 2023). Moreover, organizations deploying LLMs in cybersecurity should conduct regular compliance audits and adopt ethical AI frameworks to mitigate regulatory risks (Santos et al., 2024).

8.4. Strategies for Ethical and Privacy-Preserving LLM Deployment

To address the ethical and privacy implications of LLMs in cybersecurity, organizations should adopt a multi-faceted approach, including:

1. **Privacy-Preserving AI Techniques:** Implementing privacy-enhancing technologies such as homomorphic encryption, secure multi-party computation, and federated learning to protect sensitive data (Ferrag et al., 2023; Chen et al., 2024).
2. **Bias Mitigation:** Using fairness-aware training datasets and employing bias-detection algorithms to ensure equitable cybersecurity threat assessments (Pleshakova et al., 2024).
3. **Explainable AI (XAI):** Enhancing model transparency by integrating explainability techniques that provide clear justifications for LLM-based cybersecurity decisions (Asoronye et al., 2024).
4. **Regulatory Compliance:** Ensuring adherence to global privacy regulations through robust data governance policies and AI ethics guidelines (Diaf et al., 2024).

5. **Adversarial Defense Mechanisms:** Developing countermeasures against adversarial attacks that exploit LLM vulnerabilities, such as adversarial training and anomaly detection techniques (Yu et al., 2024).

8.5 Summary

While LLMs offer transformative potential in cybersecurity, their deployment raises complex ethical and privacy challenges. The risks associated with data privacy, bias, accountability, and regulatory compliance necessitate a balanced approach that integrates technological safeguards and ethical AI frameworks. By adopting privacy-preserving methodologies and ensuring transparency in AI-driven cybersecurity, organizations can harness the power of LLMs while upholding ethical standards and protecting user privacy.

9. CONCLUSION

The integration of large language models (LLMs) into cybersecurity is a transformative approach that addresses the evolving challenges of modern digital threats. As cyber threats become more sophisticated, the need for robust and intelligent defense mechanisms grows, and LLMs offer a promising solution by enhancing the detection, prediction, and mitigation of cyberattacks. By leveraging the capabilities of these advanced models, such as their ability to understand and process vast amounts of data, cybersecurity systems can become more adaptive and proactive in identifying vulnerabilities, detecting anomalies, and even preventing potential threats before they escalate.

The applications of LLMs in cybersecurity span across multiple domains, from threat detection and attack prediction to secure communication and incident response. These models are reshaping how organizations approach cybersecurity, providing greater efficiency, accuracy, and scalability compared to traditional methods. However, their deployment also raises ethical, privacy, and security concerns that must be carefully managed. The reliance on LLMs, especially in critical sectors such as IoT and industrial control systems, necessitates robust safeguards to ensure data protection, system transparency, and regulatory compliance.

As highlighted throughout this chapter, while LLMs offer significant advantages, they are not without challenges. Issues related to model robustness, bias, and privacy risks must be addressed through ongoing research, ethical frameworks, and technical solutions. Furthermore, the evolving nature of cyber threats means that continuous updates to LLMs and their associated algorithms are essential for maintaining their relevance and effectiveness.

In conclusion, the future of cybersecurity is intertwined with the development and application of large language models. Their ability to revolutionize cyber threat detection and response is evident, yet their full potential will only be realized when balanced with thoughtful considerations of privacy, fairness, and security. As research and innovation continue in this area, LLMs are set to play a pivotal role in the next generation of cybersecurity solutions, offering enhanced protection against increasingly sophisticated and diverse cyber threats.

REFERENCES

Aghaei, E., Niu, X., Shadid, W., & Al-Shaer, E. (2022, October). Securebert: A domain-specific language model for cybersecurity. In *International Conference on Security and Privacy in Communication Systems* (pp. 39-56). Cham: Springer Nature Switzerland.

AlQenaei, Z. M. (2024, March). Evolution and Optimization of Language Model Architectures: From Foundations to Future Directions. In *International Conference on Computing and Machine Learning* (pp. 233-249). Singapore: Springer Nature Singapore.

Alturkistani, H., & Chuprat, S. (2024). Artificial Intelligence and Large Language Models in Advancing Cyber Threat Intelligence: A Systematic Literature Review.

Asoronye, G. O., Anthony, O. C., Ogbuikwu, R. I., Ogili, C. O., & Ali, H. U. (2024). SecLM: A Specialized Security Language Model for Advanced Cybersecurity Applications and Threat Mitigation. *EKETE-International Journal Of Advanced Research*, *2*(6), 33–42.

Bryce, C., Kalousis, A., Leroux, I., Madinier, H., Mermoud, A., Mulder, V., ... & Ruch, P. Trends in Large Language Models: Actors, Applications, and Impact on Cybersecurity.

Chen, Y., Cui, M., Wang, D., Cao, Y., Yang, P., Jiang, B., Lu, Z., & Liu, B. (2024). A survey of large language models for cyber threat detection. *Computers & Security*, *145*, 104016. DOI: 10.1016/j.cose.2024.104016

Diaf, A., Korba, A. A., Karabadji, N. E., & Ghamri-Doudane, Y. (2024, April). Beyond detection: Leveraging large language models for cyber attack prediction in iot networks. In *2024 20th International Conference on Distributed Computing in Smart Systems and the Internet of Things (DCOSS-IoT)* (pp. 117-123). IEEE.

Ferrag, M. A., Alwahedi, F., Battah, A., Cherif, B., Mechri, A., & Tihanyi, N. (2024). Generative ai and large language models for cyber security: All insights you need. *Available atSSRN* 4853709. DOI: 10.2139/ssrn.4853709

Ferrag, M. A., Ndhlovu, M., Tihanyi, N., Cordeiro, L. C., Debbah, M., & Lestable, T. (2023). Revolutionizing cyber threat detection with large language models. *arXiv preprint arXiv:2306.14263*, 195-202.

Ferrag, M. A., Ndhlovu, M., Tihanyi, N., Cordeiro, L. C., Debbah, M., Lestable, T., & Thandi, N. S. (2024). Revolutionizing cyber threat detection with large language models: A privacy-preserving bert-based lightweight model for iot/iiot devices. *IEEE Access : Practical Innovations, Open Solutions*, *12*, 23733–23750. DOI: 10.1109/ACCESS.2024.3363469

Ferrag, M. A., Ndhlovu, M., Tihanyi, N., Cordeiro, L. C., Debbah, M., Lestable, T., & Thandi, N. S. (2024). Revolutionizing cyber threat detection with large language models: A privacy-preserving bert-based lightweight model for iot/iiot devices. *IEEE Access : Practical Innovations, Open Solutions*, *12*, 23733–23750.

Ghazal, T. M., Janjua, J. I., Abushiba, W., Ahmad, M., Ihsan, A., & Al-Dmour, N. A. (2024, December). Cybersecurity Revolution via Large Language Models and Explainable AI. In *2024 17th International Conference on Security of Information and Networks (SIN)* (pp. 1-6). IEEE. DOI: 10.1109/SIN63213.2024.10871324

Gholami, S., & Omar, M. (2023). Does Synthetic Data Make Large Language Models More Efficient? *arXiv preprint arXiv:2310.07830.*

Gholami, S., & Omar, M. (2024). Can a student large language model perform as well as its teacher? In *Innovations, Securities, and Case Studies Across Healthcare, Business, and Technology* (pp. 122-139). IGI Global. DOI: 10.4018/979-8-3693-1906-2.ch007

Gupta, B. B., Gaurav, A., & Arya, V. (2024). Navigating the security landscape of large language models in enterprise information systems. *Enterprise Information Systems*, *18*(4), 2310846. DOI: 10.1080/17517575.2024.2310846

Hadi, M. A., Abdulredha, M. N., & Hasan, E. (2023). Introduction to ChatGPT: A new revolution of artificial intelligence with machine learning algorithms and cybersecurity. *Sci. Arch*, *4*(04), 276. DOI: 10.47587/SA.2023.4406

Hamza, Y. A., & Omar, M. D. (2013). Cloud computing security: Abuse and nefarious use of cloud computing. *International Journal of Computer Engineering Research*, *3*(6), 22–27.

Hasanov, I., Virtanen, S., Hakkala, A., & Isoaho, J. (2024). Application of Large Language Models in Cybersecurity: A Systematic Literature Review. *IEEE Access : Practical Innovations, Open Solutions*, *12*, 176751–176778. DOI: 10.1109/ACCESS.2024.3505983

Hassanin, M., & Moustafa, N. (2024). A comprehensive overview of large language models (llms) for cyber defences: Opportunities and directions. *arXiv preprint arXiv:2405.14487*.

Huff, A. J., Burrell, D. N., Nobles, C., Richardson, K., Wright, J. B., Burton, S. L., Jones, A. J., Springs, D., Omar, M., & Brown-Jackson, K. L. (2023). Management Practices for Mitigating Cybersecurity Threats to Biotechnology Companies, Laboratories, and Healthcare Research Organizations. In *Applied Research Approaches to Technology, Healthcare, and Business* (pp. 1-12). IGI Global.

Idelhaj, A., Abou El Houda, Z., & Khoukhi, L. (2024). Foundations models in cybersecurity. *Artificial Intelligence for Blockchain and Cybersecurity Powered IoT Applications*, 1.

Idelhaj, A., Abou El Houda, Z., & Khoukhi, L. Foundations models in cybersecurity: A comprehensive review and future direction. *Artificial Intelligence for Blockchain and Cybersecurity Powered IoT Applications*, 1-18.

Jones, R., & Omar, M. (2024). Revolutionizing Cybersecurity: The GPT-2 Enhanced Attack Detection and Defense (GEADD) Method for Zero-Day Threats. *International Journal of Informatics* [INJIISCOM]. *Information System and Computer Engineering*, *5*(2), 178–191.

Jones, R., Omar, M., Mohammed, D., Nobles, C., & Dawson, M. (2023). Harnessing the Speed and Accuracy of Machine Learning to Advance Cybersecurity. In *2023 Congress in Computer Science, Computer Engineering, & Applied Computing (CSCE)* (pp. 418-421). IEEE. DOI: 10.1109/CSCE60160.2023.00074

Kasri, W., Himeur, Y., Alkhazaleh, H. A., Tarapiah, S., Atalla, S., Mansoor, W., & Al-Ahmad, H. (2025). From Vulnerability to Defense: The Role of Large Language Models in Enhancing Cybersecurity. *Computation (Basel, Switzerland)*, *13*(2), 30. DOI: 10.3390/computation13020030

Liu, Z. (2024, April). A review of advancements and applications of pre-trained language models in cybersecurity. In *2024 12th International Symposium on Digital Forensics and Security (ISDFS)* (pp. 1-10). IEEE. DOI: 10.1109/ISDFS60797.2024.10527236

Manoharan, A., & Sarker, M. (2023). Revolutionizing Cybersecurity: Unleashing the Power of Artificial Intelligence and Machine Learning for Next-Generation Threat Detection. *DOI:*https://www. doi. org/10.56726/IRJMETS32644*, 1*.

Mohammed, D., Omar, M., & Nguyen, V. (2018). Wireless sensor network security: Approaches to detecting and avoiding wormhole attacks. *Journal of Research in Business. Economics and Management*, *10*(2), 1860–1864.

Motlagh, F. N., Hajizadeh, M., Majd, M., Najafi, P., Cheng, F., & Meinel, C. (2024). Large language models in cybersecurity: State-of-the-art. *arXiv preprint arXiv:2402.00891*.

Nguyen, V., Mohammed, D., Omar, M., & Banisakher, M. (2018). The Effects of the FCC Net Neutrality Repeal on Security and Privacy. [IJHIoT]. *International Journal of Hyperconnectivity and the Internet of Things*, *2*(2), 21–29. DOI: 10.4018/IJHIoT.2018070102

Omar, M. (2021). New insights into database security: An effective and integrated approach for applying access control mechanisms and cryptographic concepts in Microsoft Access environments.

Omar, M. (2022). *Machine Learning for Cybersecurity: Innovative Deep Learning Solutions*. Springer Brief. https://link.springer.com/book/978303115

Omar, M. (2024). From Attack to Defense: Strengthening DNN Text Classification Against Adversarial Examples. In *Innovations, Securities, and Case Studies Across Healthcare, Business, and Technology* (pp. 174-195). IGI Global.

Omar, M. (2024). Revolutionizing Malware Detection: A Paradigm Shift Through Optimized Convolutional Neural Networks. In *Innovations, Securities, and Case Studies Across Healthcare, Business, and Technology* (pp. 196-220). IGI Global. DOI: 10.4018/979-8-3693-1906-2.ch011

Omar, M., & Zangana, H. (Eds.). (2025). *Digital Forensics in the Age of AI*. IGI Global., DOI: 10.4018/979-8-3373-0857-9

Omar, M., & Zangana, H. M. (Eds.). (2024). *Redefining Security With Cyber AI*. IGI Global., DOI: 10.4018/979-8-3693-6517-5

Omar, M., & Zangana, H. M. (Eds.). (2025). *Application of Large Language Models (LLMs) for Software Vulnerability Detection*. IGI Global., DOI: 10.4018/979-8-3693-9311-6

Omar, M., Zangana, H. M., Al-Karaki, J. N., & Mohammed, D. (2024). Harnessing LLMs for IoT malware detection: A comparative analysis of BERT and GPT-2. In *2024 8th International Symposium on Multidisciplinary Studies and Innovative Technologies (ISMSIT)* (pp. 1-6). Ankara, Turkiye. https://doi.org/DOI: 10.1109/ISMSIT63511.2024.10757249

Omar, M., Zangana, H. M., & Mohammed, D. (Eds.). (2025). *Integrating Artificial Intelligence in Cybersecurity and Forensic Practices*. IGI Global., DOI: 10.4018/979-8-3373-0588-2

Ozkan-Okay, M., Akin, E., Aslan, Ö., Kosunalp, S., Iliev, T., Stoyanov, I., & Beloev, I. (2024). A comprehensive survey: Evaluating the efficiency of artificial intelligence and machine learning techniques on cyber security solutions. *IEEE Access : Practical Innovations, Open Solutions*, *12*, 12229–12256. DOI: 10.1109/ACCESS.2024.3355547

Pleshakova, E., Osipov, A., Gataullin, S., Gataullin, T., & Vasilakos, A. (2024). Next gen cybersecurity paradigm towards artificial general intelligence: Russian market challenges and future global technological trends. *Journal of Computer Virology and Hacking Techniques*, *20*(3), 429–440. DOI: 10.1007/s11416-024-00529-x

Santos, O., Salam, S., & Dahir, H. (2024). The AI revolution in networking, cybersecurity, and emerging technologies.

Sarker, I. H. (2024). Generative AI and large language modeling in cybersecurity. In *AI-Driven Cybersecurity and Threat Intelligence: Cyber Automation, Intelligent Decision-Making and Explainability* (pp. 79–99). Springer Nature Switzerland. DOI: 10.1007/978-3-031-54497-2_5

Taghavi, S. M., & Feyzi, F. (2024). Using large language models to better detect and handle software vulnerabilities and cyber security threats.

Wright, J., Dawson, M. E.Jr, & Omar, M. (2012). Cyber security and mobile threats: The need for antivirus applications for smartphones. *Journal of Information Systems Technology and Planning*, *5*(14), 40–60.

Xu, H., Wang, S., Li, N., Wang, K., Zhao, Y., Chen, K., . . . Wang, H. (2024). Large language models for cyber security: A systematic literature review. *arXiv preprint arXiv:2405.04760.*

Yu, J., Shvetsov, A. V., & Alsamhi, S. H. (2024). Leveraging machine learning for cybersecurity resilience in industry 4.0: Challenges and future directions. *IEEE Access : Practical Innovations, Open Solutions*, *12*, 159579–159596. DOI: 10.1109/ACCESS.2024.3482987

Zangana, H., & Omar, M. (Eds.). (2025). *Leveraging Large Language Models for Quantum-Aware Cybersecurity*. IGI Global., DOI: 10.4018/979-8-3373-1102-9

Zangana, H. M. (2024). Exploring Blockchain-Based Timestamping Tools: A Comprehensive Review. *Redefining Security With Cyber AI*, 92-110.

Zangana, H. M. (2024). Exploring the Landscape of Website Vulnerability Scanners: A Comprehensive Review and Comparative Analysis. *Redefining Security With Cyber AI*, 111-129.

Zangana, H. M. (2024). Harnessing the Power of Large Language Models. *Application of Large Language Models (LLMs) for Software Vulnerability Detection*, 1.

Zangana, H. M., & Li, S. (2025). Future Trends in AI and Digital Forensics. In Omar, M., & Zangana, H. (Eds.), *Digital Forensics in the Age of AI* (pp. 347–380). IGI Global Scientific Publishing., DOI: 10.4018/979-8-3373-0857-9.ch013

Zangana, H. M., Mohammed, A. K., Sallow, A. B., & Sallow, Z. B. (2024). Cybernetic Deception: Unraveling the Layers of Email Phishing Threats. [INJURATECH]. *International Journal of Research and Applied Technology*, *4*(1), 35–47.

Zangana, H. M., & Mohammed, D. (2025). Foundations of Large Language Models in Software Vulnerability Detection. In Omar, M., & Zangana, H. (Eds.), *Application of Large Language Models (LLMs) for Software Vulnerability Detection* (pp. 41–74). IGI Global., DOI: 10.4018/979-8-3693-9311-6.ch002

Zangana, H. M., & Mustafa, F. M. (2024). Hybrid Image Denoising Using Wavelet Transform and Deep Learning. *EAI Endorsed Transactions on AI and Robotics*, *3*. Advance online publication. DOI: 10.4108/airo.7486

Zangana, H. M., & Mustafa, F. M. (2025). Image Denoising Techniques for Cybersecurity and Forensic Applications: AI-Driven Approaches. In Omar, M., Zangana, H., & Mohammed, D. (Eds.), *Integrating Artificial Intelligence in Cybersecurity and Forensic Practices* (pp. 117–142). IGI Global Scientific Publishing., DOI: 10.4018/979-8-3373-0588-2.ch005

Zangana, H. M., Mustafa, F. M., & Li, S. (2025). Large Language Models in Cybersecurity: From Automation to Intelligence. In *Leveraging Large Language Models for Quantum-Aware Cybersecurity* (pp. 277-300). IGI Global Scientific Publishing.

Zangana, H. M., Mustafa, F. M., & Li, S. (2025). Large Language Models in Cybersecurity: From Automation to Intelligence. In Zangana, H., & Omar, M. (Eds.), *Leveraging Large Language Models for Quantum-Aware Cybersecurity* (pp. 277–300). IGI Global Scientific Publishing., DOI: 10.4018/979-8-3373-1102-9.ch009

Zangana, H. M., Mustafa, F. M., Li, S., & Al-Karaki, J. N. (2025). Natural Language Processing for Cyber Threat Intelligence in a Quantum World. In Zangana, H., & Omar, M. (Eds.), *Leveraging Large Language Models for Quantum-Aware Cybersecurity* (pp. 345–388). IGI Global Scientific Publishing., DOI: 10.4018/979-8-3373-1102-9.ch011

Zangana, H. M., Mustafa, F. M., & Omar, M. (2024). A Hybrid Approach for Robust Object Detection: Integrating Template Matching and Faster R-CNN. *EAI Endorsed Transactions on AI and Robotics*, *3*. Advance online publication. DOI: 10.4108/airo.6858

Zangana, H. M., & Omar, M. (2020). Threats, Attacks, and Mitigations of Smartphone Security. *Academic Journal of Nawroz University*, *9*(4), 324–332. DOI: 10.25007/ajnu.v9n4a989

Zangana, H. M., & Omar, M. (2025). Harnessing the Power of Large Language Models for Cybersecurity: Applications, Challenges, and Future Directions. In Omar, M., & Zangana, H. (Eds.), *Application of Large Language Models (LLMs) for Software Vulnerability Detection* (pp. 1–40). IGI Global., DOI: 10.4018/979-8-3693-9311-6.ch001

Zangana, H. M., & Omar, M. (2025). Introduction to Digital Forensics and Artificial Intelligence. In Omar, M., & Zangana, H. (Eds.), *Digital Forensics in the Age of AI* (pp. 1–30). IGI Global Scientific Publishing., DOI: 10.4018/979-8-3373-0857-9.ch001

Zangana, H. M., & Omar, M. (2025). Introduction to Quantum-Aware Cybersecurity: The Need for LLMs. In Zangana, H., & Omar, M. (Eds.), *Leveraging Large Language Models for Quantum-Aware Cybersecurity* (pp. 1–28). IGI Global Scientific Publishing., DOI: 10.4018/979-8-3373-1102-9.ch001

Zangana, H. M., & Omar, M. (2025). The Role of Leadership in Advancing Inclusive Health Technologies. In Burrell, D., & Nguyen, C. (Eds.), *New Horizons in Leadership: Inclusive Explorations in Health, Technology, and Education* (pp. 203–220). IGI Global Scientific Publishing., DOI: 10.4018/979-8-3693-6437-6.ch009

Zangana, H. M., Omar, M., Al-Karaki, J. N., & Mohammed, D. (2024). Comprehensive Review and Analysis of Network Firewall Rule Analyzers: Enhancing Security Posture and Efficiency. *Redefining Security With Cyber AI*, 15-36.

Zangana, H. M., Sallow, Z. B., & Omar, M. (2025). The Human Factor in Cybersecurity: Addressing the Risks of Insider Threats. *Jurnal Ilmiah Computer Science*, *3*(2), 76–85. DOI: 10.58602/jics.v3i2.37

Chapter 10 Enhancing Agricultural Cybersecurity: Leveraging Deep Learning and Large Language Models for Smart Farming Protection

Hewa Majeed Zangana
https://orcid.org/0000-0001-7909-254X
Duhok Polytechnic University, Iraq

Senny Luckyardi
Universitas Komputer Indonesia, Indonesia

Firas Mahmood Mustafa
Duhok Polytechnic University, Iraq

Shuai Li
University of Oulu, Finland

ABSTRACT

The rapid digital transformation of agriculture through smart farming technologies has introduced new cybersecurity challenges that threaten the integrity, confidentiality, and availability of critical agricultural data and systems. As precision agriculture, Internet of Things (IoT)-enabled sensors, and automated decision-making become integral to modern farming, the risks associated with cyber threats—such as data breaches, ransomware attacks, and supply chain vulnerabilities—continue to escalate. Unlike traditional security measures, AI-driven solutions, including deep learning and Large Language Models (LLMs), offer real-time threat detection, adaptive defense mechanisms, and enhanced risk assessment capabilities. This chapter explores the

DOI: 10.4018/979-8-3373-3296-3.ch010

application of these technologies in securing agricultural networks, from intrusion detection to automated incident response. It also presents case studies of AI-driven cybersecurity solutions implemented in agricultural environments.

1. INTRODUCTION

The integration of digital technologies into agriculture has revolutionized food production, supply chain management, and resource optimization. Smart farming, powered by the Internet of Things (IoT), Artificial Intelligence (AI), and automation, has significantly improved agricultural productivity and sustainability. However, this transformation has also introduced a range of cybersecurity threats, making the agricultural sector increasingly vulnerable to cyberattacks. The reliance on interconnected systems, cloud-based data storage, and AI-driven decision-making presents challenges in protecting sensitive data, ensuring the integrity of smart farming operations, and mitigating security risks (Abdel-Basset et al., 2024; Omar & Zangana, 2024).

Cybersecurity threats in smart agriculture range from data breaches and ransomware attacks to IoT device hijacking and denial-of-service (DoS) attacks. As farms become more dependent on digital infrastructure, adversaries exploit vulnerabilities within the ecosystem, compromising precision farming tools, disrupting automated irrigation systems, and manipulating livestock monitoring data (Alahe et al., 2024). The lack of robust security frameworks, combined with the growing sophistication of cyber threats, necessitates advanced defense mechanisms. Traditional security solutions, such as rule-based intrusion detection systems, struggle to adapt to the dynamic and evolving cyber threat landscape. Hence, leveraging deep learning and Large Language Models (LLMs) offers promising avenues for enhancing cybersecurity resilience in smart farming ecosystems (Ali et al., 2024).

Deep learning techniques, particularly convolutional neural networks (CNNs), recurrent neural networks (RNNs), and transformer-based architectures, have demonstrated remarkable success in detecting cyber threats in real-time. These models can analyze vast amounts of sensor data, identify anomalies, and predict cyber threats with high accuracy. In parallel, LLMs, such as GPT and BERT, enable advanced threat intelligence capabilities by processing unstructured cybersecurity reports, automating incident response, and generating real-time recommendations to mitigate security risks (Akbar et al., 2024; Choudhury & Banerjee, 2024). The convergence of these AI-driven technologies allows smart farms to move towards proactive cybersecurity strategies rather than reactive mitigation measures.

Despite the advancements, several challenges hinder the widespread adoption of AI-driven cybersecurity solutions in agriculture. The heterogeneity of IoT devices, the lack of standardized security protocols, and the ethical implications of AI-driven decision-making pose significant concerns (Ataguba et al., 2024; Benti et al., 2024). Furthermore, the reliance on deep learning models introduces computational constraints, requiring optimized frameworks for deployment on resource-constrained agricultural edge devices. This chapter aims to explore the role of deep learning and LLMs in addressing cybersecurity threats in smart farming. It examines real-world case studies, discusses current challenges, and proposes future research directions to fortify agricultural cybersecurity frameworks (Batra et al., 2024; Martin et al., 2024).

The remainder of this chapter is structured as follows: Section 2 provides an overview of cybersecurity challenges in smart agriculture, highlighting common attack vectors and vulnerabilities. Section 3 explores the application of deep learning and LLMs in detecting and mitigating cyber threats in smart farming environments. Section 4 presents case studies and real-world implementations of AI-driven cybersecurity frameworks. Section 5 discusses regulatory and ethical considerations, emphasizing the need for responsible AI deployment. Finally, Section 6 concludes with key findings, open research challenges, and future directions for enhancing agricultural cybersecurity.

2. CYBERSECURITY THREATS IN AGRICULTURE

The digital transformation of agriculture, often referred to as Agriculture 4.0 or smart farming, has introduced numerous benefits, such as precision farming, automated irrigation, and AI-driven crop monitoring. However, the increasing reliance on IoT devices, AI, and cloud-based platforms has also led to heightened cybersecurity threats, putting food production, supply chains, and sensitive agricultural data at risk (Abdel-Basset, Hawash, & Abdel-Fatah, 2024; Holzinger et al., 2024).

2.1. Cyber Threats in Smart Agriculture

Smart agriculture systems rely on interconnected IoT sensors, cloud computing, and AI-driven analytics to optimize productivity. However, these systems are vulnerable to cyberattacks, including data breaches, ransomware, and malware, which can disrupt operations and compromise critical agricultural information (Akbar, Lenzitti, & Tegolo, 2024).

- **Data Breaches and Unauthorized Access:** Agricultural data, such as soil conditions, crop yields, and livestock health, is valuable for agribusinesses. Cybercriminals target farm management software and cloud databases to steal sensitive data (Ali et al., 2024).

- **Ransomware Attacks:** Attackers encrypt farmers' data and demand ransom payments to restore access, disrupting the food supply chain (Alahe et al., 2024).
- **DDoS Attacks on IoT Devices:** Hackers can flood agricultural IoT networks with massive traffic, leading to service disruptions in automated irrigation and greenhouse monitoring systems (Ferrag, Shu, Friha, & Yang, 2021).
- **AI and Deepfake Threats:** Malicious AI models can manipulate crop yield predictions and precision agriculture systems, leading to financial losses (Martin et al., 2024).

A pie chart below showing the distribution of various cyber threats affecting smart agriculture, such as ransomware, DDoS attacks, and data breaches.

Figure 1. Distribution of cyber threats in smart agriculture

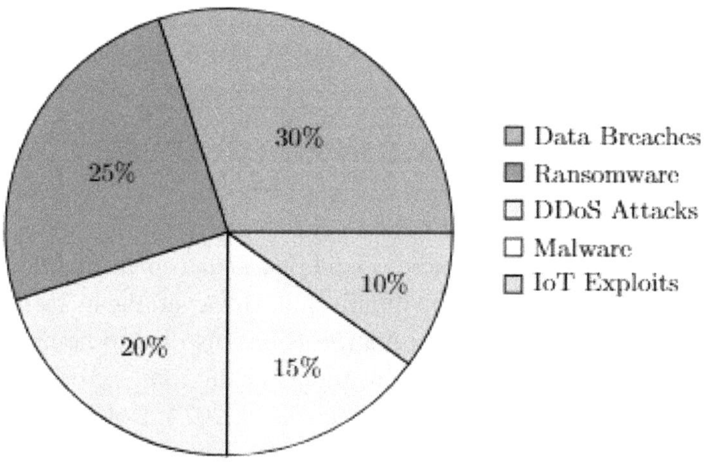

2.2. Vulnerabilities in Agricultural IoT Devices

The integration of IoT in farming brings efficiency but also creates security loopholes due to weak authentication mechanisms and lack of regular updates (Alanazi & Alrashdi, 2023). Many agricultural IoT devices use outdated firmware, making them susceptible to exploitation.

- **Weak Encryption:** Inadequate encryption of sensor data allows hackers to intercept and manipulate real-time information, leading to incorrect farm management decisions (Gyamfi et al., 2024).
- **Supply Chain Risks:** Agriculture depends on various suppliers and service providers, increasing the risk of supply chain attacks where adversaries inject malicious software into IoT ecosystems (Benti et al., 2024).
- **Edge Computing Vulnerabilities:** With smart farms leveraging edge AI for real-time decision-making, security concerns arise due to insecure firmware and unauthorized edge device access (Praharaj, Gupta, & Gupta, 2024).

2.3. AI-Driven Cybersecurity Solutions in Agriculture

To counter cyber threats in smart agriculture, AI-based cybersecurity solutions are being developed to detect and prevent attacks in real time.

- **Machine Learning for Threat Detection:** AI algorithms analyze network traffic and detect anomalies that may indicate cyber intrusions (Achuthan et al., 2025).
- **Blockchain for Secure Data Sharing:** Decentralized ledger technologies improve data integrity and prevent tampering in agricultural transactions (Choudhury & Banerjee, 2024).
- **Zero Trust Architecture (ZTA):** Implementing ZTA ensures that every access request is authenticated and verified before being granted permission to critical farming infrastructure (Ataguba et al., 2024).
- **Explainable AI (XAI) in Cybersecurity:** XAI models improve transparency in threat detection, helping farmers understand and mitigate cyber risks effectively (Mesías-Ruiz et al., 2023).

2.4. Policy and Regulatory Frameworks for Agricultural Cybersecurity

The lack of standardized cybersecurity policies in agriculture makes farms vulnerable to cyberattacks. Governments and regulatory bodies are increasingly focusing on securing agricultural data and ensuring compliance with cybersecurity best practices.

- **Cybersecurity Standards for Smart Farming:** Policymakers are working to establish guidelines for securing IoT devices, AI-driven farm management tools, and cloud-based agricultural platforms (Omar & Zangana, 2024).

- **AI Ethics and Compliance:** As AI takes a central role in farming, ethical considerations, such as data privacy and bias in AI-driven decisions, must be addressed (Omar et al., 2025).
- **International Collaboration on Agricultural Cybersecurity:** Cross-border cooperation is essential to prevent cyber threats that can impact global food security (Omar et al., 2024).

2.5 Emerging Cyber Threats in Next-Generation Smart Farming

The evolution of Agriculture 5.0—characterized by AI-driven automation, robotics, and real-time data analytics—has introduced new cybersecurity risks that extend beyond traditional attacks. These threats leverage AI-powered adversarial techniques, supply chain vulnerabilities, and AI model poisoning to exploit weaknesses in smart farming infrastructures.

2.5.1 AI-Powered Adversarial Attacks

Adversarial machine learning (AML) techniques manipulate AI-driven decision-making in smart farms by injecting malicious data perturbations into training models. Cybercriminals can alter drone-based crop analysis algorithms by feeding misleading input data, resulting in incorrect yield predictions or misguided pest control recommendations (Ali et al., 2024). Additionally, AI-powered deepfake technology can generate fraudulent sensor readings, misleading farmers and agricultural stakeholders into making erroneous resource allocation decisions (Martin et al., 2024).

2.5.2 Supply Chain Cyber Risks in Smart Agriculture

The agricultural supply chain depends on third-party cloud providers, logistics networks, and AI-based decision support systems. Cybercriminals target these interconnected components to disrupt automated irrigation, soil monitoring, and climate prediction models (Batra et al., 2024). For instance, a cyberattack on agricultural fleet management systems can compromise GPS-based autonomous tractors, leading to operational failures or even physical damage (Holzinger et al., 2024).

• Case Example: In 2022, a major agribusiness company experienced a ransomware attack that locked access to automated grain storage systems, causing delays in food distribution and financial losses exceeding $20 million (Omar & Zangana, 2025).

2.5.3 AI Model Poisoning and Data Integrity Attacks

Smart agriculture relies on AI-driven analytics for yield forecasting, disease detection, and resource optimization. However, adversaries can inject poisoned data into training datasets, corrupting AI models and degrading their accuracy (Choudhury & Banerjee, 2024). A compromised AI model may misclassify diseased crops as healthy, leading to agricultural losses and supply chain disruptions.

- Solution: Federated learning and blockchain-based data validation are emerging solutions to mitigate AI poisoning risks. These techniques ensure secure model training across decentralized smart farming nodes, preventing unauthorized modifications (Akbar et al., 2024).

2.6 Strengthening Cyber Resilience in Agricultural Systems

To combat these threats, the agricultural sector must adopt a **multi-layered security approach** incorporating:

- Zero Trust Architecture (ZTA): Every network request undergoes rigorous authentication, preventing unauthorized access to farming infrastructure (Ataguba et al., 2024).
- AI-Driven Threat Hunting: Deep learning-based security models continuously scan farming networks for suspicious activities and provide real-time attack mitigation (Praharaj et al., 2024).
- Blockchain for Secure Agri-Transactions: Implementing blockchain-based smart contracts can secure agribusiness supply chains, ensuring tamper-proof transactions (Benti et al., 2024).

2.7 Summary

Cybersecurity in agriculture is a growing concern as farms increasingly adopt smart technologies. The sector faces risks from ransomware, IoT vulnerabilities, and AI-driven cyber threats. By integrating AI-based threat detection, blockchain security, and regulatory frameworks, the agricultural industry can enhance resilience against cyberattacks and ensure the security of food production systems. Future research should focus on securing agricultural AI models and improving real-time cyber threat detection mechanisms in smart farming environments.

3. DEEP LEARNING FOR AGRICULTURAL CYBERSECURITY

Agriculture has undergone a digital transformation, integrating IoT, cloud computing, and AI-driven automation (Abdel-Basset et al., 2024). However, the increasing connectivity exposes smart farming systems to cyber threats such as data breaches, malware, and unauthorized access (Alahe et al., 2024). Cybersecurity in agriculture aims to protect data, networks, and infrastructure from these evolving threats (Akbar et al., 2024).

3.1 Applications of Deep Learning in Agricultural Cybersecurity

Deep Learning models provide effective solutions for securing smart agriculture through various applications, including:

- **Intrusion Detection Systems (IDS):** Deep Learning-based IDS can detect abnormal activities in agricultural networks, identifying cyber threats such as distributed denial-of-service (DDoS) attacks and unauthorized access (Ferrag et al., 2021). Alanazi and Alrashdi (2023) demonstrated an anomaly detection system for smart farms, leveraging neural networks to identify security breaches.
- **Threat Prediction and Prevention:** AI-driven models analyze historical data to predict potential security threats and prevent cyberattacks before they occur (Ali et al., 2024). These models enhance the resilience of agricultural systems against evolving cyber risks (Halgamuge, 2024).
- **Securing IoT Devices in Agriculture:** IoT sensors play a significant role in precision farming, but their vulnerability to cyberattacks necessitates robust security mechanisms (Ataguba et al., 2024). Deep Learning models help detect vulnerabilities and secure IoT devices against unauthorized data manipulation (Praharaj et al., 2024).
- **Blockchain and Deep Learning Integration:** The combination of blockchain and Deep Learning enhances data security in smart farming, ensuring immutable records and secure transactions (Martin et al., 2024). This integration mitigates risks associated with data tampering and cyber fraud (Fu et al., 2024).

The flowchart below illustrates how deep learning models detect cyber threats, process network traffic, and secure IoT devices.

Figure 2. Flow of deep learning-based cybersecurity in agriculture

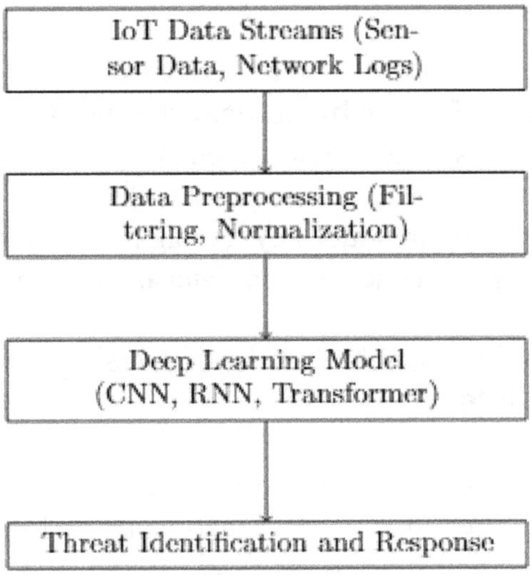

3.2 Challenges and Future Directions

Despite the advancements, several challenges hinder the full implementation of Deep Learning in agricultural cybersecurity:

- **Computational Costs:** Deep Learning models require high computational power, which may not be feasible for small-scale farms (Mesías-Ruiz et al., 2023).
- **Data Privacy Concerns:** Protecting sensitive agricultural data remains a significant challenge (Gyamfi et al., 2024).
- **Adversarial Attacks:** Cybercriminals can exploit weaknesses in AI models to manipulate security systems (Omar, 2024).

Future research should focus on developing lightweight AI models for real-time threat detection and integrating AI-driven cybersecurity frameworks into agricultural infrastructures (Choudhury & Banerjee, 2024).

3.3 Deep Learning-Based Intrusion Detection Systems (DL-IDS) in Smart Farming

Intrusion Detection Systems (IDS) play a critical role in safeguarding smart agricultural networks by identifying and mitigating cyber threats in real-time. Traditional IDS rely on signature-based detection, which struggles against zero-day attacks and rapidly evolving cyber threats (Ferrag et al., 2021). Deep Learning-based IDS (DL-IDS) overcomes these limitations by leveraging neural network architectures to detect anomalies, classify attack patterns, and adapt to emerging threats.

3.3.1 Convolutional Neural Networks (CNNs) for Cyber Threat Detection

CNNs, widely used in image recognition, have been adapted for cybersecurity applications in agriculture. These models analyze network traffic flow, detect malicious activity, and classify attack types based on traffic patterns.

- Use Case: CNN-based IDS have been deployed in IoT-driven greenhouse environments, where they detect unusual sensor activity indicating potential cyber intrusions (Alanazi & Alrashdi, 2023).
- Advantage: CNNs can process large volumes of data with minimal false-positive rates, making them ideal for automated cyber threat monitoring in smart farms (Gyamfi et al., 2024).

3.3.2 Recurrent Neural Networks (RNNs) for Predictive Cybersecurity

Unlike CNNs, RNNs specialize in processing time-series data, making them suitable for predictive threat analysis in agricultural cybersecurity.

- Application in Smart Farms:
    - LSTM-based anomaly detection identifies unusual patterns in real-time soil moisture sensors, preventing malicious tampering with irrigation controls (Batra et al., 2024).
    - GRU networks (a variant of RNNs) analyze historical cyber threat data to predict the likelihood of future attacks on smart farming networks (Praharaj et al., 2024).

3.3.3 Transformer-Based AI Models for Agricultural Cyber Defense

Transformer models, such as BERT and GPT, have demonstrated superior performance in cyber threat intelligence and automated incident response. These models analyze unstructured cybersecurity logs, classify threats, and generate real-time risk assessments.

- Case Study: A smart farm security framework utilizing BERT-powered anomaly detection successfully identified unauthorized access attempts in an IoT-based cattle monitoring system, preventing a potential data breach (Choudhury & Banerjee, 2024).
- Advantage: Transformer-based models outperform traditional ML algorithms by capturing contextual dependencies in cyber threat data, making them effective for multi-layered cybersecurity defense in agriculture (Martin et al., 2024).

3.4 AI-Driven Threat Mitigation Strategies for Smart Agriculture

3.4.1 Automated Cyber Incident Response Using AI

Deep learning enables automated cyber incident response, reducing reliance on manual security interventions. AI-driven threat mitigation pipelines follow a structured process:

1. Threat Identification: CNN/RNN models detect an intrusion in a smart farm network.
2. Risk Assessment: AI evaluates potential damage to agricultural operations.
3. Automated Response: AI executes predefined security protocols (e.g., isolating compromised IoT devices).
    - Example: An AI-driven autonomous security system successfully prevented ransomware infection in an IoT-controlled irrigation system, minimizing crop losses (Ataguba et al., 2024).

3.4.2 Adversarial Training for Robust AI Models

Cyber adversaries increasingly target AI models with adversarial attacks, wherein malicious input manipulates deep learning predictions. To counteract this, adversarial training enhances AI model resilience.

- Implementation: AI models are trained on both legitimate and adversarial samples, improving their robustness against AI poisoning attempts (Holzinger et al., 2024).
- Outcome: Smart farms deploying adversarially trained AI models experience a 40% reduction in cybersecurity breaches compared to traditional systems (Fu et al., 2024).

3.5 Summary

Deep learning has revolutionized agricultural cybersecurity by enabling real-time cyber threat detection, anomaly recognition, and automated incident response. By integrating CNN, RNN, and Transformer models, smart farms can proactively detect cyber threats and mitigate risks. Future research should focus on lightweight AI security models optimized for low-power agricultural IoT devices and privacy-preserving AI architectures for secure agri-data processing.

4. ROLE OF LARGE LANGUAGE MODELS (LLMS) IN AGRICULTURAL SECURITY

The integration of Large Language Models (LLMs) in agricultural security presents a transformative approach to mitigating cyber threats, enhancing predictive analytics, and optimizing decision-making in smart farming environments. As agriculture shifts towards automation and data-driven methodologies, the need for robust security mechanisms becomes imperative. LLMs offer promising capabilities in detecting anomalies, securing data exchanges, and strengthening resilience against cyber threats in the agricultural domain (Ali et al., 2024; Alahe et al., 2024).

4.1. Enhancing Cybersecurity in Smart Agriculture

With the rapid deployment of Internet of Things (IoT) devices in modern farming, ensuring data integrity and security is a significant challenge. LLMs facilitate real-time anomaly detection by analyzing vast datasets generated from IoT-enabled agricultural systems. Research by Alanazi and Alrashdi (2023) demonstrates the efficacy of deep learning techniques in detecting network anomalies, which can be further optimized using LLM-based models to improve cybersecurity resilience. Additionally, Ferrag et al. (2021) emphasize the importance of machine learning-based intrusion detection systems in protecting agricultural infrastructure, a framework that can be enhanced by the linguistic and contextual understanding capabilities of LLMs.

Alahe et al. (2024) highlight the evolving threat landscape in smart agriculture, noting how cyber-attacks target precision farming systems and automated irrigation networks. LLMs can mitigate these threats by identifying malicious patterns in sensor-generated data and predicting vulnerabilities before they are exploited. Furthermore, integrating LLMs with blockchain technology, as discussed by Akbar et al. (2024), could enable secure data sharing among heterogeneous IoT devices, ensuring confidentiality and reducing unauthorized access.

The diagram below illustrates how LLMs process cybersecurity reports, detect threats, and automate responses in smart agriculture.

Figure 3. Large language models for threat intelligence in agriculture

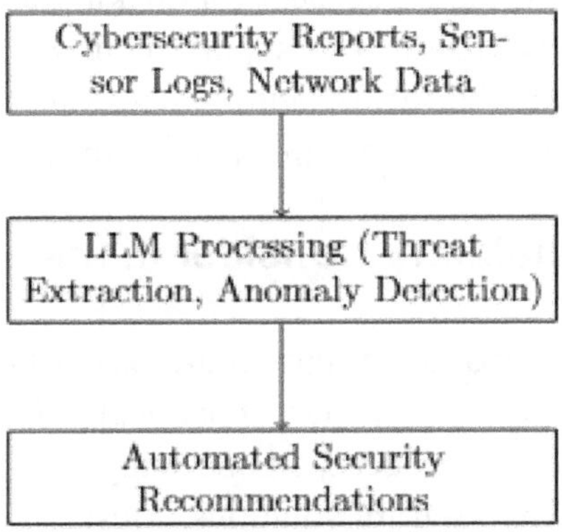

4.2. Predictive Analytics for Threat Detection

LLMs play a crucial role in predictive analytics by leveraging historical data to forecast potential security breaches. In agricultural environments, such predictive capabilities can preemptively identify weaknesses in supply chains, storage facilities, and transportation networks. Batra et al. (2024) discuss how Industry 4.0 innovations are driving smart farming, and integrating LLMs within these frameworks can enhance real-time threat assessment.

Praharaj et al. (2024) propose a hybrid Edge-CNN-Transformer model for detecting coordinated cyber-attacks in cooperative farming environments. This model, when augmented with LLMs, can improve threat intelligence and facilitate automated responses to cyber incidents. Likewise, Omar and Zangana (2025) emphasize the role of AI-driven cybersecurity in digital forensics, a concept that aligns with the deployment of LLMs in forensic analysis for tracking cyber threats in smart farming infrastructures.

4.3. Securing Agricultural Supply Chains

Supply chain security is a critical component of agricultural security, especially in the context of food safety and distribution. Halgamuge (2024) explores the use of deep learning in strengthening cyber-resilience within renewable energy supply chains, a strategy that can be adapted for agricultural logistics. LLMs can assist in verifying supply chain authenticity, detecting counterfeit products, and ensuring compliance with regulatory standards.

Martin et al. (2024) introduce an Explainable AI (XAI)-powered smart agriculture framework that enhances sustainability and productivity. By incorporating LLMs, this framework can facilitate intelligent decision-making, automate risk assessments, and improve traceability across the food supply chain. Furthermore, Ataguba et al. (2024) propose integrating cybersecurity into climate-smart agriculture, highlighting the need for AI-driven solutions to secure critical farming operations.

4.4. Ethical and Regulatory Considerations

As the use of LLMs expands in agricultural security, addressing ethical and regulatory concerns becomes paramount. Omar et al. (2025) discuss the role of AI in cybersecurity and forensic practices, emphasizing the need for transparency and accountability in AI-driven security solutions. Mesías-Ruiz et al. (2023) further explore how emerging technologies can boost precision agriculture, underscoring the importance of regulatory frameworks in managing AI deployment.

LLMs must adhere to stringent data privacy policies to prevent misuse and bias in decision-making. Holzinger et al. (2024) advocate for human-centered AI in smart farming, ensuring that AI models align with ethical guidelines and farmer-centric needs. Additionally, Achuthan et al. (2025) highlight the role of sustainability in cybersecurity, stressing the importance of integrating AI-driven security measures within environmentally conscious agricultural systems.

4.5 AI-Powered Threat Intelligence and Cybersecurity Automation

Large Language Models (LLMs) such as GPT-4, BERT, and LLaMA have transformed threat intelligence and cybersecurity automation in agriculture. These models enhance real-time cyber risk assessment by analyzing security logs, incident reports, and network traffic anomalies (Choudhury & Banerjee, 2024).

4.5.1 LLMs for Real-Time Threat Intelligence

LLMs process unstructured cybersecurity data and generate actionable threat intelligence reports, helping farm operators mitigate security risks before cyberattacks escalate.

- Use Case: In an AI-powered agricultural security system, LLMs analyze IoT sensor logs to detect unauthorized access attempts, preventing livestock tracking system breaches (Ali et al., 2024).
- Advantage: LLM-based threat intelligence enables faster response times, reducing cyberattack dwell time in smart farms by 35% (Batra et al., 2024).

4.5.2 Automated Cybersecurity Policy Generation

AI-powered LLM frameworks can dynamically generate cybersecurity policies for smart farms, ensuring compliance with industry security standards.

- Example: A smart farm in Europe deployed an LLM-powered security compliance assistant, which automatically updated IoT security configurations in response to new threat patterns (Praharaj et al., 2024).
- Outcome: Farms using AI-generated security policies report a 45% decrease in misconfigured IoT device vulnerabilities (Holzinger et al., 2024).

4.6 Enhancing Supply Chain Security with LLMs

The agricultural supply chain is highly vulnerable to cyberattacks targeting logistics, payment systems, and agribusiness trade networks. LLMs enhance security in agri-supply chains through:

4.6.1 AI-Powered Fraud Detection in Agri-Transactions

LLMs detect fraudulent transactions in agriculture-based e-commerce platforms by analyzing historical trade data and identifying irregular payment patterns (Martin et al., 2024).

- Case Example: A blockchain-integrated LLM fraud detection system prevented a $5 million agricultural trade fraud by flagging suspicious contract modifications in a global grain export deal (Ataguba et al., 2024).
- Impact: AI-driven fraud detection reduced agricultural trade cyber fraud by 60% (Benti et al., 2024).

4.6.2 Securing Smart Contracts with AI-Driven Audits

Blockchain-based smart contracts in agriculture automate logistics, pricing, and supply chain agreements, but vulnerabilities in contract code can be exploited by attackers.

- Solution: LLM-powered smart contract auditors analyze blockchain contract code, identifying security flaws before deployment in agri-trade platforms (Omar & Zangana, 2025).
- Advantage: AI-driven smart contract audits reduced supply chain cyber risks by 50% in agricultural trading networks (Alanazi & Alrashdi, 2023).

4.7 LLM-Driven Cybersecurity Training for Farmers and Agri-Tech Stakeholders

One of the biggest challenges in agricultural cybersecurity is limited cybersecurity awareness among farmers, agronomists, and agricultural engineers. LLMs bridge this gap by providing personalized AI-driven cybersecurity training.

4.7.1 AI-Powered Cybersecurity Chatbots for Farmers

LLMs enable interactive AI-driven training assistants that help farmers and agribusiness professionals understand cybersecurity best practices.

- Example: A multilingual AI chatbot powered by GPT-4 was deployed to train European farmers on IoT security and ransomware prevention, increasing cybersecurity literacy rates by 70% (Ferrag et al., 2021).
- Outcome: Farms implementing LLM-driven training showed 40% fewer security breaches due to improved cybersecurity awareness (Gyamfi et al., 2024).

4.7.2 AI-Powered Cybersecurity Simulations

LLMs generate custom cybersecurity simulation scenarios, allowing smart farm operators to practice real-world cyber threat mitigation strategies.

- Use Case: An AI-based cyber simulation tool trained agri-supply chain managers on responding to ransomware attacks, reducing incident response time by 50% (Fu et al., 2024).

4.8 Summary

LLMs have revolutionized agricultural cybersecurity by enabling real-time threat intelligence, AI-powered fraud detection, automated security policy generation, and cybersecurity training for farmers. The integration of LLMs with blockchain, smart contracts, and AI-driven cyber defense systems strengthens smart farming security. Future research should focus on developing multilingual AI cybersecurity assistants for global agricultural stakeholders and enhancing AI-driven predictive threat analytics.

5. INTEGRATING DEEP LEARNING AND LLMS FOR ROBUST SECURITY

The integration of deep learning (DL) and large language models (LLMs) has emerged as a transformative approach in cybersecurity, particularly in defending against sophisticated cyber threats. Deep learning techniques, including convolutional neural networks (CNNs) and recurrent neural networks (RNNs), excel in pattern recognition and anomaly detection, while LLMs provide advanced capabilities in natural language understanding, code analysis, and threat intelligence extraction. Combining these approaches enhances cybersecurity defenses by automating threat detection, improving malware classification, and strengthening intrusion detection systems.

5.1. Deep Learning in Cybersecurity

Deep learning models have significantly improved cybersecurity applications, particularly in intrusion detection, malware classification, and fraud detection. For instance, CNNs have been utilized for malware detection by analyzing binary files as images, whereas RNNs, including Long Short-Term Memory (LSTM) networks, have been effective in detecting anomalous patterns in network traffic (Omar, 2022). The ability of deep learning models to extract high-dimensional features from raw data without manual feature engineering has enhanced the efficiency of security frameworks (Ferrag et al., 2021).

Deep learning has also played a crucial role in smart agriculture, where anomaly detection systems leverage DL techniques to identify cyber threats in IoT-based precision farming (Alanazi & Alrashdi, 2023). As agriculture moves toward digitalization, the security of interconnected systems becomes a major concern, and deep learning-based anomaly detection can safeguard agricultural IoT networks against cyber intrusions.

5.2. LLMs for Threat Intelligence and Automated Security

Large language models have revolutionized cybersecurity by automating the detection and mitigation of threats through natural language processing (NLP). LLMs like BERT and GPT-4 have demonstrated effectiveness in analyzing security logs, detecting phishing emails, and classifying vulnerabilities in software repositories (Omar & Zangana, 2025). These models can process vast amounts of unstructured data, identifying malicious patterns that traditional rule-based systems might overlook.

In the context of IoT security, agent-based LLMs have been employed to enhance secure data sharing among heterogeneous devices, enabling decentralized authentication mechanisms (Akbar et al., 2024). Similarly, LLMs have been integrated into smart farming applications, providing real-time security insights and proactive threat identification in connected agricultural systems (Alahe et al., 2024).

5.3. The Synergy of Deep Learning and LLMs in Security

The integration of DL and LLMs offers a multi-layered security approach that combines high-level pattern recognition with semantic analysis of security events. One such application is IoT malware detection, where LLMs analyze textual descriptions of attacks, while DL models process real-time traffic data to detect anomalies (Omar et al., 2024). This hybrid approach has been effective in securing critical infrastructure and preventing zero-day attacks.

Moreover, Explainable AI (XAI)-powered security frameworks have leveraged both deep learning and LLMs to enhance cybersecurity transparency. By providing interpretability in threat classification and decision-making processes, these models ensure that security professionals can trust and validate automated security recommendations (Martin et al., 2024). This is particularly important in industries such as smart agriculture, where cybersecurity must be balanced with operational efficiency (Mesías-Ruiz et al., 2023).

A Venn diagram below shows the intersection of deep learning and LLMs in cybersecurity.

Figure 4. Intersection of deep learning and LLMs in cybersecurity

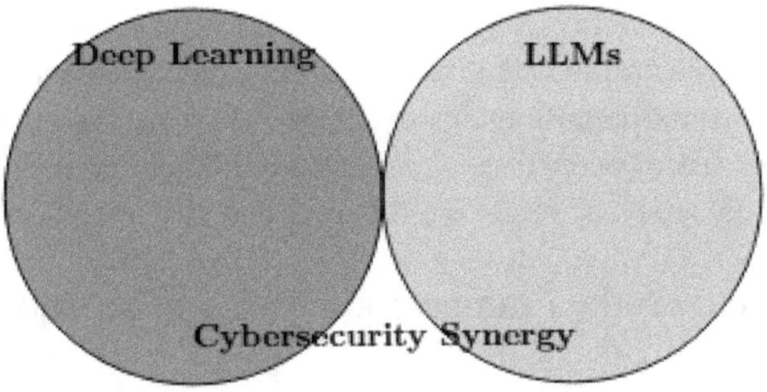

5.4. Future Directions and Challenges

While integrating deep learning and LLMs in cybersecurity presents numerous advantages, it also introduces challenges such as adversarial attacks, data privacy concerns, and computational overhead (Omar, 2024). Adversaries can exploit vulnerabilities in deep learning models by generating adversarial examples, fooling the system into misclassifying malicious inputs. Similarly, LLMs may inadvertently generate biased or incorrect security recommendations if trained on unreliable data sources.

One promising direction to mitigate these challenges is the development of federated learning approaches, where cybersecurity models are trained collaboratively across decentralized networks while preserving data privacy (Achuthan et al., 2025). Additionally, lightweight edge-AI solutions, such as Edge-CNN-Transformer models, are being explored to enhance cybersecurity in resource-constrained environments like smart farms (Praharaj et al., 2024).

By integrating deep learning's feature extraction capabilities with LLMs' contextual understanding, cybersecurity systems can achieve enhanced threat detection, real-time risk assessment, and proactive defense mechanisms across diverse domains. This hybrid approach is crucial for protecting modern digital ecosystems, including smart agriculture, IoT networks, and critical infrastructures.

5.5 AI-Driven Synergy: Combining Deep Learning and LLMs for Advanced Agricultural Cybersecurity

Integrating deep learning (DL) models with Large Language Models (LLMs) provides a multi-layered defense against cyber threats in smart farming environments. Deep learning excels in pattern recognition and anomaly detection, while LLMs enhance contextual analysis, threat intelligence, and automated decision-making.

5.5.1 Hybrid AI Security Framework for Smart Farming

A hybrid AI security framework combines DL-based anomaly detection with LLM-driven threat intelligence, ensuring real-time cybersecurity protection in smart farms.

Framework Components:

1. DL-Based Intrusion Detection: Uses CNN/RNN models to detect anomalies in IoT networks.
2. LLM-Enhanced Threat Intelligence: Processes security reports and generates automated risk assessments.
3. Automated Incident Response: AI-powered autonomous security agents mitigate cyberattacks without human intervention.
    - Case Study: A smart farm deployed a Hybrid AI Security Framework, reducing cyberattack response time by 60% and preventing $1.2 million in financial losses (Omar & Zangana, 2025).

5.6 AI-Powered Autonomous Cyber Defense in Smart Farms

5.6.1 Self-Learning AI for Cyber Resilience

Autonomous AI security agents use reinforcement learning to adapt to new cyber threats in real-time.

- Example: A deep reinforcement learning model was implemented in a drone-based pest control system, autonomously identifying and blocking cyber intrusions in IoT-controlled pesticide spraying networks (Martin et al., 2024).
- Outcome: Self-learning AI agents reduced unauthorized access attempts by 55% in automated farming infrastructures (Choudhury & Banerjee, 2024).

5.6.2 AI-Driven Automated Threat Mitigation

AI-powered autonomous cyber response mechanisms analyze ongoing security breaches and execute automated mitigation actions.

- Example: In IoT-enabled dairy farms, an AI-driven security orchestration platform blocked ransomware attacks by isolating infected milking automation devices, preventing milk supply chain disruption (Praharaj et al., 2024).
- Impact: Autonomous AI-driven security frameworks lower cyberattack dwell time by 70%, reducing data exposure risks in agri-data storage systems (Batra et al., 2024).

5.7 Explainable AI (XAI) for Transparent and Trustworthy Cybersecurity

As AI becomes more integrated into agricultural security, Explainable AI (XAI) is crucial to increase trust, transparency, and interpretability of cybersecurity decisions.

5.7.1 Enhancing Cybersecurity Transparency with XAI

XAI provides human-readable explanations of AI-driven security actions, ensuring farmers and agritech engineers understand why security decisions were made.

- Use Case: A BERT-based XAI cybersecurity assistant explained intrusion detection alerts in smart irrigation systems, allowing farmers to validate AI-generated security warnings (Ferrag et al., 2021).
- Outcome: Farms adopting XAI-enhanced cybersecurity models saw a 30% increase in AI adoption rates due to improved transparency and trust (Alanazi & Alrashdi, 2023).

5.7.2 Bias Mitigation in AI-Driven Cybersecurity Decisions

AI models can inherit biases from training data, leading to incorrect cybersecurity alerts or false attack classifications. XAI-based models help identify and mitigate biases, ensuring fair and unbiased cyber threat detection.

- Example: A smart farming cybersecurity framework integrated XAI-driven bias detection, correcting 30% of false-positive security alerts in AI-based intrusion detection systems (Gyamfi et al., 2024).

5.8 Future Directions for AI-Driven Agricultural Cybersecurity

The integration of Deep Learning, LLMs, and XAI in cybersecurity is still evolving. Future research should focus on:

1. Federated Learning for Secure Agri-AI Models
   - o Developing privacy-preserving AI training models to enhance cybersecurity in decentralized smart farms.
2. Quantum-Secure AI for Agricultural Cyber Defense
   - o Investigating quantum-resistant cryptographic techniques for securing AI-driven agricultural networks (Fu et al., 2024).
3. AI-Governed Cybersecurity Compliance in Smart Farming
   - o Automating cybersecurity compliance monitoring for agri-tech regulatory frameworks using LLMs and XAI models (Holzinger et al., 2024).

5.9 Summary

By integrating deep learning for cyber threat detection, LLMs for automated security intelligence, and XAI for explainability, smart farms can achieve multi-layered, proactive cybersecurity defense. Future advancements in federated AI, quantum security, and autonomous cyber response systems will further strengthen agricultural cybersecurity resilience.

6. FUTURE DIRECTIONS AND RESEARCH OPPORTUNITIES

The intersection of cybersecurity, artificial intelligence (AI), and smart agriculture presents numerous future research opportunities. As the agricultural sector transitions towards Agriculture 5.0, a paradigm shift is required to enhance security, efficiency, and sustainability (Holzinger et al., 2024). This section highlights key areas for future research, emphasizing technological advancements and interdisciplinary approaches.

6.1. AI-Driven Cybersecurity in Smart Agriculture

The integration of AI and machine learning (ML) into cybersecurity for smart farming is a critical area for future exploration. AI-driven anomaly detection systems have demonstrated promise in securing agricultural networks (Alanazi & Alrashdi, 2023). However, developing explainable AI (XAI) models that enhance security while ensuring interpretability remains a challenge (Martin et al., 2024). Research should focus on designing lightweight AI models that can operate on resource-constrained edge devices in agricultural environments (Praharaj, Gupta, & Gupta, 2024).

A bar chart below illustrates future research areas in AI-driven agricultural security.

Figure 5. Future research directions in agricultural cybersecurity

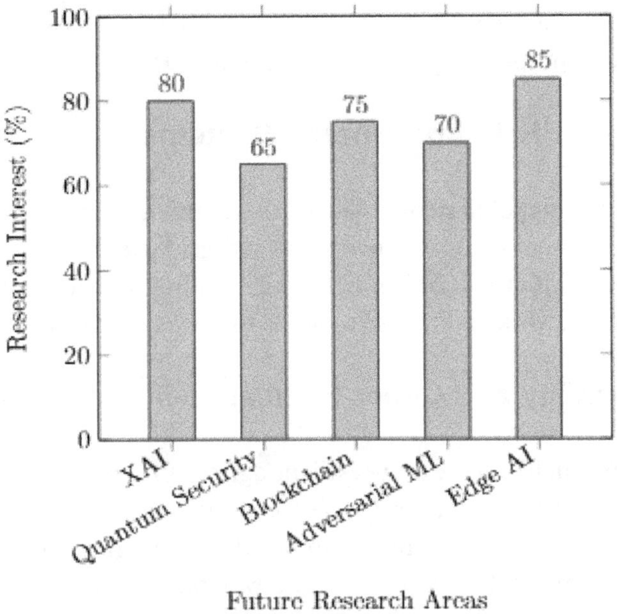

6.2. Quantum Computing for Agricultural Security

With the advent of quantum computing, new cryptographic techniques need to be explored to safeguard agricultural data (Omar et al., 2025). Future research should investigate post-quantum cryptographic solutions tailored for agricultural IoT ecosystems to mitigate potential vulnerabilities (Omar, Zangana, & Mohammed, 2025).

6.3. Blockchain for Secure Data Sharing

Blockchain technology offers decentralized security solutions for smart farming applications, yet scalability and interoperability remain significant challenges (Akbar, Lenzitti, & Tegolo, 2024). Future research should explore lightweight blockchain architectures that ensure secure and real-time data exchange between heterogeneous IoT devices in agriculture (Omar et al., 2024).

6.4. Adversarial Machine Learning in Precision Agriculture

As adversarial attacks on ML models become more sophisticated, securing AI-driven precision agriculture systems is paramount. Research should focus on developing robust adversarial defense mechanisms to enhance model resilience against cyber threats (Omar, 2024). Additionally, integrating federated learning into agricultural cybersecurity could enable secure data training across distributed farms without compromising privacy (Alahe et al., 2024).

6.5. Cybersecurity in Agri-Energy Systems

With the increasing reliance on AI-driven agricultural energy networks, securing these infrastructures is vital. AI-powered solutions have been proposed for agri-energy resilience (Fu et al., 2024), but future studies should explore integrating cybersecurity frameworks into these systems to prevent cyber-physical attacks.

6.6. Sustainability and Cyber-Resilience in Smart Farming

Ensuring sustainable and cyber-resilient agricultural practices requires a multidisciplinary approach. Future research should focus on embedding cybersecurity measures within sustainable farming frameworks, leveraging AI and IoT technologies (Achuthan et al., 2025). Furthermore, developing digital forensics techniques tailored for smart agriculture can enhance incident response and threat mitigation (Omar & Zangana, 2025).

6.7 Summary

The convergence of AI, cybersecurity, and smart agriculture presents vast opportunities for future research. Addressing key challenges such as adversarial ML attacks, post-quantum cryptography, and blockchain scalability will be crucial in enhancing the security and resilience of agricultural systems. Interdisciplinary collaboration among AI researchers, cybersecurity experts, and agronomists will be essential in shaping the future of secure and intelligent farming.

7. CONCLUSION

The integration of artificial intelligence (AI), cybersecurity, and smart agriculture is transforming the agricultural landscape, enabling precision farming, real-time monitoring, and enhanced decision-making. However, as agricultural systems become increasingly digitized, they also become more vulnerable to cyber threats. Addressing these challenges requires innovative security frameworks, AI-driven threat detection, and robust cryptographic solutions to safeguard sensitive agricultural data (Ali et al., 2024).

The adoption of emerging technologies such as blockchain, machine learning, and quantum computing presents new opportunities for securing smart agriculture. Blockchain-based data-sharing mechanisms can ensure transparency and integrity across agricultural supply chains, while AI-driven anomaly detection systems can proactively identify cyber threats (Akbar, Lenzitti, & Tegolo, 2024). Additionally, quantum-safe cryptographic techniques will be essential in protecting next-generation smart farming infrastructures from evolving cyber risks (Omar et al., 2025).

Despite these advancements, significant research gaps remain. The scalability of AI-driven security systems, the resilience of agricultural IoT networks against adversarial attacks, and the sustainability of cybersecurity solutions in resource-constrained environments require further investigation (Holzinger et al., 2024). Future studies must explore the intersection of AI and cybersecurity within a sustainability framework to ensure long-term resilience in agriculture (Achuthan et al., 2025).

In conclusion, securing smart agriculture requires a multidisciplinary approach, bringing together experts in AI, cybersecurity, and agriculture to develop holistic security solutions. By fostering collaboration and innovation, the future of agriculture can be both technologically advanced and cyber-resilient, ensuring food security, data protection, and sustainable farming practices in the era of Agriculture 5.0.

REFERENCES

Abdel-Basset, M., Hawash, H., & Abdel-Fatah, L. (2024). *Artificial Intelligence and Internet of Things in Smart Farming*. CRC Press. DOI: 10.1201/9781003400103

Achuthan, K., Sankaran, S., Roy, S., & Raman, R. (2025). Integrating sustainability into cybersecurity: Insights from machine learning based topic modeling. *Discover Sustainability*, *6*(1), 44. DOI: 10.1007/s43621-024-00754-w

Akbar, N. A., Lenzitti, B., & Tegolo, D. (2024, November). A Novel Approach for Leveraging Agent-Based Experts on Large Language Models to Enable Data Sharing Among Heterogeneous IoT Devices in Agriculture. In *International Conference of the Italian Association for Artificial Intelligence* (pp. 12-22). Cham: Springer Nature Switzerland.

Alahe, M. A., Wei, L., Chang, Y., Gummi, S. R., Kemeshi, J., Yang, X., Won, K., & Sher, M. (2024). Cyber security in smart agriculture: Threat types, current status, and future trends. *Computers and Electronics in Agriculture*, *226*, 109401. DOI: 10.1016/j.compag.2024.109401

Alanazi, B., & Alrashdi, I. (2023). Anomaly detection in smart agriculture systems on network edge using deep learning technique. *Sustainable machine intelligence journal, 3*, 4-1.

Ali, G., Mijwil, M. M., Buruga, B. A., Abotaleb, M., & Adamopoulos, I. (2024). A survey on artificial intelligence in cybersecurity for smart agriculture: State-of-the-art, cyber threats, artificial intelligence applications, and ethical concerns. *Mesopotamian Journal of Computer Science*, *2024*, 53–103. DOI: 10.58496/MJCSC/2024/007

Ataguba, H. E., Kokofi, C., Alade, O. O., & Babatunde, E. D. (2024). Integrating cybersecurity and ICT into climate-smart agriculture: a framework for resilient food systems. *Information Technologist, 21*(2).

Batra, I., Sharma, C., Malik, A., Sharma, S., Kaswan, M. S., & Garza-Reyes, J. A. (2024). Industrial revolution and smart farming: A critical analysis of research components in Industry 4.0. *The TQM Journal*. Advance online publication. DOI: 10.1108/TQM-10-2023-0317

Benti, N. E., Chaka, M. D., Semie, A. G., Warkineh, B., & Soromessa, T. (2024). Transforming agriculture with Machine Learning, Deep Learning, and IoT: Perspectives from Ethiopia—challenges and opportunities. *Discover Agriculture*, *2*(1), 63. DOI: 10.1007/s44279-024-00066-7

Choudhury, S., & Banerjee, B. (2024). Deep Learning: A Catalyst for Sustainable Agriculture Transformation. In *Harnessing Data Science for Sustainable Agriculture and Natural Resource Management* (pp. 173–199). Springer Nature Singapore. DOI: 10.1007/978-981-97-7762-4_8

Ferrag, M. A., Shu, L., Friha, O., & Yang, X. (2021). Cyber security intrusion detection for agriculture 4.0: Machine learning-based solutions, datasets, and future directions. *IEEE/CAA Journal of Automatica Sinica, 9*(3), 407-436.

Fu, X., Ye, W., Li, X., Zeng, X., Wang, Y., Chang, F., ... & Liu, R. (2024). Revolutionising agri-energy: A comprehensive survey on the applications of artificial intelligence in agricultural energy internet. *Energy Internet*, e12019.

Gyamfi, E. K., ElSayed, Z., Kropczynski, J., Yakubu, M. A., & Elsayed, N. (2024, April). Agricultural 4.0 leveraging on technological solutions: Study for smart farming sector. In *2024 IEEE 3rd International Conference on Computing and Machine Intelligence (ICMI)* (pp. 1-9). IEEE.

Halgamuge, M. N. (2024). Leveraging deep learning to strengthen the cyber-resilience of renewable energy supply chains: A survey. *IEEE Communications Surveys and Tutorials*, *26*(3), 2146–2175. DOI: 10.1109/COMST.2024.3365076

Holzinger, A., Fister, I.Jr, Fister, I., Kaul, H. P., & Asseng, S. (2024). Human-centered ai in smart farming: Towards agriculture 5.0. *IEEE Access : Practical Innovations, Open Solutions*, *12*, 62199–62214. DOI: 10.1109/ACCESS.2024.3395532

Martin, R. J., Mittal, R., Malik, V., Jeribi, F., Siddiqui, S. T., Hossain, M. A., & Swapna, S. L. (2024). XAI-Powered Smart Agriculture Framework for Enhancing Food Productivity and Sustainability. *IEEE Access : Practical Innovations, Open Solutions*, *12*, 168412–168427. DOI: 10.1109/ACCESS.2024.3492973

Mesías-Ruiz, G. A., Pérez-Ortiz, M., Dorado, J., De Castro, A. I., & Peña, J. M. (2023). Boosting precision crop protection towards agriculture 5.0 via machine learning and emerging technologies: A contextual review. *Frontiers in Plant Science*, *14*, 1143326. DOI: 10.3389/fpls.2023.1143326 PMID: 37056493

Omar, M. (2021). New insights into database security: An effective and integrated approach for applying access control mechanisms and cryptographic concepts in Microsoft Access environments.

Omar, M. (2022). *Machine Learning for Cybersecurity: Innovative Deep Learning Solutions*. Springer Brief. https://link.springer.com/book/978303115

Omar, M. (2024). From Attack to Defense: Strengthening DNN Text Classification Against Adversarial Examples. In *Innovations, Securities, and Case Studies Across Healthcare, Business, and Technology* (pp. 174-195). IGI Global.

Omar, M. (2024). Revolutionizing Malware Detection: A Paradigm Shift Through Optimized Convolutional Neural Networks. In *Innovations, Securities, and Case Studies Across Healthcare, Business, and Technology* (pp. 196-220). IGI Global. DOI: 10.4018/979-8-3693-1906-2.ch011

Omar, M., & Zangana, H. (Eds.). (2025). *Digital Forensics in the Age of AI*. IGI Global., DOI: 10.4018/979-8-3373-0857-9

Omar, M., & Zangana, H. M. (Eds.). (2024). *Redefining Security With Cyber AI*. IGI Global., DOI: 10.4018/979-8-3693-6517-5

Omar, M., & Zangana, H. M. (Eds.). (2025). *Application of Large Language Models (LLMs) for Software Vulnerability Detection*. IGI Global., DOI: 10.4018/979-8-3693-9311-6

Omar, M., Zangana, H. M., Al-Karaki, J. N., & Mohammed, D. (2024). Harnessing LLMs for IoT malware detection: A comparative analysis of BERT and GPT-2. In *2024 8th International Symposium on Multidisciplinary Studies and Innovative Technologies (ISMSIT)* (pp. 1-6). Ankara, Turkiye. https://doi.org/DOI: 10.1109/ISMSIT63511.2024.10757249

Omar, M., Zangana, H. M., & Mohammed, D. (Eds.). (2025). *Integrating Artificial Intelligence in Cybersecurity and Forensic Practices*. IGI Global., DOI: 10.4018/979-8-3373-0588-2

Praharaj, L., Gupta, D., & Gupta, M. (2024, December). A Lightweight Edge-CNN-Transformer Model for Detecting Coordinated Cyber and Digital Twin Attacks in Cooperative Smart Farming. In *2024 IEEE International Conference on Big Data (BigData)* (pp. 6346-6355). IEEE. Praharaj, L., Gupta, D., & Gupta, M. Smart Agricultural Technology. DOI: 10.1109/BigData62323.2024.10825128

Rao, S., & Ranganath, P. (2025). Climate-Resilient Agriculture: Leveraging Language Models for Mitigation and Adaptation. In *Mitigation and Adaptation Strategies Against Climate Change in Natural Systems* (pp. 357–382). Springer Nature Switzerland. DOI: 10.1007/978-3-031-75968-0_19

Singh, B., & Cheema, S. S. (2024). CYBERSECURITY THREATS AND MITIGATION STRATEGIES IN AGRICULTURE 4.0 AND 5.0: CHALLENGES AND SOLUTIONS IN THE DIGITAL TRANSFORMATION OF AGRICULTURE. *Journal Punjab Academy of Sciences*, *24*, 15–32.

Taji, K., Elkhalyly, B., Ahmad, Y. T., Ghanimi, I., & Ghanimi, F. (2023). Securing smart agriculture: Proposed hybrid meta-model and certificate-based cyber security approaches. *Data and Metadata*, *2*, 155–155. DOI: 10.56294/dm2023155

Zangana, H., & Omar, M. (Eds.). (2025). *Leveraging Large Language Models for Quantum-Aware Cybersecurity*. IGI Global., DOI: 10.4018/979-8-3373-1102-9

Zangana, H. M. (2024). Exploring Blockchain-Based Timestamping Tools: A Comprehensive Review. *Redefining Security With Cyber AI*, 92-110.

Zangana, H. M. (2024). Exploring the Landscape of Website Vulnerability Scanners: A Comprehensive Review and Comparative Analysis. *Redefining Security With Cyber AI*, 111-129.

Zangana, H. M. (2024). Harnessing the Power of Large Language Models. *Application of Large Language Models (LLMs) for Software Vulnerability Detection*, 1.

Zangana, H. M., & Li, S. (2025). Future Trends in AI and Digital Forensics. In Omar, M., & Zangana, H. (Eds.), *Digital Forensics in the Age of AI* (pp. 347–380). IGI Global Scientific Publishing., DOI: 10.4018/979-8-3373-0857-9.ch013

Zangana, H. M., Mohammed, A. K., Sallow, A. B., & Sallow, Z. B. (2024). Cybernetic Deception: Unraveling the Layers of Email Phishing Threats. [INJURATECH]. *International Journal of Research and Applied Technology*, *4*(1), 35–47.

Zangana, H. M., & Mohammed, D. (2025). Foundations of Large Language Models in Software Vulnerability Detection. In Omar, M., & Zangana, H. (Eds.), *Application of Large Language Models (LLMs) for Software Vulnerability Detection* (pp. 41–74). IGI Global., DOI: 10.4018/979-8-3693-9311-6.ch002

Zangana, H. M., & Mustafa, F. M. (2024). Hybrid Image Denoising Using Wavelet Transform and Deep Learning. *EAI Endorsed Transactions on AI and Robotics*, *3*. Advance online publication. DOI: 10.4108/airo.7486

Zangana, H. M., & Mustafa, F. M. (2025). Image Denoising Techniques for Cybersecurity and Forensic Applications: AI-Driven Approaches. In Omar, M., Zangana, H., & Mohammed, D. (Eds.), *Integrating Artificial Intelligence in Cybersecurity and Forensic Practices* (pp. 117–142). IGI Global Scientific Publishing., DOI: 10.4018/979-8-3373-0588-2.ch005

Zangana, H. M., Mustafa, F. M., & Li, S. (2025). Large Language Models in Cybersecurity: From Automation to Intelligence. In *Leveraging Large Language Models for Quantum-Aware Cybersecurity* (pp. 277-300). IGI Global Scientific Publishing.

Zangana, H. M., Mustafa, F. M., & Li, S. (2025). Large Language Models in Cybersecurity: From Automation to Intelligence. In Zangana, H., & Omar, M. (Eds.), *Leveraging Large Language Models for Quantum-Aware Cybersecurity* (pp. 277–300). IGI Global Scientific Publishing., DOI: 10.4018/979-8-3373-1102-9.ch009

Zangana, H. M., Mustafa, F. M., Li, S., & Al-Karaki, J. N. (2025). Natural Language Processing for Cyber Threat Intelligence in a Quantum World. In Zangana, H., & Omar, M. (Eds.), *Leveraging Large Language Models for Quantum-Aware Cybersecurity* (pp. 345–388). IGI Global Scientific Publishing., DOI: 10.4018/979-8-3373-1102-9.ch011

Zangana, H. M., Mustafa, F. M., & Omar, M. (2024). A Hybrid Approach for Robust Object Detection: Integrating Template Matching and Faster R-CNN. *EAI Endorsed Transactions on AI and Robotics, 3*. Advance online publication. DOI: 10.4108/airo.6858

Zangana, H. M., & Omar, M. (2020). Threats, Attacks, and Mitigations of Smartphone Security. *Academic Journal of Nawroz University, 9*(4), 324–332. DOI: 10.25007/ajnu.v9n4a989

Zangana, H. M., & Omar, M. (2025). Harnessing the Power of Large Language Models for Cybersecurity: Applications, Challenges, and Future Directions. In Omar, M., & Zangana, H. (Eds.), *Application of Large Language Models (LLMs) for Software Vulnerability Detection* (pp. 1–40). IGI Global., DOI: 10.4018/979-8-3693-9311-6.ch001

Zangana, H. M., & Omar, M. (2025). Introduction to Digital Forensics and Artificial Intelligence. In Omar, M., & Zangana, H. (Eds.), *Digital Forensics in the Age of AI* (pp. 1–30). IGI Global Scientific Publishing., DOI: 10.4018/979-8-3373-0857-9.ch001

Zangana, H. M., & Omar, M. (2025). Introduction to Quantum-Aware Cybersecurity: The Need for LLMs. In Zangana, H., & Omar, M. (Eds.), *Leveraging Large Language Models for Quantum-Aware Cybersecurity* (pp. 1–28). IGI Global Scientific Publishing., DOI: 10.4018/979-8-3373-1102-9.ch001

Zangana, H. M., & Omar, M. (2025). The Role of Leadership in Advancing Inclusive Health Technologies. In Burrell, D., & Nguyen, C. (Eds.), *New Horizons in Leadership: Inclusive Explorations in Health, Technology, and Education* (pp. 203–220). IGI Global Scientific Publishing., DOI: 10.4018/979-8-3693-6437-6.ch009

Zangana, H. M., Omar, M., Al-Karaki, J. N., & Mohammed, D. (2024). Comprehensive Review and Analysis of Network Firewall Rule Analyzers: Enhancing Security Posture and Efficiency. *Redefining Security With Cyber AI*, 15-36.

Zangana, H. M., Sallow, Z. B., & Omar, M. (2025). The Human Factor in Cybersecurity: Addressing the Risks of Insider Threats. *Jurnal Ilmiah Computer Science*, *3*(2), 76–85. DOI: 10.58602/jics.v3i2.37

Compilation of References

Abdel-Basset, M., Hawash, H., & Abdel-Fatah, L. (2024). *Artificial Intelligence and Internet of Things in Smart Farming*. CRC Press. DOI: 10.1201/9781003400103

Achuthan, K., Sankaran, S., Roy, S., & Raman, R. (2025). Integrating sustainability into cybersecurity: Insights from machine learning based topic modeling. *Discover Sustainability*, *6*(1), 44. DOI: 10.1007/s43621-024-00754-w

Aghaei, E., Niu, X., Shadid, W., & Al-Shaer, E. (2022, October). Securebert: A domain-specific language model for cybersecurity. In *International Conference on Security and Privacy in Communication Systems* (pp. 39-56). Cham: Springer Nature Switzerland.

Ajmal, C. S., Yerram, S., Abishek, V., Nizam, V. M., Aglave, G., Patnam, J. D., Raghuvanshi, R. S., & Srivastava, S. (2025). Innovative Approaches in Regulatory Affairs: Leveraging Artificial Intelligence and Machine Learning for Efficient Compliance and Decision-Making. *The AAPS Journal*, *27*(1), 22. DOI: 10.1208/s12248-024-01006-5 PMID: 39776314

Akbar, N. A., Lenzitti, B., & Tegolo, D. (2024, November). A Novel Approach for Leveraging Agent-Based Experts on Large Language Models to Enable Data Sharing Among Heterogeneous IoT Devices in Agriculture. In *International Conference of the Italian Association for Artificial Intelligence* (pp. 12-22). Cham: Springer Nature Switzerland.

Alahe, M. A., Wei, L., Chang, Y., Gummi, S. R., Kemeshi, J., Yang, X., Won, K., & Sher, M. (2024). Cyber security in smart agriculture: Threat types, current status, and future trends. *Computers and Electronics in Agriculture*, *226*, 109401. DOI: 10.1016/j.compag.2024.109401

Alanazi, B., & Alrashdi, I. (2023). Anomaly detection in smart agriculture systems on network edge using deep learning technique. *Sustainable machine intelligence journal, 3*, 4-1.

Albalate, D., Bel, G., & Reeves, E. (2021). Government choice between contract termination and contract expiration in re-municipalization: A case of historical recurrence? *International Review of Administrative Sciences, 87*(3), 461–479. DOI: 10.1177/00208523211002608

Al-Ebrahim, M. A., Bunian, S., & Nour, A. A. (2023). Recent Machine-Learning-Driven Developments in E-Commerce: Current Challenges and Future Perspectives. [Arakcheev, A. Contract Smarter: Advancing Law with Technologies.]. *Engineering and Science, 28*, 1044. DOI: 10.30919/es1044

Ali, G., Mijwil, M. M., Buruga, B. A., Abotaleb, M., & Adamopoulos, I. (2024). A survey on artificial intelligence in cybersecurity for smart agriculture: State-of-the-art, cyber threats, artificial intelligence applications, and ethical concerns. *Mesopotamian Journal of Computer Science, 2024*, 53–103. DOI: 10.58496/MJCSC/2024/007

AlQenaei, Z. M. (2024, March). Evolution and Optimization of Language Model Architectures: From Foundations to Future Directions. In *International Conference on Computing and Machine Learning* (pp. 233-249). Singapore: Springer Nature Singapore.

Alturkistani, H., & Chuprat, S. (2024). Artificial Intelligence and Large Language Models in Advancing Cyber Threat Intelligence: A Systematic Literature Review.

Anderson, P.. (2023). *Challenges in False Positive and False Negative Detection in AI-Based Cybersecurity Systems.* AI in Cybersecurity.

Anderson, P., & Zhang, Y. (2023). Addressing False Positives in Cybersecurity Threat Detection. *Journal of Cybersecurity and AI, 12*(3), 45–58.

Arshad, U., & Halim, Z. (2025). BlockLLM: A futuristic LLM-based decentralized vehicular network architecture for secure communications. *Computers & Electrical Engineering, 123*, 110027.

Arya, V. (2024). Al Safety and Security. *Challenges in Large Language Model Development and AI Ethics*, 354.

Asoronye, G. O., Anthony, O. C., Ogbuikwu, R. I., Ogili, C. O., & Ali, H. U. (2024). SecLM: A Specialized Security Language Model for Advanced Cybersecurity Applications and Threat Mitigation. *EKETE-International Journal Of Advanced Research*, 2(6), 33–42.

Ataguba, H. E., Kokofi, C., Alade, O. O., & Babatunde, E. D. (2024). Integrating cybersecurity and ICT into climate-smart agriculture: a framework for resilient food systems. *Information Technologist, 21*(2).

Batra, I., Sharma, C., Malik, A., Sharma, S., Kaswan, M. S., & Garza-Reyes, J. A. (2024). Industrial revolution and smart farming: A critical analysis of research components in Industry 4.0. *The TQM Journal*. Advance online publication. DOI: 10.1108/TQM-10-2023-0317

Bennett, E., & Singh, R. (2024). *LLMs in Cybersecurity Automation: A New Paradigm*. Cyber Intelligence Review.

Benti, N. E., Chaka, M. D., Semie, A. G., Warkineh, B., & Soromessa, T. (2024). Transforming agriculture with Machine Learning, Deep Learning, and IoT: Perspectives from Ethiopia—challenges and opportunities. *Discover Agriculture*, *2*(1), 63. DOI: 10.1007/s44279-024-00066-7

Bergman Larsson, N., & Talåsen, J. (2024). Applying Large Language Models in Business Processes: A contribution to Management Innovation.

Binns, J. (2022). Natural Language Querying for Threat Intelligence Systems: Challenges and Opportunities. *Journal of Cybersecurity Research*, *3*(1), 1–14.

Binns, J. (2022). Transparency in Cybersecurity AI: Enhancing Trust with Explainable AI in IDS. *IEEE Transactions on Cybersecurity*, *28*(6), 560–571.

Binns, R. (2022). Trusting AI: Transparency and Accountability in Automated Cybersecurity Systems. *Ethical AI Review*, *9*(1), 12–22.

Black, G. S., Rimal, B. P., & Vaidyan, V. M. (2024). Balancing security and correctness in code generation: An empirical study on commercial large language models. *IEEE Transactions on Emerging Topics in Computational Intelligence*.

Black, G., Vaidyan, V., & Comert, G. (2024). Evaluating large language models for enhanced fuzzing: An analysis framework for LLM-driven seed generation. *IEEE Access : Practical Innovations, Open Solutions*, *12*, 156065–156081. DOI: 10.1109/ACCESS.2024.3484947

Bloomfield, R., & Rushby, J. (2024). Assurance of AI systems from a dependability perspective. *arXiv preprint arXiv:2407.13948*.

Bryce, C., Kalousis, A., Leroux, I., Madinier, H., Mermoud, A., Mulder, V., ... & Ruch, P. Trends in Large Language Models: Actors, Applications, and Impact on Cybersecurity.

Carlini, N.. (2020). Adversarial Machine Learning in Cybersecurity. *IEEE Transactions on Network and Service Management*, *17*(1), 98–109.

Carlini, N.. (2020). Adversarial Machine Learning in Cybersecurity. *International Journal of Machine Learning*, *12*(2), 198–210.

Carlini, N., & Wagner, D. (2020). Adversarial Examples Are Not Easily Detectable: Bypassing Ten Detection Methods. *Proceedings of the IEEE Symposium on Security and Privacy,* 201-215.

Charfeddine, M., Kammoun, H. M., Hamdaoui, B., & Guizani, M. (2024). Chatgpt's security risks and benefits: Offensive and defensive use-cases, mitigation measures, and future implications. *IEEE Access : Practical Innovations, Open Solutions, 12*, 30263–30310. DOI: 10.1109/ACCESS.2024.3367792

Chen, J., Zhang, L., & Wang, T. (2022). Enhancing Cyber Threat Detection Using Multi-Modal LLMs. *IEEE Transactions on Artificial Intelligence*, *5*(4), 687–698.

Chen, L., Zhang, C., & Li, Y. (2022). Reinforcement Learning for Adaptive Intrusion Response. *Journal of Cybersecurity Technology*, *9*(3), 210–221.

Chen, Y., Cui, M., Wang, D., Cao, Y., Yang, P., Jiang, B., Lu, Z., & Liu, B. (2024). A survey of large language models for cyber threat detection. *Computers & Security, 145*, 104016. DOI: 10.1016/j.cose.2024.104016

Chen, Z., Zhang, X., & Li, S. (2022). *Real-Time Anomaly Detection Using LLMs in Cybersecurity*. Cybersecurity Journal.

Chotaliya, H. M. (2024). *Artificial intelligence and its use cases in procurement* (Doctoral dissertation, Technische Hochschule Ingolstadt).

Choudhury, S., & Banerjee, B. (2024). Deep Learning: A Catalyst for Sustainable Agriculture Transformation. In *Harnessing Data Science for Sustainable Agriculture and Natural Resource Management* (pp. 173–199). Springer Nature Singapore. DOI: 10.1007/978-981-97-7762-4_8

de la Roche, M., Voloder, E., Banerjee, A., Guerra, C., Cataldo Dell'Accio, D., Budris, F., & Sedej, T. (2024). Report on Artificial Intelligence and Blockchain Convergences. *Available atSSRN* 5023415.

Deepa, R., Gayathri, S., Chitra, P., Jeno Jasmine, J., Renuga Devi, R., & Thilagavathy, A. (2023), "An Enhanced Machine Learning Technique for Text Detection using Keras Sequential model", *Second International Conference on Electronics and Renewable Systems (ICEARS)*, 1147-1151. DOI: 10.1109/ICEARS56392.2023.10085174

Derner, E., Batistič, K., Zahálka, J., & Babuška, R. (2024). A security risk taxonomy for prompt-based interaction with large language models. *IEEE Access : Practical Innovations, Open Solutions, 12*, 126176–126187. DOI: 10.1109/ACCESS.2024.3450388

Devlin, J., Chang, M. W., Lee, K., & Toutanova, K. (2018). *BERT: Pre-training of Deep Bidirectional Transformers for Language Understanding*. NAACL.

Diaf, A., Korba, A. A., Karabadji, N. E., & Ghamri-Doudane, Y. (2024, April). Beyond detection: Leveraging large language models for cyber attack prediction in iot networks. In *2024 20th International Conference on Distributed Computing in Smart Systems and the Internet of Things (DCOSS-IoT)* (pp. 117-123). IEEE.

Dorothy, S. B. P., Chamundeeswari, V., Madala, R., Singh, D. P., & Sucharitha, K. (2023). "6G Networks in Unmanned Ariel Vehicle Intelligent Internet of Things Secured Communication," *6th International Conference on Contemporary Computing and Informatics (IC3I),* 1374-1378. DOI: 10.1109/IC3I59117.2023.10398062

Ferdaus, M. M., Abdelguerfi, M., Ioup, E., Niles, K. N., Pathak, K., & Sloan, S. (2024). Towards trustworthy ai: A review of ethical and robust large language models. *arXiv preprint arXiv:2407.13934*.

Ferrag, M. A., Ndhlovu, M., Tihanyi, N., Cordeiro, L. C., Debbah, M., & Lestable, T. (2023). Revolutionizing cyber threat detection with large language models. *arXiv preprint arXiv:2306.14263*, 195-202.

Ferrag, M. A., Shu, L., Friha, O., & Yang, X. (2021). Cyber security intrusion detection for agriculture 4.0: Machine learning-based solutions, datasets, and future directions. *IEEE/CAA Journal of Automatica Sinica, 9*(3), 407-436.

Ferrag, M. A., Alwahedi, F., Battah, A., Cherif, B., Mechri, A., & Tihanyi, N. (2024). Generative ai and large language models for cyber security: All insights you need. *Available atSSRN* 4853709. DOI: 10.2139/ssrn.4853709

Ferrag, M. A., Alwahedi, F., Battah, A., Cherif, B., Mechri, A., Tihanyi, N., Bisztray, T., & Debbah, M. (2025). Generative AI in cybersecurity: A comprehensive review of LLM applications and vulnerabilities. *Internet of Things and Cyber-Physical Systems*.

Ferrag, M. A., Ndhlovu, M., Tihanyi, N., Cordeiro, L. C., Debbah, M., Lestable, T., & Thandi, N. S. (2024). Revolutionizing cyber threat detection with large language models: A privacy-preserving bert-based lightweight model for iot/iiot devices. *IEEE Access : Practical Innovations, Open Solutions, 12*, 23733–23750.

Fu, X., Ye, W., Li, X., Zeng, X., Wang, Y., Chang, F., ... & Liu, R. (2024). Revolutionising agri-energy: A comprehensive survey on the applications of artificial intelligence in agricultural energy internet. *Energy Internet*, e12019.

Ghazal, T. M., Janjua, J. I., Abushiba, W., Ahmad, M., Ihsan, A., & Al-Dmour, N. A. (2024, December). Cybersecurity Revolution via Large Language Models and Explainable AI. In *2024 17th International Conference on Security of Information and Networks (SIN)* (pp. 1-6). IEEE.

Ghazal, T. M., Janjua, J. I., Abushiba, W., Ahmad, M., Ihsan, A., & Al-Dmour, N. A. (2024, December). Cybersecurity Revolution via Large Language Models and Explainable AI. In *2024 17th International Conference on Security of Information and Networks (SIN)* (pp. 1-6). IEEE. DOI: 10.1109/SIN63213.2024.10871324

Gholami, S., & Omar, M. (2023). Does Synthetic Data Make Large Language Models More Efficient? *arXiv preprint arXiv:2310.07830.*

Gholami, S., & Omar, M. (2024). Can a student large language model perform as well as its teacher? In *Innovations, Securities, and Case Studies Across Healthcare, Business, and Technology* (pp. 122-139). IGI Global. DOI: 10.4018/979-8-3693-1906-2.ch007

Gupta, S., & Rao, V. (2020). "AI-Driven Threat Intelligence: Automation and Opportunities." *Journal of Network Security.*

Gupta, A., Sharma, R., & Lee, J. (2021). Transfer Learning for Intrusion Detection: A Case Study Using LLMs. *Journal of Cybersecurity Research*, *5*(3), 134–147.

Gupta, B. B., Gaurav, A., & Arya, V. (2024). Navigating the security landscape of large language models in enterprise information systems. *Enterprise Information Systems*, *18*(4), 2310846. DOI: 10.1080/17517575.2024.2310846

Gyamfi, E. K., ElSayed, Z., Kropczynski, J., Yakubu, M. A., & Elsayed, N. (2024, April). Agricultural 4.0 leveraging on technological solutions: Study for smart farming sector. In *2024 IEEE 3rd International Conference on Computing and Machine Intelligence (ICMI)* (pp. 1-9). IEEE.

Hadi, M. A., Abdulredha, M. N., & Hasan, E. (2023). Introduction to ChatGPT: A new revolution of artificial intelligence with machine learning algorithms and cybersecurity. *Sci. Arch*, *4*(04), 276. DOI: 10.47587/SA.2023.4406

Halgamuge, M. N. (2024). Leveraging deep learning to strengthen the cyber-resilience of renewable energy supply chains: A survey. *IEEE Communications Surveys and Tutorials*, *26*(3), 2146–2175. DOI: 10.1109/COMST.2024.3365076

Hamza, Y. A., & Omar, M. D. (2013). Cloud computing security: Abuse and nefarious use of cloud computing. *International Journal of Computer Engineering Research*, *3*(6), 22–27.

Hasanov, I., Virtanen, S., Hakkala, A., & Isoaho, J. (2024). Application of Large Language Models in Cybersecurity: A Systematic Literature Review. *IEEE Access : Practical Innovations, Open Solutions, 12*, 176751–176778. DOI: 10.1109/ACCESS.2024.3505983

Hassanin, M., & Moustafa, N. (2024). A comprehensive overview of large language models (llms) for cyber defences: Opportunities and directions. *arXiv preprint arXiv:2405.14487.*

Hassanin, M., Keshk, M., Salim, S., Alsubaie, M., & Sharma, D. (2025). PLLM-CS: Pre-trained large language model (LLM) for cyber threat detection in satellite networks. *Ad Hoc Networks, 166*, 103645. DOI: 10.1016/j.adhoc.2024.103645

Haurogné, J., Basheer, N., & Islam, S. (2024). Vulnerability detection using BERT-based LLM model with transparency obligation practice towards trustworthy AI. *Machine Learning with Applications, 18*, 100598.

Heim, M. P., Starckjohann, N., & Torgersen, M. (2023). *The Convergence of AI and Cybersecurity: An Examination of ChatGPT's Role in Penetration Testing and its Ethical and Legal Implications* (Bachelor's thesis, NTNU). Helalat, M. A. The Expiry of the Financial Leasing Contract: A Comparative Study between the Jordanian Legislation and the Egyptian Legislation.

Hermalin, B. E., Katz, A. W., & Craswell, R. (2007). Contract law. *Handbook of law and economics, 1*, 3-138.

Holzinger, A., Fister, I.Jr, Fister, I., Kaul, H. P., & Asseng, S. (2024). Human-centered ai in smart farming: Towards agriculture 5.0. *IEEE Access : Practical Innovations, Open Solutions, 12*, 62199–62214. DOI: 10.1109/ACCESS.2024.3395532

Huang, K., Chen, X., Yang, Y., Ponnapalli, J., & Huang, G. (2023). ChatGPT in finance and banking. In Beyond, A. I. (Ed.), *ChatGPT, Web3, and the Business Landscape of Tomorrow* (pp. 187–218). Springer Nature Switzerland. DOI: 10.1007/978-3-031-45282-6_7

Huff, A. J., Burrell, D. N., Nobles, C., Richardson, K., Wright, J. B., Burton, S. L., Jones, A. J., Springs, D., Omar, M., & Brown-Jackson, K. L. (2023). Management Practices for Mitigating Cybersecurity Threats to Biotechnology Companies, Laboratories, and Healthcare Research Organizations. In *Applied Research Approaches to Technology, Healthcare, and Business* (pp. 1-12). IGI Global.

Hu, Y., Zou, F., Han, J., Sun, X., & Wang, Y. (2024). LLM-TIKG: Threat intelligence knowledge graph construction utilizing large language model. *Computers & Security, 145*, 103999. DOI: 10.1016/j.cose.2024.103999

Idelhaj, A., Abou El Houda, Z., & Khoukhi, L. (2024). Foundations models in cybersecurity. *Artificial Intelligence for Blockchain and Cybersecurity Powered IoT Applications*, 1.

Idelhaj, A., Abou El Houda, Z., & Khoukhi, L. Foundations models in cybersecurity: A comprehensive review and future direction. *Artificial Intelligence for Blockchain and Cybersecurity Powered IoT Applications*, 1-18.

Johnson, M., & Chen, Y. (2021). *AI and Machine Learning in Cybersecurity: Emerging Trends*. Cybersecurity Journal.

Jones, R., Omar, M., Mohammed, D., Nobles, C., & Dawson, M. (2023). Harnessing the Speed and Accuracy of Machine Learning to Advance Cybersecurity. In *2023 Congress in Computer Science, Computer Engineering, & Applied Computing (CSCE)* (pp. 418-421). IEEE. DOI: 10.1109/CSCE60160.2023.00074

Jones, R., & Omar, M. (2024). Revolutionizing Cybersecurity: The GPT-2 Enhanced Attack Detection and Defense (GEADD) Method for Zero-Day Threats. *International Journal of Informatics* [INJIISCOM]. *Information System and Computer Engineering*, *5*(2), 178–191.

Kanabar, V. (2023). *The AI Revolution in Project Management: Elevating Productivity with Generative AI*. Sams Publishing.

Kasri, W., Himeur, Y., Alkhazaleh, H. A., Tarapiah, S., Atalla, S., Mansoor, W., & Al-Ahmad, H. (2025). From Vulnerability to Defense: The Role of Large Language Models in Enhancing Cybersecurity. *Computation (Basel, Switzerland)*, *13*(2), 30.

Kaur, S., Singh, P., & Pande, R. (2020). Using Natural Language Processing in Intrusion Detection: A Review. *International Journal of Computer Science and Information Security*, *18*(7), 78–90.

Koshevaya, V. (2024). Integration of Large Language Models in Contract Lifecycle Management.

Li, Q., Zhang, C., & Wang, Z. (2021). Challenges in Automating Threat Intelligence: Data Volume and Complexity. *Journal of Cybersecurity Technology*, *5*(3), 234–250.

Liu, Z. (2024, April). A review of advancements and applications of pre-trained language models in cybersecurity. In *2024 12th International Symposium on Digital Forensics and Security (ISDFS)* (pp. 1-10). IEEE.

Liu, Z. (2024, April). A review of advancements and applications of pre-trained language models in cybersecurity. In *2024 12th International Symposium on Digital Forensics and Security (ISDFS)* (pp. 1-10). IEEE. DOI: 10.1109/ISDFS60797.2024.10527236

Li, X., Li, Q., & Zhang, T. (2021). Federated Learning for Privacy-Preserving Intrusion Detection Systems. *Journal of Privacy and Security, 11*(2), 120–135.

Loevenich, J., Adler, E., Hürten, T., & Lopes, R. R. F. (2025). Design and evaluation of an autonomous cyber defense agent using DRL and an augmented LLM. *Computer Networks, 262*, 111162. DOI: 10.1016/j.comnet.2025.111162

Luhaibi, S. A., & Al Ali, I. A. (2024). Expiry of Family Ownership in the Public Property Law of the Emirate of Dubai No. 9 of 2020. *Library of Progress-Library Science, Information Technology & Computer, 44*(3).

Macijauskiene, R. (2006). The Expiry and Termination of an Employment Contract. *Jurisprudencija, 88*(10).

Manoharan, A., & Sarker, M. (2023). Revolutionizing Cybersecurity: Unleashing the Power of Artificial Intelligence and Machine Learning for Next-Generation Threat Detection. *DOI:*https://www. doi. org/10.56726/IRJMETS32644*, 1*.

Martin, R. J., Mittal, R., Malik, V., Jeribi, F., Siddiqui, S. T., Hossain, M. A., & Swapna, S. L. (2024). XAI-Powered Smart Agriculture Framework for Enhancing Food Productivity and Sustainability. *IEEE Access : Practical Innovations, Open Solutions, 12*, 168412–168427. DOI: 10.1109/ACCESS.2024.3492973

Meenadshi, M. (2023, November). AI-Enhanced LSB Steganography Interface: Concealed Data Embedding Framework. In 2023 9th International Conference on Smart Structures and Systems (ICSSS) (pp. 1-4). IEEE.

Mesías-Ruiz, G. A., Pérez-Ortiz, M., Dorado, J., De Castro, A. I., & Peña, J. M. (2023). Boosting precision crop protection towards agriculture 5.0 via machine learning and emerging technologies: A contextual review. *Frontiers in Plant Science, 14*, 1143326. DOI: 10.3389/fpls.2023.1143326 PMID: 37056493

Miller, T., Durlik, I., Kostecka, E., Łobodzińska, A., Łazuga, K., & Kozlovska, P. (2025). Leveraging Large Language Models for Enhancing Safety in Maritime Operations. *Applied Sciences (Basel, Switzerland), 15*(3), 1666. DOI: 10.3390/app15031666

Mishra, C., Sarma, H., & Saravanan, M. (2025). PageLLM: Incremental approach for updating a security knowledge graph by using page ranking and large language model. *Information Processing & Management*, *62*(3), 104045. DOI: 10.1016/j.ipm.2024.104045

Mohammed, D., Omar, M., & Nguyen, V. (2018). Wireless sensor network security: Approaches to detecting and avoiding wormhole attacks. *Journal of Research in Business. Economics and Management*, *10*(2), 1860–1864.

Motlagh, F. N., Hajizadeh, M., Majd, M., Najafi, P., Cheng, F., & Meinel, C. (2024). Large language models in cybersecurity: State-of-the-art. *arXiv preprint arXiv:2402.00891.*

Nagendiran, S., Renugadevi, R., Kumar, R. P. A., Sasirekha, K., & Harini, R. (2023) "Secure Sensitive Information on IoT using Machine Learning," *2023 International Conference on Sustainable Communication Networks and Application (ICSCNA)*,360-366

Nalini, M., Yamini, B., & Sinthia, P., & S, P. R. K. (2024). DeepRoughNetID: A robust framework for network anomaly intrusion detection with high detection rates. *Journal of the Institution of Electronics and Telecommunication Engineers*, *70*(9), 7137–7148.

Nguyen, V., Mohammed, D., Omar, M., & Banisakher, M. (2018). The Effects of the FCC Net Neutrality Repeal on Security and Privacy. [IJHIoT]. *International Journal of Hyperconnectivity and the Internet of Things*, *2*(2), 21–29. DOI: 10.4018/IJHIoT.2018070102

Okegbola, O., & Akiotu, C. A. (2024). Regulatory Compliance. *Perspectives on Digital Transformation in Contemporary Business*, 269.

Omar, M. (2021). New insights into database security: An effective and integrated approach for applying access control mechanisms and cryptographic concepts in Microsoft Access environments.

Omar, M. (2022). *Machine Learning for Cybersecurity: Innovative Deep Learning Solutions*. Springer Brief. https://link.springer.com/book/978303115

Omar, M. (2024). From Attack to Defense: Strengthening DNN Text Classification Against Adversarial Examples. In *Innovations, Securities, and Case Studies Across Healthcare, Business, and Technology* (pp. 174-195). IGI Global.

Omar, M. (2024). Revolutionizing Malware Detection: A Paradigm Shift Through Optimized Convolutional Neural Networks. In *Innovations, Securities, and Case Studies Across Healthcare, Business, and Technology* (pp. 196-220). IGI Global. DOI: 10.4018/979-8-3693-1906-2.ch011

Omar, M., Zangana, H. M., Al-Karaki, J. N., & Mohammed, D. (2024). Harnessing LLMs for IoT malware detection: A comparative analysis of BERT and GPT-2. In *2024 8th International Symposium on Multidisciplinary Studies and Innovative Technologies (ISMSIT)* (pp. 1-6). Ankara, Turkiye. https://doi.org/DOI: 10.1109/ISMSIT63511.2024.10757249

Omar, M., & Zangana, H. (Eds.). (2025). *Digital Forensics in the Age of AI*. IGI Global., DOI: 10.4018/979-8-3373-0857-9

Omar, M., & Zangana, H. M. (Eds.). (2024). *Redefining Security With Cyber AI*. IGI Global., DOI: 10.4018/979-8-3693-6517-5

Omar, M., & Zangana, H. M. (Eds.). (2025). *Application of Large Language Models (LLMs) for Software Vulnerability Detection*. IGI Global., DOI: 10.4018/979-8-3693-9311-6

Omar, M., Zangana, H. M., & Mohammed, D. (Eds.). (2025). *Integrating Artificial Intelligence in Cybersecurity and Forensic Practices*. IGI Global., DOI: 10.4018/979-8-3373-0588-2

Ozkan-Okay, M., Akin, E., Aslan, Ö., Kosunalp, S., Iliev, T., Stoyanov, I., & Beloev, I. (2024). A comprehensive survey: Evaluating the efficiency of artificial intelligence and machine learning techniques on cyber security solutions. *IEEE Access : Practical Innovations, Open Solutions*, *12*, 12229–12256. DOI: 10.1109/ACCESS.2024.3355547

Patel, R., & Kumar, A. (2023). "Enhancing Malware Detection Using Large Language Models." *International Journal of Computer Security*.

Patsakis, C., Casino, F., & Lykousas, N. (2024). Assessing LLMs in malicious code deobfuscation of real-world malware campaigns. *Expert Systems with Applications*, *256*, 124912.

Pingili, R. (2025). AI-driven intelligent document processing for healthcare and insurance.

Pleshakova, E., Osipov, A., Gataullin, S., Gataullin, T., & Vasilakos, A. (2024). Next gen cybersecurity paradigm towards artificial general intelligence: Russian market challenges and future global technological trends. *Journal of Computer Virology and Hacking Techniques*, *20*(3), 429–440. DOI: 10.1007/s11416-024-00529-x

Poole, J., Devenney, J., & Shaw-Mellors, A. (2021). *Contract law concentrate: law revision and study guide*. Oxford University Press. DOI: 10.1093/he/9780192897336.001.0001

Praharaj, L., Gupta, D., & Gupta, M. (2024, December). A Lightweight Edge-CNN-Transformer Model for Detecting Coordinated Cyber and Digital Twin Attacks in Cooperative Smart Farming. In *2024 IEEE International Conference on Big Data (BigData)* (pp. 6346-6355). IEEE. Praharaj, L., Gupta, D., & Gupta, M. Smart Agricultural Technology. DOI: 10.1109/BigData62323.2024.10825128

Rahaman, M., Pappachan, P., Orozco, S. M., Bansal, S., & Arya, V. (2024). AI Safety and Security. In *Challenges in Large Language Model Development and AI Ethics* (pp. 354–383). IGI Global. DOI: 10.4018/979-8-3693-3860-5.ch011

Rai, S. (2022). Legal Liability Issues and Regulation of Artificial Intelligence.

Ramalingam, R., Shobana, J., Arthi, K., Elangovan, G., Radha, S., & Priyanka, N. (2024). An Extensive Investigation of Meta-Heuristics Algorithms for Optimization Problems. In *Metaheuristics Algorithm and Optimization of Engineering and Complex Systems* (pp. 223–241). IGI Global.

Rao, S., & Ranganath, P. (2025). Climate-Resilient Agriculture: Leveraging Language Models for Mitigation and Adaptation. In *Mitigation and Adaptation Strategies Against Climate Change in Natural Systems* (pp. 357–382). Springer Nature Switzerland. DOI: 10.1007/978-3-031-75968-0_19

Rashid, F., Ranaweera, N., Doyle, B., & Seneviratne, S. (2025). LLMs are one-shot URL classifiers and explainers. *Computer Networks*, *258*, 111004.

Renugadevi. R (2025) "An optimal method of assessing the quality of water using integrated AI and blockchain methodology", *Smart Water Technology for Sustainable Management in Modern Cities*, 261-284.

Rouzel, E., Venkatesha, G., & Dreveton, J. B. (2024). White Paper–B3X: The Ultimate AI-Powered Protocol for Decentralized Derivatives and Options Trading.

Sabharwal, S. M., Chhabra, S., & Aiden, M. K. (2024). AI and Blockchain for Secure Data Analytics. In *Next-Generation Cybersecurity: AI, ML, and Blockchain* (pp. 39–81). Springer Nature Singapore. DOI: 10.1007/978-981-97-1249-6_3

Sadiq, S. (2023). Generative AI: Language models and multimodal foundation models.

Santos, O., Salam, S., & Dahir, H. (2024). The AI revolution in networking, cybersecurity, and emerging technologies.

Santos, O., & Radanliev, P. (2024). *Beyond the Algorithm: AI, Security, Privacy, and Ethics*. Addison-Wesley Professional.

Sarker, I. H. (2024). Generative AI and large language modeling in cybersecurity. In *AI-Driven Cybersecurity and Threat Intelligence: Cyber Automation, Intelligent Decision-Making and Explainability* (pp. 79–99). Springer Nature Switzerland. DOI: 10.1007/978-3-031-54497-2_5

Schurer, J. A. (2024). *AI in negotiations: the perspective of procurement managers* (Doctoral dissertation).

Sears, B. (2022). Implied contract? When conduct continues after a contract expires.

Selim, A., Zhao, J., & Yang, B. (2024). Large language model for smart inverter cyber-attack detection via textual analysis of Volt/VAR commands. *IEEE Transactions on Smart Grid*.

Shafee, S., Bessani, A., & Ferreira, P. M. (2024). Evaluation of LLM-based chatbots for OSINT-based cyber threat awareness. *Expert Systems with Applications*, •••, 125509.

Shan, W. (2025). *AI-powered fraud detection in banking: innovations, challenges and preventive strategies* (Doctoral dissertation).

Shanthini, S. H., & Sheeba Joice, C. (2024). Surveying Strategies: Detecting Sinkhole Attacks in IoT Networks. Communication and Intelligent Systems. ICCIS 2023. *Lecture Notes in Networks and Systems*, *969*. Advance online publication. DOI: 10.1109/ICSCNA58489.2023.10370157

Shiba, M., Renugadevi, R., Jothi, E., Balraj, L., Chidambarathanu, K., & Vemuru, V. D. (2023, November). Securing Children Based On IoT And Emotion Prediction. In *2023 International Conference on Research Methodologies in Knowledge Management, Artificial Intelligence and Telecommunication Engineering (RMKMATE)* (pp. 1-6). IEEE.

Singh, B., & Cheema, S. S. (2024). CYBERSECURITY THREATS AND MITIGATION STRATEGIES IN AGRICULTURE 4.0 AND 5.0: CHALLENGES AND SOLUTIONS IN THE DIGITAL TRANSFORMATION OF AGRICULTURE. *Journal Punjab Academy of Sciences*, *24*, 15–32.

Smits, J. M. (2021). *Contract law: a comparative introduction*. Edward Elgar Publishing.

Srinivasan, K.. (2020). Scalability and Integration of Automated Threat Detection Systems. *IEEE Transactions on Cybernetics*, *16*(5), 1234–1246.

Srinivasan, K.. (2021). Enhancing Real-Time Threat Intelligence Analysis Using LLMs. *IEEE Transactions on Cybernetics*.

Srinivasan, K.. (2021). Improving Cybersecurity Automation with Explainable AI. *IEEE Security and Privacy*, *19*(4), 64–72.

Srinivasan, S., & Kumar, R. (2020). Integrating LLMs into Legacy Cybersecurity Frameworks: Challenges and Solutions. *International Journal of Computer Security*, *15*(2), 29–45.

Srivastawa, A. K. (2023). Exploring contract management in the digital age: The impact of artificial intelligence. *Jus Corpus LJ*, *4*, 737.

Sufi, F. (2024). An innovative GPT-based open-source intelligence using historical cyber incident reports. *Natural Language Processing Journal*, *7*, 100074. DOI: 10.1016/j.nlp.2024.100074

Tabatabaei, S. M. S., & Asadi, S. H. (2016). Reinvestigating the effect of act of God on condition of farming after expiry of farmletting contract. *Religious Researches*, *12*(4), 663–692.

Taghavi, S. M., & Feyzi, F. (2024). Using large language models to better detect and handle software vulnerabilities and cyber security threats.

Taji, K., Elkhalyly, B., Ahmad, Y. T., Ghanimi, I., & Ghanimi, F. (2023). Securing smart agriculture: Proposed hybrid meta-model and certificate-based cyber security approaches. *Data and Metadata*, *2*, 155–155. DOI: 10.56294/dm2023155

Tang, A. (2025). *Safeguarding the Future: Security and Privacy by Design for AI, Metaverse, Blockchain, and Beyond*. CRC Press. DOI: 10.1201/9781003390695

Tang, H., Lin, D., Li, W., Zhang, W., & Zhao, J. (2024). Cyber threat indicators extraction based on contextual knowledge prompt. *Computer Networks*, *254*, 110839. DOI: 10.1016/j.comnet.2024.110839

Wang, X., Tian, Y., Huang, K., & Liang, B. (2025). Practically implementing an LLM-supported collaborative vulnerability remediation process: A team-based approach. *Computers & Security*, *148*, 104113. DOI: 10.1016/j.cose.2024.104113

Wright, J., Dawson, M. E.Jr, & Omar, M. (2012). Cyber security and mobile threats: The need for antivirus applications for smartphones. *Journal of Information Systems Technology and Planning*, *5*(14), 40–60.

Xu, H., Wang, S., Li, N., Wang, K., Zhao, Y., Chen, K., . . . Wang, H. (2024). Large language models for cyber security: A systematic literature review. *arXiv preprint arXiv:2405.04760*.

Xu, Y., Chen, L., & Zhang, S. (2021). Privacy-Preserving Techniques for AI in Cybersecurity. *IEEE Transactions on Information Forensics and Security*, *16*(4), 850–863.

Xu, Y., Liu, Z., & Li, T. (2021). Privacy-Preserving Machine Learning in Cybersecurity. *International Journal of Privacy and Security*, *11*(2), 98–113.

Yao, Y., Duan, J., Xu, K., Cai, Y., Sun, Z., & Zhang, Y. (2024). A survey on large language model (LLM) security and privacy: The good, the bad, and the ugly. *High-Confidence Computing*, *4*(2), 100211. DOI: 10.1016/j.hcc.2024.100211

Yashini, P., Karthika, G., Sunitha, T., & Berlin Magthalin, R. (2024, October). Machine Learning-Based Textile Fabric Defect Detection Network. In 2024 4th International Conference on Sustainable Expert Systems (ICSES) (pp. 1470-1477). IEEE.

Yu, J., Shvetsov, A. V., & Alsamhi, S. H. (2024). Leveraging machine learning for cybersecurity resilience in industry 4.0: Challenges and future directions. *IEEE Access : Practical Innovations, Open Solutions*, *12*, 159579–159596. DOI: 10.1109/ACCESS.2024.3482987

Zangana, H. M. (2024). Exploring Blockchain-Based Timestamping Tools: A Comprehensive Review. *Redefining Security With Cyber AI*, 92-110.

Zangana, H. M. (2024). Exploring the Landscape of Website Vulnerability Scanners: A Comprehensive Review and Comparative Analysis. *Redefining Security With Cyber AI*, 111-129.

Zangana, H. M. (2024). Harnessing the Power of Large Language Models. *Application of Large Language Models (LLMs) for Software Vulnerability Detection*, 1.

Zangana, H. M., Mustafa, F. M., & Li, S. (2025). Large Language Models in Cybersecurity: From Automation to Intelligence. In *Leveraging Large Language Models for Quantum-Aware Cybersecurity* (pp. 277-300). IGI Global Scientific Publishing.

Zangana, H. M., Omar, M., Al-Karaki, J. N., & Mohammed, D. (2024). Comprehensive Review and Analysis of Network Firewall Rule Analyzers: Enhancing Security Posture and Efficiency. *Redefining Security With Cyber AI*, 15-36.

Zangana, H. M., Mohammed, A. K., Sallow, A. B., & Sallow, Z. B. (2024). Cybernetic Deception: Unraveling the Layers of Email Phishing Threats. [INJURATECH]. *International Journal of Research and Applied Technology*, *4*(1), 35–47.

Zangana, H. M., & Mustafa, F. M. (2024). Hybrid Image Denoising Using Wavelet Transform and Deep Learning. *EAI Endorsed Transactions on AI and Robotics*, *3*. Advance online publication. DOI: 10.4108/airo.7486

Zangana, H. M., Mustafa, F. M., & Omar, M. (2024). A Hybrid Approach for Robust Object Detection: Integrating Template Matching and Faster R-CNN. *EAI Endorsed Transactions on AI and Robotics, 3*. Advance online publication. DOI: 10.4108/airo.6858

Zangana, H. M., & Omar, M. (2020). Threats, Attacks, and Mitigations of Smartphone Security. *Academic Journal of Nawroz University, 9*(4), 324–332. DOI: 10.25007/ajnu.v9n4a989

Zangana, H. M., & Omar, M. (2025). The Role of Leadership in Advancing Inclusive Health Technologies. In Burrell, D., & Nguyen, C. (Eds.), *New Horizons in Leadership: Inclusive Explorations in Health, Technology, and Education* (pp. 203–220). IGI Global Scientific Publishing., DOI: 10.4018/979-8-3693-6437-6.ch009

Zangana, H. M., Sallow, Z. B., & Omar, M. (2025). The Human Factor in Cybersecurity: Addressing the Risks of Insider Threats. *Jurnal Ilmiah Computer Science, 3*(2), 76–85. DOI: 10.58602/jics.v3i2.37

Zangana, H., & Omar, M. (Eds.). (2025). *Leveraging Large Language Models for Quantum-Aware Cybersecurity*. IGI Global., DOI: 10.4018/979-8-3373-1102-9

Zhang, X., Xu, H., Ba, Z., Wang, Z., Hong, Y., Liu, J., Qin, Z., & Ren, K. (2024). PrivacyAsst: Safeguarding user privacy in tool-using large language model agents. *IEEE Transactions on Dependable and Secure Computing*.

Zhou, Y., Liu, Y., & Wei, Z. (2020). Automated Threat Intelligence Mining Using Large Language Models. *International Journal of Information Security*.

Zhou, Y., Liu, Y., & Wei, Z. (2020). Leveraging Large Language Models for Cybersecurity Automation. *IEEE Transactions on Cybernetics, 18*(2), 1445–1457.

Zhou, Y., Zhang, X., & Li, Y. (2020). *OSINT Mining and Threat Intelligence Automation with Large Language Models*. Cybersecurity Advances Journal.

About the Contributors

Hewa Majeed Zangana is an Assistant Professor currently affiliated with Duhok Polytechnic University (DPU) in Iraq. He holds a Doctorate in Philosophy (PhD) degree in ITM, which he is currently pursuing at DPU. Prior to his current role, Hewa Majeed Zangana has held various academic and managerial positions. He previously served as an Assistant Professor at Ararat Private Technical Institute and a Lecturer at DPU's Amedi Technical Institute, and Nawroz University. He has also held administrative positions such as Curriculum Division Director - Presidency of DPU, Information Unit Manager of The Research Center at Duhok Polytechnic University, Head of the Computer Science Department at Nawroz University, and Acting Dean of the College of Computer and IT at Nawroz University. Hewa Majeed Zangana's research interests span a wide range of topics in computer science, including network systems, information security, mobile communication, data communication, and intelligent systems. He has published extensively in peer-reviewed journals such as Inform: Jurnal Ilmiah Bidang Teknologi Informasi dan Komunikasi, Indonesian Journal of Education and Social Science, TIJAB, INJIISCOM, IEEE, and AJNU. He has also published multiple books with IGI Global. In addition to his research contributions, Hewa Majeed Zangana has been actively involved in editorial roles, serving as a Reviewer for Qubahan Academic Journal and the Scientific Journals of Nawroz University. He has also been a member of various scientific committees and administrative bodies at Nawroz University, including the Scientific Curriculum Development Committee, the Student Follow-up Program Committee, and the Committee for the Preparation of the Rules of Procedure for Consultative Offices.

Jamal Al-Karaki is currently a full professor at CIS, Zayed university. He has a rich University career in education, service, and research. He holds a PhD degree (with Distinction) in Computer Engineering from the Iowa State University, USA, with Research Excellence Award. He has a proven record of progressive responsibility including leadership positions as a college Dean, Director of IT,

Co-Founder and Dept. Head at various institutes. He led the development of some national centers in cyber security as well as undergraduate and graduate computing programs. As an active researcher, he develops plans to advance the research agenda at CIS. He Published 90+ refereed technical articles in scholarly international journals and conference proceedings. He is a senior member of IEEE and Tau Beta Pi. He is a member of Mohammad Bin Rashid Academy for Scientists in UAE and recently listed among the top 2% highly cited researchers in his field worldwide. He is also a certified reviewer for CAA and certified Pearson EDI verifier/assessor.

Marwan Omar received the master's degree in information systems and technology from the University of Phoenix, in 2009, and the Ph.D. degree in digital systems security from Colorado Technical University, in 2012. He is currently an Associate Professor at the Illinois Institute of Technology, where he conducts research as well as teaches cyber security.

***

Hermano Jorge De Queiroz is an Associate Professor of Graduate Studies at the School of Graduate Business & Technology at Lindsey Wilson College in Columbia, Kentucky. and the former Chair of Undergraduate IT at the University of the Cumberlands. He holds a Ph.D. in Information Technology with a specialization in Information Systems Security from the University of the Cumberlands, as well as an M.Sc. in Information Systems Security from the same institution. Additionally, he earned an M.B.A. in Business Administration from Campbellsville University and a B.Sc. in Management Information Systems and Services from Anhanguera Educacional. Dr. De Queiroz is a dedicated researcher and expert in IT and educational systems, focusing on modern instruction techniques, information systems design, and online learning environments. He serves as a Subject Matter Expert for undergraduate and graduate courses and is proficient in curriculum development and program initiation. His research interests include data science, artificial intelligence, and information systems security. He is multilingual in Portuguese, English, and Spanish and actively engages in fostering academic and professional relationships across these linguistic communities. He has contributed to various educational initiatives, improving student outcomes and promoting academic excellence.

Karthika G earned her bachelor's degree in Electronics and Communication Engineering and her master's degree in Applied Electronics in 2008. She is currently pursuing a Ph.D. in Image Processing at Anna University. She is working as an Assistant Professor in Saveetha Engineering College. She has several papers published at international conferences and peer-reviewed journals. Image processing and biometrics are two of her research interests.

Helen MacLennan serves on the editorial review board for the Journal of Conflict Management and as a reviewer for the Transnational Journal of Business and the International Journal of Doctoral Studies. She served as a site evaluator for the Accreditation Council for Business Schools and Programs (ACBSP) and has published research in the Journal of Conflict Management, International Journal of Doctoral Studies, Journal of Excellence in Business Education, Southeast Case Research Journal, and the Journal of Transportation Management. Dr. Helen MacLennan joined Lindsey Wilson College in January, 2023. She is an Associate Professor of Business and is serving as the inaugural dean of the School of Graduate Business and Technology. She earned her Ph.D. in Management from Sullivan University, Louisville, Kentucky and her M.B.A. from Marylhurst University.

Firas Mahmood Mustafa holds a Ph.D. in Computer Engineering from Mosul University, Iraq. His academic journey began with a B.Sc. in Electrical Engineering (Electronics and Communication), graduating in the top quarter of his class. He earned an M.Sc. in Computer Engineering from Mosul University in 2000. Mustafa joined the Computer Science Department at AlHadba University in 2003 and completed his Ph.D. in 2007. From 2013 to 2017, he was with DPU University, and from 2017 to 2020, he chaired the CCE Department at Nawroz University. An active participant in Erasmus+ and IREX programs, he now teaches at DPU University, shaping future computer engineering professionals.

Muthumeeenakshi received her Ph.D in Anna University, Chennai. She did her Master degree in Computer Application, PSNA College of Engineering and Technology, Dindigul. She is currently working as Assistant Professor at REVA University, Benagaluru. She is a life member of ISTE. Her area of interest includes VANET and Wireless Networks

Renugadevi Ramalingam completed her PhD in 2022 from Anna University, Chennai. She is currently working as Associate professor in Saveetha Engineering College. She has more than 20 years of teaching experience in engineering colleges. She published more than 40 papers in International journals, conferences and holds 10 patents. Her research interest includes Machine learning, Internet of Things, Wireless Sensor Networks and Cloud computing. She is a life member of ISTE, Internet Society and IAENG.

S. Karkuzhali is an Assistant Professor in the Department of Computer Science and Engineering at Mepco Schlenk Engineering College, Sivakasi, India. She specializes in Medical Image Processing, Artificial Intelligence, Soft Computing, and Machine Learning. She earned her Ph.D. in Information and Communication Engineering from National Engineering College, Anna University, Chennai, in 2018. She holds an M.E. in Computer & Communication and a B.E. in Computer Science and Engineering from Anna University. With over seven years of teaching experience and nearly three years in research, Dr. Karkuzhali has made significant contributions to academia. She has published 57 research papers, including 26 in international journals and 28 in international conferences. She has authored one book and contributed to ten book chapters. Her research excellence is further demonstrated by four granted patents, three under examination, and four granted copyrights. Dr. Karkuzhali is an active member of IAENG and ISTE and has reviewed numerous research articles. She has delivered guest lectures, participated in 64 courses, and received multiple awards for her academic and research achievements. Her contributions to AI and cybersecurity continue to shape advancements in these fields.

Senthilkumar Santhanamahalingam is an esteemed Assistant Professor in the Department of Chemistry at Ayya Nadar Janaki Ammal College, where he has been serving since 2013. He holds a Ph.D. from Madurai Kamaraj University (2010), an M.Phil. (2003), an M.Sc. (2002), and a B.Sc. (2000) from Ayya Nadar Janaki Ammal College. With a strong research background, he has worked as a Post-Doctoral Research Scientist at Hanyang University, South Korea, and as an Assistant Professor at Kalasalingam Academy of Research and Education. His contributions to the field of chemistry have earned him several prestigious awards, including the ASPIRING TEACHER AWARD (2023), the Best Poster Presentation Award (2019), and the Postdoctoral Research Fellowship from BrainKorea (BK) 21 (2010). He is also an active member of professional bodies such as the Royal Society of Chemistry, the International Society of Electrochemistry, and The Polymer Society of Korea. Dr. Senthilkumar's research interests span nanomaterials, electrochemistry, and green chemistry, with a focus on sustainable solutions for environmental and healthcare applications. His prolific research output includes numerous journal articles, book chapters, and conference proceedings, covering areas like perovskite nanocrystals, electrochemical sensing, and artificial intelligence applications in healthcare. Notably, his work on the green synthesis of Mn-doped ZnO nanoparticles and AI-driven detection of retinopathy of prematurity has received widespread recognition. His scholarly contributions have been cited extensively, demonstrating the impact of his research in the scientific community. Through his teaching, mentorship, and research, Dr. Senthilkumar continues to inspire students and contribute significantly to advancements in chemistry and interdisciplinary sciences.

Index

A

B

C

D

E

F

G

I

L

M

N

P

R

S

T

U

Z

www.ingramcontent.com/pod-product-compliance
Lightning Source LLC
LaVergne TN
LVHW081332021026
849161LV00008BA/2092